Luminous Bliss

Pure Land Buddhist Studies
a publication of the Institute of Buddhist Studies
at the Graduate Theological Union

Luminous Bliss

A Religious History of Pure Land Literature in Tibet

With an annotated English translation
and critical analysis of the Orgyan-gling gold
manuscript of the short
Sukhāvatīvyūha-sūtra

Georgios T. Halkias

University of Hawai'i Press / Honolulu

Paperback Edition 2017

Printed in the United States of America
22 21 20 19 18 17 6 5 4 3 2 1

Library of Congress Cataloging-in-Publication Data
Halkias, Georgios.
Luminous bliss : a religious history of Pure Land literature in Tibet : with an annotated English translation and critical analysis of the Orgyan-gling gold manuscript of the short Sukhāvatīvyūha-sūtra / Georgios T. Halkias.
p. cm.—(Pure Land Buddhist studies)
Includes bibliographical references and index.
ISBN 978-0-8248-3590-3 (hard cover : alk. paper)
1. Pure Land Buddhism—China—Tibet Autonomous Region. 2. Buddhist literature, Tibetan—History and criticism. 3. Tripitaka. Sutrapitaka. Sukhavativyuha (Smaller) I. Tripitaka. Sutrapitaka. Sukhavativyuha (Smaller). English. II. Title. III. Series: Pure Land Buddhist studies.
BQ8514.4.C62H35 2013
294.3'85—dc23
2012007446

ISBN 978-0-8248-7282-3 (pbk.)

The Pure Land Buddhist Studies series publishes scholarly works on all aspects of the Pure Land Buddhist tradition. Historically, this includes studies of the origins of the tradition in India, its transmission into a variety of religious cultures, and its continuity into the present. The series is committed to providing a venue for diverse methodological approaches, including but not limited to anthropological, sociological, historical, textual, biographical, philosophical, and interpretive, as well as translations of primary and secondary works. The series will also seek to reprint important works so that they may continue to be available to the scholarly and lay communities. The Pure Land Buddhist Studies series is made possible through the generosity of the Buddhist Churches of America's Fraternal Benefit Association. We wish to express our deep appreciation to the Institute of Buddhist Studies for its support.

University of Hawai'i Press books are printed on acid-free paper and meet the guidelines for permanence and durability of the Council on Library Resources.

Printer-ready copy prepared by Marianne Dresser.

This work is dedicated to my parents.
To loving Aggeliki, inspiring Triantafyllos,
and the wisdom incarnation of Terton Rigzin Chogyal Dorje.

Contents

Preface

Pure Land Buddhism—considered broadly as the cults of Amitābha, Amitāyus, Aparimitāyus, and the cosmology of a pure buddha land, whether associated with any of those figures or any other buddha—has been an integral part of the Mahayana tradition effectively from its inception. This series seeks to make available scholarly works that examine all aspects of that tradition across the entire range of Buddhist cultures. The series also seeks to provide an opportunity for the examination of that tradition from any methodological perspective as well.

Georgios Halkias' *Luminous Bliss* is a religious history of Pure Land Buddhism in Tibet that highlights the textual and ritual traditions. In doing so, he locates the development of the concept of a Pure Land within broader Indian and Central Asian Mahayana themes, many of which have been central to the intellectual development of the tradition right into the present. In this work Halkias presents a historical orientation to the development of the Pure Land tradition in Tibet from the ninth century onward, and a critical textual study of one of the texts central to the tradition.

An additional important contribution of this work is that Halkias examines the way in which Pure Land sutra-based aspirations and tantric practices have mutually supported each other in Tibet. This provides additional nuance to our understanding of the tradition, calling into question the all-too-easy equation of Pure Land Buddhism with devotionalism, whether Indian (*bhakti*) or European (piety). The breadth of Halkias' work, however, is based on a detailed philological study of representative texts and a systematic description of meditative techniques upheld over the last millennium by all the major schools of Tibetan Buddhism, which establishes a standard for future studies of Pure Land literature in all of the Buddhist languages.

My thanks to Marianne Dresser and Cynthia Col for their work on this volume.

Richard K. Payne
Series Editor

Acknowledgments

The creation of *Luminous Bliss* would not have been possible without the material support and moral encouragement of many people and institutions interested in the documentation and study of Tibetan Pure Land traditions. Like other works of its kind, this book is the outcome of many causes and conditions coming together. My heartfelt thanks go to a number of Tibetan Buddhist scholars and adepts who over the years have generously shared their knowledge to answer my questions and patiently guide me through the various interpretations of Pure Land faith and practice in Tibet. Among them, His Holiness the Seventeenth Karmapa Orgyen Trinley Dorje (Dharamsala), for his pith instructions on the conceptualization of pure lands as expressions of pure vision, as opportunities for generating joy in the minds of beings, and ultimately, as being inseparable from the nature of mind; Lama Zopa Rinpoche (Kathmandu), for outlining a gradual path (*lam-rim*) of cultivation that leads to the attainment of *dharmakāya* (*chos-sku*), the ultimate realization of Amitābha's Pure Land; Zamdong Rinpoche (Sarnath), for emphasizing the need to develop five powers to secure awakening in the Pure Land, and for illuminating the difference between Amitābha's *nirmāṇakāya* (*sprul-sku*) projections and Amitāyus' *saṃbhogakāya* (*longs-sku*) transmissions in Vajrayana contexts; Tulku Ngedon Rinpoche (Bylakuppe), for illustrating with lucid examples the unchanging emptiness that characterizes all buddha fields; Khenpo Lobsang Rinpoche (Dharamsala), for highlighting the salience of Sukhāvatī in the Treasure tradition; Geshe Sonam Rinchen (Dharamsala), for clarifying the relation between Mahayana tenets and Tibetan Pure Land practices; and Geshe Lama Gelek Jinpa (Kathmandu), for explaining the representation of pure lands in the traditions of the Great Perfection.

Above all and without measure, I am grateful to His Eminence Ayang Rinpoche from Eastern Tibet, who inspired the inception of this work. In 1999, during his annual teachings on *phowa* (*'pho-ba*), he introduced me for the first time to the unfathomable depths of Tibetan Buddhism and to the traditions of Sukhāvatī in the bKa'-brgyud and rNying-ma schools. He is a timeless expression of the blending of luminosity and bliss in the practice of Buddha Amitābha. I am also thankful to Rinpoche's students, an international community of Pure Land practitioners, for sharing their personal insights and encouraging this work.

My sincere thanks go to Abbot Sayadaw Nyaneinda of the Burmese Vihar in Bodh Gaya for providing a welcoming and contemplative environment during my repeated visits to the area. It is because of him that I had a chance to meet and learn from a number of visitors and long-term residents of his monastery about the application of Pure Land ideals among Western practitioners of Tibetan Buddhism.

It is impractical to list all the people who have contributed directly or indirectly to the successful realization of this book. I apologize to those not mentioned and remain grateful to all; especially Mr. Gene Smith (1936–2010), for his legendary efforts to preserve and disseminate Tibetan manuscripts online (Tibetan Buddhist Resource Center) and for availing to me his vast knowledge of Tibetan genres of religious literature; Prof. Ryoshun Kajihama at Setsunan University (Osaka), for his collegiality and for sharing his pioneer research in Japan on sutra and commentarial trends of Tibetan Pure Land; Dr. Ulrike Roesler (Oxford), for evaluating sections of this work and for being a good friend over the years; Prof. Charles Ramble (Paris), for supervising my doctoral research on Tibetan Pure Land traditions at the Faculty of Oriental Studies, University of Oxford; Dr. Cathy Cantwell (Oxford), for meticulously examining and appraising the doctoral version of this work and offering precious suggestions for its future improvement; Dr. Robert Mayer (Oxford), for his guidance and inspiring lectures; Dr. Brandon Dotson (Munich), for his precious recommendations and comments and for being a supportive colleague over the years; Dr. Dan Martin (Jerusalem), for sharing his extensive knowledge and reviewing earlier sections of this work; Prof. Christopher Beckwith (Indiana) for kindly sharing his expertise, offering invaluable insights, and remaining a good friend over the years; Prof. Peter Schwieger (Bonn), for his pioneer studies on Tibetan Pure Land traditions and for appraising my DPhil thesis; Prof. Paul Williams (Bristol), for evaluating my doctoral research and sharing his expertise on Indo-Tibetan Buddhism; Prof. Richard Gombrich (Oxford), for his stimulating lectures at Balliol College and for examining this work in its earlier stages; Prof. Vesna Wallace (California), for her intellectually enriching and inspiring visit at the Faculty of Oriental Studies, Oxford; Mr. Tsering Gongkatsang (Oxford), for his patience and good sense of humor during our reading sessions in Tibetan; Mr. Ralf Kramer (Oxford), for his unmatched archival skills that have helped many bewildered students through the selection of Tibetan texts at the Indian Institute Library; Mr. Burkhard Quessel (London), for his warmth, knowledge, and guidance through the Tibetan collection at the British Library; Ms. Sue Swee Chin Small (London), for her guidance through the Tibetan sources in the Chinese and East Asian collection at the Library of the School of Oriental and African Studies; Dr. Sam Van Schaik (London), for making accessible Dunhuang material at the British Library (International Dunhuang Project); Tashi Tsering at Amnye Machen Institute (Dharamsala), for his insights on Tibetan history and the formation of monastic lineages; the librarians at the Library of Tibetan Works and Archives (Dharamsala), and especially Ācārya Lobsang Shastri, for guiding me through the catalogues and texts in Tibetan; the librarians at the Central Institute of Higher Tibetan Studies (Sarnath), and especially Director Ācārya Jampa Samten, for encouraging me to study the Orgyan-ling manuscripts; Prof. Hisao Inagaki (Kyoto), for supporting the creation of this work and making available his many publications on Pure Land Buddhism; and last, but not least, Dr. Tadeusz Skorupski (London), for his pioneer studies on Tibetan Pure Land sutra and tantra traditions and for his moral support over the years.

This book would not have been possible without the generosity of the Jōdo Shinshū Ōtani-ha Foundation (Kyoto), which awarded me a three-year doctoral fellowship at the University of Oxford and invited me to Japan to learn about the thriving lineages of Japanese Pure Land Buddhism. I am grateful to Prof. Charles Burnett for supporting my study of Himalayan history and religion during my research at the Warburg Institute (University of London); to Dr. Tadeusz Skorupski for encouraging my research on the cultural heritage of Ladakh during my British Academy Postdoctoral Fellowship at the School of Oriental and African Studies (University of London); and to Prof. Volkhard Krech and his team at the Käte Hamburger Kolleg, Dynamiken der Religionsgeschichte zwischen Asien und Europa (Ruhr-Universität-Bochum), for creating a congenial and intellectually rewarding environment to conduct research on Central Asian Buddhism.

I am fortunate to have received, over the years, financial support for archival and fieldwork research in India and Europe from the following institutions: Arts and Humanities Research Council (London); British Academy (London); School of Oriental and African Studies (London); Society for South-Asian Studies (London); Spalding Trust (London); Frederick Williamson Memorial Fund (Cambridge University); Faculty of Oriental Studies (University of Oxford); and Wolfson College (University of Oxford).

Lastly, I am thankful to Prof. Richard Payne (California) and the editorial staff of the University of Hawai'i Press for their patience and invaluable feedback throughout the publication process. I remain indebted to all the readers and friends from the United Kingdom, Greece, Spain, Germany, India, Japan, and the United States, who have generously offered their suggestions and support over the years.

Finally, while it goes without saying, any misunderstandings, omissions, and errors contained in this book are solely of my own making.

Buddhisms and Other Conventions

Italics: Titles of texts, literary collections, and foreign words.

Hyphenation is not used in titles of texts but it is employed in all Tibetan terms (e.g., *bde-smon*) and proper nouns (e.g., Tsong-kha-pa), and in most foreign terms (e.g., *buddha-kṣetra*).

Transliteration: Wylie system for Tibetan; Pinyin for Chinese. The first root letter in Tibetan compounds is capitalized in titles of texts and in proper nouns (e.g., sMin-gling) but not in Tibetan terms (e.g., *rtsa-rlung*).

( ): All foreign terms in parentheses are in Tibetan, unless otherwise indicated. Parentheses also include glosses and comments.

[ ]: Interpolations and clarifications.

The term "Mahayana" (Great Vehicle) refers to a religious orientation, not a single unitary phenomenon, which has diverse social and geographical origins and multiple religious and philosophical expressions. Nevertheless, as a matter of usage it has come to be regarded as a coherent movement despite its polysemic and nonsectarian antecedents. The problem of pinning down precisely to what the term may refer has been addressed by many scholars, more recently by Ruegg (2004). In this book, as in scholarship and more demotic pronouncements on the subject, Mahayana is understood as a generic category connecting Buddhist schools, texts, and practices that, while they were not necessarily always in mutual support of each other, can be said to champion the soteriological vocation of bodhisattvas.

Conventionally speaking, the term "Pure Land Buddhism" provokes associations with the cult of Buddha Amitābha and his buddha field, Sukhāvatī. Apropos and in order to avoid confusion, it has been adopted in this book despite some conspicuous reservations, such as the fact that it was coined originally to highlight East Asian developments of Mahayana Buddhism. Furthermore, Mahayana literature features numerous buddhas and pure lands and the common use of "Pure Land Buddhism" excludes other celestial buddhas presiding over their enlightened world-systems, such as the Medicine Buddha, Maitreya, and Akṣobhya, among others. There is enough internal diversity in the scriptural reasoning and conceptual morphology of Pure Land Buddhism in India, China, Japan, and Tibet to challenge the initial formulation of the term altogether. Pure Land Buddhism is not the Buddhism of pure lands that, according to Jan Nattier,

> consists of all Buddhist teachings that look forward to the possibility of rebirth in another world-system (*lokadhātu*) or Buddha-field (*buddha-kṣetra*), where a [b]uddha is presently teaching the Dharma. (2000, 74–75)

Under the rubric of "Tibetan Buddhism" we may identify several Buddhist schools and sub-schools spread across many regions and existing at different times. Tibetan Buddhism encompasses numerous sources of cultural production including, but not limited to, vibrant monastic institutions with distinct and shared Mahayana lineages of teachers and doctrines, a vast corpus of philosophical and ritual texts, and an assortment of soteriological and non-soteriological contemplative techniques grouped together in yet another deceptive (though necessary) "-ism." It may also be understood to refer to lay communities of devotees primarily in Tibet, but also in the Himalayan regions of India, Nepal, Bhutan; across Asia, in Mongolia, China, and other Asian regions; and in other parts of the world, including Europe, America, and Australia. In this work, Tibetan Buddhism denotes all of the above, while it is conceptually and scripturally synonymous with Vajrayana—a religious orientation that stands for a heterogeneous collection of esoteric texts and practices geared toward the speedy development of one's own inborn potential for liberation.

Abbreviations

Tibetan Canonical Editions

Kanjur
D = sDe-dge (Derge)
F = Phug-brag (Phudrag)
H = Lha-sa (Lhasa)
N = sNar-thang (Narthang)
Og = rTa-dbang Gold (Orgyan-Gold)
O = rTa-dbang hand-written (Orgyan)
K = Peking
L = London

Tanjur
D = sDe-dge (Derge)
N = sNar-thang (Narthang)

Collections and Resources

DM 1 = *bDe smon phyogs bsgrigs* (*Anthology of Aspiration Prayers*, vol. 1)
DM 2 = *bDe smon phyogs bsgrigs* (*Anthology of Aspiration Prayers*, vol. 2)
GB = *gSung 'bum gyi dkar chag* (*Index of Karma chags-med's Collected Works*)
IDP = International Dunhuang Project [http://idp.bl.uk/]
JSK = *A Tibetan-English Dictionary* (Jäschke)
LK = *dKar chag lDan dkar ma* (*Denkarma Catalogue*)
MV = *Mahāvyutpatti* (*Bye brtag tu rtogs par byed pa chen po*)
NAR = Narita Catalogue of Tibetan Works
NC = *gNam chos thugs kyi gter kha sngan brgyud zab mo'i skor* (*Celestial-Treasure Cycle*)
NCG = *gNam chos bde chen zhing sgrub* (*Means of Attaining Sukhāvatī*)
OTDO = Old Tibetan Documents Online [http://otdo.aa.tufs.ac.jp/]
Pel.Tib. = *Pelliot Tibétain* Catalogue
PT = *dKar chag 'Phang thang ma* (*Phangthangma Catalogue*)
RKS = Resources for Kanjur Studies [http://www.istb.univie.ac.at/kanjur/]
T = *Taishō shinshū daizōkyō* [http://21dzk.l.u-tokyo.ac.jp/SAT/index_en.html]
TBRC = Tibetan Buddhist Resource Center [http://www.tbrc.org/index.xq]

TOH = Tohoku Catalogue of Tibetan Works
TRP = *rTsib ri spar ma Catalogue*

Sutras (*mDo*)

DKG = *bDe ba can gyi bkod pa'i mdo* (abbr. *bDe-mdo*). Tibetan short *Sukhāvatīvyūha-sūtra*.
LV = Sanskrit edition of the long *Sukhāvatīvyūha-sūtra*.
OKG = *'Od dpag med gyi bkod pa'i mdo*. Tibetan long *Sukhāvatīvyūha-sūtra*.
SV = Sanskrit edition of the short *Sukhāvatīvyūha-sūtra*.
Tshe-mdo = *Tshe dang ye shes dpag tu med pa zhes bya ba theg pa chen po'i mdo* (Skt. *Aparimitāyur-jñāna-nāma-mahāyāna-sūtra*).
VN = *Vimalakīrtinirdeśa-sūtra*. Tibetan edition.

Reference Titles to Sanskrit Texts

Buddha-Matrix Sutra (*Tathāgatagarbha-sūtra*)
Compendium of Scriptures (*Sūtrasamuccaya*)
Descent to Lanka (*Laṅkāvatāra-sūtra*)
Diamond Cutter (*Vajracchedikā-sūtra*)
Discourse on the Ten Stages (*Daśabhūmikavibhāṣā-śāstra*)
Flower Ornament Sutra (*Avataṁsaka-sūtra*)
Golden Light Sutra (*Suvarṇaprabhāsa-sūtra*)
Immeasurable Life and Wisdom Sutra (*Aparimitāyur-jñāna-nāma-mahāyāna-sūtra*)
King of Prayers (*Bhadracaryā-praṇidhāna-rāja*)
Lotus of Compassion Sutra (*Karuṇāpuṇḍarīka-sūtra*)
Lotus Sutra (*Saddharmapuṇḍarīka-sūtra*)
Meditation on Amitāyus (**Amitāyurdhyāna*)
Mahayana Compendium (*Mahāyāna-saṃgraha*)
Samādhi of Heroic Progress (*Śūraṃgamasamādhi-sūtra*)
Stages of Meditation (*Bhāvanākrama*)
Sublime Continuum (*Uttaratantra-śāstra*)
Sutra on the Ten Stages (*Daśabhūmika-sūtra*)
Teachings of Vimalakīrti (*Vimalakīrtinirdeśa-sūtra*)
Treatise on Sukhāvatī (**Sukhāvatīvyūhopadeśa*)

Abbreviations

bp. = *bam-po* (unit of length)
BCE = Before the Common Era
ca. = circa

CE = Common Era
Ch. = Chinese
fol. = folio, folia
n. = endnote/footnote
Jpn. = Japanese
lit. = literal, literally
MS, MSS = manuscript, manuscripts
pron. = pronounced
Skt. = Sanskrit
sl. = *śloka* (unit of length)
Tib. = Tibetan

§ = divisional heading
* = reconstruction

"All buddha fields rise from one's own mind and have infinite forms, sometimes pure, sometimes defiled; they are in various cycles of enjoyment and suffering."

—*Flower Ornament Sutra*

Preface

Religious texts are as much about the circumstances of their production as they are about their interpretation and contemplative application. In this study, I tried to anticipate some historical aspects in the constitution of Tibetan Pure Land literature and signal, when possible, the dynamic relation between soteriology and contemplation and their impending synthesis in Buddhist orthopraxy.

In Buddhist traditions a detached reading of religious texts and sober analysis of doctrines are not valued as an end in themselves. This approach ultimately tallies with Buddhist practice as a cognitive process with psychological reverberations and physiological repercussions that supersede the literary and theological redaction of religion to a disembodied collection of texts and tenets. Buddhist texts are not simply testimonies of doctrine but serve as diagrams of soteriology reflecting a constant struggle between silence, the highest embodiment of the Buddha's teachings, and the limitations of the written word. As manuals for unlocking and shaping our inner worlds of intentionality, they trigger occasions for liberation that cannot be conveyed by language registers; they resort to reason, analogy, and illustration to transcend the very act of reading as a vindication of perfunctory understanding. Internalizing the contemplation of the Buddha is said to induce subtle insights into the acategorical configurations of reality, and to challenge false identifications with the self taken as a substantive, self-referential center of consciousness. The cultivation of the realization of "no-self" (a doctrinal pillar of Buddhism) precipitates a process of de-individualization and a progressive manner of loss that culminates in a new situationality whose very irreversibility offers a view into the timeless expanse of the present moment.

Awakening with one's senses to the insubstantiality of phenomena is a systemic process, a body-mind and time-space adaptation that does not reside in the statements that express it, nor in the visibilities that fill it. Nevertheless, it may be indexed along "four reliances" or hermeneutic guidelines that articulate a new species of awareness: *rely on the teaching, not the teacher; on the meaning, not the letter; on the definitive meaning, not the interpretive meaning; and on wisdom, not consciousness.*

grub-pa rab-gnas lcags-stag
Completed in the Year of the Iron Tiger (2137)

Introduction

This book is written as a record of the religious literature as inspired by an impressive solar deity, which emerged from a Mahayana polytheistic universe and attained over the centuries trans-local eminence and unequivocal soteriological authority. Its transformation into a pan-Asian religious phenomenon, known as Pure Land Buddhism, is closely linked with the astral legends of buddha fields (Skt. *buddha-kṣetra*), or pure lands. Despite the salient role of pure lands for the expression of Mahayana Buddhism in India and its growth beyond, for the most part their cultic legacy has had little impact on Western academic studies of Buddhism, which, if they dealt with the subject at all, have been preoccupied with the advent of Buddha Amitābha and his Pure Land in China and Japan.

There are several explanations for this neglect and lack of emphasis. To start with, there are regrettably few accurate and readable translations of indigenous Pure Land scriptures currently available in Chinese, Japanese, and Tibetan—a reality of the scholarly world that reflects a lack of academic curiosity in a tradition that superficially resembles monotheism.[1] Moreover, the obscure origins of buddha fields and their insignificant presence in Śrāvakayāna Buddhism have led a number of scholars and proponents of a European construction of a "pure and original Buddhism" to adopt a condescending or dismissive attitude toward the soteriology of pure lands, which is often disparaged as the wishful thinking of simpletons grasping for a better life in heavenly realms after death.[2]

A serious charge raised by purists against the doctrine of future birth in a pure land is that it appears antithetical to the strict codes of self-reliance promulgated in Śrāvakayāna Buddhism. Furthermore, failing to appreciate the various degrees of nuance concerning pure lands may seem to challenge the Mahayana ideal of bodhisattvas, whose foremost intention is to endure countless incarnations and personal trials in order to bring liberation to others in this world. To this list of reservations we may add the denigration of Pure Land traditions for being merely "devotional," as if devotional religion is a category different from and subordinate to Buddhism. In response, Galen Amstutz rightly contends, "All Buddhism is devotional, [for] it deals with experiential transformations which in all cases pose ideals empirically 'external' to the starting status of the devotee"

(1998, 72–73). This is as much a truism in Mahayana as it is in so-called Theravāda Buddhism.[3] Peter Bishop expands upon these concerns:

> The one-sided technocratic fantasy about Tibetan Buddhism can also be seen in the comparative failure of Pure Land Buddhism to stimulate the Western imagination. Despite the overwhelming popularity of Pure Land beliefs in Tibet (and in all other Mahayana countries), it has received very little emphasis in Western commentary. This may be because such Buddhism is not readily reduced to a technique, nor is it conducive to scientific status, and in addition it relies almost totally upon faith. Hence Pure Land beliefs do not easily fit the dominant scientific image that the West seems to want of Buddhism. (1993, 87)

Bishop, however, may be guilty of the very stereotypes he critiques if he is suggesting that Pure Land soteriology has not been subjected to a discerning and prodigious interweaving of Mahayana doctrines and contemplative prescriptions by many Tibetan and East Asian scholars of Buddhism.[4] Moreover, Western commentators have not been blind to the importance of Pure Land literature in Tibetan Buddhist contexts, as signaled in the works of Matthew Kapstein (2003), Tadeusz Skorupski (1995), and Peter Schwieger (1978).

It is my aspiration that this work, a religious history of Pure Land literature in Tibet, will illuminate and problematize some salient aspects of this neglected tradition and clarify many of the misconceptions concerning the soteriological orientation of pure lands in Indo-Tibetan Buddhism. This work has had a long gestation; an earlier version was submitted as a doctoral thesis at the Faculty of Oriental Studies, University of Oxford, in 2006.[5] Its present incarnation incorporates substantial revisions and new material, which may be attractive to a wider readership interested in the Indian origins and Tibetan developments of the genre of Pure Land literature known as *bDe-smon* (pron. de-mön). Broadly defined, the *bDe-smon* encompasses a wide range of scriptures, such as Pure Land aspirational prayers, commentarial literature on Pure Land theology, and Vajrayana forms of devotion to the deity, which articulate a shared typology of liberation and faith in the buddha field of Buddha Amitābha.

There are, of course, many meaningful ways of handling the textual material with which the present study will not be concerned. This book will not address the various ways of reception of these narratives: their social, philosophical, and anthropological articulation across different times, places, and cultural locations. Nor will it offer a comprehensive study of the literary genres in which pure land narratives are inserted, any more than providing a structural examination of these narratives as myths, psychoanalytic categories, or objects of cross-cultural comparison.

Arguably, a religious history of Buddhist traditions in Tibet should attempt to strike a balanced representation of traditional Tibetan references (i.e., literary, political, doctrinal, and so on) and current academic research, which may question the veracity of historical narratives composed for and by Tibetans. In Tibet as elsewhere, collective memory may not always be historically credible, but since both sides of articulation serve to instantiate positions drawn from an inventory of possibilities—idealized representations of religious sentiments as history on the one hand, and the reduction of religion to the material conditions of its appropriation on the other—they are given elaboration in this book. Pure Land Buddhism in Tibet is as much about the ways in which it is traditionally configured as a syncretism of tenets, motifs, and rituals as it is as a subject of critical inquiry into the historical circumstances of the cult's categorization and persistence. The question is not whether myth and history can coexist side by side, but the ways they do coexist in Tibetan traditionalism with its specific forms of fidelity toward narrative continuity and wholeness against the foreclosing literary rationalization and reduction of contemporary historiography.

The writing of any religious history of texts is an eclectic process of differentiation and selection, and I have taken special care to substantiate visibilities of religious creed in Tibetan texts representative of Sukhāvatī's cultic and theological coherence. Hence, the present variety of literature is in agreement with what the Tibetan commentarial tradition considers its major and most admired works of the genre. Furthermore, the choices in this book draw from canonical and paracanonical sources, scriptural collections, and ritual cycles of teachings from all major schools of Tibetan Buddhism, and represent for the most part institutionalized exoteric and esoteric traditions of Tibetan Pure Land spanning from the ninth century to the present. Interviews with Tibetan Buddhist scholars and practitioners, as well as my own participation in Pure Land rituals and teachings conducted in India, Germany, and Greece from 1999 to 2011, informed a wider frame of religion not limited to the subtleties of Mahayana doctrine but also in relation to more arresting kratophanies, the manifestations of the deity's alleged power—its capacity for providing protection, healing, prophecy, and spiritual success in this world and in the afterlife.

It should be clear from the start that the term "Tibetan Pure Land Buddhism" is employed both as a generic term for useful comparisons with analogous developments in India and China (i.e., Pure Land Buddhism vis-á-vis the Mahayana "cult of the book"), and as an empirically specific category for differentiating other Tibetan cults linked with their own divinities, collection of rituals, scriptures, communities, and so forth. Nothing in the material presented in this book can be seen to imply or remotely suggest that there has ever been a sectarian, self-conscious movement of Pure Land Buddhism in Tibet. Nor can we speak in any meaningful way of Tibetan Pure Land orientations independently of the doctrinal and contemplative aims of Buddhism in Tibet at large. Therefore, there has been no conscious effort to sustain an argument that binds the textual sources in an overarching notion of historical contextualization, while I have refrained from elaborating over the construction and deconstruction of the terms "Tibetan," "Pure Land," and "Buddhism," as these are merely designations that derive their sense and meaning in comparative and historically embedded contexts.

Given the diversity of ritual, credal, and literary redactions of Pure Land literature and its relation to the many subdisciplines of Tibetan studies, I often delved into several other areas, such as history, politics, art, archaeology, and textual studies, but I have refrained from lengthy discussions in the main text concerning the latest interpretations and academic debates. I have utilized endnotes in several ways, resulting in informative but often lengthy sub-texts. Some readers may wish to skip the notes, bearing in mind that they are intended for those who will find the bibliographical references, clarification of concepts and terms, allusions to scholarly discussions, and suggestions amenable to future comparative and general research.

The sections of this work form independent readings that are related to each other in instructive ways; however, it is assumed that this book will be read sequentially to encourage progressively more informed approaches to the interpretation of the Tibetan sources, and often clarifications offered in earlier sections are not repeated in later parts. *Luminous Bliss* is arranged in three sections. Part One, "Early Pure Land Traditions in India, Tibet, and Central Asia," is divided in two chapters. It deals with the formulation of Pure Land soteriology in India and the circumstances of its adaptation in Tibet and Central Asia. Part Two, "Pure Land Texts in Tibetan Contexts," also in two chapters, offers an English translation of the short *Sukhāvatīvyūha-sūtra* imported from India during the times of the Tibetan empire and concludes with a survey of Tibetan Pure Land texts in the dGe-lugs-pa, bKa'-brgyud, rNying-ma, and Sa-skya schools of Buddhism. Part Three, "Pure Lands and Pure Visions," again in two chapters, presents a translation of some of the most innovative tantric practices related to the Tibetan cult of Sukhāvatī from the Treasure tradition.

The work is thus organized into six chapters. "Chapter One: Indian Mahayana Origins and Departures" sketches the soteriological functions of buddha fields in Indian Mahayana literature, followed by the different epithets, features, localities, and forms of the deity and its abode in the literary and archaeological sources. After an overview of Tibetan representations of Buddha Amitābha, the chapter concludes with an introduction of two authoritative Pure Land commentaries in East Asia that were allegedly composed in India but are unknown in Tibet.

"Chapter Two: Pure Lands and the Tibetan Empire" outlines the avenues through which Buddhism was transplanted to Central Asia. The competitive encounters between the Tibetan empire and the Tang dynasty serve as historical background to the presence of the Tibetans in Central Asia and their propagation of Tibetan forms of Buddhism in the colonies of Miran, Turfan, Khotan, and Dunhuang. This chapter situates the importation of Sukhāvatī beliefs in Tibet as part of a widespread transmission of Indian Mahayana traditions and their adaptation as the official religion of the Tibetan empire.

"Chapter Three: The Dharma That Goes against the Ways of the World: The Short *Sukhāvatīvyūha-sūtra* with an English Translation from Tibetan" is dedicated to the short *Sukhāvatīvyūha-sūtra,* a core Pure Land text widely read in Tibet and East Asia. This chapter introduces the contents and Tibetan editions of the sutra translated in Central Tibet from Sanskrit sometime in the ninth century CE, and concludes with an annotated English translation. A critical analysis of the sutra is presented in Appendix I.

"Chapter Four: Tibetan Pure Land Commentaries" opens with a discussion of the causes for taking birth in Sukhāvatī and introduces the Tibetan genre of Pure Land Buddhism, the *bDe-smon.* Texts of this genre include prayers of aspiration for taking birth in Sukhāvatī (*bde-smon*) and commentaries (*'grel-ba*) composed by eminent Tibetan Buddhist scholars that reflect a typical synthesis of Mahayana sutra-type ascriptions and the ritual observances of the deity endorsed by the esoteric traditions.

"Chapter Five: Tantric Transfer in Sukhāvatī" examines Vajrayana rituals devoted to Buddha Amitābha and Amitāyus. The chapter centers on a unique contemplative practice from the Treasure tradition, the technique of transferring one's consciousness to the buddha field Sukhāvatī (*'pho-ba*), and concludes with a brief history and English translation of *The Standing Blade of Grass* composed by Nyi-zla sangs-rgyas in the fourteenth century, which details instructions for the method of transference to Sukhāvatī.

"Chapter Six: The Celestial Treasures of Buddha Amitābha" focuses on Pure Land texts and contemplative instructions drawn from the Treasure literature of the rNying-ma and bKa'-brgyud schools. The chapter highlights the importance of the liturgical collection of the Celestial Teachings derived from the pure visions of gNam-chos mi-'gyur rdo-rje (1645–1667). The chapter concludes with an English translation of Mi-'gyur rdo-rje's Celestial Treasure, *Sukhāvatī Sādhana: Empowerment and Oral Instructions,* followed with a translation of *Invoking the Guardians of Sukhāvatī,* a unique visualization and invocation ceremony of Sukhāvatī Protector deities composed by the renowned Tibetan scholar Karma chags-med (1613–1678).

Following the Epilogue, "From Sukhāvatī to Tibet and Back," are three appendices: "Appendix I. A Critical Analysis of the Orgyan-gling Gold *bDe-mdo*" offers a diplomatic study of the short *Sukhāvatīvyūha-sūtra* utilizing as its root text the Orgyan-gling gold MS. "Appendix II. *Means of Attaining the Sukhāvatī Kṣetra:* Editions and Liturgical Texts" introduces some known editions and scriptures of the *gNam chos bde chen zhing sgrub* collection. "Appendix III. An Anthology of Pure Land Texts from the Treasure Tradition" lists some representative "revealed" texts of the Pure Land variety.

Part I

Early Pure Land Traditions in India, Tibet, and Central Asia

Tibetan depiction of Sukhāvatī, Amitābha's Pure Land

Chapter One

Indian Mahayana
Origins and Departures

The Soteriology of Buddha Fields

Around the beginning of the Common Era, hundreds of years after the death of the historical "architect" of Buddhism, Buddha Śākyamuni, a small and active minority of Indian Buddhists, belonging in all probability to a number of different monastic ordination lineages (Pāli *nikāya*), continued to elaborate on preexisting soteriological options, and over the course of centuries articulated them into an original and enormous body of scriptures—Mahayana sutras—that reflected a variety of philosophical approaches and ritual and contemplative practices.[1] A common thread that unified these lineages featured a universal aspiration to reach "supreme and perfect awakening" (Skt. *anuttarā samyaksaṃbodhi*), as did Śākyamuni, who, according to birth stories of his past lives (Jātaka), was once a being (Skt. *sattva*) set toward awakening (Skt. *bodhi*), a bodhisattva that became a buddha. Proponents of buddhahood were self-identified as exponents of the Mahayana ("Great Vehicle"), in contrast to contemporary Buddhist factions, the *śrāvakas*, who were denigrated as the Hinayana ("Small Vehicle") for focusing on one's own liberation, nirvana, the state of an arhat.

The partisans of Mahayana idealism questioned self-serving estimations of the *summum bonum* of Buddhist practice by challenging the division between "self-liberation" and "other-liberation." They held the view that these two seemingly distinct soteriological endeavors converge in the altruistic vocation of bodhisattvas who vowed to become buddhas in order to deliver all sentient beings from unwanted states of suffering. Mahayana orientations share much in common with the philosophical principles and ethical discipline of Śrāvakayāna Buddhism but arguably differentiate themselves from the latter on the grounds of soteriological intentionality.[2] Their scriptures emphasize the spiritual pursuits and glory of bodhisattvas, which, in conceptual terms and practical expression, eventually meant acknowledgement of the interdependent origination of self and phenomena (Skt. *pratītyasamutpāda*) through a rigorous course of training aimed at refining six "perfections" (Skt. *pāramitās*): generosity (Skt. *dāna*), morality (*śīla*), patience (*kṣānti*), vigor (*vīrya*), concentration (*dhyāna*), and discriminating understanding (*prajñā*).[3]

As we will examine in the following sections, in a number of Mahayana sutras the unrivaled path of a bodhisattva is conceptually analogous with the production, purification, and maturation of a buddha field (Skt. *buddha-kṣetra;* Tib. *sangs-rgyas kyi zhing;* Ch. *foguo*).[4] These identifications accommodate a number of doctrinal issues, not least that buddha fields are outside the forces of compulsive becoming, the suffering and frustration of cyclic existence (samsara). These symbolic kernels of Buddhist enlightenment were ethically elaborated to represent exalted virtues, such as altruism and renunciation embedded in the bodhisattva's vows of "ecumenical liberation." Buddha fields are characterized by a semantic polysemy that suited Mahayana expressions of worship and devotion and resonated with prevailing Indic (and non-Indic) beliefs in heavenly realms and eternal life. The conceptualization of buddha fields as pure abodes, idealized locations where the buddhas perpetually teach the Dharma, inspired meditators, artists, and thinkers to contemplate new ways of representing and engaging with their exalted forms. Buddha fields came to represent the goal and consummation of the Mahayana path, while the possibility of encountering buddhas and celestial bodhisattvas residing in heavens compensated for the spiritual vacuum left by the absence of Śākyamuni Buddha and provided an incentive for contemplative training.

> Certain bodhisattvas emerged from deep meditation with tales of visions they had experienced, visions of a universe far more vast than had previously been supposed. Throughout the ten directions, they claimed, were other world-systems like our own, each with its own hierarchy of gods and human beings. Most important for aspiring bodhisattvas, however, was the news brought by these early visionaries that in some of these world-systems buddhas were currently living and teaching. Thus while our own world-system is currently devoid of a buddha (though the Dharma itself is still present and accessible), other buddhas were now held to exist in the present, albeit in world-systems located (to use contemporary scientific parlance) many millions of light years away. These new visions thus introduced the dramatic possibility of encountering a living buddha in the near future—indeed in one's very next life, through being reborn in his realm.[5]

Overall the Pure Land material is narrative, with its integrity and realism strongly informed by its soteriological content. Hence, in time buddha fields turned into objects of instruction[6] and vehicles to channel spiritual sentiments of longing to "see and hear" the buddhas. The pure lands of the buddhas embellished the imagination of Mahayanists and offered them ways to conceptualize their liberation in a spiritual geography conjoining this world with a sacred life beyond. However, narratives exploiting the spiritual potential of otherworldly realms are not limited to the Mahayana scriptures.[7] The doctrine of other worlds is found in Pāli texts, in which all who have gone through the stages of realization known as the "fruition of stream-winning" (*sotāpatti-phala*), the "fruition of once-returning" (*sakadāgāmi-phala*), and the "fruition of non-returning" (*anāgāmi-phala*) will eventually be born in celestial heavens after death.[8] This being said, the heavenly worlds of Śrāvakayāna Buddhism are well within samsara, "impermanent and pervaded with final frustration and suffering," while buddha fields (which are not heavens) manifest as opportunities for enlightenment for a Pure Land believer who becomes a "non-returner" (*anāgāmin*) after death.[9] Mahayana texts feature a number of topics ranging from pure land geography and toponymy to soil, flora, fauna, and architecture; and the lavish availability of victuals and provisions, an infinite repertoire of Buddhist teachings, the make-up of a spiritual community, and ample ceremonial opportunities to meet buddhas in the pure lands and make offerings to them as one would do in real life. Pure Land eschatology champions several attractive destinations: Abhirati, the Land of Extreme Joy; Sukhāvatī, the Land of Bliss; Vaiḍūryanirbhāśa, the Land of Luminous Lapis Lazuli; Ghanavyūha, the Land of Mystic Splendor; and Padmagarbha, the Land of the Womb of the Lotus.

In the ways pure lands constitute a rhetoric of liberation, they are contrasted with the contaminated world of our everyday experience—hence, some buddha fields may be impure (Skt. *aviśuddha*) or mixed (Skt. *miśraka*).[10] In the *Lotus of Compassion Sutra,* in circulation by the mid-third century CE when the first Chinese translation of it was made, our world is devalued as an impure buddha field distorted by five corruptions: the degeneracy of our times, our views and blind passions, and the degeneracy of all people and life on earth.[11] However, at any given time buddhas may wish to transform an impure world into a pure land and vice versa, while bodhisattvas create flawless environments within impure universes. Ultimately, the edifying distinction between purity and impurity is a subjective interpolation, for all *buddha-kṣetras* are *ipso facto* pure (Skt. *viśuddha*), while one and the same buddha field may be experienced as defiled or immaculate according to the disposition of those who dwell in it.[12]

The *Akṣobhyavyūha-sūtra* is the earliest Mahayana text to link the soteriological potency of buddha fields with a bodhisattva's vows.[13] According to the sutra, a long time ago a devout Buddhist monk vowed to attain full enlightenment, an aspiration he realized upon becoming Buddha Akṣobhya reigning over his pure land Abhirati (lit., "Extreme Joy") located in the eastern sector of our universe. This pure land, free of illnesses, lies, ugliness, smelly things, and non-Buddhists,[14] is an ideal after-death destination for those wishing to progress toward arhatship without distraction. Obviously, arhatship falls short of the Mahayana ideal of "supreme and perfect awakening," but the "Small Vehicle" appeal of this text points to an early phase in the construction of Pure Land orientations in India, when soteriological ends had not yet been fashioned as an exclusive feature of Mahayana.

In the following discussion we will examine three related and overlapping themes crucial to the formulation of buddha fields that might well be described as the generic pre-history of a religious development, cultic as well as doctrinal, whereby the spiritual vocation of bodhisattvas came to encompass the subtleties of Mahayana doctrine, particularly but not exclusively in Indian sources. According to many Mahayana cults of devotion, buddha fields are the celestial abodes of the buddhas, "timeless" and "perfected" realms where the gospel of enlightenment eternally recurs. The second motif symbolizes a bodhisattva's pious asceticism, his earnest desire to purify buddha fields in the course of his Mahayana training. The purity of buddha fields is ritually dependent upon a bodhisattva's ethical dedication and is synonymous with the purification of his mind.[15]

Shinkan Murakami elaborates on the term *vyūha* as a critical concept that exemplifies the earnest wish to arrange, construct, and purify a buddha field as a kind of Mahayana utopia, a symbolic manifestation of the Buddha's nirvana. He explains that *vyūha* originally meant a combination of elements that comes about through the power of "imagination, earnest desire, wish, vow, or in other words, mental creation, which is taken to be achieved by the magical powers of the Buddha[s] or Bodhisattva[s], often by their power of concentration."[16] In the *Sutra on the Ten Stages, vyūha* conveys the powers of a bodhisattva to transform his dwellings and environment into a spectacular mental arrangement. Vajragarbha, who expounds most of the sutra, enters into meditative concentration and manifests buddha fields in the nature of his own body.[17]

The last theme has a wide cultic appeal, for here buddha fields are reconstituted as after-death opportunities, such as the pure land of Bhaiṣajyaguru

where the dead are led to his heaven by Sūryaprabha and Candraprabha, his attending bodhisattvas. Pure lands figure as ideal landscapes of the afterlife in stark contrast to the Buddhist hell realms and the imminent possibility of falling into a bad rebirth. The discourse on buddha fields is implicitly and at times explicitly mediated by two antipodes: the consummation of the bliss of liberation on the one hand, and its opposite unfolding as layers of "samsaric" torments from Avīci (the lowest hell realm) to other hellish worlds inhabited by mind, and further on to the Sisyphean reality of hungry ghosts, the animal realm characterized by fear and dullness, the human universe shaped by a wanton proliferation of desire, and so on.

The symbolic and tangible aspects of soteriological landscapes entwined with discourses on ecumenical compassion. The salvation of all beings in a buddha field was a timely and plausible development, since a bodhisattva attains awakening never just for himself but as an example for others to do the same.[18] "Awakened worlds" and "worlds of awakening" are two sides of the same theological elaboration, for buddha fields are simultaneously active extensions of a bodhisattva's great compassion (Skt. *mahākaruṇā*) and the manifest fulfillment of his vows (Skt. *praṇidhāna*).[19] The bodhisattva who cultivates supreme *bodhi* and safeguards the welfare of all sentient beings eventually attains awakening in his own pure land.[20]

There are a number of salient and, at first, bewildering features in the theological formulation of pure lands—interpreted from a substantivist position as tangible objectives for afterlife enthusiasts, and as situational registers for the bodhisattva's intentionality and nameless realization of the buddha. While the supplication of specific deities to secure access in their buddha fields is not common in earlier Indian texts, such as the *Akṣobhyavyūha*, it finds voice in later productions like the short and long *Sukhāvatīvyūha* sutras and the *Immeasurable Life and Wisdom Sutra*.[21] Over time, hypostasized expressions of devotion, like the "recollection of the buddha" (*sangs-rgyas rjes su dran-pa;* Skt. *buddhānusmṛti*) and accumulation of spiritual capital (merit), served as means for a happy transition after death and an assured admission in a pure land. Refined interpretations of Mahayana doctrine and veritably pragmatic exchanges between worshiper and deity coexisted side by side in Indian Buddhist traditions, as they did in Chinese and Tibetan Buddhist contexts.[22]

Pure Lands as Skillful Means

The *Teachings of Vimalakīrti* (Skt. *Vimalakīrtinirdeśa-sūtra*) was translated into Chinese for the first time in the late second century CE and it is among the oldest Mahayana sources for understanding how Indian Buddhists conceptualized pure lands. This work was held in high esteem in China, Tibet, and Central Asia and it contains a substantial section devoted to the explication of the doctrine of nonduality. The narrative centers on the bodhisattva-persona of Vimalakīrti, an Indian layman who had previously taken birth in Akṣobhya's *buddha-kṣetra* and who is an authority on the topic.

> Son of good family, the field of high resolve (*adhyāśaya*) is the Buddhakṣetra of the Bodhisattva: the instant he obtains enlightenment, beings who have accumulated all the stores of good roots (*kuśalamūlasaṃbhāra*) are born in his Buddhakṣetra. (VN I, §13)[23]

For Vimalakīrti, buddha fields are expressions of a bodhisattva's intentionality, since they are in no way distinct from his resolve to attain enlightenment (field of high resolve); while birth in the pure lands is reserved for those who have accumulated prerequisite merit (stores of good roots) through a righteous life and contemplative way of being.[24] Buddha Śākyamuni instructs Ratnākara on the unusual level of commitment required to attain a pure buddha field:

> [Bodhisattvas aiming for the buddha fields should] possess all the stores of good roots and [be] gifted with all the good intentions; are observant of the ten paths of good conduct; are established in goodwill, compassion, joy and equanimity; are free from malicious thoughts; are skilled in all the means and practices of deliverance, the four applications of mindfulness, the four right efforts, the four bases of psychic power, the five dominant faculties, the five powers, the seven limbs of enlightenment and the eight limbs of the Path, and so forth. (VN I, §13)[25]

There are additional concerns associated with the soteriology of buddha fields, their modality of presentation and phenomenal arising. Pure lands are realized by bodhisattvas in the ways they appear to the minds of those who are to be trained and disciplined in the Great Vehicle.[26] In the *Samādhi of Heroic Progress* (Skt. *Śūrangaṃasamādhi-sūtra*), an early Mahayana scripture composed anonymously near the beginning of the first millennium,[27] *mahāsattva*-bodhisattvas secure "perfectly adorned buddha fields" not for themselves but for the welfare of all sentient beings. They are conceived as altruistic provisions of compassion, expressions of a skillful teleology, for pure lands are extensions of the skill-in-means (Skt. *upāyakauśalaya*) of bodhisattvas and creative expressions of their resourcefulness in bringing an end to suffering (VN I, §13).

And just as a bodhisattva imparts to the world his understanding of reality, his wisdom, in the same way he shares his merit in skillful ways by transferring it to those in need (Skt. *pariṇāmanā*). Spiritual capital (merit) is commonly accrued after the performance of a virtuous act and this positive accumulation may in turn be exchanged for the welfare of sentient beings.[28] Despite the law of karma that may inhibit such elaborations, dedications of merit have played and continue to play a cohesive role in Mahayana devotional lifestyles. They abound in votive formulas and are appended at the colophons of many Mahayana sutras.[29] They provide a religious incentive for the writing, copying, and distribution of Buddhist sutras, which are frequently sponsored by devotees in order to acquire merit that can be transferred to aid the living or the recently deceased—a widespread Mahayana activity that contributed to what Schopen (1975) has termed the "cult of the book." Cultic activity in these circumstances is as much an occasion for reflection upon the signification of the cult object, such as of conjuring effects and precipitating intervention by forms of exchange that range between supplication and propitiation of the deity in question, as it is a way of partaking in the meritorious activity of offering.

There are many dedications and aspirations in Mahayana texts written with the intention of attaining birth in a pure land. The *Ratnagotravibhāga-śāstra,* a major fifth-century commentarial treatise on the doctrine of buddhanature (Skt. *tathāgatagarbha*), concludes with a typical dedication prayer: "By the merit I have acquired through [writing] this [treatise], may all living beings come to perceive the Lord Amitāyus endowed with infinite light."[30] The ingenious notion of skill-in-means in Mahayana is construed here (and elsewhere) as an expression of compassion that reflects an unprecedented flexibility to suit the Buddha's teachings in an infinite inventory of possibilities beyond the personal, social, and historical constraints of their delivery. This is possible because "skillful means" are ultimately anchored neither in themselves, nor in their agents, nor in others.[31]

The Emptiness of Pure Lands

In an apparently interpolated passage from the *Descent to Lanka* (Skt. *Laṅkāvatāra-sūtra*), translated into Chinese in the early fifth century, there is a retrospective prophecy of the philosopher Nāgārjuna expounding on the philosophical doctrines of Mahayana before passing on to Sukhāvatī:

> Mahāmati, know that there will be one who can hold up the eye (of the Dharma). In the southern part of this country called Vedali there will be a Bhikshu of great and excellent reputation known as Nāgāhvaya[32] who will destroy the one-sided view of being and non-being. He will while in the world manifest the unsurpassable Mahayana, and attaining the Stage of Joy, pass to Sukhāvatī.[33]

While it is doubtful that this passage substantiates Nāgārjuna's sympathy for Pure Land doctrines, as claimed by Shin Buddhists in Japan,[34] for the purposes of this discussion it is instructive to examine the formulation of buddha fields from the perspective of Nāgārjuna's discourse on emptiness, since the multiformity that characterizes a bodhisattva's mental disposition features unlimited combinations of compassionate responses in skillful contexts, predicated by sapient realization of the nonexistence of inherent *dharmas*. In the *Madhyamakakārikā,* a central text for the articulation of Mahayana philosophy, Nāgārjuna unambiguously states that emptiness (Skt. *śūnyatā*) is realized as dependent origination (Skt. *pratītyasamutpāda*).[35] He explains that the emptiness of all *dharmas* (phenomena and noumena) is their conditional mode of arising in dependence on the convergence of causes and conditions. There are no independent claims of truth in this world, and this is also the case with buddha fields, which are relational constructions lacking intrinsic substance (Skt. *svabhāva;* "own-being").[36]

The emptiness of buddha fields is professed by Vimalakīrti, since from the perspective of nondual understanding they are "nothing to see" in themselves (VN XI, §1). As we have seen, bodhisattvas realize the ontological insubstantiality of *buddha-kṣetras* yet cultivate them for those seekers who aspire for liberation (VII, §6). In a related passage Śākyamuni deconstructs the errant notion that buddha fields exist in any way disconnected from the benefit rendered by them to sentient beings:

> To the extent that Bodhisattvas favour beings do they acquire buddhakṣetras. To the extent that beings produce all sorts of pure qualities do Bodhisattvas acquire buddhakṣetras. To the extent that beings are disciplined by these pure buddhakṣetras do Bodhisattvas acquire buddhakṣetras. . . . To the extent that beings, entering these buddhakṣetras, produce noble dominant faculties do Bodhisattvas acquire buddhakṣetras. And why is it so? Sons of good family, the buddhakṣetras of the Bodhisattvas draw their origin from the benefits rendered by them to beings. (VN I, §12)

The *Diamond Cutter* (Skt. *Vajracchedikā-sūtra*) of the Prajñāpāramitā collection outright rejects the assertion that buddha fields can or should be formulated as concrete individualities. The cultivation of the perfection of *prajñā* results in a state of consciousness that cognizes the absence of "self" or intrinsic nature in all processses and entities, which are devoid of ultimate identity.

> If any Bodhisattva should speak thus: "I will establish a Buddha field," he would speak falsely. And why? The establishment of a Buddha field, Subhūti,

> as non establishments have they been taught by the Tathāgata. Therefore they are called "field-establishments."[37]

In the *Large Sutra on Perfect Wisdom,* Śākyamuni confides to Ānanda that "the Tathagata Akshobya, these disciples, those persons belonging to the Bodhisattva vehicle, and that Buddha field, do not come within the range of the eye . . . for all *dharmas* are unknowable, unseeable, and incapable of doing anything."[38] The fields of the buddhas are not routine objects of knowledge nor can they have a tangible effect on our world strictly from their own side. The bodhisattvas who gain access to these relational orchestrations do not conceive of them in any inherent way, for they are not independent of a deliberate contemplation of the benefit rendered by them to others. According to the *Samādhi of Heroic Progress,* bodhisattvas in the tenth and last stage of awakening are masters of the meditation known as the *śūraṃgamasamādhi.* At this time, they "circulate through all the buddhakṣetras, but do not conceive of the buddhakṣetras."[39] In the mystical language of the *Flower Ornament Sutra* (Skt. *Avataṁsaka-sūtra*), buddha fields arise in arrangements of mutual revelation to each other, while their involutions mirror infinite formations of spontaneous perfection:

> All lands are interpenetrating in the Buddha-land, and they are countless in number, a phenomenon beyond our understanding; there is nothing which does not fill up every quarter of the universe, and things are inexhaustible and immeasurable and move with perfect spontaneity. All the Buddha-lands are embraced in one Buddha-land, and each one of the Buddha-lands embraces all the others in itself.[40]

However hard one may try to articulate buddha fields in conventional terms, in the long *Sukhāvatīvyūha* Śākyamuni instructs Ānanda:

> And in that buddha field, Ānanda, one will not find even the word or the designation for fire, sun, moon, planets, constellations, or stars, or for gloom and blinding darkness. One will not find anywhere even the designation for day and night, except in the Tathāgata's use of conventional language. (LV §83)[41]

In a typical Mahayana fashion the edifying distinction between object and subject collapses, for in an ultimate sense neither *buddhakṣetras* nor the sentient beings that aspire for them should be reified by a religiously predisposed imagination. Buddha fields are devoid of any worldly or otherworldly corporeality outside a conceptual specificity that is etiologically nothing more than a purified construction in the spotless minds of those confronted with their own luminosity.

The *Mahayana Compendium* (Skt. *Mahāyāna-saṃgraha*) portrays bodhisattvas in the act of contemplating the truth of phenomena as mental projections (Skt. *vijñaptimātratā*), because samsara and nirvana are mental constructions since "a name and an object are nothing but mind-talk."[42] Similarly, for the Buddhist scholar Asaṅga buddha fields are a "masterful and well-purified conscious construction." Asaṅga's interpretation inspired Asvabhāva to compose a commentary in the first half of the sixth century CE, in which he defends the proposition that the manner through which buddha fields are characterized is a conscious and well-purified process.

> *It is characterized by masterful and well-purified conscious construction* means that the Buddha land is characterised by masterful and well-purified conscious construction because it is only conscious construction [that generates] the image of a pure land. Apart from conscious construction there are no gems or anything else, but they appear as such through a well-purified conscious construction [of wisdom images].[43]

Asvabhāva's position echoes Diṅnāga, who states in his sixth-century minor commentary on the *Prajñāpāramitā* that from the perspective of absolute truth it is impossible to partake of the buddha fields.

> [Be]cause they are a mere denomination which is the mental outflow of the Buddha; on account of their not having any material consistency (from the point of view of the absolute truth) and of the eminency which they imply, the arrangement (*vyūha*) of these fields is said to be essentially a non-arrangement (*a-vyūha*).[44]

Pure lands do not simply mirror symmetries of Buddhist doctrine. And even if they do, they are susceptible to an inflation of interpretations, nuances, tenets, and desires. The vision of pure lands and the doctrines that ought to give them meaning do not always find a place to meet, either by those who yearn to see them or by those who read them as signifiers for something else. Their unpredictable variation signals an interstice and a perpetual play of absence: their way of being is ultimately a non-relation.[45]

The Sutras of Pure Land Faith

Three Mahayana sutras are at the core of Pure Land traditions in the East and most of Asia. The long and short *Sukhāvatīvyūha* sutras were composed in India roughly in the second century CE and are considered canonical texts in the Chinese and Tibetan Buddhist traditions.[46] A third text, a fifth-century work known as the *Meditation on Amitāyus* (Skt. **Amitāyur-dhyāna-sūtra* or **Amitāyur-buddhānusmṛti-sūtra*), is not found either in India or Tibet, but enjoyed considerable prestige in Central Asia and China.

The long and short *Sukhāvatīvyūha* sutras bear the same title in Sanskrit, but their contents vary considerably and they are in fact two different texts. Their Chinese and Japanese titles offer no clarity as to the differences between them—the short *Sukhāvatīvyūha* is commonly known as the *Sutra on Amita Buddha* (Ch. *Amituo jing;* Jpn. *Amida kyō*) and the long *Sukhāvatīvyūha* as the *Sutra on Amitāyus Buddha* (Ch. *Wu liang shou jing,* Jpn. *Muryōju kyō*).

The Tibetan titles of the *Sukhāvatīvyūha* sutras resolve this ambiguity. The title of the short sutra reflects the contents of the Sanskrit text. It reads *bDe ba can gyi bkod pa'i mdo* (Skt. *Sukhāvatīvyūha-sūtra*), while the long sutra centers on the life and vows of Buddha Amitābha and bears the title *'Od dpag med kyi bkod pa'i mdo* (Skt. *Amitābhavyūha-sūtra*).[47]

The relative antiquity of the long and short *Sukhāvatīvyūha* sutras is a subject of ongoing debate. Evidence from linguistic and philological analysis suggests that both texts were compiled in northwest India during the rise of the Kuṣāṇa empire (50–250 CE).[48] In the opinion of some experts, the long sutra was translated into Chinese first and is the older of the two.[49] Others maintain that the short sutra is the earliest Indian text composed in its original form sometime in the first century BCE,[50] or that they may belong to different traditions altogether.[51]

The *Sukhāvatīvyūha* sutras of the earliest date are available in Chinese. The Sanskrit and Tibetan versions belong to a much later period. A philological examination of the Chinese translations prompted experts to suggest that they were originally composed in Gandhārī.[52] Salomon (1999, 3) coined the term "Greater Gandhāra" to articulate a broad cultural zone covering several areas that contributed to the rise of Gandhārī civilization. While this zone should encompass the place for the composition of the *Sukhāvatīvyūha* sutras, traces of these texts have yet to be discovered in Greater Gandhāra. So far the discovery of an incomplete recension of the long *Sukhāvatīvyūha* originates from Afghanistan, possibly the Bamiyan area.[53]

According to traditional Chinese accounts, between 64 and 67 CE the Han emperor Mingdi initiated the introduction of Buddhism to China and sent emissaries to India to collect Buddhist doctrines and texts. During his reign an Indian missionary named Kāśyapa Mātaṅga recalled an older tradition in which Emperor Aśoka (ca. 270–232 BCE) had allegedly sponsored Buddhist sanctuaries in China.[54] This sounds like the telling of a pious tale, but we can be relatively certain that the broader expansion of Buddhism in China took place from the middle of the second century with the aid of Gāndhārī, Sogdian, and even Parthian agents, such as the famous prince An-shi-gao, an eminent Buddhist emissary, who arrived in China in 148 CE and is credited with the translation of the *Amitāyus-sūtra* into Chinese.[55] The discovery of Buddhist inscriptions in Kharoṣṭhī and Gāndhārī script near two leading hubs of Chinese Buddhism, Luoyang and Chang'an, suggests that Gāndhārī Buddhist texts must have been among the first to reach China.[56] In fact, many Chinese Buddhist texts may be of Central Asian provenance, since the first translators of the Chinese Buddhist canon came from Kuṣāṇa settlements in Bactria and Sogdiana.[57]

The long *Sukhāvatīvyūha* is extant in seven complete recensions: one Sanskrit text from a manuscript collection in Nepal; one translation from Sanskrit in the Tibetan Kanjur; and five extant Chinese translations from Sanskrit.[58] The first translation from Chinese is said to have been executed during the Zao Wei dynasty (221–266 CE), long before the standardization of Buddhist vocabulary in Chinese. A previously unknown translation of the long sutra not recorded in the Chinese Tripiṭaka has surfaced in a fragment from Turfan.[59]

In East Asia, the most commonly read Chinese translation is entitled *Wu liang shou jing* (T. 360) and is attributed to the Sogdian monk Saṃghavarman.[60] This attribution, however, has been recently contested on the basis of earlier Chinese catalogues, notably the *Collection of Records Concerning the Tripiṭaka* (*Chu san zang ji ji*) compiled by Sengyu in 510 CE. If this is correct, then the *Wu liang shou jing* is a later translation dating to Buddhabhadra and Baoyun in the fifth century.[61]

In Blum's estimation (2002, 149), all five Chinese translations known to us were made from the same original source. Fujita's comparative analysis of the sutras suggests that the first two Chinese translations preserve an early form of the sutra, whereas "the next two, together with the Sanskrit and Tibetan recensions, show a more evolved form [and] the fifth an even more developed one" (1996, 7). He maintains that the earliest Chinese translation of the long *Sukhāvatīvyūha* was made in 222 or 253 CE, either by Zhiqian or Lokakṣema, and the last in 991 by the Tripiṭaka master Faxian, who traveled as a pilgrim to India.

There are four complete recensions of the short *Sukhāvatīvyūha* extant: a text surviving in Sanskrit, a Tibetan translation, and two Chinese translations. The Chinese version by Kumārajīva (344–413) was translated during the Yao Qin period (384–417); it bears the title *Amituo jing* (T. 366) and is the one most commonly read.[62] The other version, translated in 650 CE by Master Xuanzang, is entitled *Cheng zan jing tu fo she shou jing* (T. 367). It contains the highest degree of variation in comparison to the other extant Chinese editions.[63] The translation attributed to Guṇabhadra (394–468), a brahmin from Central India, is no longer extant.

Among some Uighur scriptures discovered in Dunhuang there is a collection of manuscripts with the abbreviated title *Abitaki*. The Uighur texts are in four volumes and include different types of citations to Amitābha. Recent studies show that they were translated from sources originally written in Chinese that bear no relation to Kumārajīva's translation of the sutra (T. 366).[64] According to Shimin (2004), they belong to a lost book, *The Great White Lotus Society Sutra* (*Da bai lian she jing*), of the Chinese Pure Land school consisting of four chapters.

In addition to the long and short sutras, the East Asian Pure Land corpus includes a third text, the *Meditation on Amitāyus* (Ch. *Guan wu liang shou fo jing*).[65] This apocryphal work survives in one Chinese version (T. 365) attributed to Kālayaśas (383–442).[66] It knows no Sanskrit, Tibetan, or variant Chinese editions and may be of Central Asian origin embellished in China, or written in Chinese by the Central Asian master Kālayaśas from 420–440, during the Song dynasty (420–479).[67] While its contents illustrate typical Indian Mahayana views, it is unlikely that this text was composed in India. The Tibetan compilers of the Tibetan Tripiṭaka may have been aware of its non-Indian origins and decided to exclude it.[68]

In comparison with the *Sukhāvatīvyūha* sutras, the *Meditation on Amitāyus* is arguably the most sophisticated and detailed exponent of Pure Land doctrines. It describes thirteen gradual visualizations of the Pure Land and its inhabitants, and delineates nine grades of birth in Sukhāvatī—for those who are skilled in meditation; for those who cannot meditate all that well, yet who follow a strong ethical practice; and for those who can do no more than recite Amitābha's name.[69] In China and Japan, the *Meditation on Amitāyus* had a much greater impact than the *Sukhāvatīvyūha* sutras, and it inspired unique commentarial traditions and interpretations of Pure Land faith.

Unending Luminosity and Life

For over two millennia, Buddha Amitābha has been the most beloved buddhas in all of Mahayana history, the master of Sukhāvatī, a blissful reality located to the west of our world-system (Skt. *sahā-lokadhātu*).[70] The term "Pure Land Buddhism" was originally coined in reference to his worship in East Asian regional contexts, but it more widely refers to a pan-Asian religious movement that embraces scriptures, beliefs, and rituals specific to his cult across Asia. Veneration of Amitābha was observed virtually in all countries where Mahayana traditions of Buddhism flourished, including China, Japan, Tibet, and Central Asia, and there are numerous references to him in Buddhist sutras and treatises (Skt. *śāstras*).[71] Amitābha and his Pure Land were known in China as early as the third century and in Korea by the sixth century, but it is in Japan especially that Pure Land Buddhism offered an autonomous source of religious authority and shaped sectarian denominations that today account for more believers than any other Japanese Buddhist tradition.[72]

Amitābha ("Unending Light") and Amitāyus ("Unending Life") are two names (not epithets) that theologically refer to the same buddha worshiped in two complementary aspects as light-giver and life-provider, conqueror over darkness and death. Etymologically, his names derive from a single Sanskrit root, the term *amita* or *amṛta* (*a-mṛta,* "immortal").[73] Technically speaking, however, the light and life of this buddha is beyond measure; it is neither infinite nor eternal. In the early Chinese translations of the long *Sukhāvatīvyūha-sūtra,* Amitābha will eventually pass on to nirvana and will be succeeded by the bodhisattva Avalokiteśvara. Following the dissolution of Avalokiteśvara, Mahāsthāmaprāpta will become the sovereign lord of Sukhāvatī.[74] Sukhāvatī is thus renewed indefinitely by Avalokiteśvara and Mahāsthāmaprāpta, both of whom succeed the founder of the Pure Land and preserve his messianic message of universal light and unending spiritual life. As pointed out by Tucci,

> unending life and infinite light, ζωή and φῶς, have too great an importance for religious history, in India and outside India, for us to exclude that under this myth may be hidden an extremely complex history and two originally independent cycles. (1949, 349)[75]

In the long *Sukhāvatīvyūha-sūtra* luminosity takes on a cosmological dimension invested with soteriological power. Light is that which pervades all buddha fields, quelling "passion, hatred and delusion" and "the fire in the realms of hell."[76] Amitābha's halo of light is greater in size than hundreds of thousands of millions of trillions of buddha fields, as vowed by Bodhisattva Dharmākara before becoming the enlightened buddha known as Amitābha.

> Blessed One, may I not awaken to unsurpassable, perfect, full awakening if, after I have awakened to unsurpassable, perfect, full awakening, the halo of light I display in this buddha field of mine should be measurable—and this means if it could be measured by any means, even with extraordinary measures such as the size of hundreds of thousands of millions of trillions of buddha fields. (LV §28, 13)

Similarly, the Buddha's life is immeasurable (LV §28, 15), as is the lifespan of the inhabitants of Sukhāvatī (LV §28, 14). Dharmākara's fifteenth and fourteenth vows pledged before Buddha Lokeśvararāja illustrate these two points respectively.

> Blessed One, may I not awaken to unsurpassable, perfect, full awakening if, after I have awakened to unsurpassable, perfect, full awakening, one could set a limit to my lifespan, even if it meant counting for as many as hundreds of thousands of trillions of cosmic ages. (LV §28, 15) Blessed One, may I not awaken to unsurpassable, perfect, full awakening if, after I have awakened to unsurpassable, perfect, full awakening, one could set a limit to the measure of the lifespan of living beings in this buddha field of mine, except in those cases when one would shorten one's life by the power of one's own vows. (LV §28, 14)

In Chinese sources the name Amitābha appears earlier than that of Amitāyus,[77] but both Sanskrit names are identified for the first time in the *Sukhāvatīvyūha* sutras and are presumed to have been used independently before that time.[78] In Tibetan sources Amitābha is usually rendered as 'Od-dpag-med (lit., "measureless light") and Amitāyus as Tshe-dpag-med (lit., "measureless life"), or Tshe-tshad-med in manuscripts from Dunhuang. The *Mahāvyutpati,* a bilingual Tibetan-Sanskrit lexicon composed for standardizing Tibetan translations of Sanskrit Buddhist texts, does not list the name Amitāyus. sNang-ba mtha'-yas, an equally old Tibetan translation of Amitābha dating to the time of the Tibetan empire, is also excluded from the *Mahāvyutpati.*[79]

The earliest datable literary reference of the name Amitāyus is in the *Samādhi of Direct Encounter with the Buddhas of the Present* (Skt. *Pratyutpanna-buddhasaṃmukhāvasthita-samādhi*). This popular Mahayana sutra, compiled sometime in the second century, was probably composed in Gāndhāra, the home of its translator into Chinese, the Indo-Scythian Lokakṣema (T. 418).[80] This text enjoyed considerable prestige in China and Japan;[81] it was translated into Tibetan sometime in the ninth century and is preserved in the Tibetan Buddhist Tripiṭaka.[82]

The *Samādhi of Direct Encounter* is a persuasive Mahayana text that encourages "recollecting the buddha" (Skt. *buddhānusmṛti;* Tib. *sangs-rgyas rjes su dran-pa;* Ch. *nianfo*) as an effective means for attaining birth in Sukhāvatī. The recollection of the buddha may have been performed in front of a concrete image, a statue, painting, or a paradise scene.[83]

> In accordance with what they have learned they concentrate on the thought: "That Lord, the Tathāgata, Arhat and Perfectly Awakened One Amitāyus now resides, lives, dwells and teaches the Dharma, surrounded and attended on by a host of bodhisattvas, in the world-system of Sukhāvatī, one hundred thousand koṭis of Buddha fields to the west of this Buddha field;" and they concentrate their thoughts on the Tathāgata with undistracted minds. . . . "Lord, what dharmas must bodhisattvas and mahāsattvas possess to be reborn in this world system [of yours]?" . . . Having been asked this question, the

> Lord and Tathāgata Amitāyus said to those bodhisattvas: "Sons of good family, if the calling to mind of the Buddha (*buddhānusmṛti*) is practiced, cultivated, developed and rehearsed, then one is reborn in this world-system."[84]

The practice of *buddhānusmṛti* enjoyed wide currency among Buddhist communities in Central Asia and China, "spanning a host of derivative practices and being itself transformed beyond recognition."[85] Its deployment for the salvific purpose of attaining birth in Sukhāvatī was not restricted to the invocation of Buddha Amitāyus but was also directed toward other buddhas, such as Śākyamuni and Bhaiṣajyaguru.[86] In later times, it would seem that the propitiation of deities and visualization of their buddha fields offered a palatable alternative to the intimidating dialectic of the doctrine of emptiness and the sobering rationalism of scholar-monks dispensing their "knowledge-remedies."[87] It is not hard to envisage why deity practices that centered on the afterlife would have acquired a broader geographical and social remit of operation, crossing geographical and political boundaries to reach a wide social spectrum.

Archaeological and Literary Records

The literary standing of Amitābha and his Pure Land Sukhāvatī in India, and his theological and cultic elaboration across Asia, do not resonate with Indian archaeological records. The earliest epigraphical reference to Amitābha is in an inscribed image pedestal discovered at Govindnagar near Mathurā (present-day Muttra). According to the inscription dated to the Kuṣāṇa period of 104 or 171 CE:[88]

> At the 26th day of the second month in the 28th year of the great king Huviṣka (or Huveṣka), at this occasion, by grandson of the Caravan-leader Satvaka, grandson of the merchant Balakīrta (or Balakatta), son of Budhabala (or Budhapila): Nāgarakṣita, the Lord Buddha Amitābha's image *was set up for the worship of all the Buddhas.* Through this root of merit may all the living beings obtain supreme knowledge of the Buddha.[89]

The Amitābha inscription in Mathurā, which was a Buddhist stronghold of the Sarvāstivādin school, may be the first archaeological evidence for the existence of Mahayana Buddhism in India.[90] While early forms of Pure Land devotion seem to coincide with the development of Mahayana Buddhism in the Kuṣāṇa period, curiously Amitābha's name does not reappear in inscriptions before the seventh century. It has been suggested that the ecumenical inscription at Govindnagar "set up for the worship of all the Buddhas" may have been limited to this instance.[91]

There have been a number of claims concerning the impact of Indian Pure Land traditions in the material culture of Gandhāra, but most of these have been challenged. Huntington (1980) identified Buddha Amitābha in a stele from Mohamed-Nari in the Lahore Museum in Pakistan, but Juhyung Rhi (2003) cast serious doubt on his identification. Schopen and Salomon (2002) have questioned the alleged reference by Brough (1982) to Amitābha in a Kharoṣṭhī inscription on a Gandhāran relief, but their objections are not equally shared by other scholars.[92]

While the evidence from Gandhāra resists scholarly consensus, there is a critique attributed to Asaṅga, a native of the region, which castigates the appeal of Pure Land teachings as a lure for the "spiritually inferior" and "morally indolent people."[93] Asaṅga's reservation toward Pure Land doctrines is shared by Vasubandhu the Elder in the *Mahāyāna-saṃgraha-bhāṣya,* a commentary on Asaṅga's *Mahayana Compendium.*[94] We cannot be certain how important or influential these critiques may have been among Indian scholars, but they seem to suggest that Pure Land traditions had spread in Gandhāra.[95]

References to Amitābha's cult in two popular Mahayana sutras may indicate some tension between Pure Land traditions and other Mahayana orientations in India. The *Lotus of Compassion Sutra* ranks Śākyamuni above all other buddhas, especially over Amitābha, on the grounds of compassion, given that Śākyamuni did not dwell in a pure land but took birth in our impure Sahā world in order to teach.[96] Pure Land doctrines are not foreign to the *Buddha-Matrix Sutra,* which seems, albeit only indirectly, to devalue them.[97] In the final section of the sutra we read that Avalokiteśvara and Mahāsthāmaprāpta, the two central figures in Amitābha's retinue, along with Mañjuśrī and Vajramati, did not (and possibly could not) attain enlightenment through the teachings on the *tathāgatagarbha* doctrine. The relevant passage reads:

> Passing beyond countless kalpas
> There was a Buddha named Brilliant King,
> Constantly radiating great brilliance
> Universally illuminating measureless Lands.
> Boundless Light Bodhisattva
> Under that Buddha first perfected the way,
> And stated a request about this sutra
> The Buddha accordingly extensively taught it.
> Those who encountered it were exceedingly Victorious
> And those hearing this sutra
> All extensively obtained saṃbodhi,

Excluding four bodhisattvas:
Mañjuśrī, Avalokiteśvara
Mahāsthāmaprāpta and Vajramati
These four bodhisattvas
All previously heard this Dharma.[98]

Unfortunately, our knowledge suffers still from the lack of source material and synthetic studies that would map the formulation and localization of Amitābha's cult in relation to other deity cults in India, their regional and trans-local zones of diffusion, the constituencies of Amitābha's worshipers, and his theological articulation over time. In the absence of further evidence, it would appear that the development of Pure Land orientations in India was a marginal phenomenon that was diffused with other Mahayana traditions or one that may have coalesced outside strictly Mahayana contexts. After all, with one dubious exception, there are virtually no accounts by Chinese Buddhist pilgrims having ever met Pure Land practitioners during their journeys in the Indian subcontinent. There is a single story by the Chinese pilgrim Huiri, who wrote in the eighth century that his Indian masters encouraged him to pursue Pure Land teachings as the quickest way to behold a vision of Amitābha. However intriguing this narrative, it should be treated with caution, because his "reports could very well be a pious accounting of a Pure Land devotee who, upon his return to China became one of the major Pure Land proponents of the mid-Tang period."[99]

While Amitābha's cult met with great success outside India's borders the material and literary sources neither categorically exclude nor substantiate his communal worship in India. It may be that interpreting the prominence of a deity based on its iconography is a phenomenon secondary to its cultic salience centered on practices of supplication and propitiation. The Amitābha cult developed when Indian Buddhism was exposed to a different religious and cultural climate than that of India proper. We will now turn our attention to the historical circumstances that coincide with rise of the Kuṣāṇa empire and the spirit of religious pluralism and imperial ecumenism it brought in its course.

The Mahayana Past of a Solar Deity

The emergence of Mahayana traditions in India occurred under conditions of imperial expansion and centralization, regional interconnection, and international trade, whatever their extent and nature. Clearly, Mahayana did not occur exclusively within the framework of established Buddhist traditions, but did so in the context of its encounter with other Indian religions and foreign cultures then prevalent in India. This point is relevant in light of syncretistic elements in the *Sukhāvatīvyūha* sutras, which were composed during the times of the Kuṣāṇa empire, a remarkable period in Indian history marked by cross-cultural contacts and religious tolerance.

The dynasty of the Kuṣāṇas united peoples of different nationalities, languages, and religions and opened the way for Indian civilization to spread in Central and Eastern Asia.[100] Its foundation is traced to the Yuezhi (Tokharians), old settlers of the Tarim basin who in 176–175 BCE were pushed away from their ancestral lands by the Xiongnu, a powerful nomadic people and dangerous competitors to Han supremacy in Central Asia. Sogdiana witnessed large migrations of the Yuezhi, who led attacks against the Parthians and occupied northern Bactria in 124–123 BCE Less than a century later, the charismatic Yuezhi leader Kujula Kadphises united by force the four constituent chiefdoms of Tokharistan and founded what came to be known as the Kuṣāṇa empire.[101]

Buddhism had arrived in Northwest India and Gandhāra in pre-Kuṣāṇa times during the reign of Emperor Aśoka, who sponsored several Buddhist missions inside and beyond the territories of the Mauryan empire.[102] His royal edicts record that imperial envoys were dispatched across India to the southern island of Ceylon (present-day Sri Lanka) and to the thriving Indo-Greek kingdoms. The Indians had been acquainted with the Greeks from the incursions of Alexander III in 327 BCE and from the Hellenized cities he had established in Bactria and Northwest India.[103] During Aśoka's time, the Greeks in his provinces were held in high esteem, not least for serving as traders and emissaries between India and the vast Greek world of Persia and the Mediterranean basin ruled by Alexander's successors, the Diadochoi (Greek Διάδοχοι).[104]

At least three of Aśoka's royal inscriptions (a minor rock edict and parts of edicts nos. XII and XIII) were written in Greek,[105] supporting a growing body of evidence that Aśoka intended to proselytize his own and neighboring Iranian and Greek subjects to the ethical ways of Buddhism. The success of such efforts could explain, in part, constitutive elements in Mahayana Buddhism, infused with the cosmopolitan spirit of universality favored by the Greeks of Hellenistic times and the creation of a school of Greco-Buddhist art that flourished in Gandhāra.[106]

After the decline of the Mauryan empire, the Greco-Bactrian kingdom grew into a large state that subsumed parts of Western India, Eastern Iran, and Central Asia.[107] Commercial exchanges between China and the Greco-Bactrian kingdom may have begun as early as the first part of the second century BCE, during the reign of the Greek king Demetrios.[108] According to the archaeological evidence however, not until the second century CE was Buddhism disseminated from Bactria to Kāshgar and further to the east, from Northwest India to Kashmir and Khotan and across the oasis cities south of the Taklamakan desert.[109] The ecumenical spirit of the Kuṣāṇas may be traced, in part, to a cosmopolitan milieu that featured active Hellenized communities. While the Kuṣāṇa aristocracy tried to assimilate the royal ideology of the Greco-Bactrian kings, new forms of religious worship developed in the Surkhan Darya valley.[110]

The Kuṣāṇa emperors generally did not seek to eradicate popular religious traditions or to systematically impose their own religious traditions on their conquered territories. Instead they promoted inclusive religious and official imagery, a process also reflected in their development of science, philosophy, art, and architecture.[111] Numismatic evidence confirms a conscious religious pluralism in an organizational setting that featured coins with pre-Zoroastrian deities, as well as Zoroastrian, Greek, Egyptian, Mesopotamian, and Indic gods and goddesses. This explosion of religious plurality betokens elaboration in the context of large-scale acculturating political instances, whereby marginal regional deities came to acquire social and institutional consistency beyond local cultic practice, all the while preserving original features of iconography and ritual. The institutional support of Buddhism across the empire and beyond its borders is attributed to the Kuṣāṇa emperor Kaniṣka, whose patronage of Buddhist cults and establishment of Buddhist monasteries and monuments is linked with the spread of Buddhism in the Tarim basin during his reign.[112]

Given the polyethnic and multireligious constitution of the Kuṣāṇa empire featuring Greek, Persian, and Central Asian communities, there have been several hypotheses concerning foreign influences in the make-up of the *Sukhāvatīvyūha* sutras. It has been argued that there are unequivocal Iranian elements in the heliocentric formation of the Amitābha deity on the basis of shared motifs with the Zoroastrian solar god Ahura Mazdā, who abides in his luminous heaven, and parallels have been drawn between Zrvanakarana and Amitāyus.[113] There have also been readings in favor of Hindu influences drawn from Vedic literature or the *Bhagavadgītā*.[114] Other scholars have been keen to assign exclusive Buddhist origins to the inception of Amitābha. This position is exemplified by Fujita (1996, 11–16) who credits the Mahāsāṃghikas for the Mahayana concept of "universal buddhahood" and the "bodhisattva ideal"—two precursors to the formation of Buddha Amitābha.

It is not the purpose of this discussion to provide a comprehensive list of associations among deities of different provenance, nor to provide a history of such syncretism or map its geographical spread associated with religious mythographies during the Kuṣāṇas. As we have seen earlier in this chapter, the cult of Amitābha and his Pure Land can be adequately explained doctrinally as an endemic evolution of Indian Mahayana. However, a "theological compatibility" does not exclude foreign influences from Persian, Hellenistic, and Indian religious cults, beliefs, and practices. The solar character and astral attributes of Amitābha suggests the domestication of non-Buddhist material that was assimilated doctrinally within an indisputably Buddhist framework. As we will examine in later sections, this may become empirically evident with regard to iconographic associations that show how constant and common religious syncretism has been, and the degree to which solar deities reflected a universal attraction for the sun and for luminosity that inspired theological and metaphorical elaborations of the divine and sublime.

Though rich and diverse as the origins of Amitābha may be, his Buddhist past is concocted in some fifteen Jātaka tales distributed across several Mahayana sutras.[115] The better-known Mahayana account of the luminous buddha is found in the long *Sukhāvatīvyūha-sūtra.* This Jātaka-type narrative is centered on a bodhisattva by the name of Dharmākara who pledges before Buddha Lokeśvararāja (lit., "King of the Lords of the World") to become enlightened in his buddha field through the formulation of bodhisattva vows uttered as conditional statements, such as "May I never attain enlightenment if my vows (x, y, z . . .) are not fulfilled."[116] This model of religious confirmation and succession is common to several Mahayana texts, and even Buddha Śākyamuni is depicted as an aspiring bodhisattva pledging his vows before an ancient buddha named Dīpaṇkara (lit., "Creator of Light"), who confers on him a prophecy of his future enlightenment. The archetypal encounter between a buddha and an "aspiring buddha" reinforces a number of literary tropes, not least an opportunity for the bodhisattva to acquire vast merit (Skt. *puṇya*) in the act of enunciating his pledges before an ultimate field of merit, a living buddha.

In the long *Sukhāvatīvyūha-sūtra,* Dharmākara's encounter with Buddha Lokeśvararāja serves as a didactic tour de force, one that incites Dharmākara to "roar with a lion's roar" and inspire an assembly of like-minded aspirants to adopt similar Mahayana vows in order to bring about the perfection of buddha fields according to the spiritual needs of their communities.[117]

> Dharmākara approached the Tathāgata, in salutation touched the feet of the Blessed One, the Tathāgata Lokeśvararāja, with his forehead, and said: "I have now assembled the most perfect wondrous qualities and ornaments of a buddha field." When this has been said . . . the Tathāgata Lokeśvararāja said to the monk Dharmākara: "Speak then, O monk. The Tathāgata approves . . . now is the time to do so, O monk. Bring joy to the assembly, stir the assembly, roar with a lion's roar, so that, upon hearing this, Bodhisattvas, Mahāsattvas, of the present and of times to come, will adopt vows like yours, vows to achieve the perfection of a buddha field." (LV §§26, 27)

Amitābha's past lives feature in other Jātaka narratives that interweave mythical or long-forgotten elements about noble descendants and glorious incarnations. It is here that we learn of the enlightenment of the monk Āyuṣpariśuddha, the monk Samadarśanālaṃbana, the prince Acintyaguṇaratnaśrī, the king Candradatta, the king Puṇyodgata, and the king Arciṣmat, among others.[118] These hagiographies differ from the long *Sukhāvatīvyūha* and with each other in significant details, suggesting that the conceptualization of Buddha Amitābha did not originate with the composition of the *Sukhāvatīvyūha* sutras any more than the worship of Amitābha defined exclusively the religious orientation that came to be known as Pure Land Buddhism. It appears that this deity was bound to regions and to important Indian social groups, but was worshiped nevertheless by a variety of people at different and common locations, while one senses the occurrence of kratophanies that are hard to identify and measure concretely, beyond a list of names and their corresponding families.

In the Garden of the Gods

> There was the garden of the gods; all round him stood bushes bearing gems. Seeing it he went down at once, for there was fruit of carnelian with the vine hanging from it, beautiful to look at; lapis lazuli leaves hung thick with fruit, sweet to see. For thorns and thistles there were haematite and rare stones, agate, and pearls from out of the sea. While Gilgamesh walked in the garden by the edge of the sea Shamash saw him, and he saw that he was dressed in the skins of animals and ate their flesh. He was distressed, and he spoke and said, "No mortal man has gone this way before, nor will, as long as the winds drive over the sea." And to Gilgamesh he said, "You will never find the life for which you are searching." Gilgamesh said to glorious Shamash, "Now that I have toiled and strayed so far over the wilderness, am I to sleep, and let the earth cover my head for ever? Let my eyes see the sun until they are dazzled with looking. Although I am no better than a dead man, still let me see the light of the sun." (*The Epic of Gilgamesh*)

The *Sukhāvatīvyūha* sutras embellish lavish descriptions of Sukhāvatī, a heavenly palace with elegant gardens and soothing ponds with colorful floating lotuses, adorned with an abundance of precious jewels, and imbued with divine sounds. These inordinate illustrations of Amitābha's garden-like heaven, common to many religious traditions, have given rise to hypotheses concerning foreign constituents that may have gone into its Buddhist delivery. Current opinions concerning the origins of Sukhāvatī tend either to reflect diffusionist models in which portions of doctrines and ideas presumed to have been taken from other religious systems, or they rely on endemic models that may satisfactorily account for new developments in the religious pluralism of India at that time.

There are striking parallels between Sukhāvatī and Zoroastrian heavens, Ecbatana, Uttarāpatha, and other foreign depictions of celestial abodes.[119] Barber (2002) traces the beginnings of Sukhāvatī to Hindu conceptions of heavens, while other scholars discern similarities with the castle Kusāvatī in the *Mahāsudassana-sutta.*[120] In fact, one does not need to search far to find comparable concepts in Indian or world religious literature, for that matter. Celestial abodes that resemble Sukhāvatī abound in Buddhist sutras, i.e., the city of Gandhavatī in the *Aṣṭasāhasrikā Prajñāpāramitā,* the buddha lands of the *Saddharmapuṇḍarīka,* the gardens in the *Gaṇḍavyūha,* the eastern land Abhirati in the *Akṣobhyavyūha,* and so on.[121]

Hirakawa (1963) put forward influential arguments that link the origins of Amitābha's Pure Land with the cult of the stupa.[122] Just like Mus (1998) before him, who drew typological associations between Buddhist reliquaries, *maṇḍalas*, and the city of the *cakravartin* at the Barabuḍur site in Indonesia, Hirakawa discerned in the stupa's sevenfold *vedikā* design a prototype for the architectural layout of Sukhāvatī adorned with seven terraces. His hypothesis draws support from the fact that stupas in India were active centers of daily ritual activity and were commonly sited in surroundings with beautiful ponds, gardens, and rows of trees,[123] elements reminiscent of the landscape imagery that made Amitābha's buddha field so attractive in Buddhist iconography and the popular imagination.

Etymologically speaking, the term "Sukhāvatī" features the Sanskrit term *sukha,* which in early Buddhist texts refers to both worldly happiness and spiritual bliss.[124] Thus, Sukhāvatī is infused with the bliss of the nirvana realm (Skt. *nirvanadhātusaukhya*), and in the long *Sukhāvatīvyūha* those who take birth in Sukhāvatī are blissfully born "miraculously and cross-legged on lotus flowers."[125] The opened lotus (Skt. *padma*) attained enormous religious importance for Buddhism and was frequently employed in images from Gandhāra, possibly during the latter half of the second century.[126] However, its prevalence as a spiritual symbol of creation with photic connotations is attested to in Egypt and India prior to the growth of Buddhism.[127]

There are many Buddhist references to the lotus. A lotus bloomed in the wake of each step taken by the child Śākyamuni, a symbol of his unmistakeable purity and divinity, in the manner of celestial gods in Hinduism. Over time, the lotus became intimately identified with Buddhist art and literature and came to symbolize the arrival of a buddha in the world. In the *Flower Ornament Sutra,* a luminous lotus symbolizes such a moment:

> Furthermore, when the worlds are beginning, there is a great flood filling the billion-world universe, producing enormous lotus flowers, called array of jewels of virtues of the manifestation of Buddha, which cover the surface of the waters, their radiance illumining all worlds in the ten directions. Then the overlord god, the gods of the pure abodes, and so on, seeing these flowers, know for certain that in this eon there will be that many buddhas appearing in the world.[128]

There are references in Buddhist scriptures concerning those who after death will attain spontaneous birth (Skt. *upapāduka*) on a thousand-petaled lotus in front of the King of Dharma if they create buddha figures seated on a lotus.[129] The lotus is an exemplary emblem of purity in Buddhism, for it is untainted by the muddy waters of the world from which it grows. In the popular Buddhist text *Milindapañha* (*Questions of King Milinda*), preserved in Pāli and Chinese translations, the Indo-Greek king Menander (ca. 155–130 BCE) of Śākala (present-day Sialkot in the Punjab) is instructed by the Buddhist monk Nāgasena:

> Just, O king, as the lotus, though it is born in the water, and grows up in the water, yet remains undefiled by the water [for no water adheres to it]; just so, O king, should the strenuous Bhikshu, earnest in effort, remain undefiled by the support that he receives, or by the following of disciples that he obtains, or by fame, or by honour, or by veneration, or by the abundance of the requisites that he enjoys. . . . As the lotus, O king, is untarnished by the water, so is Nirvāṇa untarnished by any evil dispositions. This is the one quality of the lotus inherent in Nirvāṇa.[130]

Like the gods of the Hindu pantheon, buddhas and bodhisattvas are frequently depicted holding a lotus, as in images of Avalokiteśvara, or rising out of exalted lotuses. In Hindu traditions some celestial deities are described as "lotus-born," such as Brahma, the Vedic god of creation, and Śrī Lakṣmī, consort of the god Viṣṇu.[131] In Indra's heaven, Trāyastriṃśa, one is born from lotuses.[132] Lotus-born (*padma 'byung-gnas*) is also the name of the Indian master Padmasambhava from Uḍḍiyāna (present-day Swat) who, according to Tibetan tradition, arrived in central Tibet after being summoned by Emperor Khri Srong-lde-brtsan (ca. 755–794) to assist in the establishment of Tibet's first monastery at bSam-yas. His miraculous birth takes place on a lotus floating in Lake Dhanakosha (see Epilogue).

In the long *Sukhāvatīvyūha-sūtra,* all those who take birth in the Pure Land do so without conception and sexual exchange of genital fluids, but do arise spontaneously (Skt. *aupapāduka*) in the manner of Mahayana deities from the opening blossom of a spiritual womb, a floating lotus.[133] Birth in a pure land acquires the quality of a visual spectacle. This reduction of the experience of awakening to the visible serves the objectification of enlightenment within the realm of the ocular, and it is precisely this sort of appropriation that renders the objectification of the buddha field into a contemplative act of visualization and consummation. Furthermore, this spectacular mode of immaculate reception in a Buddhist paradise and the aesthetic specificities of this vision are mediated by one's faith in the sutra's teachings. An unpleasant surprise awaits those who harbor doubt and hesitation, for should they have sufficient merit to be born in Sukhāvatī but entertained doubts on how this may be possible, after death they are consigned to a kind of spiritual purgatory, disoriented and locked in isolation for 500 years inside closed calyxes of immense lotuses resembling gigantic Venus flytraps, which purges the "doubting Thomases" of their lack of trust before releasing them into Amitābha's Land of Bliss.

> [W]ith a mental image of the palaces and the gardens of the Land of Bliss, and no excrement or urine is discharged from their bodies, no phlegm or mucus, and nothing disagreeable to the mind is found on their bodies or in their dwellings, still for five hundred years they are deprived of seeing Buddhas, hearing the Dharma, seeing Bodhisattvas, speaking about and ascertaining the Dharma, and practicing any of the best virtues taught in the Dharma. Although they do not rejoice there or find satisfaction, still, when their previous transgressions have been exhausted, they then, at last, leave that calyx; and, as they leave it, they cannot tell if they are leaving from above, from below, or across. (LV §140)

Amitābha in Tibetan Representation

The importation and adaptation of religious imagery or its local manufacture according to adapted models, which might have syncretic iconographic contents, seem to have been a common practice in Tibet whenever material conditions permitted, and might provide interesting directions for the interpretation of the cult of Amitābha and the future study of the representational varieties of his worship in Tibet. The Tibetan-styled Buddha Amitābha is depicted in the color of the setting sun with a peaceful countenance and two arms.[134] He is commonly dressed with three kinds of monastic robes and is seated crossed-legged on an open lotus with hands in the gesture of meditation (Skt. *dhyāna-mudrā*), holding an alms bowl (Skt. *piṇḍapātra*). On both sides of his lotus throne we discern his mount (Skt. *vāhana*), a pair of peacocks and a full-blown lotus between them.[135] In tantric lore, Buddha Amitābha symbolizes the wisdom of discerning perception (Skt. *saṃjñāskhandha*) that neutralizes the poison of attachment (*'dod-chags;* Skt. *kāma*), the desire that "grasps hungrily at everything," and the transformation of passion into compassion. In the same traditions, he is associated with the fire element that excites passion, and with the quality of luminosity that makes things visible. Amitābha symbolizes the psychosomatic transmutation of gross and subtle forms of desire into discriminating judgment. His indivisible oral register, his seed syllable, is a red syllable *hrīh* visualized standing still on a lotus or rotating horizontally at the throat *cakra* (*'khor-lo*). His full mantra, *oṃ amidhewa hrīh,* when uttered in correct form and order, formulaically and repetitively expressed, is designed to unlock the energies and capacities of the powers invoked, such as bestowing mastery over all aspects related to ordinary and wisdom speech.

There are numerous references to Buddha Amitābha scattered across Tibetan ritual texts and in association with mortuary rites.[136] In tantric scriptures he is represented as the master of one of five buddha domains (*rigs-lnga;* Skt. *pañcakula*), the family of the lotus,[137] in which his Pure Land does not occupy any overt part or may represent the location where he taught the tantra of enlightened speech.[138] Amitābha exemplifies the capacity for verbal communication, and during Tantric meditations he is visualized at the center of the throat, the subtle *cakra* of enjoyment depicted with sixteen spokes radiating outwardly.[139] In this capacity, he is ritually supplicated to bestow consecration (*rab-gnas*) on words, letters, and printed matter. The consecration is commonly done by envisioning him in union with his consort (*yab-yum*), the personification of his wisdom aspect (Skt. *prajñā*), and dissolving them both into light as they undergo transformation into the form of letters.[140] In this posture, his arms are crossed behind her back holding a thunderbolt (*rdo-rje;* Skt. *vajra*) and a handbell (*dril-bu;* Skt. *ghaṇṭa*), while Pāṇḍarāvāsuni (Gos-dkar-mo), also red in color, sits on his lap holding a skull and a chopper (or wheel).[141] In an esoteric work of the rNying-ma school, the five buddha families are said to be emanations of Buddha Amitābha miraculously born of his own will from a lotus in the center of the milky ocean (*'o ma can gyi mtsho*).[142]

There are ample associations of Amitābha with a number of meditational deities that belong to his own family (*maṇḍala*) occasioning distinct theological and mythographic interpretations.[143] This raises the question whether a study of Amitābha's provenance in Tibet should take into account cultic practices that depict him in important ritual and thematic ways with deities from his own family, such as Padmasambhava and Tārā, who are not mentioned in the *Sukhāvatīvyūha* sutras.[144] The triadic syncretism of Amitābha, Avalokiteśvara, and Padmasambhava is revered in the rNying-ma and bKa'-brgyud schools and is to be understood as a theological elaboration with cultic ramifications, given that "lay religious practice turns almost exclusively on these figures, who are regarded as the three embodiments (*sku-gsum;* Skt. *trikāya*) of a single Buddha."[145]

While there does not seem to be sufficient reason to impute to this Tibetan synthesis of worship a coherent and stable form, there are many legendary associations between Amitābha and Avalokiteśvara, whose six-syllable mantra (*oṃ maṇi padme hūṃ*) purifies lower rebirths and causes one to be born in Sukhāvatī.[146] A popular legend in Tibet relates how Avalokiteśvara's faith was shaken after having beheld the sight of countless beings swarming toward the horrors of the lower realms of rebirth. Because of this, he renounced his bodhisattva vows and soon after his body and head shattered into a thousand pieces. Buddha Amitābha gathered and blessed the broken pieces and refashioned Avalokiteśvara with eleven faces and a thousand hands, like a thousand-petaled lotus. Then he situated himself on top of Avalokiteśvara's head and praised him thus, "I bow to you because your thousand hands are the hands of the thousand universal emperors and those eyes in each of the palms of the hands are the eyes of one thousand buddhas who will appear in this fortunate aeon."[147] The emblematic insertion of Amitābha's head on top of Avalokiteśvara's headdress seems to have been established before the Gupta period[148] and is widespread in Tibetan statues and paintings of the eleven-headed and thousand-armed Avalokiteśvara, an importation from Nepal.[149] The appropriation of this motif is all the more conspicuous in the life-size portrait statue of the Tibetan emperor Srong-tsen Gampo (ca. seventh century) in the Potala Palace in Lhasa, an iconography that, one would presume, betokened an imperial regime with divine sanction.[150]

The iconic synthesis of Indian Mahayana deities, known as the "Sukhāvatī triad" from Mathurā in the Kūṣana period,[151] prevailed as a popular subject of Tibetan religious paintings (*thang-ka*). Amitābha is situated in the center of his Pure Land flanked symmetrically on his right by a standing white Avalokiteśvara, and on his left by Mahāsthāmaprāpta in blue color, and at times accompanied by eight bodhisattva attendants.[152] This octad is quite common in Tibetan depictions of Amitābha and Buddha Vairocana.[153] In rNying-ma literature there is a reference to alchemical systems in which eight magicians emanate from Buddha Amitāyus.[154]

Buddha Amitābha and Amitāyus are popular subjects of representation in the Tibetan and Himalayan traditions, and are commonly evoked at appropriate times and places for expiatory, divinatory, apotropaic, votive, or devotional purposes, or indeed a combination of some or all of these. Tibetan-style depictions of Amitābha abound in statues and murals in the northwest Indian Himalayas (Alchi, Shey, Tabo), in central Tibet (bSam-yas, Jo-khang), and in Central Asia (Dunhuang), while woodcut illustrations of the Buddha are found in the Tibetan canonical collections of the Kanjur and Tanjur. Buddha Amitāyus and Buddha Amitābha may be depicted at times together in their different visual forms. Amitāyus is usually represented sitting on an open lotus in red or golden color with his hands on his lap in the meditation gesture (Skt. *dhyāna-mudrā*), holding the vase of long-life ambrosia (*tshe-bum*), his special emblem.[155] He is adorned in *saṃbhogakāya* fashion with lavish vestments, a beautiful crown, jewel ornaments, silk garments, and so forth, and when accompanied with a "silk arrow" (*mda'-dar*) he is propitiated in conjunction with divination rituals. On rare occasions he is framed on each side by the bodhisattvas Avalokiteśvara and Mahāsthāmaprāpta, while there are also depictions of him in tantric union with his consort in the center of his *maṇḍala*.[156]

Unique is the representation of a nine-deity Amitāyus *maṇḍala* attributed to the eleventh-century Indian Buddhist scholar Jetāri, the author of the *Nine-deity Maṇḍala of Amitāyus according to the System Transmitted by Ācārya Jetāri* (*Tshe dpag med lha dgu slob dpon dze ta ri'i lugs kyi dkyil 'khor*) preserved in the *Compendium of Tantras* (*Rgyud sde kun btus*, vol. 2, 113–210). An intricate thangka in the possession of the Rubin Museum of Art (no. 720), dated to the first part of the fifteenth century, portrays Amitāyus in his principal form at the center of a nine-deity *maṇḍala* surrounded by his eight identical forms seated on eight-petaled lotuses—in the east (below) is Vajra Amitāyus, south (left) Ratna Amitāyus, west (above) Padma Amitāyus, and north (right) Karma Amitāyus.[157]

In the present state of our knowledge, we cannot tell how the pictorial differentiation between Amitābha and Amitāyus developed, and whether the Tibetans continued a tradition elaborated by some Indian schools or if they were the first to formulate it.[158] In Indian Mahayana sources we find no evidence for a separate identity of Amitābha and Amitāyus; as we have seen, the long *Sukhāvatīvyūha* equates their names indiscriminately.[159]

There are some striking iconographic parallels between Amitābha and Sūrya, the Indian sun deity. Images from Gāndhāra show that Sūrya was susceptible to transformations and artistic innovations. At times he appears with wings holding lotus flowers, or standing on a chariot like the Greek god of the sun, Helios, lead by four or two horses, and framed by two female (and later male) attendants.[160] During the Kuṣāna period, Sūrya is represented squatting in a cart drawn by two horses, wearing an embroidered coat, trousers, and turban, and holding a lotus bud in his right hand and a dagger in his left.[161] In the later Gupta period, the sun god is depicted fully seated and holding lotus flowers in both hands. Tibetan images of Buddha Amitābha resemble late Gupta themes, where Sūrya is portrayed seated cross-legged in the *padmāsana* posture with two male attendants at his sides, Daṇḍa (Yama) and Piṅgala (Agni), a halo around his head, and his hands in *dhyāna-mudra.*[162]

It appears that Indian Buddhists worshiped the sun god and performed solar-cult rites. The *Bṛhat-Saṁhitā,* a technical encyclopedia on secular sciences, lists "benevolent Buddhist priests of serene mind" among those qualified to perform the ceremony for the solar deity during the installation of sun images.[163] The image of Sūrya in a Buddhist monastic complex in Bamiyan in Greater Gandhāra, dating from the third–fourth centuries CE, resembles Buddha Amitābha, whose name, after all, is a synonym for Sūrya.[164]

Although this is not the place to explore in detail these instances, it seems quite plausible that solar deities are of a widespread geographical origin with a capacity to take on a variety of functions common to a number of stellar gods, including granting wishes, offering protection, and so forth. This raises the question whether we are dealing with one deity or with a variety of deities located in or imported from different places, and whose "astral characteristics" furthermore suggest a case of appropriation for solar theology, especially in regions having long-term contact with other cultures and among travelers and traders relying on the position of heavenly bodies for navigation and livelihood. The name Amitābha signals a divine appellation shared by a number of heliocentric deities (i.e., Helios, Sūrya, etc). It may very well be that there was not always a clear hierarchy among a profusion of Buddhist, Hindu, and foreign divinities in India, quite apart from the prestige that would have attached them to kings and leading family lineages, while we cannot exclude the possibility that households and individuals worshiped several divinities at different times, some of which may have held similar operations and appellations, regardless of their places of origin or differences in iconography.

Indian Pure Land Commentaries in East Asia

Our survey of Indian Pure Land themes would not be complete without brief mention of two controversial commentaries attributed to renowned Indian Buddhist scholars and patriarchs of Pure Land traditions in East Asia.[165] These Chinese commentaries are unknown in Sanskrit and Tibetan literature, and for this reason scholars remain skeptical and dismissive of their alleged Indian origins.[166]

The first apocryphal text is attributed to Nāgārjuna (ca. 150–250 CE), entitled *Discourse on the Ten Stages* (*Daśabhūmikavibhāṣā-śāstra*). This commentary on the "ten stages of awakening" draws from Chapter Twenty-Six of the *Flower Ornament Sutra.* There is no alternative Chinese translation of the *Discourse on the Ten Stages* and the one currently available (T. 26) was allegedly translated from Sanskrit by Kumārajīva (344–413).[167] The *Discourse on the Ten Stages* contains thirty-five chapters in total, but Chapter Nine, entitled "Easy Practice," is the one most widely read and quoted in support of Pure Land orthodoxy in East Asia.

In this chapter, Nāgārjuna seems to suggest that one may swiftly attain the first bodhisattva level (Skt. *bhūmi*), the "stage of joy" (*pramuditā-bhūmi*), by following an easy path of training: "Those who wish to enter the Stage of Non-retrogression quickly should reverently hold [the buddhas] in mind and recite their names."[168] This "easy" mode of spiritual practice served as one of the primary bases for the development of Pure Land exegetical traditions in East Asia.[169]

The second commentary that had considerable impact on East Asian Pure Land traditions is linked to the Yogācāra tradition and Master Vasubandhu. This work is known as the *Treatise on Sukhāvatī* and is said to have been translated into Chinese from Sanskrit (T. 1524) by the Buddhist monk Bodhiruci (ca. 529) from north India.[170]

The *Treatise on Sukhāvatī* recommends that one recollect Buddha Amitābha, visualize his land, and make the wish to be born there. In order to accomplish this, Vasubandhu elaborates on "five contemplative gates" (Ch. *wu-nian men*), namely: 1) worship, 2) praise, 3) aspiration, 4) visualization, and 5) transference of merit. The commentary focuses on the fourth contemplative gate, which includes visualizing seventeen merits associated with Sukhāvatī, eight merits related to Amitābha, and four merits of bodhisattvas.[171]

These alleged Indian classics, the *Treatise on Sukhāvatī* and the *Discourse on the Ten Stages,* exerted indisputable influence on the doctrinal interpretation of Pure Land Buddhism in China and Japan. They have been glossed in a variety of ways, not least to support exclusive religious attitudes and channel popular expressions of devotion, especially the chanting of the name of Buddha Amitābha, as sufficient means of Buddhist practice. For all their impact and popularity in East Asia, these *śāstras* are virtually ignored by compilers of Tibetan canonical literature, such as the polymath librarian Bu-ston rin-chen grub (1290–1364). Tibetan monastic schools of Buddhism claim authorship to a large and diverse corpus of aspiration prayers and commentaries, and yet in none of these indigenous works of Buddhist literature do we find any explicit reference to these contested East Asian Pure Land commentaries attributed to Nāgārjuna and Vasubandhu.[172]

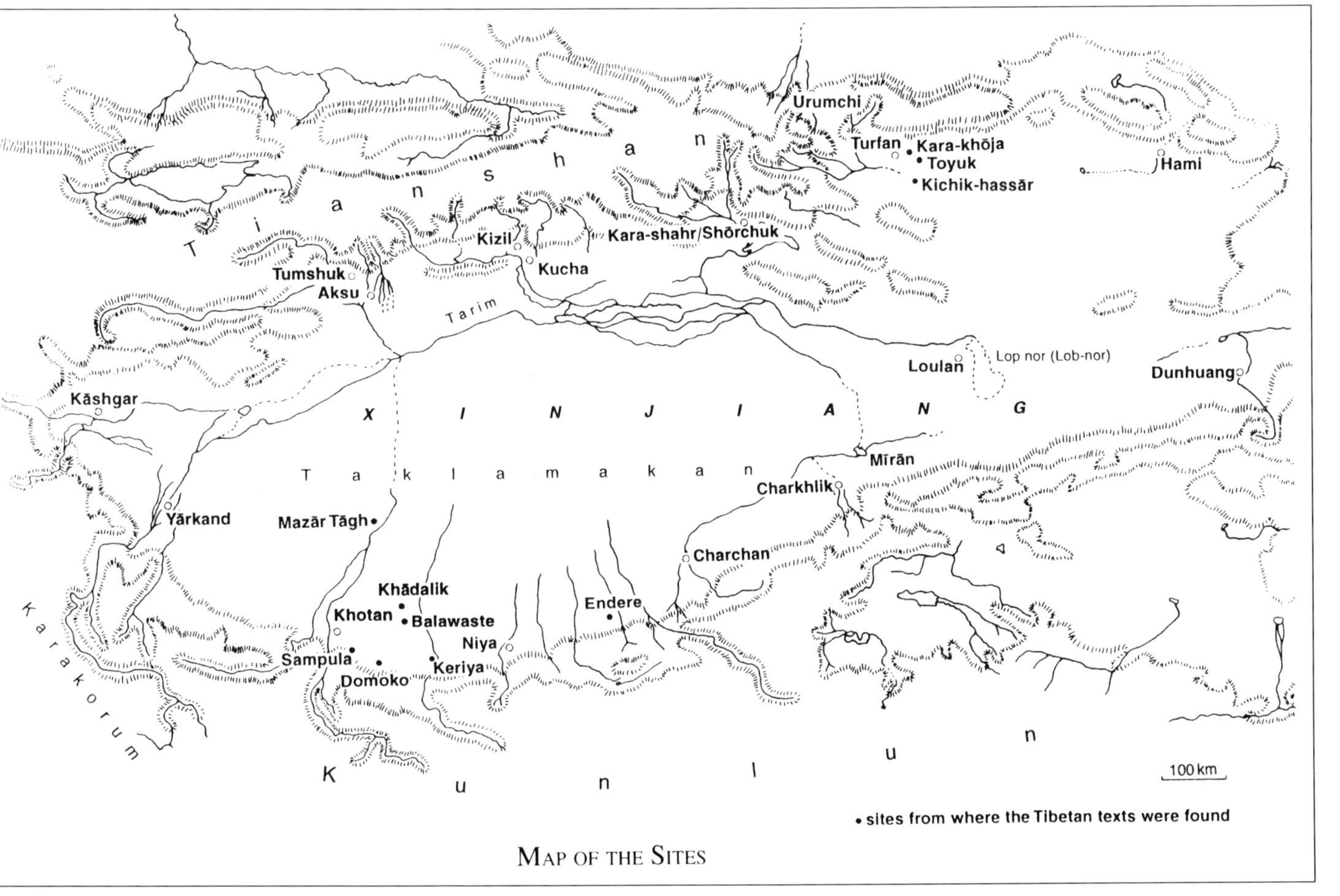

Tarim basin sites where Tibetan texts were discovered. Courtesy of the British Library (Takeuchi 1998).

Chapter Two

Pure Lands and the Tibetan Empire

The Tibetans and the Tang Dynasty

The arrival of the Tibetans in Central Asia is marked by a series of confrontations with the Tang dynasty (618-907). In Tang histories, Tibet was situated eight thousand *li* west of the Tang capital of Chang'an, and in the words of one scholar, it challenged "more severely than any other non-Chinese state in the Tang period Chinese security and sense of superiority."[1]

> In contrast to the nomadic peoples who typically refrained from attempting to occupy the territory of settled peoples, the Tibetans were noted for their territorial ambition. They expanded in all directions, confronting the Chinese in the Qinghai region where the Tuyuhun had their kingdom as well as in the Western Regions, in addition to their constant incursions on the Chinese frontiers.[2]

From the early seventh century until the first half of the ninth, the Tibetans maintained a powerful presence in Central Asia that challenged the geopolitical ambitions of the Tang. In the span of a century, Tang and Tibet concluded seven sworn treatises (Ch. *meng*) for peace in 706, 732, 762, 765, 767, 783, and 821–822; two of the treaties were violated by the Chinese and five by the Tibetans.[3]

Following the second reign of Khri Srong-brtsan (ca. 646–649), the Tibetan emperor Khri Mang-slon-mang-rtsan (ca. 649–676) "gained a strategic advantage that the Chinese obviously did not appreciate until it was too late."[4] Tibet's military strength had grown substantially. It included fighting infantries marching to battle in single file, and an efficient system of patrols and sentries composed of infantrymen dispatched for the defense and control of the main roads, mountain passes, post stations, and cities.[5] In 663, the Tibetans launched an attack against the 'A-zha (Ch. Tuyuhun), south of the Koko Nor region, disrupting a buffer zone between Tang China and Tibet and ushering their infiltration into the trade markets of the Tarim basin. In 678, the Tibetans confronted and crushed 180,000 Tang troops at Koko Nor and were soon in control of the whole of

China's western frontier and the lucrative trading networks attached to the Silk Road.[6]

The Tang initiated further military confrontations with Tibet in 694 and 695, culminating in a devastating defeat for the Chinese troops in Suluohan in 696. The Chinese government, having previously refused three Tibetan requests for peace, changed its policy and Empress Wu (684–705) dispatched Guo Yuanzhen to meet the Tibetan minister Mgar-khri-'bring and commence negotiations.[7] Mgar-khri-'bring was a tough negotiator. He demanded that the Tang empress dismantle the four garrisons in the Western Regions and free the Tarim states from Chinese rule. In effect, he threatened that Tibet would continue to intrude on Tang frontiers in Ganzhou and Liangzhou, weakening Tang rule, one way or another, in order to force the empire to give up its trading monopoly of the Silk Road. Mgar-khri-'bring and Guo Yuanzhen were not able to reach an agreement. The Chinese, who controled the Western Regions, were not willing to give up the garrisons that secured the steady flow of commodities to and from the western capital of Chang'an.

Periods of peace and war alternated between Tibet and China, and by the end of Emperor Xuanzong's reign, Tang seemed to have had the upper hand. But this did not last long. The An Lushan Rebellion (755–763) turned the balance of power in favor of Tibet.[8] This heavy blow to Tang national unity triggered another assault by Arab and Persian pirates—in 758, they attacked Canton, looting the royal granaries and storehouses and forcing the Tang government to flee.[9]

Taking advantage of the Tang's political instability and dwindling financial resources, the Tibetans conquered Liangzhou in 758 and installed their own military government (*khrom*).[10] In 763, they detained two Chinese envoys of high rank and seized the western capital of Chang'an, positioning their own prince on the Tang throne.[11] The occupation of the city lasted only two weeks, but the Tibetans, stationed seventy-eight miles west of Chang'an, continued to attack the western capital. They mounted military campaigns for more than two decades, forcing the government to declare martial law in the city on at least four occasions between 764 and 768.

The Tang recovered its capitals in 757 and suppressed the successors of An Lushan in early 763, but the rebellions had devastating effects on the empire's physical integrity, economy, and morale. The Chinese had lost direct control of much of their former territory. The Tibetans, Quarluqs, and Uighurs usurped Chinese colonies in Central Asia, while major areas of China, no longer under Tang control, refused to pay taxes to the emperor. The Tibetan conquest of the northwest territories had dire consequences for the Tang economy, which incurred the loss of silk production, trading monopolies, and the availability of pasturelands for horses.[12]

Sino-Tibetan hostilities more or less ended with the signing of one last treaty between China and Tibet in 821–822. Unlike previous agreements, this landmark record, a bilingual inscription on a stone pillar outside the Jo-khang at Lhasa, recognized both parties as self-sovereign over their respective territories to the east (China) and west (Tibet).[13] "The Nephew-Uncle Pillar Inscription" (*dbon-zhang rdo-rings*) reads:

> In the east is China, extending to the great ocean, the king of the region where the sun rises, unlike other *barbarians*, by the excellence of its dominion and religious customs and the greatness of its wisdom and method, a match even for Tibet in war and a partner in *friendship*.[14]

The 821–822 treaty was signed during the reign of the Tibetan emperor Khri gTsug-lde-brtsan (815–841) and states that the relationship between "uncle" China and "nephew" Tibet had been established centuries ago when the brother or son of Emperor Srong-btsan-sgam-po took the Chinese princess Wencheng Gongzhu (who departed for Tibet in 641) as an imperial consort, and later Khri lDe-gtsug-brtsan (704–ca. 754) betrothed the Chinese princess Jincheng Gongzhu to seal imperial interests.

Peaceful relations prevailed between Tang and Tibet for the most part, interrupted by an incident in 830 and another in 831, when the Tibetan vice-commissioner of Weizhou submitted to the Chinese. He was sent along with his people to Tibet and was executed by the Tibetan court. During this time, Tibet dispatched at least fifteen diplomatic missions to Tang and Tang sent ten to Tibet.[15]

According to Tibetan accounts, in 842 the last Tibetan emperor, Khri-'U'i-dum-brtan, better known as Glang-dar-ma (841–842), was assassinated by lHa-lung dpal-gyi-rdo-rje, a Buddhist monk. This caused royal succession to fall in dispute and Tibetan central authority to disintegrate. Many fortified Tibetan cities in the area of Hexi fell to the Tang in 849. In 851, Dunhuang and Khotan were free from their Tibetan masters. The last imperial Tibetan fortress in Central Asia fell in 866.[16]

Territorial ambitions and the lucrative opportunities of transcontinental trade brought Tibet into the international limelight and in direct contact with the Arabs, the Uighurs, the 'A-zha, and the Chinese. Tibet's adoption of Buddhism as an imperial religion coincided with its military expansion in Central Asia—where the Tibetans had first encountered the foreign religion of the Buddha and adopted it as their own from the eighth century onward.[17]

Indo-Sino-Tibetan Trends

Central Asia holds a place of unparalleled importance for the growth and spread of Buddhist communities and cultures under various political regimes, at different times, and among people of diverse ethnicities: Chinese, Tibetans, Khotanese, Tokharians, Sogdians, Uighurs, and Turks. In the words of one author, for medieval India and Tibet there is "no area comparable to Central Asia for its combination of intellectual, ritual, mythic, and social impact."[18] The Tibetan presence in the Tarim basin corresponds to a later phase in the development of Central Asian Buddhism that fostered the movement of Chinese and Central Asian Buddhist missionaries and traders arriving at the newly formed religious center at bSam-yas and the vibrant markets of Lhasa. In this historical milieu we encounter the finest expression of Chinese and Tibetan forms of Pure Land worship across the oasis states of the Taklamakan desert. Although Central Eurasian trade, Buddhist missionaries, and patronage are some obvious factors that contributed to the propagation of Pure Land Buddhism, its success lies in the nature of its doctrines. Pure Land teachings dispense a universal remedy against the most fundamental human anxiety about death and the beyond, offering a blissful ontological alternative and a cosmological and ritual infrastructure to assist the departed and those who must go on living. The soteriological features of buddha fields addressed the preoccupations of the people of Tibet and Chinese Turkestan concerning death, the afterlife, and the longevity of the family.[19] Furthermore, Pure Land orientations in China and among the Chinese people of Central Asia resonated with preexisting beliefs in Daoist terrestrial paradises believed to be located in the far west in the Kunlun Mountains, the abode of the Divine Queen Mother of the West (Ch. Xiwangmu), who ruled over the immortals.[20]

Kucha

The period from the third to the eighth centuries witnessed the rise and fall of powerful kingdoms along the Tarim basin and across two major routes frequented by caravans and traders. To the north of the Taklamakan desert, the Northern Route curved eastward through the cities of Tumshuq, Aksu, Kucha, Turfan, and Hami; to the south, the Southern Route linked Yarkand, Khotan, Loulan, Niya, Endere, Miran, and Dunhuang. The growth in overland commerce facilitated continual exchanges between religious groups and merchant cultures. Sogdian Buddhist texts discovered in Dunhuang and Turfan featured Mahayana sutras and commentaries, Jātakas and Avadānas, and tantric scriptures and *dhāraṇī.* It has been suggested that these texts resemble those circulating in Kuṣāṇa (Ch. Ta Yuezhi) and in Parthia, implying cross-cultural exchanges between Sogdians, Bactrians, Parthians, and Kuṣāṇas at that time.[21]

Gangetic India was physically connected with the Silk Road through a branch of the Southern Route that linked Kashgar with Balkh and from there over the Hindu Kush into Gandhara and on to the Indus. Another branch left Yarkand, traveling south and across the Karakorum to Leh, the capital of Ladakh, and from there to the plains of India. The oasis state of Kucha (Ch. Juizi) was situated on the Northern Route. It was the home of Tokharian speakers of a western Indo-European language whose cultural influence extended through Karashahr (Agni in ancient and medieval times), Turfan, and further east.

By the third century, the town of Kucha was fortified with a set of triple walls enclosing many ornate Buddhist temples and stupas. According to Xuanzang's report, the royal palaces in Kucha were splendidly decorated with gold and jade, "shining like the dwellings of the gods." At that time, the city was an important center of learning for *śrāvakayāna* Buddhism, especially of the Sarvāstivāda school. All Kuchean manuscripts from the fifth to the ninth centuries belong to this school, with no textual traces of Mahayana. The first Buddhist manuscripts attest to the use of Sanskrit in the second century.[22] A good number of fragments of Buddhist Sanskrit texts, translated into one or both Tokharian languages, have been recovered from Kucha, Karashahr, and Turfan.[23]

Kumārajīva (344–413) and other native missionaries of Kucha are usually associated with the spread of Mahayana Buddhism in China and Central Asia.[24] In seventh-century Kyzyl, we find evidence for the presence of Mahayana Buddhism. There are wall paintings of Maitreya enthroned in Tuṣita Heaven and depictions of the "Miracle of Śrāvastī."[25] Ideas and people traveled between oasis states, as evidenced in shared Central Asian Buddhist motifs. For example, artifacts from Kyzyl and Turfan share the same theme of a two-headed buddha, which probably refers to the legend of the Buddha performing a miracle for the benefit of two paupers.[26]

Refined representations of Pure Land devotion are identified during the Chinese occupation of Kumtura. Religious scenes especially of Buddha Amitābha were clearly popular subjects in certain fragments of wall paintings. A fine example is that of Queen Vaidehī, who chose to be born in Sukhāvatī, according to the *Meditation on Amitāyus Sutra.* She is depicted meditating on the sun. A good number of depictions from Kumtura resemble Pure Land images in the Dunhuang oasis.[27]

Turfan

Further east, to the north of the Lop Desert, the oasis city of Turfan lays in a depression 505 feet below sea level. With summer temperatures soaring to upward of 117 degrees (F), the Chinese called it Huozhou, the "Prefecture of Fire."[28] Turfan, like other oasis states, depended for its survival on irrigation systems fed by snowmelt from the Tian Shan Mountains. Faxian explains that outside the comfort of an oasis the traveler was greeted by vast desert with

> many evil demons and hot winds . . . no flying birds above, no roaming beasts below, but everywhere, gazing as far as the eye can reach in search of the onward route, it would be impossible to know the way, but for the dead men's decaying bones which show the direction.[29]

Due to its strategic position, Turfan (Qocho or Kocho; Gaochang) suffered a long history of colonization by the Chinese from as early as 60 BCE until the seventh century CE.[30] The King of Kocho (Gaochang) was not ethnically Chinese, and when the Chinese pilgrim Xuanzang met him in the seventh century, he may have been surprised to discover that the government of the kingdom followed Chinese administrative structures and used Chinese language for all official purposes. The king had maintained his political independence by allying with the western Turks but his sovereignty was cut short in 640 CE, when Tang troops annexed the kingdom.[31]

During their meeting Xuanzang instructed the king on the *Sutra of the Benevolent Kings* (Ch. *Ren wang jing*), which was said to protect nations from calamities. In return, the king of Gaochang showered Xuanzang with many gifts to support his travels to India and requested that he serve as an international envoy for the delivery of merchandise to the kings he was to encounter along his route.[32]

Most of the texts discovered in the Astana necropolis, north of Gaochang, were written in Chinese, confirming Xuanzang's reports.[33] Some of the tomb artifacts are simple inventories and contracts that list grave goods (including cash) for the deceased to use in the afterworld. Among the Astana fragments, there are several Buddhist texts and a sutra extant only in Chinese, the *Sutra of Seven Daughters*.[34] It deals with the subject of death and the afterlife and narrates the story of seven female protagonists who are exposed to many gruesome aspects of death in a graveyard. In the narrative, the sisters eventually meet Śākyamuni Buddha, who delivers a sermon on the impermanence of life and the karmic consequences of one's actions for the afterlife: "Those who carry out good deeds and avoid the profane will ascend to heaven after death, while those who do evil will enter the mud of the fields."[35]

For nearly a century, between the mid-sixth and mid-seventh centuries, Turfan reflects vibrant Chinese traditions of Pure Land Buddhism. The *Sutra of Meditation on Maitreya Bodhisattva's Rebirth on High in the Tuṣita Heaven*, composed in Turfan and translated into Chinese in 455 CE, shows that rebirth in the presence of Maitreya may be just as desirable as in Sukhāvatī.[36] The mural paintings in cave-temple 20 illustrate scenes from the popular *Meditation on Amitāyus Sutra* (Ch. *Guan wu liang shou jing*) that may have been a local product of Turfan.[37] An eighth-century Buddhist temple shows naked children playing on the balustrades of terraces in Amitābha's Pure Land and others born from lotuses.[38] A previously unknown translation of the long *Sukhāvatīvyūha-sūtra*, not included in the Chinese Buddhist Tripiṭaka, is identified among the fragments of Chinese texts discovered in Turfan.[39]

Miran

Miran (Ch. Yuni) was located on the eastern edge of the Kroraina kingdom (Ch. Shanshan), 250 miles south of Turfan and midway between Loulan, to the south of the Lop desert, and Niya on the Southern Route to Khotan. During Kroraina rule, Miran was an active center of Buddhism with several monasteries and ornate stupas decorated with painted friezes and sculptures.

The Chinese chroniclers Faxian and Songyun, who visited the region, report on the predominance of Indian culture, attested to by Miran artifacts showing unmistakable influence from Gāndhāra, reinforced by the use of Kharoṣṭhī script in a local variant known as Kroraina Prākrit used in administrative documents here and in neighboring Niya.[40] Among the most striking artifacts to be discovered are twenty-four winged angels with unmistakable Western features decorating a wall painting of a Buddhist temple. They are refined expressions of Gāndhārī style with Indo-Iranian, Hellenistic, and Bactrian elements mixed with Nestorian Christian motifs. Sir Aurel Stein must have been startled to stumble upon them among illustrations of the Buddha's life. They are fine examples of heterogeneous cultures and religions that coalesced at the crossroads of trade and colonization, and of the lasting influence that Northwest India and Bactria exerted on the development of Buddhism in Eastern Central Asia.[41]

Because of its close proximity to the Hexi Corridor and to the trading routes with China and Tibet, the Tibetans made Miran, "Great Nob" (Tib. Nob chen-po), into a major administrative center of the region.[42] For over fifty years, from the late eighth to the mid-ninth centuries, the Tibetan empire controlled the Southern Route and most of the Hexi corridor in China's Gansu province. Tibetan imperial policy brought about the revival of Miran's old irrigation system and the transformation of the city into a military, administrative, and commercial center of the Lop Nor area. Paper was already in use in the Tibetan empire, and texts found in the Tibetan fort (*rdzong*) include official documents, contracts, and military communications between Tibetan units of watchmen.[43]

The majority of Tibetan sources that have been discovered are administrative records, with the exception of a few fragmentary texts on divination and scriptures of Pure Land orientation, including a *dhāraṇī* dedicated to Buddha Amitābha (Sang-rgyas snang-ba-mtha-yas), two fragments of the *Ārya-Aparimitāyur-nāma-sūtra,* and an altogether different version of the same sutra in pieces from the same roll.[44] Apart from this limited variety of Buddhist texts there is no evidence of a revival of Buddhism in Miran during the Tibetan occupation. It would appear that Miran functioned primarily as a military and trading post on the Southern Route, and the discovery of Pure Land scriptures may suggest their use in relation to postmortem rites conducted by Tibetan colonists for their deceased brethren soldiers.

Khotan

The kingdom of Khotan (Ch. Yudian) was strategically located at the junction of the southern and oldest branch of the Silk Road joining China, India, and the West. Khotan was a prosperous land whose vibrant markets teemed with local manufacturers and artisans of silk, carpets, felt, paper, and jade, attracting many merchants and fortune-seekers from Central Asia and beyond. There were gold and copper mines in the mountains to the south of Khotan, and the area remained prosperous and renowned for a long time as a center for exporting high-quality jade flowing down from the Khunlun Mountains in the Yurung-kash ("White Jade") and Kara-kash ("Black Jade") rivers. Early Chinese histories report that the king of Khotan was required to draw the first jade from the river before his people could begin to harvest for the season.[45] We have a fair description of seventh-century Khotan through the eyes of the Chinese pilgrim Xuanzang, who visited on his way to India in search of Buddhist teachings.

> The country is about 4,000 *li* (about 2,000 kilometers [1,243 miles], according to Sven Hedin) in circuit, the greater part is nothing but sand and gravel, the arable portion of the land is very limited. It is suitable for the cultivation of cereals and produces an abundance of fruits. It manufactures carpets, felts of fine quality, and fine-woven light silks. Moreover, it produces white and dark

> jade. The climate is soft and agreeable, but there are windstorms which bring with them clouds of dust. The manners and customs show a sense of propriety and justice. The inhabitants are mild by nature and respectful, they love to study literature, and distinguish themselves by their skill and industry. The people are easy going, giving to enjoyments, and live contented with their lot. Music is much practiced in the country, and men love the song and the dance. Few of them wear garments of wool and fur, most dress in light silks and white clothes. Their appearance is full of urbanity and their customs are well regulated.[46]

Khotan was also a major exporter of Buddhism. Chinese and Tibetan histories preserve legends that link Khotan's foundation with Emperor Aśoka and the Mauryan empire. However, there are no archaeological records to substantiate early Mauryan incursions in the Tarim basin.[47] Bilingual Sino-Kharoṣṭhī coins discovered in the ancient capital of Yotkan date the first Indian settlements to the first century CE

According to the *Arhat's Prophecy of Khotan* (*Li yul gyi dgra bcom pas lung bstan pa*), the King of Khotan (to the west of Huthen) followed Chinese systems of administration, while his councilor Yasha ruled the country from the eastern river, following Indian clerical laws and conventions.[48] The *Annals of Khotan* (*Li yul gyi lo rgyus*) reports:

> Li (Khotan) being a land where India and China meet, the common language agrees with neither India nor China. The letters agree successively with India. The manners of the laity agree for the most part with China: the clerical manners and the clerical language agree for the most part with India.[49]

By the late fourth century Khotan was a thriving center of Mahayana Buddhism supporting fourteen monasteries—one of which, the famous Gomatī, is said to have housed some 3,000 monks.[50] It was common for the Khotanese royalty and aristocracy to be ordained as Buddhist monks or nuns, winning for their families the title and honor of belonging to a "bodhisattva-lineage."[51] Much of our information on Khotan derives from the accounts of two eminent Chinese pilgrims, Faxian and Xuanzang, who visited the kingdom in the fourth and the seventh centuries respectively. From their accounts, we learn that Khotan observed Buddhist holidays and ceremonies and was a renowned hub of Mahayana scholarship, attracting students from China, India, and Central Asia.[52] There were apparently stupas built in front of every other house, many of which contained the bones of bodies cremated and deposited in the reliquaries, with the exception of the king's body, which was buried in a coffin in the desert.[53] The kings of Khotan claimed descent from Vaiśravaṇa, the Guardian King of the North in Buddhist cosmology, and an important temple was built in his name.[54]

Buddhist monasteries in Central Asia served as centers of learning in the widest sense, since the preservation of the doctrine of the Buddha entailed the reproduction and dissemination of Buddhist scriptures. Khotan had its own paper industry and was an international market for the reproduction and sale of Sanskrit Buddhist manuscripts. In the early sixth century, the Chinese pilgrim Songyun reports that he brought to China 170 volumes of Mahayana texts from Khotan.[55] Zhu Shixing mentions that he came to Khotan to study Buddhism and managed, in just a few years, to collect 9,000 bundles of Sanskrit scriptures, which he sent to China through his disciple Furuodan.[56] While many Buddhist texts were copied locally in Khotan, according to Xuanzang a good number were imported from Kashmir—an operation that entailed acquisition of merit for those who copied them and profit for those who sold them.[57]

Cultural and religious exchanges between China and Khotan took place in both directions. Zhu Shixing journeyed to Khotan in 260 CE to acquire the *Prajñāpāramitā in 25,000 Verses,* and the Khotanese scholar Mokṣala translated this text into Chinese in 291 CE.[58] By the early eighth century, there was a substantial Chinese community in Khotan engaged in the translation of Buddhist texts into Chinese.[59] On the other side, a good number of Khotanese scholars visited China and served as translators of Sanskrit texts into Chinese; the names Devaprajñā, Gītamitra, Śikṣānda, Mokṣala, and Śīladharma are among those mentioned in the Chinese Tripiṭaka.[60] By the tenth century Dunhuang and Khotan enjoyed strong diplomatic ties through the marriage of Khotan's King Viśa' Saṃbhava to a Chinese princess from the prominent Cao family of Dunhuang. During this time, the Khotanese began to visit famous Chinese Buddhist teachers, and documents discovered in Dunhuang suggest a Khotanese settlement.[61]

Khotanese monks could read and write sutras in Sanskrit or Prakrit and used a southern Turkestani Brāhmī script for composing indigenous Buddhist literature.[62] Although there is no evidence for a Khotanese Buddhist canon, monastic centers engaged in the reproduction and classification of Indian Buddhist texts in large collections that would later acquire canonical status, such as the *Mahāratnakūṭa* and the *Mahāvataṃsaka.*[63] In contrast to Chinese and Tibetan translations of Sanskrit Buddhist texts, Khotanese translations favored variation instead of consistency and it was common for a Khotanese translator to translate the same passage differently within a single text.[64] Translations of Sanskrit sutras into Khotanese-Saka featured the *Vimalakīrtinirdeśa,* the long *Sukhāvatīvyūha,* the *Bhaiṣajyaguru,* the *Saddharmapuṇḍarīka,* and the *Aparimitāyus.*[65] Other translations included the *Anantamukha-nirhāra-dhāraṇī* and a Khotanese poem in praise of Amitāyus (Armyāya in late Khotanese), of which thirty-six out of an original sixty verses survive.[66] The epilogue to a Khotanese version of the *Pradakṣinā-sūtra,* a text on the benefits of stupa worship, details the aspiration, presumably of the person who had the sutra copied, to behold buddhas everywhere and that his merit be dedicated to take birth in Sukhāvatī, where Buddha Amitāyus will utter a prophecy of his future buddhahood.[67]

The Tibetans fostered close relations with the kingdom of Khotan, which they called the "Land of Li" (Li-yul) since the time of the Tibetan emperor Srong-btsan-sgam-po. They occupied Khotan twice, in 670 and in 791, because of its strategic location on the Southern Route.[68] Tibetan control of the southern trading networks lasted for nearly sixty years. The Tibetan empire started disintegrating in 842, but Khotan remained under its rule until 851.

Tibetan records from the area show that Khotan's governmental infrastructure, from the king down to local officials, was left intact during Tibet's colonial rule. According to Chinese-Khotanese bilingual texts composed under Chinese rule and Khotanese texts composed in the Tibetan period, the people of Khotan served as local officials during Chinese and Tibetan administration (up to and after 790, respectively).[69] It appears that during Tibetan rule the kingdoms of the Tarim basin retained their political integrity in exchange for tribute, supplies of troops, and material necessities requested by the Tibetan authorities. Khotanese men from the lower social strata were recruited and incorporated into Tibetan units of watchmen as auxiliaries and cooks. Order and control was sternly maintained; there were cases of Khotanese watchmen being executed for attempting to desert their posts, while others were given a second chance, as in the case of an assistant cook who succeeded in commuting his death sentence by paying 4,500 copper coins to the senior Tibetan members of his station.[70]

Tibetan documents discovered in Mazār-tāgh confirm that Tibetan military posts were in continuous communication with the city of Khotan and there were ongoing exchanges with Tibetan soldiers in other oasis towns of the Tarim basin and in Tibet proper.[71] The Tibetans maintained an orderly system of watchtowers and installed military garrisons along the trade routes from Khotan to Dunhuang manned with soldiers arriving from Central Tibet.[72] In the same texts, Khotan is described as a land of abundance in everything "because of the merits of the [Khotanese] king, as well as because of the Tibetan Masters, who are guarding this land of Khotan."[73]

Secular and Buddhist texts were translated from Tibetan into Khotanese and some Khotanese texts into Tibetan, while Khotanese architects were invited to Lhasa to build Buddhist monasteries.[74] Tibetan-Khotanese relations however, were not always harmonious. According to the *Inquiry of Vimalaprabhā,* a Khotanese text extant in Tibetan translation, the "red-faced" Tibetans may have burned and looted Khotanese Buddhist monasteries and monuments.[75]

> At what time the Red-Faces (Tibetans) and the Chinese shall fight, at that time may we cause the Li country (Khotan) in no way to perish . . . and beings who shall have fled there from other countries may we cause there to obtain a settlement and to pay ransom for the Li country, in order that with their assistance the great stupas and retreats of the Saṃghas burned by the Red-Faces may be restored; may we cause them with the Chinese reciprocally to give and receive brides.[76]

Dunhuang

> On Dunhuang myriad acres of level fields flanked by sands on four sides,
> The walled fortress of the Han became the domain of Tibet.
> Songs and ballads now return to the Tang tunes again,
> On the road dances the spring breeze with willow catkins.
> Ladies donning the coiffure with Tianbao-style topknot,
> By the streams, like before, plant mulberry and hemp.
> Gallant troops constantly beat the battle drums,
> Fighting generals toil in vain as the Xianyun tribes brag on.[77]

Dunhuang is a small town in the westernmost part of present-day Gansu province. One of the most important aspects of ancient Dunhuang was its central location on the Silk Road. Situated at the juncture of the Northern and Southern Routes as they divide around the Taklamakan Desert, it served as a major trading post for caravans, merchants, missionaries, and pilgrims on their way to the Chinese western border. In the words of one scholar,

> [I]t was here that the great civilization of China shared with the Central Asian peoples' scriptures and sculptures, horses and garrisons, jade stones and jade beauties. It was both her wound and her wonder.[78]

Dunhuang was founded in 111 BCE, during the reign of Emperor Wu, as a military post, and after the fall of the Han (206 BCE–220 CE), it remained under the control of the Sui and Tang dynasties.[79] When An Lushan attacked the Chinese capital, the Chinese troops in the western garrisons were hastily recalled to quell the rebellion, and the Tibetans took advantage of the unguarded city. By 781 they had conquered Sha-cu ("City of the Sands"), the preferred name for Dunhuang during the Tang period.[80] Tibetan texts continued to be composed there up until the tenth century, but with the gradual conversion of Central Asia to Islam from the ninth century onward, Dunhuang was by then a major international Buddhist center in decline.

Dunhuang's monastic caves are a treasury of 800 years of Buddhist painting, literature, and sculpture, preserving fine examples of Chinese Buddhist paintings and Chinese and Tibetan manuscripts. In its heyday, there were at least seventeen Buddhist monasteries and nunneries, with the largest housing up to forty monks and sixty nuns and about half these numbers of resident novices.[81] The majority of Chinese texts discovered there are related to the major denominations of Chinese Buddhism that flourished during the Tang dynasty.[82] Canonical texts of the Pure Land tradition are also represented—the long and short *Sukhāvatīvyūha* sutras and the apocryphal *Meditation on Amitāyus,* along with several Pure Land liturgical texts.[83] The One Thousand Buddhas cave complex provides the most fertile source for Pure Land imagery.[84] As in Turfan, Pure Land scenes in Dunhuang date from the first half of the seventh century.[85]

The earliest examples of Pure Land themes depicting Amitābha and his celestial paradise are found in Cave 220 and reflect the continuation of the Chinese High Tang tradition.[86] The paintings in this cave-temple were sponsored by the Zhai in 642 and contain religious and political narratives tied to the history of the family.[87] Illustrations of Sukhāvatī in the south wall appear to have been inspired from the apocryphal *Meditation on Amitāyus Sutra,* while portrayals of the Tang emperor and his court officials on the east wall reflect the loyalty of the Zhai family to the Tang court. Future studies on other Dunhuang cave-temples may reveal similar narratives.[88]

In Dunhuang we find several copies of Kumārajīva's and Xuanzang's translations of the *Sukhāvatīvyūha-sūtra,* both in Chinese and in Tibetan script.[89] There are also numerous scrolls of the *Aparimitāyus-sūtra,* a booklet entitled *Hymns for Repeating the Buddha's Name at the Five Assemblies* (*Wu hui nian fo zan*) dated to 955 CE, the *Hymn Texts of the Western Pure Land* (*Si fang jing tu zan wen*), and related meditation texts and *dhāraṇī.*[90] In the colophons of many sutras are references to the widespread practice of reproducing Buddhist texts in order to accumulate merit and the dedication of such merit toward birth in Amitābha's buddha field.

A prayer from 522 CE contains a dedication for someone recently departed that "he may mount to the realm of the absolute and his body travel to the Pure Land . . . and that likewise all sentient beings may share in this merit and attain perfect intelligence."[91] The following inscription dated to

710 CE tells of a Madame Deng, who copied the *Sukhāvatīvyūha-sūtra* for the benefit of the Tang emperor and empress and for all living beings.

> On the 11th day of the 12th month, the female devotee Madame Têng reverently caused a copy of the Amita Sutra to be made, firstly for the benefit of our Divine Emperor and Empress that their sovran (sic) influence may never be exhausted; and secondly, on behalf of the living beings of our universe, that they may one and all reach the Western regions (i.e., Amitābha's paradise) and together share in the highest degree of felicity.[92]

In the colophon of a fairly well-preserved *dhāraṇī,* apparently translated from a Sanskrit text on May 19, 720, we are assured that its recitation will lead one to behold a vision of Buddha Amitābha and take birth in his Pure Land. Like most *dhāraṇī,* its efficacy is proportional to the number of recitations. It also prescribes typical Buddhist rituals, such as scattering flowers, offering incense, and praying before an image of the Buddha.

> The preceding dhāraṇī has already been translated and issued for circulation. If, after cleansing the mouth in the morning with a willow twig, scattering flowers and incense before the image of the Buddha, kneeling and joining the palms of the hands, it be daily recited seven, fourteen, or twenty-one times, the four grave sins, the five wicked acts, and other trespasses may be wiped out, the existing body will be afflicted by no untimely calamities, one's final destiny will be in the realm of immeasurable longevity, and reincarnation in a female form will be escaped forever. Now that the Sanskrit text has been reexamined, and the Indian Vinaya monk Buddhasangha and others have been consulted, we know that the majestic power of this *dhāraṇī* is beyond all conception: if recited one hundred times in the evening and again at noon, it destroys the four grave sins and the five wicked acts, and will pluck out the very roots of sin, ensuring rebirth in the regions of the West. If in sincerity of spirit one is able to complete 200,000 recitations, then perfect intelligence is born, and there will be no backsliding; if 300,000, then one will see Amitābha Buddha face to face, and with absolute certainty be reborn in the Pure Land of Tranquility and Bliss.[93]

The tradition of meritorious dedications continued in Dunhuang; a color painting on silk, dated 910 CE, depicts the celestial bodhisattva Avalokiteśvara along with an inscription requesting that the Chinese empire be peaceful, that Buddhism remain in China, and that the donor's elder sister, teacher, and deceased parents take birth in the Pure Land.[94]

A good number of prayers to Amitābha and his buddha field and Tibetan esoteric scriptures of the Indo-Tibetan variety may have been composed during the Tibetan occupation of Dunhuang (ca. 781–851).[95] The encounter between Chinese and Tibetan Buddhists in Dunhuang (and other parts of Central Asia) reflects the meeting of two important historical phases in the evolution of Buddhism outside India—the former were acquainted with older Indian lineages of Buddhism that reached China in the early centuries of the first millennium, and the latter with newly acquired doctrines and practices imported from eighth-century India. Indisputably, there must have been a reciprocal fascination for each other's heritage and interpretations of Indian Buddhism that sparked prolific collaborations in Dunhuang and also in Tibet, as testified by Sino-Tibetan (or partly bilingual) manuscripts of Buddhist scriptures (sutra, *śāstra, vinaya*), library inventories, names of temples and copyists, lists of doctrinal terminology, *dhāraṇī,* and mantras.[96]

Chinese Buddhist temples kept Chinese and Tibetan manuscripts in their libraries and lodged Tibetan Buddhist monks, nuns, and pilgrims visiting Dunhuang in the summer or during festivals. Other examples of Sino-Tibetan interactions include a Chinese register of the main temples in Dunhuang transcribed in Tibetan, a collection of prayers for the Tibetan military governor in Guangzhou, and an untitled manuscript that lists several Tibetans among the dignitaries present on the occasion of the construction of a Chinese Buddhist temple. Donations granted for the reproduction of major Buddhist scriptures were often jointly made by the Sino-Tibetan sangha from the Chinese families Yin, Li, Pei, Shi, Song, Zhang, Wang, Cao, and so forth, and the Tibetan families from the sNying-choms, sTong-sar, and rGod-sar divisions.[97] The reproduction of Tibetan and Chinese Buddhist manuscripts was carried out by professional bilingual scribes. For their services they were allotted measured sheets of paper.[98] Their compensation was in kind, in rations (*tshal-ma*), while "the work was carried out under the superintendence of the monasteries, which upon completion deliver the volumes and send in their accounts."[99]

Central Eurasian Markets of Knowledge

The coalescing and multifaceted phenomenon we may call Central Asian Buddhism can be assessed in terms of the unique contributions of its individual players and their interactions with each other (i.e., Gāndhārī, Chinese, Tibetan) and in terms of its representative traditions (i.e., Hinayana, Mahayana, Vajrayana). Given the extent and intensity of interreligious and intrareligious contacts, Buddhism in Central Asian contexts may be best reconstructed as a multidirectional complex that spans nearly a millennium and features Eurasian exchanges among diverse polities, economies, and civilizations.

The distribution of Buddhist scriptures in the Tarim basin signals a concentration of *śrāvakayāna* traditions in Turfan, Kucha, and Karashahr. On the other hand, Mahayana and Vajrayana literature dominates the oases of Khotan, Dunhuang, and Kashgar, where the famous translator Kumārajīva converted to Buddhism.[100] It could be misleading however, to determine the kinds of Buddhism circulating from texts alone, since both Mahayana and Hinayana scriptures were stored, studied, and copied in the same monasteries. The importation, reproduction, and exportation of Buddhist manuscripts in Central Eurasia was invariably linked to literate members of the sangha, patrons, pilgrims, and traders operating across regional and transregional networks of distribution. The acquisition and translation of Buddhist texts in a variety of languages (i.e., Sanskrit, Chinese, Khotanese, and Tibetan), suggests mechanisms for soliciting funds through lay and royal donations, and by profitable exchanges in silk and other precious and semiprecious merchandise. Silk was the most important item traded along the Central Eurasian caravan routes, and its value greatly exceeded that of other commodities, providing a handsome income to local and foreign rulers, monasteries, merchants, artisans, and residents of the oasis city-states.[101]

Recent studies of the silk trade illustrate that Central Eurasian commerce was a complex phenomenon of transactions involving multiple parties and religious cultures and institutions.[102] Buddhist monasticism and trade supported each other in intricate ways, since the profit gained through business could be converted into symbolic capital (religious merit) by sponsoring Buddhist establishments and monks and supporting merit-earning activities, such as commissioning temples, murals, and so on. As we have seen, the demand for religious merit was readily met through the reproduction of Buddhist sutras.[103] Chinese and Indian Buddhist monks who resided in Tang China received bolts of silk and silk robes from the emperors for their religious services, while the purchase of Buddhist relics from India could fetch prices of as much as 4,000 bolts of silk.[104]

In Kucha, seventh-century texts written in Tokharian-B record large quantities of coins deposited in Buddhist monasteries, which served as vital centers of economic activity.[105] The Chinese are credited with the introduction of coins in eastern Central Asia, but cash was not the dominant form of currency. Silk and grain were frequently exchanged by monks, farmers, and merchants. A Dunhuang document lists monasteries receiving as income the crops of certain farms whose owners or occupants are referred to in Tibetan as *yon-bdag* (donors or patrons).[106] The arable fields belonging to Dunhuang monasteries were exempt from taxation, and monks cultivated and traded in wheat and millet for sale in the community.[107] But they were not the only ones; Buddhist monks in Loulan and Niya also engaged in trade, unhindered by the restrictions of the Vinaya: "they lived at home with their wives and children, owned property, and donned Buddhist vestments only for occasional ceremonies."[108] The sangha of Loulan followed various traditions of Buddhism, and while some monks may have been drawn to more renunciant lifestyles, others seem to have been adept at all sorts of worldly affairs, hiring out means of transportation, offering loans and banking services, and participating in the international silk trade. Many Buddhist communities thrived along the Silk Road. Some monastics became prosperous by retaining their family property (including slaves), while others unabashedly indulged in moneylending and luxuries, purchased girls, and forged marital alliances with other Buddhist families.[109]

From their very inception, Buddhist movements were self-conscious of their soteriological mission to propagate the teachings of liberation to others—and, with the Buddha's blessing, to do so "in one's own tongue."[110] This is as true today as it was then, and Indian Buddhist texts were readily translated into many foreign languages. Buddhist monasteries functioned as centers of knowledge and in Dunhuang they operated schools in which students studied Buddhist literature and the Confucian classics.[111] Khotan became renowned for its Buddhist publishing houses and scholarship, and attracted visitors, students, and scholars from India, Tibet, Central Asia, and China.

The spread and growth of Buddhist traditions in Central Eurasia was a multi-layered and dynamic process that changed radically over the centuries. In the early centuries of the first millennium, China's neophyte status as an eager recipient of Buddhist wisdom shifted to a far more active and dominant role beginning in the early sixth century. Chinese translations of Buddhist texts flooded Central Asia and stimulated the translation of Buddhist literature in Central Asian vernaculars, a process that probably began in Kucha and Agni and spread to other areas, including Khotan, in the seventh and eighth centuries.[112] The unique collection of texts, epitaphs, and artifacts from the Turfan necropolis demonstrate that Buddhism did not come to Central Asia at a constant pace or from only one direction. It came from both east and west, China and India.[113]

Chinese literature and art from Turfan and Dunhuang provide evidence for the Chinese impact on the development of Pure Land faith in the Tarim basin during the seventh century. As we will see in this chapter, the circulation of Tibetan translations and indigenous compositions of Pure Land

Buddhism in Central Tibet and across the Tarim basin suggests that Tibetans were not passive importers of Buddhist literature from India, China, and Central Asia. By the eighth century Tibet had emerged as a major Buddhist empire that supported an enormous production of Tibetan translations of Buddhist texts for reproduction and distribution not just across the Tibetan plateau but well beyond its geographical borders, in the Himalayan regions of Nepal and India and in the heart of eastern Central Asia.

The Buddhist Emperors of Tibet

For the most part, Tibetans recount their history in terms of Buddhism (*nang-pa'i chos;* lit., "the religion of the insiders") and its introduction to Tibet in two major phases. They identify the early spread of the Buddhist doctrine (*bstan-pa snga-dar*) during the reign of the Tibetan emperors (*btsan-po*), followed by a later revival (*bstan-pa phyi-dar*) that coincides with the rise of Tibetan monasticism in medieval Tibet of the early eleventh century. The second revival of Buddhism transpired after the fragmentation of the Tibetan empire (*sil-bu'i dus*) into clan-based regional powers. An intermediate period of propagation (*bstan-pa bar-dar*), which arguably occurred after the first transmission, reflects an ongoing movement of indigenizing Indian, Chinese, and Central Asian traditions of Buddhism.[114]

The early spread of the doctrine is traditionally attributed to the first Tibetan emperor, Srong-btsan-sgam-po (early seventh century–ca. 649 CE). In Tibetan narratives Srong-btsan-sgam-po is glorified as the first Buddhist sovereign (*chos-rgyal;* Skt. *dharmarāja*) of Tibet. In fact he was a formidable warrior who conquered Zhangzhung territories, fought against the 'A-zha, and consolidated Tibet into an important Central Asian empire that over the next 200 years would come to claim the commercial networks of the ancient Silk Road and Himalayan borderland trade, parts of Western China, and much of Inner and Central Asia.[115]

The Tang *Annals* record that Emperor Srong-btsan-sgam-po sent envoys and tribute to the Chinese emperor, petitioning for a matrimonial alliance. In 641 he received at his court Princess Wenzheng along with an entourage of Chinese scholars, scribes, and bureaucrats. Seven years later, he invited skilled artisans from China to manufacture paper and ink for use in the administration of his state. His request was granted by the Chinese emperor, serving as proof that writing was practiced during the reign of the first Buddhist emperor of Tibet.[116]

> Previously in Tibet, there was no writing, but it was during the time of this Btsan-po—from the reign of Btsan-po Khri Srong-brtsan—that the entire good

> basis of Tibet's customs was created: Tibet's great legal and governmental system, the [system of] ministerial rank, the division of ranks into both great and small, the rewards for the good, the punishments for the wicked and deceitful, the equal division of fields and pasturelands into *thul-ka, dor-ka* and *slungs,* and the standardization of the weights and measures *bre, p[h]ul* and *srang,* etc. All men felt a great gratitude for his kindness and in return they called him "Srong-brtsan the Profound."[117]

The instigation of a national system of laws, measurements, and writing must have taken place between 630 and 648, the latter being the terminus ad quem, since paper and ink manufacturers were sent by the Chinese emperor in that year.[118] The official introduction of paper in Tibet eventually replaced the tally (*khram*) previously used in the imperial administrative machine. The first dated attestation of the word paper (*shog*) in Tibetan literature appeared in 744–745, while its use for bureaucratic functions would have presupposed prior knowledge of reading and writing in Tibetan script.[119]

The introduction of paper also paved the way for the translation and reproduction of Buddhist scriptures, and it is possible that Indian and Chinese Buddhist texts circulating at the Tibetan court inspired the instigation of paper-based communication in the Tibetan administration. The promotion of writing and literature may be the most compelling evidence of an early and intimate connection forged between Buddhism and imperial power in Tibet.[120] While the Tang *Annals* make no reference to the origins of the Tibetan script and remain silent about the admission of Buddhism at the Tibetan court, Tibetan post-dynastic histories include ample testimonies concerning Emperor Srong-btsan-sgam-po dispatching his minister Thon-mi Sambhoṭa to India to study languages, from which he devised, with the assistance of Indian scholars, the Tibetan script and related grammatical treatises.[121] Srong-btsan-sgam-po thus emerged in popular narratives as a man of letters, credited with the first Tibetan translations of Indian Buddhist texts.[122]

By the seventh century, Buddhism was well rooted among diverse communities, rulers, and merchant groups in India, Nepal, China, and Central Asia, and there was no shortage of missionaries and monks eager to propagate the Buddhist doctrines in a welcoming court. The religion of the Buddha had gained the reputation of fostering an ideological system and ceremonial setting that elevated secular rulers to the status of Buddhist deities and granted them the Indian honorific title of *cakravartin* ("wheel-turning king"). This prestigious identification replaced native claims of divine kingship with a new economy of sovereignty, in which the ruler was secretly empowered and ritually placed in the center of a new sacred cosmology, a *maṇḍala.* Like a buddha, situated in the middle of a timeless geography, the converted royalty reinvented itself as a universal monarchy with the clergy's blessings.

There are many reasons that account for the attraction of Buddhism for a newly formed empire in Central Asia. Beside a missionary ideology that suited the aristocracy well, Buddhism brought along highly efficient monastic institutions that fulfilled many functions—not least, serving as centers of both religious learning and secular knowledge of medicine, languages, crafts, and the arts. Buddhist monasteries provided administrative resources, financial skills, and a reserve male population, and had the added advantage of being strategically situated and technically constructed as forts.[123] In this respect, they were ideal places to store commodities for safekeeping (i.e., food, weapons, money, records, etc.), while the rigorous discipline and monastic protocol prescribed by the Vinaya fostered microsocieties of men cohabiting in relative harmony and dedicated to the welfare of the community and the state.

During Srong-btsan-sgam-po's reign, Tibet witnessed the construction of Buddhist temples and a program of literacy that supported what may have been the first state translations of Buddhist texts into Tibetan script. In time, a certain mythos grew around the persona of Srong-btsan-sgam-po, who was perceived as a semidivine ruler equal to Avalokiteśvara, the celestial bodhisattva of compassion. There are undeniable Pure Land themes in the Avalokiteśvara-Amitābha constellation and Tibet's first *cakravartin* that can been traced back to imperial times and to the adaptation of Buddhism in Tibet.[124] To these we may add the title Bao-wang (an epithet of Amitābha) bestowed on Srong-btsan-sgam-po by the Tang emperor Gaozong, whose reign began in 649, and a miniature image of Buddha Amitābha that crowns a life-size portrait statue of Srong-btsan-sgam-po in the Potala Palace in Lhasa, which some scholars date to the ninth century.[125]

Tibetan inscriptions and texts verify that the Tibetan sons of heaven modeled themselves on the *cakravartin* ideal and were identified as celestial bodhisattvas prior to the collapse of the Tibetan empire.[126] There is a post-imperial interpolation of Srong-btsan-sgam-po pleading with his parents to grant him power to rule on the grounds that he had vowed to Buddha Amitābha to discipline Tibet through the teachings of Buddhism.[127] In the *History of Tibet,* the Fifth Dalai Lama (1617–1682) does not shy away from envisaging his own religious-political regime, like that of Srong-btsan-sgampo, as the contemporaneous emanation of Avalokiteśvara and a living embodiment of Tibet's patron-deity. His mission, which he presented in accord with that of his imperial predecessor, was to transform Tibet into Amitābha's Pure Land.[128] He relates how Srong-btsan-sgam-po sent out emanations to build twelve temples dedicated to Amitābha (*mi-'gyur-ba'i gzer*) and a self-arisen image of the deity was carved clearly as it appeared on a rock in Zla-ba Tshal to a craftsman from Nepal.[129]

Srong-btsan-sgam-po's legacy as a patron saint of Buddhism was followed by Emperor Khri Srong-lde-brtsan (756–ca. 800), exalted in traditional narratives as the second *chos-rgyal* of Tibet. And for good reason: in the late eighth century he declared Buddhism the official religion of the Tibetan empire by erecting inscriptions and issuing two royal edicts swearing to preserve the creed of the Buddha and actively support the Tibetan Buddhist sangha.[130] Against a background of contesting religious ideologies, the pillar inscription at bSam-yas attributed to him casts valuable light on the legitimation of this process:

> May the shrines of the Three Jewels established in the temples of Ra-sa and Brag-mar and this practice of the religion of the Buddha never be abandoned or destroyed. The requisite properties that have been provided shall not be diminished or reduced. From now onwards each generation of the *btsan-po* (emperor), fathers and sons, shall make a vow in this way. And in order that there shall be no detraction from that oath and that it shall not be changed, the supra-mundane gods, the gods of this world, and the spirits are all invoked as witnesses. The *btsan-po,* father and son, ruler and ministers all have sworn. A detailed account of this edict exists separately.[131]

Khri Srong-lde-brtsan was a formidable emperor and a devout Buddhist. Traveling with his own retinue of Buddhist monks in the court, he extended generous support to the Jo-khang and Ra-mo-che temples and to the Tibetan monasteries of bSam-yas and Khra-'brug.[132] He took a keen interest in the interpretation and dissemination of Buddhist literature and established the Buddhist Council (*mdun-sa*), an institution responsible for overseeing the official translations of Buddhist texts into Tibetan. Because of these activities, he is invariably referred to as an incarnation of Mañjuśrī, the celestial bodhisattva of wisdom and knowledge.

Post-imperial references to Amitābha's lore occur also during Khri Srong-lde-brtsan's reign, recounting the following mystical signs after the consecration of the temple at bSam-yas:

> In the afternoon, at dusk, from the top of the temple a light appeared, which became bigger and bigger and illuminated all of upper and lower Brag dmar, shining like the moon. The mKhan po said: "This is the light of Amitābha's

> coming. Tomorrow a temple of Amitābha shall be built as an upper storey above the dBu rtse."[133]

Khri Srong-lde-brtsan paved the way for the acceptance of Buddhism in the Tibetan court and for its growth among the laity. The sKar-chung Inscription, attributed to his son and royal successor Khri lDe-srong-brtsan (ca. 800–815), constitutes a renewal of Khri Srong-lde-brtsan's vows to maintain confidence in the Three Jewels. He repeats the exact words used by his father in the bSam-yas Pillar Inscription and concludes with a statement that a detailed version of the edict has been deposited alongside the edict attributed to his father's time.[134]

> Therefore from now onwards, for ever and ever, following the pronouncement in the time of the supernaturally wise divinity, the *btsan-po,* the father, Khri Srong-lde-brtsan that each generation should take a vow not to abandon and not destroy the shrines of the Three Jewels and the practice of the religion of the Buddha, the *btsan-po,* father and sons, rulers and ministers, all together have sworn an oath that they shall act in accordance with the words of the edict and the inscription on the stone pillar.[135]

Khri gTsug-lde-brtsan (815–841), also known in Tibetan as Ral-pa-can, is the last glorified Dharma Ruler (*chos-rgyal*) of the empire. He is traditionally identified with the celestial bodhisattva of powerful means, Vajrapāṇi, because of the religious reforms he vigorously enacted, restoring Buddhist temples and initiating a major literary revision movement to standardize Tibet's Buddhist heritage. As we will see later in this chapter, under his auspices the first systematic attempts at cataloging Tibetan translations of Buddhist texts and purging apocrypha were undertaken. Pure Land sentiments echo during his reign; an old document mentions hundreds of Tibetan and Chinese scrolls of the *Immeasurable Life and Wisdom Sutra* (*Aparimitāyur-jñāna-sūtra*) being offered by the Sino-Tibetan saṅgha of Dunhuang to the "Divine Prince" (*lha-sras*) Khri gTsug-lde-brtsan, possibly on the occasion of his safely passing to the Pure Land of Buddha Amitābha.[136]

The emperors Srong-btsan-sgam-po, Khri Srong-lde-brtsan, and Khri gTsug-lde-brtsan serve as archetypes of a synthesis between sovereignty and Buddhist missionary ideology and hold a conspicuous place in Tibet's religious history. There is no doubt that Buddhist expertise contributed to the administrative reorganization of the Tibetan empire.[137] In less than apocalyptic terms, Tibetan histories unanimously recount that Khri gTsug-lde-brtsan's successor, the infamous Emperor Glang-dar-ma, assassinated him and initiated an anti-Buddhist campaign that brought the subversion of Buddhism and the downfall of the empire. Scholarship has questioned the accuracy and import of this incident, which does not appear to have been the main cause for a reported lessening of state support of the Buddhist clergy. Davidson (2005, 8–116) argues that Eastern traditions of Vinaya continued to flourish despite Glang-dar-ma's alleged devastation, while Dunhuang Tibetan documents, such as the Pel. Tib. (999), demonstrate that Buddhism received royal sponsorship until the reign of Khri 'Od-srung (ca. 846–ca. 893). In light of this contradictory evidence, it may well be that Tibetan religious tradition preserves a communal reenactment of a scapegoat ritual in which the evil Glang-dar-ma is ousted from collective history and receives the blame for the ills that had befallen the Tibetan empire. The story also serves as a figurative interpolation on the part of the Tibetan historiographical tradition, which cherishes the belief that the harmony and prosperity of the state flourishes solely in the hands of a Buddhist ruler.[138]

Soteriological Conflicts at bSam-yas

The institutionalization of Buddhism in Tibet is closely tied to the state that supported the spread of religion within the empire and beyond its borders. This was reinforced in a variety of ways, including the public erection of Buddhist markers (i.e., pillars, temples, monasteries, stupas, etc.) and forging theophoric associations with the emperors; the importation, translation, reproduction, and study of Buddhist scriptures; sponsorship of religious crafts and art; and, more importantly, by inviting and welcoming foreign Buddhist teachers to visit Tibet and attend to the spiritual needs of the royal court. Many itinerant scholars, artists, monks, mystics, and missionaries of Buddhism who visited Tibet during this period came from India, Nepal, China, and Central Asia. Most of them have long been forgotten, but a few are remembered for their distinct contributions to Tibet's early religious history and their tremendous impact on Tibetan culture.

The Indian pundit Śāntarakṣita (mKhan-chen zhi-ba mtsho, 725–788) was a prominent teacher who spent the last fifteen years of his life in Tibet. He served as the abbot of Tibet's first Buddhist monastery at bSam-yas, ordained the first seven Tibetan monks, and introduced a rigorous system of study drawn from the philosophical traditions of Indian learning at the great Buddhist universities of Nālandā and Vikramaśīla. He composed several important works, some of which exercised considerable intellectual influence in Tibet, including the *Compendium of Principles* (*Tattvasaṃgraha*), the *Ornament of the Middle Way* (*Madhyamakālaṃkāra*), and the *Madhyamakālamkāravṛtti,* his own commentary on the latter. He is still fondly remembered by Tibetans as the "Ācārya Bodhisattva," as he and his brilliant Indian pupil Kamalaśīla (ca. 740–795) were the first scholars to transmit the Indian traditions of Madhyamaka and Yogācāra in Tibet.

Kamalaśīla composed several commentaries on his teacher's works and on the philosophy of Madhyamaka, an ontology of the "Middle Way" between the extremes of asserting the absolute existence of phenomena on the one hand (eternalism), and their nonexistence on the other (nihilism). His most influential work for the articulation of Buddhist orthopraxy in Tibet is the *Stages of Meditation* (*sGom pa'i rim pa;* Skt. *Bhāvanākrama*), which outlines a gradual contemplative path to Buddhist realization. These texts were composed following the aftermath of the Indo-Sinitic debate in 792–794 CE at the monastic compound at bSam-yas.[139] The alleged dispute between the Indian and Chinese Buddhist factions is a well-known literary development in Tibetan religious histories. A popular version is recounted in some detail in the *Testimony of Minister Ba* (*dBa' bzhed*); Ba was a minister and a member of the dBa' clan, one of the elite Tibetan families at that time.[140]

According to the *Testimony of Minister Ba,* the Indian faction was led by the abbot-successor of Śāntarakṣita, the Tibetan monk Ye-shes dbang-po (dBa' gsas-snang), and other Tibetan supporters from the dBa' (sBa) clan. The Chinese reaction was instigated by the Chinese Buddhist missionary Hva-śang Mahayana, who is presented in surviving Dunhuang documents as the seventh lineage holder following Buddha Śākyamuni, Kāśyapa, Bodhidharma, and so on. Among Hva-śang's followers, there were Chinese Buddhist monks residing at bSam-yas and Lhasa, Tibetan disciples such as the monk Ting-nge-'dzin of the Myang clan, and Tibetan noble ladies, including Queen Byang-chub-ma, who had become a Buddhist nun after the death of her son.[141] Internal political rivalry may have underlined the whole affair, with the Indian faction being alarmed by the attention Hva-śang was attracting in high places.

For the *Testimony of Minister Ba,* the "golden apple of Eris" presented to Emperor Khri Srong-lde-brtsan (756–ca. 800) was none other than the doctrinal differences between the two parties. Śāntarakṣita's followers advocated a gradual approach (*rim gyis-pa*) to buddhahood and viewed realization as a process that unfolds in stages and through practice. On the other side, Hva-śang's partisans upheld a simultaneist (*gcig car-ba*) perspective of enlightenment "here and now," a philosophical position that repudiated all ritual and conceptual efforts.

Khri Srong-lde-brtsan, who may have been sympathetic to Hva-śang's doctrines, attempted to resolve the conflict, to no avail.[142] The Chinese faction continued to mount protests and threatened public acts of self-mortification and collective suicide. The Tibetan emperor heeded the advice of the abbot Ye-shes dbang-po, who recommended inviting Śāntarakṣita's brightest pupil, since Śāntarakṣita has passed away, to settle the matter in a public debate (or a series of debates) with the Chinese. Kamalaśīla was asked to resolve the conflict, which had divided the pro-Indian Tibetan clans of dBa' against the Chinese-allied 'Bro and Myang clans.

Representatives of the Indian and Chinese parties met at a small temple called Byang-chub sems-bskyed-gling in bSam-yas Monastery to defend their competing doctrines and methods. Hva-śang argued for the practice of quietism, through which liberation from samsara is achieved instantaneously by refraining from all intentional action and mental apprehension (*mi rtog-pa*). Kamalaśīla refuted this position on the grounds that following it is tantamount to giving up discriminating wisdom (*so-sor rtog-pa'i shes-rab*), an important component of Buddhist dialectics.

Khri Srong-lde-brtsan issued an edict at the aftermath of the debate in favor of the Indian Madhyamaka team. The *Testimony of Minister Ba* reports,

> Hence, as far as theory is concerned, this shall follow the view of Nāgārjuna. As far as cultivation (*sgom pa*) is concerned, mental quiescence meditation (*zhi gnas;* Skt. *śamatha*) and penetrative insight (*lhag mthong;* Skt. *vipaśyanā*) shall be practiced on the basis of the three wisdoms.[143]

Moreover, Khri Srong-lde-brtsan ordered the establishment of a College for Tibetan Translators and the foundation of three additional colleges tasked with training Tibetans in the correct understanding of the Buddha's doctrine. He further decreed that Mahāyoga and Vajrayana scriptures should not be translated, except those texts belonging to the Kriyā and Upaya Tantras, an exception personally requested by Ye-shes dbang-po.

According to Chinese testimonies of the bSam-yas debate, Kamaśīla and his party lost.[144] While it is possible that the defeat of the Chinese simultaneist tradition was exaggerated by later Tibetan religious histories (*chos-'byung*), it is certain that the so-called "bSam-yas incident" did not instigate the eclipse of Chinese Buddhism in Tibet. Chan doctrines did not cease to circulate in central Tibet and among Tibetans in Central Asia.[145] Simultaneist teachings continue to resonate with Tibetan systems of non-conceptual contemplation, like the Great Perfection and Mahāyoga—a "resonance" noted and critiqued by Tibetan scholars who launched polemics against the rNying-ma teachings on the ground of their doctrinal proximity to Hva-śang's system of meditation (*hva-śang gi lugs*).[146]

The *Learned Feast* (*mKhas pa'i dga ston*), an acclaimed Tibetan history completed by dPa'-bo gtsug-lag 'phreng-ba in 1565, details how after the bSam-yas debate, Khri Srong-lde-brtsan requested Kamalaśīla to condense the Buddha's teachings into a definitive system (*gtan-la-phab-pa*) with a threefold application that includes learning, reflection, and meditation (*thos, bsam, sgom*) on the "selflessness" (*bdag med-pa*) of phenomena. Kamalaśīla heeded the emperor's request and contributed important works, among them the *Stages of Meditation,* which contains gradual instructions for meditation on key Mahayana topics such as generating great compassion and *bodhicitta,* meditating on "mental quiescence" (*śamatha*) and "penetrative insight" (*vipaśyanā*), practicing the six perfections (*pāramitā*s) with "skillful means" (*upāyakauśalaya*), and accumulating "merit" (*puṇya*). At the last stage of this gradual path, *buddha-kṣetra*s arise in the mental continuum of a bodhisattva, the result of having fully integrated the force of wisdom (*prajñā*) with compassion (*karuṇā*). Kamalaśīla's interpretation draws from the *Samādhi of Heroic Progress,* the authority of which was invoked by the Indian faction during the bSam-yas debate to support their gradualist thesis.[147]

For Kamalaśīla *buddha-kṣetra*s are magical creations (*sprul-pa;* Skt. *nirmāṇa*) mastered by a bodhisattva for the sake of completing the "spiritual maturity of beings" and entering into full enjoyment of the Dharma at the tenth and final stage of his spiritual evolution.[148] During this time, a bodhisattva displays one hundred aspects of spiritual mastery, such as causing an ordinary field (*kṣetra*) to expand into immeasurable fields, reducing immeasurable fields to a single ordinary field, inserting immense *buddha-kṣetra*s into a single pore of skin, and extending one's body to all the *buddha-kṣetra*s without exception.[149]

Whatever may have been the historical circumstances, the *Stages of Meditation* appeared at a critical time in the formulation of Tibetan Buddhism, when Buddhist scholars and monks from different regions and traditions engaged in intrareligious discussions concerning the correct interpretation and application of Buddhist doctrine. As we will see in the following section, Nāgārjuna's philosophy of the Middle Way was favored by the court translators and the Tibetan aristocracy. Kamalaśīla's gradual system of orthopraxy won the hearts of the Tibetans, who adopted his teachings along with a typical Mahayana interpretation of buddha fields arising from a total integration of compassion with emptiness experienced during the final stage of a bodhisattvas' spiritual attainment.

Imperial Registers and Their Texts

The state's official adaptation of Buddhism and patronage of Buddhist monastic cultures caused significant changes in Tibet's social fabric and fostered an intellectual environment in which a sharp increase in Buddhist literacy took place.[150] In order to contextualize the prevailing doctrinal trends of Mahayana Buddhism that were sanctioned in the empire, we must take a closer look at the range and types of the scriptures imported, and the collective efforts of the Indo-Tibetan and Sino-Tibetan translator-scholar teams. Unfortunately, very little is known of the latter.

The first translations of Buddhist scriptures were recorded in inventory lists kept in Tibetan monasteries and royal depositories. In all probability, these first inventories were consulted for the state-sponsored production of three imperial registers, or catalogues (*dkar-chag*), that took their names from the places of their composition.[151] According to a widespread system of reckoning, the oldest of the three was composed at the fortress-palace Stod-thang ldan-dkar.[152] The *Denkarma Catalogue* (*dkar-chag lDan dkar ma or Lhan dkar ma*) is attributed to the Tibetan translators dPal-brtsegs and Nam-mkha'i-snying-po, who were active during the second reign of Khri lDe-srong-brtsan (ca. 802–815). This is the only imperial register preserved in the Tibetan Buddhist Tripiṭaka.[153] A second catalogue, the *Samye Chimpuma* (*dkar-chag bSam yas mchims phu ma*), is attested to in historical sources, but to date it has not been found.[154] The last of the three, the *Phangthangma Catalogue* (*dkar-chag 'Phang thang ma*), was composed in the dog year (*khyi-lo*) in the upper Yar-lung valley at the royal palace of 'Phang-thang southeast of the Yum-bu-bla-sgang. The Tibetan translators dPal-brtsegs, Chos-kyi-snying-po, Devendra, and dPal-gyi-lhun-po are credited with its composition.[155]

The imperial catalogues from Denkar and Phangthang are invaluable testimonies to the official introduction and systematization of Buddhist literature during the eighth and ninth centuries. There are several doxographic layers to the taxonomies designed by the Indo-Tibetan translation teams, but full attention to this matter is best reserved for another work. Suffice to say that nearly a thousand Buddhist texts were classified according to the vehicle to which they belong (Hinayana/Mahayana), their size (small/large), genre (sutra, *dhāraṇī, śāstra*), or subject matter (i.e., Vinaya, Madhyamaka).[156] The bulk of the Tibetan scriptures recorded in the *Denkarma* and *Phangthangma Catalogues* are translations from Sanskrit, with a few works singled out as translations from Chinese sutras and commentaries. This reflects an active market and demand for Sanskrit manuscripts and a traditional Tibetan preference for Indian texts. Naturally, competence in Sanskrit language was essential to this extensive translation enterprise, and Tibetan scholars went beyond a passive reception of Indian texts and pursued the study of various aspects of Sanskrit grammar.[157]

From the colophons of the sutras we learn that Tibetan translators worked together with foreign scholars (*lo-paṇ*) mainly from India, but also from Uḍḍiyāna (present-day Swat), 'Bru-źa (Gilgit), Nepal, Khotan, and China.[158] For their work they solicited the assistance of many scribes who remain anonymous, and sorted through a substantial corpus of imported scriptures with perhaps duplicate or triplicate versions of the same texts in Sanskrit, Central Asian, and Chinese languages. The successful completion of this enormous task would have required considerable physical, mental, and financial resources, since the compilation of these catalogues accorded with a rigorous process of literary revision of all Tibetan translations throughout the Tibetan-speaking world. The *Testimony of Minister Ba* preserves an account of these times.

> During the reign of the Son of the God Khri gTsug lde btsan (Ral pa can), numerous Indian scholars were invited and the three [translators], Ka, Cog, [sNa], translated the texts of the doctrine which had not been translated before. Before translating them, [the manner of translating itself] was also systematized thanks to the Great Revision.[159]

The so-called Great Revision of Tibetan literature was seen to completion by Khri gTsug-lde-btsan, and seems to have been the outcome of three imperial injunctions (*bkas-bcad*) related to the codification of religious language that occurred prior to the reign of Khri gTsug-lde-brtsan in 763, 783, and 814.[160] Small teams of one or two Tibetan translators (*lo-tsā-ba*) and approximately the same number of Indian scholars (Skt. *paṇḍita*) were authorized to revise the old and new Tibetan translations—that is, to purge them of errors and inconsistencies according to a uniform religious terminology and translation techniques fixed for the new language of translations (*skad-gsar-bcad*). The official standardization of this process and the guidelines laid out in the *Vyutpatti* treatises were under the tutelage of the Buddhist Council, the bCom-ldan-'das-kyi-ring-lugs-kyi-'dun-sa.[161] Scherrer-Schaub (2002, 288) explains:

> In 783–795 the ecclesiastic chancery already followed an established hierarchical procedure: the colleges of translating and explaining Buddhist texts had to refer proposed terminology for approval to the high ecclesiastic representative

> and the college of translators attached to the palace. . . . The canonical and Dunhuang versions, possibly reflecting the 814 situation, bear evidence to a flourishing ecclesiastic bureaucracy.

The historical and religious significance of the imperial registers for Buddhist studies is undeniable.[162] The Kadampa master bCom-ldan ral-gri (1227–1305) and the polymath librarian Bu-ston (1290–1364) consulted them to create their own inventories of Tibetan canonical collections,[163] and a fair number of taxonomies and hundreds of texts listed in the early catalogues found their way in the Tibetan Tripiṭaka.[164] On a practical level, an operation of this scale would not have been possible without sufficient funds and a high degree of centralized organization and expertise. It is possible that inventories of Sanskrit Buddhist manuscripts from Kashmir and Khotan were consulted for the creation of Tibet's earliest known Buddhist canonical collections, while foreign experts were solicited, perhaps from China, where Buddhist texts had already seen a long history of translation, revision, and classification by local and foreign Buddhist masters.[165]

The *Sukhāvatī* Sutras in Tibetan Translation

The earliest records for the translation of the long and short *Sukhāvatī-vyūha* sutras from Sanskrit into Tibetan are the *Denkarma* and *Phangthangma Catalogues.* They were probably translated not long before the composition of the *Denkarma Catalogue,* which lists both. The origin of the Sanskrit texts consulted by the Tibetan translators is unknown to us and they were perhaps procured from India, Nepal, or Khotan.[166] From the colophons of the sutras we learn that they were edited during the Great Revision and made to conform to the official standards for translating Sanskrit Buddhist texts into Tibetan as decreed by the Buddhist Council and prescribed in the *Mahāvyutpati* and the *sGra sbyor bam po gnyis pa* treatise in two volumes.[167]

In the *Denkarma Catalogue* the long *Sukhāvatīvyūha-sūtra* is listed with the Tibetan title *'Od dpag med kyi bkod pa* (Skt. **Amitābhavyūha-sūtra*) and placed in the section "Mahayana sutras of the Ratnakūṭa class."[168] The size of the sutra is recorded "three *bam-po* and nine-hundred *śloka*" long.[169] The *Phangthangma Catalogue* includes the long sutra in the section "Mahāsūtras according to size" (§IV, no. 89) with a slightly different title and length: *De bzhin gshegs pa 'od dpag med kyi zhing gi bkod pa* (Skt. **Tathāgata-Amitābha-kṣetravyūha-sūtra*), three *bam-po* long. The different titles and varying sizes in the catalogues suggest that two different Sanskrit texts were consulted for the translation of the long *Sukhāvatīvyūha-sūtra* in Tibetan.

Following the *Denkarma* arrangement of texts, most Tibetan Kanjurs situate the long *Sukhāvatīvyūha-sūtra* in the "Ratnakūṭa" section with the long title *'Phags pa 'od dpag med kyi bkod pa shes bya ba theg pa chen po'i mdo* (Skt. *Ārya-Amitābhavyūha-nāma-mahāyāna-sūtra*). The Stog Kanjur places it in the "Mahā-Ratnakūṭa" section and its length in the colophon corresponds to that given in the *Denkarma Catalogue* (three *bam-po* and 900 *śloka*). The long *Sukhāvatīvyūha-sūtra* is listed in Bu-ston's catalogue of the Kanjur and Tanjur (no. 112), in the Ulan Bator copy of the *rGyal-rtse Them-spangs-ma* (*dKon-brtsegs*, vol. 48), in the *Record of Teachings Received* (*gSan-yig/ Thob-yig*) of sMin-gling gter-chen, (1634?–1714) (no. 30), and in the Fifth Dalai Lama's (1617–1682) *gSan-yig* (no. 33).[170]

The *Denkarma Catalogue* registers the short *Sukhāvatīvyūha-sūtra* with the title *bDe ba can gyi bkod pa* (Skt. *Sukhāvatīvyūha*) in the section "Miscellaneous Mahayana sutras less than one *bam-po*" (§VI, no. 196), 136 *śloka* long. The *Phangthangma Catalogue* is in complete agreement and provides the same title and size, arranging the sutra in the section "Small Sutras less than one *bam-po* long" (§V, no. 188). In later Tibetan canonical collections, the title of the short *Sukhāvatīvyūha-sūtra* is standardized to *'Phag pa bde ba can gyi bkod pa zhes bya ba theg pa chen po'i mdo* (Skt. *Ārya-Sukhāvatīvyūha-nāma-mahāyāna-sūtra*). Listings of the short *Sukhāvatīvyūha-sūtra* are included in Bu-ston's Catalogue (no. 183), in the rGyal-rtse Them-spangs-ma (*mDo-mangs*, vol. 74), in the *Record of Teachings Received* by sMin-gling gter-chen (no. 96), and the Fifth Dalai Lama's *gSan-yig* (no. 100).[171]

All known editions of the Tibetan Buddhist canon include the short and long *Sukhāvatīvyūha* sutras.[172] There is, however, some inconsistency concerning their Tibetan translators. The Derge, Lhasa, and Stog colophons of the long *Sukhāvatīvyūha* refer to Ye-shes-sde as the "chief translator and editor," in partnership with the Indian monks Dānaśīla and Jinamitra.[173] The Peking Kanjur lists the Tibetan "chief translator of definitive meaning" Klu'i-rgyal-mtshan. Given that the Derge, Lhasa, and Stog editions are reliable stemma representatives for the Tshal-pa and Them-spang-ma lineages of the Kanjur, they can be trusted on this issue (see Chapter Three). Dānaśīla and the monk Ye-shes-sde collaborated with Jinamitra, the Indian *paṇḍita* of "vast scholarship," in the translation of related Pure Land literature.[174] Since there are no substantial differences between the Derge, Lhasa, Stog, and Peking editions of the long sutra, there is no reason to assume that two different translations were made in the ninth century. It may very well be that both accounts are accurate, if Klu'i-rgyal-mtshan was involved in the production of the sutra at a later stage, for example, during its revision.[175]

We are confronted with similar discrepancies in the colophons of the short *Sukhāvatīvyūha-sūtra.* The Derge, Lhasa, and Stog editions list the Indian scholar Dānaśīla and Tibetan translator Ye-shes-sde, while the Pudrag and Cone editions acknowledge the Indian scholars Prajñāvarman and Surendrabodhi in collaboration with Ye-shes-sde.[176] As is the case with the long *Sukhāvatīvyūha-sūtra,* the Pudrag edition of the short sutra does not differ in any considerable way from the Derge edition, and there is no reason to suspect two separate translations.

Unfortunately, there is not much in the colophons concerning the lives of the Tibetan translators and their Indian teachers. There is scant information in Tibetan historical sources, but even there we find very little about our Tibetan translators. Where did they receive training in Sanskrit and/or Chinese, who sponsored their studies, and what was their social and economic standing? Likewise, we have little evidence concerning the daily lives of the Indian Buddhist scholars residing and teaching in Tibet. Some, like the Kashmiri monks Dānaśīla and Jinamitra, were apparently fluent in Tibetan.[177] There is little doubt concerning their dedication and tireless commitment to the spread of Buddhism in Tibet. The Tibetan tradition acknowledges them as the "three kind translators and scholars" (*drin can lo paṇ gsum*), often referring to Jinamitra, Dānaśīla, and Ye-shes-sde. Another tradition celebrates Zhang-nam Ye-shes-sde, sKa-ba dPal-brtsegs, and Cog-ro Klu'i-rgyal-mtshan as simply the "Three"—implying the three great ones.[178]

Tibetan translators rose to fame during the regime of Emperor Khri lDe-srong-brtsan (ca. 800–815), and many continued with their activities during the reign of his son, Khri gTsug-lde-brtsan (ca. 815–841). Some of them were quite learned in Mahayana Buddhism and composed their own commentaries on Madhyamaka, inspired by Śāntarakṣita's legacy.[179] The "chief translator" Ye-shes-sde is credited with the *Distinctive View,* a treatise on Buddhist tenets (*grub-mtha'*) and the doctrines of Madhyamaka. This work occupies an important place in the earliest examples of Tibetan philosophical literature.[180] Ācārya Klu'i-rgyal-mtshan composed the *Definitive Meaning of Madhyamaka,*[181] and the "illustrious translator of grammar" (*sgra sgyur gyi lo tsha ba*), Ācārya sKa-ba dPal-brtsegs, authored a Madhyamaka commentary entitled *Explanation on the Gradual View.*[182] Another *ācārya* unknown to us, named bKra-shis, composed a hefty summary of Śāntarakṣita's *Madhyamakālaṃkāra,* possibly as mnemonic device,[183] and even the apostate Tibetan emperor Glang dar-ma is listed in the *Phangthangma Catalogue,* under the name Emperor dBa' dun-brtan, as the author of a Madhyamaka commentary.[184]

Pure Land Literature in Early Tibet

Dhāraṇī (*gzungs*) is a widespread genre in Buddhist literature. Most of the *dhāraṇī* imported to Tibet appear to be of Indian origin, with noted exceptions singled out in the *Phangthangma Catalogue;* one sutra with its attached *dhāraṇī* is recorded to have been from China and Khotan.[185] Concerning their role in Buddhist scriptures, Davidson argued that *dhāraṇī* are polysemic texts sensitive to both function and context. Their main operation reflects a process of encoding/decoding information; one is usually said to enter (Skt. *mukha*) a *dhāraṇī* and not merely recite it.[186] In different contexts, *dhāraṇī* serve diverse goals, ranging from soteriological ends (liberation, birth in a pure land) to apotropaic means (purifying negative karma and averting its ripening), enhancing activities (accumulating merit, increasing lifespan, wealth, power), and protection from harm (physical and mental, external obstacles). Their pedagogical mission draws from their use as mnemonic devices and summaries of texts. While some *dhāraṇī* are, strictly speaking, devoid of theological meaning, others may be integrated into meditations of the *śamatha* type, trigger the recollection of the Buddha (Skt. *buddhānusmṛti*), and ultimately aid the cultivation of nonreferential contemplation. One gains confidence through the recitation of mantras; in the *Bodhisattva Stages* (Skt. *Bodhisattvabhūmi*) we read:

> He is supremely mindful of those mantra phrases spoken by the Tathāgata to whit: *IṬI MIṬI KIṬI BHIKṢĀ ṂTI PADĀNI SVĀ HĀ.* He considers, ponders and investigates the reference value of the mantra phrases, and becomes correctly accomplished by practicing the purport of the mantra phrases relying on himself and not listening to another.
>
> Accordingly, he concludes, "there is no denotative value determinate in these mantra phrases, for they are referentially indeterminate (nirartha)! Thus, their semantic force is exactly their referential indeterminacy! Beyond that, there is no other semantic value to be discovered." And by this referential indeterminacy the significance of these mantra phrases becomes well penetrated.[187]

A good number of *dhāraṇī,* dating from the time of the Tibetan empire onward, are associated with Mahayana and Vajrayana deities, including Avalokiteśvara, Vajragarbha, Samantabhadra, Vajrapāṇi, Vajrabhairava, Mañjuśrī, the White Canopy Uṣṇīṣa, Amitāyus, and the Seven Buddhas, among others.[188] Many *dhāraṇī* are of anonymous authorship, but some are attributed to prominent Indian masters such as Vasubandhu, Āryadeva, Śāntarakṣita, Kamalaśīla, Kalyānavarman, and Jñanagarbha. In the *Phangthangma Catalogue* they are classified according to their size and kind;

they may be long (*chen-po*), of various sizes (*che-phra*), or of various types (*gzungs-sna-tshogs*), such as essential mantra-*dhāraṇī* (*gzungs-sngags kyi snying-po*) and genera (*gzungs*).[189]

Tibetans employed *dhāraṇī* to propitiate, supplicate, and appease not only Buddhist deities but also supernatural beings such as the eight goddesses, the seven zombies (*ro-langs*), the Yeti (*mi-rgod*), and the black goddess. In the category of *vidyā* mantras we find texts dedicated to worldly kings and the king of *nāgas*, while other verbal strings are voiced to enhance one's wealth, intelligence, progeny, or even to cure hemorrhoids, smallpox, and eye diseases. The *Phangthangma Catalogue* also lists *dhāraṇī* appended to specific sutras as mnemonic devices of a sort; these include the *dhāraṇī* of the *Sutra of Entering the City of Vaishali*, the *Stainless Sutra*, and the *Tathāgatagarbha-sūtra*.[190]

There are two popular *dhāraṇī* associated with Buddha Amitābha/Amitāyus and his Pure Land; the *Aparimitāyur-jñāna-sūtra* and the *Ārya-Anantamukha-nirhāra-dhāraṇī* (*'Phags pa sgo mtha' yas pa sgrub pa'i gzungs*). The latter was prevalent in India, Central Asia, and China and features in the Tibetan imperial catalogues and in the Kanjur.[191] It was held in high prestige in China and was translated for the first time into Chinese (T. 1011) by the polyglot Zhiqian (223–253 CE), and at least eight more times from the third to the eighth centuries.[192] The *Ārya-Anantamukha-nirhāra-dhāraṇī* survives partly in Sanskrit and Khotanese, but an extensive commentary on it by Jñānagarbha is preserved only in Tibetan.[193]

The *Anantamukha-dhāraṇī* seems to contain the earliest reference to Amitāyus in Chinese literature.[194] It mentions his name in relation to a certain prince in the west who became Buddha Amitābha. He who is diligent in its practice will accomplish "infinite entrances" into the world of *dhāraṇī*. This accomplishment is listed as one of the four entrances; the other three are "skill in the faculty of beings," "uncompounded skill in karma and fruition," and the "expression of the deep Dharma."[195] In Tibet the *Anantamukha-dhāraṇī* inspired large commentaries and explanatory works recorded in the *Denkarma* and *Phangthangma Catalogues*.[196]

Amitāyus *dhāraṇī* are not recorded before the third century CE, and those of earlier origins are listed in Chinese collections and in both Tibetan imperial registers.[197] Their titles in the imperial registers do not specify their contents, but judging from their size they were probably of various lengths. The *Phangthangma Catalogue* features a short and long *sādhana* to Amitāyus (no. 916) and a text that enumerates the attributes and characteristics of Amitābha authored in Tibetan by someone called Vairocanarakṣita (no. 879).[198]

Besides *dhāraṇī,* other relatively unstudied works with a Pure Land orientation are included in Lalou's 1939 catalogue of the *Pelliot Tibétain Collection.*[199] Among these, Pel. Tib. 758 has come to the attention of scholars because it is a Tibetan translation of Kumārajīva's Chinese translation of the Sanskrit short *Sukhāvatīvyūha-sūtra* (T. 366). Akamatsu dates this incomplete manuscript to the end of the eighth century, making it among the earliest known Tibetan translations of the short *Sukhāvatīvyūha-sūtra.*[200]

Another interesting text from the collection is Pel. Tib. 16, which mentions an Amitābha statue in the consecration of the temple of De-ga gyu-tshal.[201] This text draws from the *Sukhāvatīvyūha* sutras and recommends the recitation of Amitābha's name for the purification of all negative deeds (*sdig-pa*)—a meritorious act that leads one to take birth in Amitābha's buddha field (*sangs-rgyas kyi zhing*), supreme among all other buddha fields.

> Installed [in the temple] is the image of Buddha Amitābha, whose field is supreme among those of all buddhas, so that even the names for the three evil destinies and the eight obstacles are unknown. Being adorned with all the adornments of divine enjoyment, even the name for passing sorrow (nirvana) cannot be known there! For it is a field adorned with all and perfect world-transcending happiness. Because [Amitābha] is especially compassionate on behalf of beings, by just reciting his name all sins are purified and one is blessed to be born in that buddha field.[202]

Tibetan literature with a Pure Land orientation features Mahayana sutra (*mdo*), *stotra* (*bstod-pa/brgyad-pa*), mantra (*sngags*), *dhāraṇī* (*gzungs*), and tantric texts of the *sādhana* and *homa* variety.[203] However, Amitābha's popularity in Tibet and the Tibetan colonies of Central Asia should be measured in relation to other attractive Mahayana deities and their sutras, such as the cosmic Buddha Vairocana, who was widely worshiped in Sino-Japanese and Central Asian artistic productions drawn from the *Avataṃsaka-sūtra.*[204] There is a growing body of evidence concerning the flourishing cult of Buddha Vairocana in Tibet and the political appropriation and representation of this buddha in Tibetan religious art of the early period.[205]

The Ārya-aparimitāyur-mahāyāna-sūtra

The most compelling evidence for the widespread circulation of Pure Land beliefs among Tibetans comes from the Pel. Tib. 999 MS acquired in 1908 by Paul Pelliot from library cave 17 in Dunhuang. It dates to the mid-ninth century and contains important historical information on the reigns of Tibetan emperors and their sponsorship of Buddhist texts.[206] The beginning of the manuscript states that formerly the people of Sha-cu (Dunhuang) sponsored many Chinese and Tibetan copies of the *Immeasurable Life and Wisdom Sutra* (*Aparimitāyur-jñāna-sūtra*) for the occasion of offering them to the "divine prince" (*lha-sras*) Khri gTsug-lde-brtsan. The donation record mentions the reproduction of 136 Chinese and 480 Tibetan scrolls of the *Aparimitāyur* stored in the library of the Linghongsi *vihāra*. The manuscript records some 2,700 local residents who had collected funds to commemorate the occasion of 'Od-srung's (842 or 843-ca. 890) ascension to the Tibetan throne. In this document he is mentioned as the son of Lady Phen, one of the wives of Khri gTsug-lde-brtsan, who ruled the kingdom in the interim as dowager queen. The document concludes with a list of those in charge of the project: the Chinese dignitary monk Hongben and a Tibetan monk called dBang-mchog.[207] Richardson (1992, 7) sums up nicely the history of this period:

> At this time the country was wracked by violent fighting between rival ministers. Shangkungje of Dba's was out for himself, while Shangpipi of 'Bro whose family had long connections with the Tibetan royal house and whose origin was in the neighbourhood of Sha-cu, can be seen as supporting Lang Darma's successor 'Od srung for whom and for his mother the lady 'Phan prayers continued to be offered. In Pell T. 999 as mentioned above, 'Od-srungs' name is linked with that of Khri-Gtsug lde-brtsan. The religious dignitary principally responsible for the offering was the abbot (Hong pien) who later led the return of the Chinese of Sha-cu to allegiance to the Chinese Emperor on the collapse of the Tibetan authority in 850.

Although Pel. Tib. 999 does not provide further details, it would seem to suggest that the *Aparimitāyur-sūtra* was copied in large numbers as part of a nationwide prayer for the birth and longevity of the "divine prince" or, more likely, if copied during the reign of 'Od-srung, for aiding Khri gTsug-lde-brtsan's passage to Sukhāvatī.[208]

The dedication of the *Aparimitāyur-sūtra* testifies to the prominence of this proto–Pure Land text that was reproduced in conspicuously large numbers across the Tarim basin. In all, Tibetan translations of the *Immeasurable Life and Wisdom Sutra* occupy nearly 950 scrolls, many of which were multiple copies in a bundle acquired by Sir Aurel Stein during his expeditions to Central Asia between 1906 and 1908.[209] The *Immeasurable Life and Wisdom Sutra* also exists in Chinese, Tangut, and Central Asian translations.[210] The sheer volume of Chinese and Tibetan copies in Eastern Central Asia suggests that it was produced on several occasions and for a variety of reasons, not least for transferring merit on the behalf of the deceased on their journey to the netherworld.[211]

The *Immeasurable Life and Wisdom Sutra* (*Tshe dang ye shes dpag tu med pa zhes bya ba theg pa chen po'i mdo;* Skt. *Aparimitāyur-jñāna-nāma-mahāyāna-sūtra*) is in fact a *dhāraṇī*-sutra.[212] It centers on the deity Aparimitāyus and expounds on the benefits associated with the recitation of his *dhāraṇī.* In the Tibetan and Chinese traditions Aparimitāyus is equivalent to Buddha Amitāyus, but it remains unclear if Aparimitāyus was originally an independent Indian Mahayana deity.[213] As we will see in Chapter Five, the Tibetan translation of the sixth-century *Ārya-aparimitāyur-jñāna-hṛdaya-nāma-dhāraṇī* unambiguously declares that Sukhāvatī is the buddha field of Aparimitāyus. This claim is also reiterated in Tibetan tantric literature related to this deity.

The sermon of the *Immeasurable Life and Wisdom Sutra,* like that of the *Sukhāvatīvyūha-sūtra,* takes place in Śrāvastī, in the Jeta Grove of the merchant Anāthapiṇḍika. It is delivered by the Bhagavān, Buddha Śākyamuni, who engages the youthful Mañjuśrī in front of a large gathering of 1,250 monks and many bodhisattvas. The Buddha shares with his audience an epiphany of a world-system located in the zenith where Tathāgata Aparimitāyurjñāna abides and dispenses Buddhist remedies for dealing with fear, old age, and death. The *pharmakon* is a special gift to humankind, a *dhāraṇī* uttered by Aparimitāyurjñāna that can extend one's life by no less than a hundred years.

The *Immeasurable Life and Wisdom Sutra* resembles the short *Sukhāvatīvyūha-sūtra* in other ways. Both texts invoke countless buddhas to serve as cosmic witnesses to the text's antiquity and authenticity. In another sense, the invocation of countless buddhas may be seen to empower the reader who recites "with one mind and a single intention" the 108 syllables of Aparimitāyus' *dhāraṇī.*

The *Immeasurable Life and Wisdom Sutra* concludes with praise of each of the six Mahayana perfections. The repeated emphasis to have this work copied and transmitted reinforces Schopen's argument for the Mahayana cult of the book, which was prevalent in Tibet.[214] There are many advantages associated with the recitation of Aparimitāyus' *dhāraṇī.* Those who hear the *dhāraṇī,* recite it, write it down, or worship it in any form will reap the benefits of long life and gain protection from enemies and untimely death. There are also undeniable soteriological incentives attached to its recitation. For example, one can purify negative deeds and, most important, attain birth in Sukhāvatī.[215] The alleged benefits of this *dhāraṇī* may have served as a cause for popularizing Pure Land doctrines among illiterate Tibetans, who could not read the Buddhist sutras. In fact, in many cases the names of Chinese scribes are listed at the end of the Tibetan *dhāraṇī*-sutras discovered in Central Asia.

Despite the importance of the *Immeasurable Life and Wisdom Sutra* for understanding the formation of Indo-Tibetan and Central Asian Pure Land traditions, this text has been ignored in relevant studies.[216] To the best of my knowledge, the first and only attempt toward a critical edition of the *Tshe-mdo* (*Life Sutra*) was done by Sten Konow along with an English translation of the Tibetan text in 1916.[217] Konow's pioneer effort is not free of errors in the transcription and interpretation of the Tibetan text, which necessitates revisiting the contents of this Indo-Sino-Tibetan Buddhist classic. The English translation below is based on an anonymous Tibetan translation of the *Aparimitāyur-jñāna-nāma-mahāyāna-sūtra* preserved in the *rGyud* section of the Derge edition of the Tibetan Kanjur.[218] A version of the same text seems to be listed in the *Phangthangma Catalogue* with the title *Ārya-Aparimitāyur* (*'Phags pa tshe dpag tu med pa,* sl. 120) under the heading "Miscellaneous *Dhāraṇī* of Various Sizes" (§XV, no. 334).[219]

The Immeasurable Life and Wisdom Sutra

Derge no. 674 (ba, vol. 91, fol. 216–220, pp. 431–440)

[431] In the language of India: *Ārya-aparimitāyur-jñāna-nāma-mahāyāna-sūtra.* In the language [432] of Tibet: *'Phags pa tshe dang ye shes dpag tu med pa zhes bya ba theg pa chen po'i mdo.*

Homage to all the buddhas and bodhisattvas!

Thus I have heard, at one time the Exalted [Śākyamuni] resided in the city of Śrāvastī, in the garden of Anāthapiṇḍada, the grove of Prince Jeta, with one thousand three hundred fifty monks of the great sangha and a multitude of great bodhisattvas all seated together.

At this time, the Bhagavān addressed Mañjuśrī, the youthful: "Mañjuśrī, above us there is a world-system (*'jig-rten gyi khams*) of immeasurable qualities (*yon-tan dpag tu med-pa*). In that world abides the one called the Tathāgata Ārhat, the Perfectly Enlightened Buddha, Unmistakable King of Immeasurable Life and Wisdom teaching to people mastery over the extension of life.

Listen, youthful Mañjuśrī, "The people of Jambudvīpa have short lives, barely reaching one hundred years, while many of them lose their lives in untimely death." And yet, Mañjuśrī, "whoever writes or causes one to write this sutra that praises the qualities of the Tathāgata Aparimitāyurjñāna and whoever would hear it and recite it, enter it into a book, keep it at home, worship it by offering flowers, incense, garlands, and sand, his life will increase one hundred years even if it had been exhausted."

Mañjuśrī, "Whoever hears the one hundred and eight syllables[220] of the *Unmistakable King of Immeasurable Life and Wisdom*, his life will increase and so it will for him who keeps it in mind when his life fades away with great suffering."

[432] In this way, Mañjuśrī, "the sons or daughters of a good family wishing for a long life should listen to the one hundred and eight syllables of the Tathāgata Aparimitāyurjñāna, write them down, or cause them to be written, and thus obtain virtue and prosperity."

oṃ namo bhagavate / aparimitāyuḥ jñāna subinitsiṭa tejo rājāya / tathāgatāya / arhate / samyaksaṃ buddhaya / tadyathā [oṁ puṇye puṇye / mahā puṇye / aparimita puṇye / aparimitayuh puṇye jñāna saṃbhāropatsiti] / oṃ sarva saṃskāra pariśuddha dharmate gagana samudgate sarva bishuḍhe mahānaya pari bāre svāhā.[221]

Mañjuśrī, "Whoever writes or causes one to write all one hundred and eight syllables of the Tathāgata, keeps them in mind, and recites them, his life will increase one hundred years even if it had been exhausted. Having died, he will be born in the buddha field of the Tathāgata Aparimitāyurjñāna, the world-system Sukhāvatī (*bde-ba-can*) possessing immeasurable qualities (*yon-tan dpag tu med-pa*)."[222]

oṃ namo bhagavate / aparimitāyuḥ jñāna subinitsiṭa tejo rājāya / tathāgatāya / arhate / samyaksaṃ buddhaya / tadyathā [oṁ puṇye puṇye / mahā puṇye / aparimita puṇye / aparimitayuh puṇye jñāna saṃbhāropatsiti] / oṃ sarva saṃskāra pariśuddha dharmate gagana samudgate sarva bishuḍhe mahānaya pari bāre svāhā.

At this time, nine hundred million buddhas with one mind and a single intention recited the *Aparimitāyur-jñāna-sūtra. Oṃ namo bhagavate . . . pari bāre svāhā.*

At this time, eight hundred and forty million buddhas with one mind and a single intention recited the *Aparimitāyur-jñāna-sūtra. Oṃ namo bhagavate . . . pari bāre svāhā.*

[434] At this time, seventy-seven million buddhas with one mind and a single intention recited the *Aparimitāyur-jñāna-sūtra. Oṃ namo bhagavate . . . pari bāre svāhā.* At this time, sixty-five million buddhas with one mind and a single intention recited the *Aparimitāyur-jñāna-sūtra. Oṃ namo bhagavate . . . pari bāre svāhā.* At this time, fifty-five million buddhas with one mind and a single intention recited the *Aparimitāyur-jñāna-sūtra. Oṃ namo bhagavate . . . pari bāre svāhā.* At this time, forty-five million buddhas with one

mind and a single intention recited the *Aparimitāyur-jñāna-sūtra. Oṃ namo bhagavate . . . pari bāre svāhā.*

At this time, thirty-five million buddhas with one mind and a single intention recited the *Aparimitāyur-jñāna-sūtra. Oṃ namo bhagavate . . . pari bāre svāhā.*

[435] At this time, twenty-five million buddhas with one mind and a single intention recited the *Aparimitāyur-jñāna-sūtra. Oṃ namo bhagavate . . . pari bāre svāhā.*

At this time, ten million buddhas, equal in number to the grains of sand in ten rivers like the Ganga, with one mind and a single intention recited the *Aparimitāyur-jñāna-sūtra. Oṃ namo bhagavate . . . pari bāre svāhā.*

Whoever writes, causes one to write, or keeps in mind the *Aparimitāyur-jñāna-sūtra,* his life will increase one hundred years even if it had been exhausted. *Oṃ namo bhagavate . . . pari bāre svāhā.*

Whoever writes or causes one to write the *Aparimitāyur-jñāna-sūtra* will never again take birth in hell, among animals, or in the realm of Yama (i.e., will no longer be subject to transmigration). He will never be born without freedom and will recollect all his previous births. *Oṃ namo bhagavate . . . pari bāre svāhā.*

[436] Whoever writes or causes one to write the *Aparimitāyur-jñāna-sūtra* will resolve the eighty-four-thousand collections of Dharma.[223] *Oṃ namo bhagavate . . . pari bāre svāhā.*

Whoever writes or causes one to write the *Aparimitāyur-jñāna-sūtra* will resolve and become fully established in the eighty-four thousand collections of Dharma. *Oṃ namo bhagavate . . . pari bāre svāhā.*

Whoever writes or causes one to write the *Aparimitāyur-jñāna-sūtra* will purify the five heinous acts. *Oṃ namo bhagavate . . . pari bāre svāhā.*

Whoever writes or causes one to write the *Aparimitāyur-jñāna-sūtra* will purify his negative karma even if it as great as Mount Meru. *Oṃ namo bhagavate . . . pari bāre svāhā.*

Whoever writes or causes one to write the *Aparimitāyur-jñāna-sūtra* will not be harmed by Māra and his family, by celestial beings (*lha*), or by *rakṣās* and demons. *Oṃ namo bhagavate . . . pari bāre svāhā.*

[437] Whoever writes or causes one to write the *Aparimitāyur-jñāna-sūtra* as prophesied [in the scriptures], when he is about to die ninety-nine million buddhas will actually appear before him, stretch out their arms [to welcome him], and [once there] he will be able to travel from this buddha field to other buddha fields. Concerning this, you should entertain no doubt nor have two minds about it. *Oṃ namo bhagavate . . . pari bāre svāhā.*

Whoever writes or causes one to write the *Aparimitāyur-jñāna-sūtra,* the Four Guardian Kings (*rgyal-po chen-po bzhi*) will accompany him and offer their protection against all evil. *Oṃ namo bhagavate . . . pari bāre svāhā.*

Whoever writes or causes one to write the *Aparimitāyur-jñāna-sūtra* will take birth in the buddha field Sukhāvatī of the Tathāgata Amitābha ('Od-dpag-tu-med pa). *Oṃ namo bhagavate . . . pari bāre svāhā.*

In whatever place the sutra is written down, that place will become like a stupa worthy of respect. Any animals, such as birds or deer, who hear it [recited] will attain unexcelled and perfect enlightenment. *Oṃ namo bhagavate . . . pari bāre svāhā.*

[438] Whoever writes or causes one to write the *Aparimitāyur-jñāna-sūtra* will never be born again in a woman's body. *Oṃ namo bhagavate . . . pari bāre svāhā.*

Whoever gives one *karshapana* (Indian coin) for the teachings of the *Aparimitāyurjñāna-sūtra,* it is as if surrendering seven precious jewels to fill the buddha fields of the entire universe with generosity. *Oṃ namo bhagavate . . . pari bāre svāhā.*

Whoever makes offerings to this sutra will be able to understand the meaning of all the supreme teachings of the Buddha. *Oṃ namo bhagavate . . . pari bāre svāhā.*

For example, even if one could count the merit accrued from offering seven precious jewels to Vipaśyin (rNam-par-gzigs), Śikhin (gTsug-tor), Viśvambhu (Thams-cad-skyob), Krakucchanda (Log-par-dad-sel-'khor-ba-'jig), Kānakamuni (gSer-thub), Kāśyapa ('Od-srung), and Śākyamuni (Sā-kya-thub-pa), the collection of merit accrued by making offerings to Aparimitāyurjñāna is [in comparison] immeasurable. *Oṃ namo bhagavate . . . pari bāre svāhā.*

[439] Likewise, even if one offers a pile of jewels as large as Mount Meru in an act of generosity, the merit accrued by making offerings to the Aparimitāyurjñāna is immeasurable in comparison. *Oṃ namo bhagavate . . . pari bāre svāhā.*

Even if one could count each drop of water in the four great oceans, the merit accrued from Aparimitāyurjñāna is immeasurable in comparison. *Oṃ namo bhagavate . . . pari bāre svāhā.*

Whoever writes or causes one to write the *Aparimitāyur-jñāna-sūtra,* and pays homage and makes offerings to it, it is like paying homage and making offerings to all the Tathāgatas and their buddha fields across the ten directions. *Oṃ namo bhagavate . . . pari bāre svāhā.*

Through the power of generosity (*sbyin-pa*) of the pure exalted buddhas, the lions of men, having internalized (*rtogs-pa*) the power of generosity, enter the compassionate city where the message of this power (i.e., generosity) is heard.[224]

Through the power of morality (*tshul-krims*) of the pure exalted buddhas, the lions of men, having internalized the power of morality, enter the compassionate city where the message of morality is heard.

Through the power of patience (*bzod-pa*) of the pure exalted buddhas, [440] the lions of men, having realized the power of patience, enter the compassionate city where the message of patience is heard.

Through the power of perseverance (*brtson-'grus*) of the pure exalted buddhas, the lions of men, having realized the power of perseverance, enter the compassionate city where the message of perseverance is heard.

Through the power of meditation (*bsam-gtan*) of the pure exalted buddhas, the lions of men, having realized the power of meditation, enter the compassionate city where the message of meditation is heard.

Through the power of wisdom (*shes-rab*) of the pure exalted buddhas, the lions of men, having realized the power of wisdom, enter the compassionate city where the message of wisdom is heard.

oṃ namo bhagavate / aparimitāyuḥ jñāna subinitsiṭa tejo rājāya / tathāgatāya / arhate / samyaksaṃ buddhaya / tadyathā [oṁ puṇye puṇye / mahā puṇye / aparimita puṇye / aparimitayuh puṇye jñāna saṃbhāropatsiti] / oṃ sarva saṃskāra pariśuddha dharmate gagana samudgate sarva bishuḍhe mahānaya pari bāre svāhā.

Having thus spoken, the Bhagavān, Mañjuśrī the youthful, the great *śrāvaka*s, bodhisattvas, gods, humans, *asura*s, and *gandharva*s, and all the inhabitants of the world, were delighted and praised his teachings.

The *Ārya-aparimitāyur-jñāna-dhāraṇī* is complete.

An Aspiration Poem from Dunhuang

The importance of mortuary rites in pre-Buddhist Tibet is alluded to in some of the earliest Tibetan documents. A vital passage from the Old Tibetan Chronicle discovered at Dunhuang narrates the violent death of Gri-gum btsan-po, the first Tibetan sovereign.[225] He was allegedly the first mortal king to perish on Tibetan soil, as his forebears had previously passed directly to the heavens through a "head rope" (*dbu-thag*), leaving no earthly remains behind. These stories about the early kings of Tibet are revealing. They did not descend "to inhabit the earth, but as in certain Chinese legends, to govern it."[226]

The mortal death of the first king in pre-Buddhist Tibet signaled an era of elaborate royal burial practices and a phase of anxiety about death and its aftermath.[227] Similar preoccupations about the death of the ancient gods are found in the *Tale of the Cycle of Birth and Death* (*Skye shi'i lo rgyus*). This text from Dunhuang coincides with the transitional period following the introduction of new Buddhist concepts about death and related rituals in Tibet.[228]

> Formerly all the gods possessed of body (*gzugs yod lha*) hoped that their life would be eternal: for innumerable eons they had never seen the law of birth and death (*skye shi'i chos*) because they had a long life of numerous years. The Lord of this world (*de'i khams rje*) was called 'Od 'bar rgyal, "King of Blazing Light." The dwelling place that he occupied . . . was made solely of light and shone dazzlingly bright. . . . One day the life of 'Od 'bar rgyal was exhausted and the moment of the fall arrived for him. His magical power (*'phrul stobs*), his indescribable virtues (*yon tan*) and the beautiful blazing light of his body disappeared (*yal*). He stopped speaking, moving or breathing. Everyone found it extraordinary and asked each other what was the fault and what was the law. Nobody knew the meaning of the law (*chos don*). His thousand sons, ten thousand parents and all his retinue were plunged into an ocean of suffering and, beating their bodies, showed the signs of the most profound sadness. They wished that the king would return [to life] and be as he was before (*slar 'ong sngon bzhin yod du re*).[229]

The belief of birth in heavenly realms was not altogether abandoned even in later times when Mahayana doctrines were widespread. A Tibetan text from Dunhuang connected with funeral rites subscribes to the "teaching of the path of the god's realm" (*lha yul du lam bstan pa*), in which the deceased must journey through several heavens before arriving at Buddhism's highest end.[230]

Models of divine kingship played an important role in the political traditions of Tibet, as they did in Chinese and Eurasian contexts.[231] Heavenly beliefs and mortuary rites in pre-Buddhist Tibet were probably shaped through contact with Central Eurasian peoples participating in what Beckwith (2009) has termed the Central Eurasian Culture Complex.[232] Whatever may have been the lines of transmission, old Tibetan beliefs about the afterlife were not eclipsed by the advent of Buddhism in the Tibet court.[233] Early Indo-Tibetan forms of Buddhism would struggle and eventually succeed to build upon older notions of divine kingship refashioned in a new light through the doctrine of reincarnation and the conviction of afterlife in a pure land, a neoteric objective and flawless heaven.

In a bundle of copies of the *Aparimitāyur-jñāna-sūtra* brought back by from Dunhuang by Stein there was an incomplete Tibetan text (two folia) that offers a welcoming addition to a significant body of evidence concerning the prevalence of Tibetan Pure Land practices in the Tarim basin. This previously unstudied manuscript suggests associations between Pure Land aspirations and Mahāyoga/Chan ideas that may have been connected to postmortem rites. MS IOL Tib J 310.1207 is among the earliest precursors to the Tibetan genre of Pure Land literature, the *bDe-smon*. In all likelihood it is an indigenous Tibetan composition and not a translation from Sanskrit or Chinese, even while it displays influence from both traditions.

Every stanza of the text is marked with the repetition of the aspiration "May [you] take birth in that pure land" (*rnam dag zhing der skye bar 'gyur*). In Tibetan translations from Sanskrit, Sukhāvatī is commonly rendered as the "field of a buddha" (*sangs-rgyas kyi zhing*) or a "world-system" (*'jig-rten gyi khams*). The expression "pure land" resonates with the Chinese term *jingdu*, but is not found in Indian Buddhist literature, nor does it have a known Sanskrit antecedent. In Sanskrit *buddha-kṣetra* (buddha field or domain of a buddha) does not contain the meaning of "purity" in its etymology. According to Asaṅga, the practice of purifying a *buddha-kṣetra* is understood in terms of of purifying one's mind of dualistic fixation and false distinctions—an understanding that may have inspired the formulation of buddha fields as pure.[234]

It has been suggested that the term "pure land" was first coined in China, borrowing from the Indian concepts of "purified buddha field" (Skt. *pariśuddhaṃ buddha-kṣetram*) and "impure buddha field" (Skt. *kliṣṭaṃ buddha-kṣetram*), both of which are attested to in Indian Buddhist texts.[235] The Tibetan term for pure land, *rnam-dag zhing*, does occur in Tibetan Buddhist literature much later, as in the *Praise to the Protector Amitābha: Opening the Door to the Sublime Field* composed by Tsong-kha-pa blo-bzang grags-pa (1357–1419).[236]

The poem's uniform metric structure runs approximately in four-line stanzas per folio of seven-syllable verse, all ending with the same refrain "May [you] take birth in that pure land!" Each phrase is separated by the vocative interjection "Amyitapur!", a repetition alluding to the fact that the text was ritually chanted. The meaning of the utterance, as noted by Silk, is the liturgical invocation of "Amita Buddha! Namo Amita Buddha in Chinese language."[237]

Without recourse to the complete manuscript and without knowledge of the ritual and social circumstances of its usage, it is impossible to make any conclusive statements about the date of its composition and its intended function. Some internal evidence hints that we are dealing with a ritual text related to mortuary rites conducted by religious specialists. Stanza three in folio four resonates with the *Tibetan Book of the Dead,* which grew out of similar beliefs concerning the dissolution of the aggregates (*phung-po*), elements (*khams*), and sense fields (*skye-mched*), followed by prayers and instructions recited to the dead while in the intermediate state between death and rebirth (*bar-do*).

Other layers in the poem suggest that it served instructional or pedagogical purposes, given its presentation of key Mahayana practices such as the generation of great compassion (stanza 1), the accumulation of merit and wisdom (stanza 2), and ascetic practices that may have been influenced by tantric traditions at the time of its composition (stanzas 1 and 2). In either case, it is clear that the intended audience was Buddhist adepts, possibly even yogis familiar with charnel ground practices (stanza 1), sleeping in sitting meditation posture (stanza 2), *śamatha* meditations (stanza 2), and Mahāyoga/Chan-type directions in nonconceptualization (stanzas 3, 4, and 5).

Reconstruction and Translation

The original manuscript is stored in the Tibetan collection of Dunhuang manuscripts at the British Library in London. It is written in *dbu-can* script and comes untitled in loose-leaf pothī format. It contains archaic Tibetan orthographical features typical of many manuscripts from Dunhuang, but cannot be reliably dated by present codicological or palaeographical methods, which are in only a nascent stage as concerns Dunhuang manuscripts in general and Tibetan manuscripts in particular.[238]

An English translation (without the frequent interjection "Amyitapur!") is followed by an interlinear Tibetan-to-English translation arranged in themes, and a short commentary not included in the original text.

Amyitapur!
May you take birth in that pure land!

Meditate on great enlightened compassion.
In order to meditate on natural purity,
Uphold the vows of a cemetery-dweller.
May you take birth in that pure land!

Accumulate merit and wisdom
In order to attain single-pointed concentration

Train in the discipline of sleeping in a sitting posture.
May you take birth in that pure land!

The faultless sphere of phenomena
Manifests things as they are in actuality because,
They bind together in semblance to the ground.
May you take birth in that pure land!

Not abiding in forms and concepts,
Relinquish all that is and is not.
Meditate on the *dharmas* beyond concepts.
May you take birth in that pure land!

The ultimate reality of all buddhas,
Is the true state without limit and end.
Meditate beyond the three times.
May you take birth in that pure land!

Having passed beyond the aggregates and the elements,
Liberated from all sense fields,
Apprehend the two extremes. . . .

Interlinear Translation

Sequence of Contents
- Descriptive headings not included in the original text
- Numbering of folio
- Transliteration of Tibetan stanza in italics
- English translation
- Notes to the original text

Symbols and Conventions
- * = ornamental, *yig-mgo*
- I = reverse vowel, *gi-ku-rlog*
- Y = *ya* attached to *ma, ma-ya-btags*
- ' = short *a* attached at the end of verses, *'a-rten*
- /:/ = mid-line *tsheg*
- // = double *shad*
- [ ] = folio and line, reconstructions of illegible, missing, or misspelled text
- [x] = letter struck with a line by scribe
- ( ) = explanations and Tibetan terms

Structure and Meter

Two noncontinuous folia, blank on reverse
Five lines per folio

[Folio 1]
Charnel Ground Practices

[line 1] * */:/ a mYi ta pur // rnam dag zhing der skye bar 'gyur // a mYi ta pur // snying rje byang cub cher bsgoms te // a mYi ta pur //* [line 2] *rang bzhIn dag par bsgoms pa'i phyIr // a mYi ta pur // dur khrod*[u] *pa'i sdom byas na // a mYi ta pur // rnam dag zhing der skye* [line 3] *bar* [s]*'gyur //*

Amyitapur!
May you take birth in that pure land!

Amyitapur!
Meditate on great enlightened compassion.
Amyitapur!
In order to meditate on natural purity
Amyitapur!
Uphold the vows of a cemetery-dweller.
Amyitapur!
May you take birth in that pure land!

The first stanza emphasizes the motivation of Mahayana practitioners to meditate on great compassion toward all sentient forms. The use of *der* (lit., "in that") expresses familiarity with the pure land in question, which is, in all probability, Sukhāvatī in this context. The aspirant should meditate on the inherent purity of all phenomena adhering to the commitments (*sdom-pa*) of an ascetic who resides in cemeteries, graveyards, and charnel grounds.[239] References to the natural purity of reality alludes to a Mahāyoga orientation, and given the circulation of Vajrayana literature in Dunhuang, tantric rites may have been performed in charnel grounds.

Merit, Wisdom, and *Śamatha*

a mYI ta pur // bsod nams shes [*rab*] *tshogs bsags te // a mYi ta pur // rtse gcig sems kyis* [line 4] *bya'I phyir // a mYI ta pur // cog bu pa'i sdom sbyangs na' // a mYi ta pur // rnam dag zhing der skye bar 'gyur //*

Amyitapur!
Accumulate merit and wisdom
Amyitapur!

In order to attain single-pointed concentration
Amyitapur!
Train in the discipline of sleeping in a sitting posture.
Amyitapur!
May you take birth in that pure land!

The repetition of the phrase "May you take birth in that pure field" (*rnam dag zhing der skye bar 'gyur*) is common in later Tibetan Pure Land prayers. In Mahayana, the two accumulations (*tshogs-gnyis;* Skt. *dvasambhara*) feature 1) merit accumulation (*bsod-nams kyi tshogs;* Skt. *puṇyasambhara*), which serves as the cause for obtaining the form body of the Buddha (Skt. *rupakāya*); and 2) wisdom accumulation (*shes-rab kyi tshogs;* Skt. *prajñānasambhara*), which serves as the cause for obtaining the truth body of the Buddha (Skt. *dharmakāya*). An ascetic abides in meditation in three postures (sitting, walking, and standing). This is included in the *dhutanga* practices discussed earlier. It necessitates sleeping in the meditation posture and not lying down. In our verse, it is the cause for cultivating *śamatha*, one-pointed concentration.

The Mode of Appearance of Phenomena and the Ground

a mYi ta pur // [line 5] *chos kyi dbyings la mYi nyams shing // a mYi ta pur // yang dag ji bzhIn mngon ba'i phyir // a mYi ta pur // gzhi bzhIn s[d]om ba'* [na] [*a mYi ta pur*] [*rnam dag zhing der skye bar 'gyur*]

Amyitapur!
The faultless sphere of phenomena
Amyitapur!
Manifests things as they are in actuality because,
Amyitapur!
They bind together in semblance to the ground.
[Amyitapur!]
[May you take birth in that pure land!]

The sphere of phenomena, the *dharmadhātu* (*chos kyi dbyings*), encompasses both phenomena and numena. They "manifest, become visible" (*mngon-ba*) in their "actual, ultimate way" (*yang-dag*), because (*phyir*) they bind together (*sdom*) in a "root, ground, basis" (*gzhi*), semblance (*bzhin*).

The State of Nonconceptualization
[Folio 2] [Line 1]

(verse continued from preceding third line of non-extant folio:) . . . *bsrungs byas na // a mYi ta pur // rnam dag zhing der skye bar 'gyur // a mYi ta pur //*

tham[s] cad chos la mYi gnas shing // a mYi ta [line 2] *pur // yod dang mYed pa rna[m]s [spangs] ste // a mYi ta pur // bsam rtogs 'das pa'i [m]chos bsgoms na' // a mYi ta pur // rnam dag* [line 3] *zhing der skye bar 'gyur //*

. . . having protected.
Amyitapur!
May you take birth in that pure land!

Amyitapur!
Not abiding in forms and concepts.
Amyitapur!
Relinquish all that is and is not.
Amyitapur!
Meditate on the *dharmas* beyond concepts.
Amyitapur!
May you take birth in that pure land!

The first part of this stanza ("having protected") follows from the third line of a previous folio not available for consultation. The term "all *dharmas*" (*thams-cad chos*) refers to all phenomena that enter our field of experience, such as forms arising from our sense perceptions and concepts concerning the truth, manner, and agency of this experience. Substantializing modalities of existence and nonexistence are known as the two extremes in Buddhism, referring to the errant positions of eternalism and nihilism. These instructions resonate with early Mahāyoga and Chan nonconceptual systems of contemplation.

The Ultimate Reality of the Buddhas

a mYi ta pur // sangs rgyas rnams kyi chos nyid de // a mYi ta pur // mtha' dang [m]u med yang dag nyid // a mYi [line 4] *ta pur // dus gsum 'das pa'I sgom byas na' // a mYi ta pur // rnam dag zhing der skye bar 'gyur //*

Amyitapur!
The ultimate reality of all buddhas
Amyitapur!
Is the state without limit and end.
Amyitapur!
Meditate beyond the three times.
Amyitapur!
May you take birth in that pure land!

The ultimate reality (*chos-nyid*) realized by those awakened is the "true state" (*yang-dag-nyid*) without boundaries, beginning, or end. The nonreferential contemplation of limitless space and timelessness is again reminiscent of nonconceptual meditations found in Chan and Mahāyoga traditions.

Liberation from the Sense Fields

a mYi ta pur // phung po khams [line 5] *las 'das pa ste // a mYI ta pur // skye mche*[*d*] [*na*]*ms las rnam par grol // a mYI ta pur // mtha*['] *gnyis dmYIgs* [*na*] [*a mYi ta pur*] [*rnam dag zhing der skye bar 'gyur*]

Amyitapur!
Having passed beyond the aggregates and elements,
Amyitapur!
Liberated from all the sense fields,
Amyitapur!
Apprehend the two extremes. . . .
[Amyitapur!]
[May you take birth in that pure land!]

This is a likely reference to the five aggregates (*phung-po lnga;* Skt. *skandhas*) that comprise the physical and mental constituents of a sentient being, and their corresponding elements (*khams*). If read in an exclusive way, it could suggest that the poem was recited by a ritual specialist to someone who has passed beyond the five aggregates of physical form, sensation, conception, formation, and consciousnesses, and the corresponding elements of earth, water, fire, and so on. During the process of death, after the dissolution of the aggregates and elements follows the disintegration of the analogous sense fields (*skye-mched*), i.e., the senses of sight, hearing, smell, and so forth.

Part II

Pure Land Texts in Tibetan Contexts

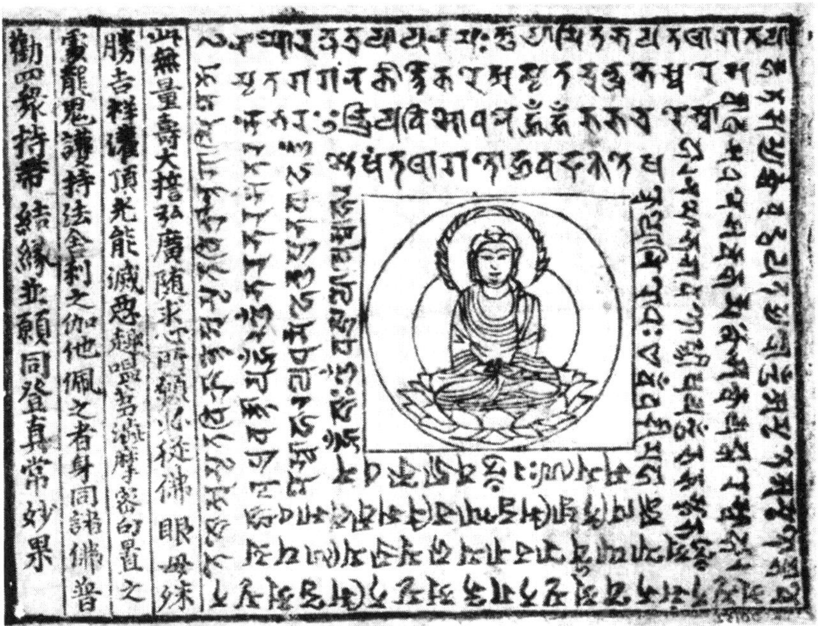

Woodblock print of Amitābha, seated within a square of Sanskrit text (*dhāraṇī*). Chinese inscription on the left, Kizil, cave 17, ca. tenth century CE. Printed in ink on paper. Courtesy of British Museum.

Chapter Three

The Dharma That Goes against the Ways of the World: The Short *Sukhāvatīvyūha-sūtra* with an English Translation from Tibetan

Editions of the *Sukhāvatīvyūha-sūtra* in the Kanjur

The Tibetan canonical collections of Buddhist scriptures are a colossal accumulation of nearly 4,500 texts. These works occupy a vital position in the religious literature of Tibet and Buddhist literature in Tibetan translation, and also include a small number of original works authored by Tibetans. The Tibetan Tripiṭaka is divided into the Kanjur (bKa'-'gyur; lit., "translation of the word"), which comprises teachings said to have been propagated by Buddha Śākyamuni (Skt. *buddhavacana*), and the Tanjur (bsTan-'gyur; lit., "translations of commentaries"), which features commentarial literature on Buddhist sutras and tantras and scriptures on rituals, hymns, and technical compositions on grammar, poetry, logic, medicine, astrology, divination, and so forth.

The most influential collection of *buddhavacana* in Tibetan was compiled at Narthang Monastery in the region of gTsang in the fourteenth century.[1] The production of a handwritten Kanjur was an enormous enterprise, which would not have been possible without the resources and expertise of mChims 'Jam-dpal-dbyangs, who served as the chaplain to Buyantu-qan (1311–1320) and used his position at the Yuan court to solicit substantial donations. It necessitated the collection of Buddhist manuscripts from many monasteries across Tibet, and the expertise of religious specialists who had to ascertain the authenticity of the texts and supervise their distribution in the Vinaya (*'Dul-ba*), Sutra (*mDo*), and Tantra (*rGyud*) sections that commonly comprise the Kanjur.[2] The making of the first Narthang collection was an impressive endeavor, as Eimer (1988, 66) explains:

> A learned monk needs about five months in order to copy one volume of the Kanjur. The task of revising the manuscript copy takes an additional month. Here one has to bear in mind the fact that full set of the early version of the

> Kanjur consists of 111 volumes. Therefore, a great number of well-trained monks were assembled at Narthang monastery. All these scribes needed housing, food and assistance, not to mention paper and ink; and they were not only engaged in copying the Kanjur, but they were also busy preparing exemplars of the Tanjur with its more than 200 volumes.

The Narthang handwritten collection is no longer available and the earliest complete and accessible version of the Tibetan Kanjur dates to the seventeenth century.[3] While a prototype can be traced to the fourteenth-century Narthang compilation, there is no consensus among experts on whether this collection, which was never printed, is the sole basis for two well-established transmission lines of the Kanjur. The first transmission line is known as the Tshal-pa, named after Tshal-gung-thang Monastery in dBus, where an edition of the Kanjur that included the old tantras (*rnying-rgyud*) was produced between 1347 and 1351. The second line is the Them-spangs-ma, which is based on a collection compiled in 1431 in the region of rGyal-rtse at dPal-'khor-chos-sde Monastery and is in agreement with the *Collected Works* of Bu-ston that excludes the old tantras.[4]

The history of the transmission of the Buddhist Kanjurs is a very complex enterprise, given their overlapping lines of descent and the reciprocal influence they exerted on each other.[5] Several Kanjurs exhibit notable contamination from both the Tshal-pa and Them-spangs-ma lines, like the collections from sDe-dge (1733) and sNar-thang (1730–1732). Moreover, a growing number of independent or local Kanjurs discovered in Tibet and its Himalayan borders do not exactly fit a twofold lineage schema, nor can they be traced to the old sNar-thang prototype.[6] Local Kanjurs often contain unique recensions and translations of individual texts that may go back to lines of textual transmission that predate the mainstream canons.[7]

In Appendix I, a critical analysis of the Orgyan-gling gold MS of the short *Sukhāvatīvyūha-sūtra* (*bDe-mdo*) relies on eight Kanjurs, including two less-studied regional collections, the Phug-brag and the handwritten Orgyan-gling. The eight Kanjurs are briefly introduced below with their sigla.[8]

1. The Orgyan Gold-MS Kanjur (Og)

The exact date of the Orgyan gold-MS has not been established. Based on its faded physical form and ancient orthographical features—the frequent use of *myi, myed, stsogs,* and reverse *gi-gu*—it appears older than the Orgyan handwritten copy of 1699–1700. Most of our knowledge of the Orgyan Kanjurs is indebted to Jampa Samten's study.[9] The gold-MS was selected as the root text for the critical comparison because it arguably comes from a relatively older and more complete collection of the two (see Appendix I).

The Orgyan Kanjurs (Og = gold and O = handwritten) were discovered in rTa-dbang (pron. Tawang) at dGa'-ldan rnam-rgyal lha-rtse Monastery in present-day Arunachal Pradesh. The dGa'-ldan rnam-rgyal, most commonly known as rTa-dbang Monastery, was established by the Fifth Dalai Lama, Blo-bzang rgya-mtsho (1617–1682), to serve as a religious and administrative center for the dGe-lugs school in the area of Mon-yul before his passing away in 1680 or 1681.[10] His incarnation, Tshangs-dbyangs rgya-mtsho (1683–1706), the Sixth Dalai Lama, was discovered in the rTa-dbang region.

According to the *Religious History of the Mon* (*Mon chos-'byung*), said to have been originally composed in the Tibetan fire-male-dragon year (896–897) by Ngag-dbang phun-tshogs and the king (*rgyal-po*), there were cultural and political contacts between Tibet and the country of the Mon (Mon-yul) that date to the times of the Tibetan empire. The region of Mon-yul includes parts of north Arunachal Pradesh and Bhutan that were ruled by the descendants of Lha-sras gtsang-ma, the son of Emperor Khri lDe-srong-btsan, who was banished from Central Tibet to rTa-dbang by Emperor Glang dar-ma.[11]

Neeru Nanda, who served as an Additional Deputy Commissioner in rTa-dbang from 1974–1977, offers an eyewitness account of the Orgyan Kanjurs at the time:

> The gompa [monastery] is built like a huge fortress on a high hill with a very commanding and impregnable location. . . . The main image of the gompa is of the seated Buddha, an immensely tall and imposing figure at least 15 feet high. . . . In the library, upstairs in the middle cluster of building, the scriptures are kept. These are printed on handmade paper which is locally manufactured from the bark of the *sugu* tree (*daphne botanica*) and preserved in excellent condition—long, oblong bundles tied in cloth of faded red and yellow silk. The books are merely show-pieces now, since the gompa has no scholar worth the name who can study and translate them. The main showpiece of the library is a book written in letters of gold. Two pages have been displayed in glass cases and are beautiful, each page decorated with a drawing of a god or goddess, also done in gold and studded with minute jewels, with the scriptures written in the dull glow of ancient gold dust.[12]

The Central Institute of Higher Tibetan Studies (CIHTS) in Sarnath, India, has microfiche copies of both the gold and handwritten rTa-dbang Kanjurs. The gold Kanjur (*gser-chos*) contains eighty-six volumes of varying size written on thick, black-coated paper in alternating lines of gold and silver. Its index (*dkar-chag*) has not been found. The stock register at the monastery at rTa-dbang records a total of ninety-four volumes, eighty-nine in good condition and five that are damaged.

The comparison of the Og *bDe-mdo* edition with the other seven Kanjurs yielded thirty-six independent readings, including several repetitions. It shares no significant readings with any of the Kanjurs consulted, and displays no discernable preference for siding either with the Tshal-pa or the Them-spangs-ma lines.[13] The Og DKG appears to be an independent witness.

2. The Orgyan Handwritten MS Kanjur (O)

This Orgyan Kanjur was commissioned in 1699 by the Fifth Dalai Lama's regent, sDe-srid Sangs-rgyas-mtsho, and was completed before the eighth day of the sixth month of 1700. It is beautifully handwritten on thick paper in black ink by skillful scribes from central Tibet and contains sixty volumes inclusive of the old tantras (*rnying-rgyud*). For reasons discussed in his article, Samten (1994, 394–395) suggests that O may have been a copy of Og. However, the present study yields fifty-four singular readings and only two in which it agrees independently with the Og. It is clear that the Orgyan handwritten edition of the sutra is not a direct copy of the Og. There are four readings where it sides independently with L, but it generally displays no clear preference for siding either with the Tshal-pa or the Them-spangs-ma lines. The O and F editions share nine independent readings with each other. This may be significant, since the O and F Kanjurs share three variant translations and two texts not found in any other Kanjur, while displaying a clear sectarian influence over the Tantra section.[14]

3. The Peking Qian-long Edition (K)

The Peking Qianlong xylograph was sponsored by Emperor Qianlong (1735–1796) during the Manchu Qing dynasty. This Kanjur dates to 1737 and is available in the Otani reprint edition.[15] The Peking line of canons starts with the 1410 Yongle edition, followed by a number of other reprints, i.e., the Berlin manuscript (1680), the Kangxi (1684–1692), and the Qian-long (1717–1720) xylographs. All known Tshal-pa descendants belong to Kanjurs published in Peking under the sponsorship of Chinese emperors, or to those collections produced on the basis of the 'Phying-ba stag-rtse MS, namely, the Jang-sa-tham (Li-thang) (1609–1614) and Co-ne xylographs (1721–1731).[16] The K *bDe-mdo* edition yielded five independent readings that are scribal misspellings (nos. 116, 176, 395) and variant transliterations of Sanskrit words (nos. 24, 34).

4. The Derge Kanjur (D)

The Derge canon dates to 1733 and it is highly acclaimed among Kanjurs for its accuracy and consistency.[17] Its contents and structure generally follow the Tshal-pa tradition, and like the Co-ne collection it is mainly based on the 'Jang-sa-tham woodblock edition. Its editors also adopted readings from the Them-spangs-ma line through the lHo-rdzong manuscript.[18] The Derge edition occupies a unique position because its editor, Si-tu Gtsug-lag chos-kyi-snang-ba, followed the Them-spangs-ma arrangement for the *rGyud* section, sporadically inserting additional texts.[19]

As with other Peking editions, like the Co-ne, Berlin MS, Li-thang, Urga, Yongle, and so on, the Derge edition belongs to the Tshal-pa line.[20] It yielded eight independent variants, most of which are alternative transliterations of Sanskrit terms.

5. The Lhasa Kanjur (H)

The Lhasa xylograph is a modern edition of the canon dated to 1934. Along with the Urga Kanjur (1908–1910) it belongs to a later progeny of Kanjurs of mixed descent.[21] Its testimony may be ignored for text-critical purposes, since its variants are clearly derived from the N and D Kanjurs, or from independent rules of spelling, punctuation, and grammar. As anticipated by Harrison (1992), the Lhasa *bDe-mdo* sometimes follows D and other times N, with a slight preference for N on five different occasions.

6. The Narthang Kanjur (N)

The Narthang xylograph dates to 1730–1732 and should not to be confused with the old Narthang Kanjur discussed earlier. It represents a most unusual case of mixed parentage in that different volumes or sequential texts follow either the Tshal-pa line or the Them-spangs-ma editions scrupulously.[22] It yielded eight independent readings, most of which are variant transliterations of Sanskrit terms. In its shared variants, it follows closely after the Tshal-pa (K) instead of the Them-spangs-ma (L) line; this is evident in the distribution of *shad.*

7. The Phudrag MS Kanjur (F)

The Phudrag MS Kanjur is a local, cumulative collection compiled between 1697 and 1705 at Phug-brag (sPu-brag) Monastery in Ladakh, India.[23] It does not seem to share direct links with either the Them-spangs-ma or the Tshal-pa Kanjurs. A close study of the *Heart Sutra* suggests that it cannot be attached to the stemma at any given place.[24] A critical analysis of the F *bDe-mdo* yields ninety-three independent readings, many of which are scribal corruptions. It agrees more or less with L, as it does with Kanjurs of the Tshal-pa group and those of mixed descent (D, N, and H), supporting the findings of text-critical scholarship that argues for its unique and independent status.

8. London MS Kanjur (L)

The London manuscript (dated ca. 1712) is the fourth copy of the Shel-dkar MS, and along with the sTog Palace Kanjur, Ulaan Bataar, Thang-po-che, and Tokyo Kanjurs, it descends from the same Them-spangs-ma source.[25] It is located at the British Library (Or. 6724). The London *bDe-mdo* sides with the Them-spangs-ma line yielding thirty-six independent readings.

Contents and Divisions of the Sutra

The short *Sukhāvatīvyūha-sūtra* is a typical Mahayana text noted for its brevity and elegance, and it is recited in many Buddhist temples in Asia and the West even today.[26] It came to the attention of Western readers in 1880 when Müller's authoritative edition of the Sanskrit manuscript was published by the Royal Asiatic Society in London and later reprinted in the appendix of the 1883 Oxford edition of the long *Sukhāvatīvyūha-sūtra.*[27]

The Tibetan edition of the following English translation agrees, for the most part, with Müller's edition of the Sanskrit text. However, the Tibetan and Sanskrit versions diverge from each other in important ways, suggesting that the Indian scholar Dānaśīla and the Tibetan translator Ye-shes-sde consulted a Sanskrit version of the short *Sukhāvatīvyūha* that differs from the one published by Müller. This is not altogether surprising. When writing was employed to transmit Indian sutras, this did not necessarily mean that a text was definitively fixed in one single, original redaction with only scribal or aural variants supervening in the course of its transmission. By the ninth century, the Indo-Tibetan scholar-translator teams may have had to collate or read among several Sanskrit versions of the short *Sukhāvatīvyūha,* which were in circulation in India, Nepal, and Central Asia, before finalizing what became the present edition of the *bDe-mdo.*[28]

The *bDe-mdo* starts with a formula common to many works of the genre. Following a list of its title in Sanskrit and Tibetan, the sutra offers homage to the buddhas and bodhisattvas (I–II), a short preamble on the location of the sermon (III), and an enumeration of members in the audience (IV–V). The rest of the text frames Sukhāvatī as a desirable spiritual destination that reads like a travelogue to another world. The narrative furnishes further details on the location (VI), description (VIII), and definition (VII) of the Pure Land, the names of its presiding sovereign (IX), the large community of its inhabitants (X), and the benefits for taking birth there (XI).

A substantial section (XII–XXIII) of the work is devoted to the validation of Pure Land beliefs. This segment of the sutra represents, in fact, its mission statement, drawing from the Mahayana lore of immeasurable buddhas. Many buddhas drawn from all directions of the universe are invoked by name to provide testimony of Amitābha's buddha field. They are summoned as supreme authorities (expert witnesses, in a legal sense) to authenticate the doctrines presented in the text.[29]

The *bDe-mdo* reads very much like a monologue, with the Elder Śāriputra (Pāli. Sāriputta Thera) fixed as a silent interlocutor in the background of Śākyamuni's sermon. Section XX stands out for introducing (once, and only in the Tibetan version) Śāriputra's response to the narrative. His reply enunciates an affirmation in praise of Śākyamuni's teachings that could have been given by any convinced reader or hearer of the sutra.

The text is a well-structured narrative composed by those learned in Mahayana soteriology and argumentation. Its reference to a multitude of deities reflects an early stage in the development of Mahayana, when the cult of Amitābha was part of a larger system of beliefs that featured many buddhas and buddha fields. Buddha Akṣobhya is mentioned by name in the text, and it is likely that this buddha and his pure land were already known to the audience.

References to *śrāvakas* (disciples of early Buddhism) are not unprecedented in Mahayana literature. However, in what seems to be either a proselytizing Mahayana gesture or yet another strategy to legitimize the text, *śrāvakas* oddly enough are mentioned as residents of Sukhāvatī (X) and, together with a welcoming congregation of bodhisattvas, they gather to accompany the dying to the Pure Land (XI).

The English translation includes headings and sectional divisions (I–XXIV), which are not found in the Tibetan text but are included below to provide structure to the narrative and its contents.

Contents

VIII. Perfectly Adorned with the Qualities of a Buddha Field
IX. The Buddhas Immeasurable Life and Immeasurable Light
X. The Countless Inhabitants of Sukhāvatī
XI. Dedication of Virtue for Birth in Sukhāvatī

Celestial Testimonies
XII. Testimonies of the Buddhas of the East
XIII. Testimonies of the Buddhas of the South
XIV. Testimonies of the Buddhas of the West
XV. Testimonies of the Buddhas of the North
XVI. Testimonies of the Buddhas of the Zenith
XVII. Testimonies of the Buddhas of the Nadir

The Authenticity of the Sutra and Its Benefits
XVIII. The "Dharma Embraced by all Buddhas"
XIX. Enlightenment in Sukhāvatī
XX. The Inconceivable Qualities of the Buddhas
XXI. The Age of Decline and Śāriputra's Response
XXII. The Dharma That "Goes against the Ways of the World"

Statements of Completion
XXIII. The Praise of the Chorus
XXIV. Coda

An Annotated English Translation of the *bDe-mdo*

The English translation of the *bDe-mdo* is based on the Derge edition of the Kanjur. For the most part it follows closely the Tibetan syntax, while there has been a conscious attempt not to compromise the flow of the English narrative. For example, frequent repetitions of the name "Śāriputra," which may have served as a mnemonic device, have been edited from the English translation.

Unless otherwise indicated, Sanskrit names of the buddhas accord with Ducor's (1989, 141–149) edition of the Sanskrit sutra. Names in Tibetan transliteration are given when there is no equivalent Sanskrit name in the bilingual *Mahāvyutpatti* lexicon or in Ducor's edition. Folia numbers to both the Derge and the Orgyan gold-MS are supplied in brackets; the gold-MS is utilized as the root text for the critical analysis of the sutra in Appendix I.[30]

Root Text

D: sDe-dge, *mDo-sde,* vol. Ja, fol. 195b4–200a.2

[ ] clarifications, interpolations, and references not found in the Tibetan text
( ) Sanskrit or Tibetan names and terms

Captions

I. Sanskrit and Tibetan Titles

[D: 195b; Og: 205a1] In Sanskrit: *Ārya-Sukhāvatīvyūha-nāma-mahāyāna-sūtra.* In Tibetan: *'Phags pa bde ba can gyi bkod pa zhes bya ba theg pa chen po'i mdo*

II. Homage

Homage to all the buddhas and bodhisattvas!

The Forum and Audience

III. Cosmological Setting of the Sermon

Thus I have heard, at one time the Awakened [Buddha Śākyamuni][31] was in the city of Śrāvastī, in the garden of Anāthapiṇḍada, the grove of Prince Jeta,[32] with a large assembly of 1,250 monks and elders, and great *śrāvakas* who had attained arhatship.

IV. Enumeration of Elders

Namely, [among those present] were: the Elder Śāriputra, Mahā-Maudgalyāyana, Mahā-Kāśyapa, Mahā-Kātyāyana, Mahā-Kapphiṇa, Mahā-Kauṣṭhilya, Revata, Śuddhipanthaka, Nanda, Ānanda, Rāhula, Gavāṃpati, Bharadvāja, Kālodayin, Vakkula, and Āniruddha, those and many other great *śrāvakas* and bodhisattvas.[33]

V. Enumeration of Bodhisattvas and Other Exalted Participants

[D: 196a; Og: 205a4] [Also present were] the Youthful Mañjuśrī, the bodhisattva-*mahāsattva* Maitreya,[34] the bodhisattva-*mahāsattva* Gandhahastin, the bodhisattva-*mahāsattva* Nityodyukta, and the bodhisattva-*mahāsattva* Anikṣiptadhura. And among them, there were many other bodhisattvas and great beings. There was Indra, the King of Gods,[35] and Brahmā, the Lord of the Sahā world, and countless other gods[36] surrounding the Awakened when he addressed the Elder Śāriputra.[37]

The Travelogue of Sukhāvatī

VI. Millions of World-systems Away

Śāriputra, "Sukhāvatī is located to the west, amid other buddha fields millions of world-systems away.[38] The Tathāgata, Arhat, and Perfectly

Enlightened Buddha Amitāyus resides in this buddha field and transmits the Dharma."

VII. The Land of Bliss

"Now what do you think," Śāriputra, "why is this world-system blissful?" Śāriputra, "this world is called Sukhāvatī because living beings do not experience any physical or mental suffering, but only inexhaustible conditions for [experiencing] bliss. For that reason, this world is called Sukhāvatī."

VIII. Perfectly Adorned with the Qualities of a Buddha Field

Śāriputra, "in every direction this blissful world is decorated and enclosed by seven railings, seven rows of palm trees with nets of bells, spectacular and beautiful to behold."[39] Śāriputra, "this buddha field is enriched with four kinds of precious substances: gold, silver, beryl, and crystal. In this way, Sukhāvatī is perfectly adorned with a spectrum of all the qualities of a buddha field."

[D: 196b; Og: 205b4] Moreover, Śāriputra, "in Sukhāvatī there are pools filled with water endowed with eight qualities, covered with precious lotuses made of seven kinds of precious substances.[40] They are strewn with golden sand and filled up to their banks so that even a raven is able to drink from them. And on the four sides of each of these pools, there are four striking staircases made of gold, silver, beryl, and crystal. Near the pools there are precious trees bearing seven treasured substances—namely, gold, silver, beryl, crystal, red pearl, emerald, and coral.[41] They are shining and beautiful to behold.

Lotus flowers grow in the ponds. There are golden ones of gold color, shining with golden light and gold appearance; blue ones of blue color, shining with blue light and blue appearance; yellow ones of yellow color, shining with yellow light and yellow appearance; red ones of red color, shining with red light and red appearance; white ones of white color, shining with white light and white appearance; multicolored ones of different colors, shining with variegated light and multicolored appearance." Śāriputra, "these lotuses grow the size of chariot wheels! In this way Sukhāvatī is perfectly adorned with a spectrum of all the qualities of a buddha field."

"Moreover, Śāriputra, in the world of Sukhāvatī the soil is of pleasing golden color, and celestial sounds from heavenly musical instruments continuously resound." Śāriputra, "in this way Sukhāvatī is perfectly adorned with a spectrum of all the qualities of a buddha field."

[D: 197a; Og: 206a3] "Furthermore, in that buddha field a shower of celestial *mandara* flowers[42] pours down three times a day and three times a night. Those who are born there travel every morning to other buddha fields to pay worship to hundred-thousand-myriad buddhas. And having showered each Tathāgata with hundred-thousand-myriad flowers, they return to their world to spend the rest of the day." Śāriputra, "in this way Sukhāvatī is perfectly adorned with a spectrum of all the qualities of a buddha field."

"In the world of Sukhāvatī there are swans, cranes,[43] and peacocks. They gather three times a day and three times a night and each one sings in its own voice, expounding on the [five] faculties, the [five] powers, and the [seven] limbs of awakening.[44] Whoever is born here hears their songs and turns his mind toward the Buddha, Dharma, and Sangha."[45]

Śāriputra, "what do you think? Do you really believe that these birds are animals? And why is it that you should not hold this view? It is because in this buddha field, the designations hell-being, animal birth, and realm of death (*preta*) do not exist.[46] The flock of birds is an emanation of the Tathāgata Amitāyus expressing the language of Dharma." Śāriputra, "in this way Sukhāvatī is perfectly adorned with a spectrum of all the qualities of a buddha field."

Furthermore, Śāriputra, "in this buddha field one hears a delightful language from the wind that stirs the palm trees and nets of bells. It is as if a musician is playing a celestial instrument composed of infinite musical parts. When humans hear it, a recollection of the Buddha (*buddhānusmṛti*), Dharma, and Sangha pervades their bodies. Śāriputra, "in this way Sukhāvatī is perfectly adorned with a spectrum of all the qualities of a buddha field."

IX. The Buddhas Immeasurable Life and Immeasurable Light

[D: 197b; Og: 206b2] "What do you think," Śāriputra? "Why is the Tathāgata called Immeasurable Life?" Śāriputra, "the Tathāgata Amitāyus, has a limitless lifespan and for that reason he is called the Tathāgata Immeasurable Life." Śāriputra, "and why is the Tathāgata called Immeasurable Light?" "The reason that the Tathāgata is called Immeasurable Light is because his light pervades, without any hindrance, all buddha fields."

Ten eons have passed since the Awakened, Tathāgata Amitābha, attained unsurpassable, perfect, and complete enlightenment."

X. The Countless Inhabitants of Sukhāvatī

Furthermore, Śāriputra, "one cannot venture to count the company of those following the Awakened [Amitābha] who are all pure *śrāvaka*s and arhats." Śāriputra, "those born in this buddha field are non-returners, pure bodhisattvas one lifetime away from enlightenment. The numbers of these bodhisattvas cannot be measured and for this reason they are said to be immeasurable." Śāriputra, "in this way Sukhāvatī is perfectly adorned with a spectrum of all the qualities of a buddha field."

XI. Dedication of Virtue for Birth in Sukhāvatī

"Therefore, Śāriputra, a son or daughter of good lineage should dedicate his or her root virtues with devotion for the sake of taking birth in this buddha field.[47] And why? Having dedicated their virtues they will encounter excellent persons like themselves." Śāriputra, "by inferior root virtue one will not be born in the field of the Tathāgata Amitāyus."

[D: 198a; Og: 207a1] Śāriputra, "the sons or daughters of a good lineage who hear the name of the Tathāgata Amitāyus the Awakened [One], by keeping it in mind without distraction for one, two, three, four, five, six, or seven nights, then at the moment of death, if they do not hold wrong views at that time, they will be greeted by the Tathāgata Amitābha ('Od-dpag-med).[48] They will be surrounded by a gathering of *śrāvakas* and a large number of bodhisattvas on their way to Sukhāvatī, the buddha field of the Tathāgata Amitābha. Therefore, Śāriputra, any sons and daughters of good lineage who have discerned the essential meaning should offer with devotion aspiration prayers to be born in this buddha field."

Celestial Testimonies

XII. Testimonies of the Buddhas of the East

Śāriputra, "just as I, the Tathāgata, say this now, other Awakened Ones, Tathāgatas to the East, namely, the Tathāgata Akṣobhya,[49] Tathāgata Merudhvaja, Tathāgata Meru, Tathāgata Mahāmeru, Tathāgata Mahāmeruprabhāsa, Tathāgata 'Jam-sgra (*Mañjusvara),[50] Tathāgata Mañjugosha, and many more equal to the grains of sand in the waters of the Ganges River in the eastern direction, each one gives expression to the buddha fields.[51] You should have confidence in this teaching, which extols inconceivable qualities and is embraced by all buddhas."

XIII. Testimonies of the Buddhas of the South

[D: 198b; Og: 207b2] "Likewise in the South, there are the Tathāgata Candrasūryapradīpa, Tathāgata Yaśaḥ, Tathāgata Yaśaḥprabha, Tathāgata Ārcisskandha, Tathāgata Merupradīpa, and Tathāgata Anantavīrya. These and other Awakened Ones, equal to the grains of sand in the waters of the Ganges River in the southern direction, each one gives expression to the buddha fields. You should have confidence in this teaching, which extols inconceivable qualities and is embraced by all buddhas."

XIV. Testimonies of the Buddhas of the West

"Likewise in the West, there are the Tathāgata Amitāyus, Tathāgata Amitaskandha, Tathāgata Amitadhvaja, Tathāgata Mahāprabha, Tathāgata'Od-zer-snang-ba (Raśmiprabha), Tathāgata Ratnaketu, and Tathāgata

Śuddharaśmiprabha. These and other Awakened Ones, equal to the grains of the sand in the waters of the Ganges River in the western direction, each one gives expression to the buddha fields. You should have confidence in this teaching, which extols inconceivable qualities and is embraced by all buddhas."

XV. Testimonies of the Buddhas of the North

[D: 199a; Og: 207b8] "Likewise in the North, there are the Tathāgata Mahārciskandha, Tathāgata Thams-cad-sgrol-ba-dbyangs (Vaiśvānaranirghoṣa), Tathāgata Duṣpradharṣa, Tathāgata Ādityasaṃbhava, Tathāgata Jalinīprabhā, and Tathāgata'Od-kyi-'byung-gnas (Prabhākara). These and other Awakened Ones, equal to the grains of sand in the waters of the Ganges River in the northern direction, each one gives expression to the buddha fields. You should have confidence in this teaching, which extols inconceivable qualities and is embraced by all buddhas."

XVI. Testimonies of the Buddhas of the Nadir

"In the same manner, in the nadir there are the Tathāgata Siṃha, Tathāgata Yaśaḥ,[52] Tathāgata Yaśaprabhasa,[53] Tathāgata Dharma, Tathāgata Dharmadhara, the Tathāgata Dharmadhvaja. These and other Awakened Ones, equal to the grains of sand in the waters of the Ganges River in the nadir, each one gives expression to the buddha fields. You should have confidence in this teaching, which extols inconceivable qualities and is embraced by all buddhas."

XVII. Testimonies of the Buddhas of the Zenith

[D: 199b; Og: 208a8] "Likewise, in the zenith there are the Tathāgata called Brahmaghoṣa, the Tathāgata Nakṣatrarāja, Tathāgata Gandhottama, Tathāgata Gandhaprabhāsa, Tathāgata Spos-kyi-phung-po (*Gandhaskandha), Tathāgata Ratnakusumasaṃpuṣpitagātra, Tathāgata Śālendrarāja, Tathāgata Ratnotpalaśrī, Tathāgata Sarvārthadarśa, and Tathāgata Sumerukalpa. These and other Awakened Ones in the zenith, equal to the grains of sand in the waters of the Ganges River in the zenith, each one gives expression to the buddha fields. You should have confidence in this teaching, which extols inconceivable qualities and is embraced by all buddhas."

The Authenticity and Benefits of the Sutra

XVIII. The "Dharma Embraced by All Buddhas"

Śāriputra, "what do you think? Why is this teaching called 'embraced by all buddhas?' Śāriputra, any sons and daughters of a good lineage who hear, have heard, and will hear this Dharma and the names of those Awakened [Ones] will be embraced by all buddhas."

XIX. Enlightenment in Sukhāvatī

Śāriputra, "whoever prays, has prayed, or will pray to the world of Sukhāvatī, the buddha field of the blessed Tathāgata Amitābha, has not and will never fall short of attaining unsurpassable and perfect enlightenment."[54]

XX. The Inconceivable Qualities of the Buddhas

Śāriputra, "just as I now extol the inconceivable qualities of these blessed buddhas, in the same way, Śāriputra, these blessed buddhas profess my own qualities, which are just as inconceivable."

XXI The Age of Decline and Śāriputra's Response

To this Śāriputra responded, "it is extraordinary that during the age of decline and increasing afflictions, of degenerate beings and views, when the lifespan of humans has decreased, that the blessed Śākyamuni, the King of Śākyas, obtained unsurpassable and perfect enlightenment in this Sahā world and taught the Dharma that goes against the ways of the world."

XXII. The Dharma That "Goes against the Ways of the World"

[D: 200a; Og: 208b6] The Awakened [One] said, "Śāriputra, during the five degenerations of this Sahā world I succeeded in the most difficult of tasks—that of attaining unsurpassable and perfect enlightenment and teaching the Dharma that goes against the ways of the world."

Statements of Completion

XXIII. The Praise of the Chorus

Having completed his sermon, *āyuṣmāt* Śāriputra, the great *śrāvaka*s, bodhisattvas, gods, humans, *asura*s and *gandharva*s, and all the inhabitants of the world were delighted with and praised what was uttered by the Awakened [One].

XXIV. Coda

The *Ārya-Sukhāvatīvyūha-nāma-mahāyāna-sūtra* is complete.[55]

Chapter Four

Tibetan Pure Land Commentaries

Birth in Sukhāvatī and Its Four Causes

In the Tibetan commentarial tradition, the long and short *Sukhāvatīvyūha* sutras are invoked as authoritative texts for elaborating on Pure Land doctrines. This especially true when it comes to Dharmākara's nineteenth vow in the long *Sukhāvatīvyūha-sūtra,* which is frequently cited for visualizing and formalizing the causes for birth in Sukhāvatī. The relevant passage reads:

> Awakened One, may I not awaken to full, complete, and perfectly manifest enlightenment, if when I attain enlightenment whichever living being hears my name, directs his mind for the purpose of birth in the buddha field and in countless other buddha fields, totally dedicates his roots of virtues, and ten [times] generates [this] thought, is born in these buddha fields—except for those sentient beings who commit heinous crimes and who have become obscured by the defilement of abandoning the excellent Dharma.[1]

The nineteenth vow is linked to another passage from the long sutra that encapsulates four causes for birth in Sukhāvatī. Unanimously quoted in Tibetan commentarial literature, this short excerpt features Śākyamuni's instructions to his pupil Ānanda.

> O Ānanda, any sentient being who recollects the Tathāgata and his aspects, generates immeasurable roots of virtue, fosters the mind of enlightenment, completely dedicates [his merits for that cause], and prays to be born in the Land [of Bliss], when the time of death nears he will face the Tathagāta, Arhat, Perfectly Enlightened Amitābha, surrounded by a gathering of monks.[2]

As we will see, for many Tibetan scholars there are four causes to secure birth in Sukhāvatī, but their opinions about the most important cause among these often diverge. They concur that prayers of aspiration to take birth in Amitābha's field are only one of four causes. The other three include: 1) recollection of Buddha Amitābha and his enlightened qualities (Skt.

buddhānusmṛti), which may entail visualization of the enlightened aspects of his Pure Land; 2) accumulation of virtue (and merit); and 3) dedication of merit with a Mahayana aspiration.

The recitation of the *Seven Limb Prayer,* which is part of the *King of Prayers* (*Bhadracaryā-praṇidhāna-rāja*), encapsulates the proper way of dedicating merit and thus fulfilling one of the causes of birth.[3]

> May whatever little virtue I have gained
> From prostrating, offering, confessing,
> Rejoicing, requesting, and beseeching,
> Be dedicated so that all [beings] attain perfect enlightenment.[4]

The *Bhadracaryā-praṇidhāna-rāja,* also known as *Samantabhadra's Prayer,* is favored by Tibetan Pure Land commentators for including two seminal references to Buddha Amitābha. The first citation is a prayer to be born in Sukhāvatī from a lotus and receive directly from Buddha Amitābha a prophetic prediction (*lung bstan-pa;* Skt. *vyākaraṇa*) of future awakening. The second passage recommends that the merit accrued from the recitation of the prayer be dedicated to all sentient beings caught in samsara so that they may safely reach Amitābha's Pure Land.

> In that excellent and joyful *maṇḍala* of the Conqueror (Buddha),
> May I be born from a splendid and truly beautiful lotus,
> Where I will directly perceive Buddha Amitābha, who will foretell my own enlightenment.
> And after receiving his prediction, with countless emanations and with mental fortitude, may I benefit numerous beings in all directions.[5]

> By the boundless and excellent merit gained through the dedication of the "Aspiration to Noble Deeds" [*King of Prayers*], may countless migrating beings, who are sinking in the torrents of suffering, reach the supreme domain of Amitābha.[6]

Tibetan commentators drew their inspiration, though not exclusively, from the long *Sukhāvatīvyūha* and the *King of Prayers,* and like their Indian Buddhist predecessors, they understood Pure Land theory and praxis to be co-extensive with the soteriological goals of Mahayana Buddhism. Karma chags-med and Glag-bla bsod-nams chos'-grub utilized the "four causes" as a platform for discoursing on the entire Mahayana path in a *lam-rim* (gradual) fashion with detailed instructions on how to integrate Pure Land contemplation in daily Buddhist practice. In their seminal commentarial works they strike a remarkable balance between faith, devotion, and reason in the efficacy of Amitābha's salvific vows and the benefits of his Pure Land.

The Tibetan Genre of Pure Land Literature

Tibetan religious literature is quite varied and there are many genres to reflect the internal diversity and dynamic cohesion among philosophical and ritual texts often subsumed in larger Buddhist cycles and collections of teachings. Strictly speaking, Pure Land eulogies claim a unique place in Tibetan Buddhist literature and form a genre known as the *bde-smon* (pron. de-mön), an abbreviation of *bde-ba-can gyi smon-lam,* meaning aspirational prayers (*smon-lam*) to Sukhāvatī (*bde-ba-can*).

In line with the Tibetan tradition, the *bde-smon* genre is broadly defined, as a particular class of religious compositions that articulate the intention and aspiration (and often the methods) to realize Sukhāvatī.[7] Works of this genre often conclude with a dedication of merit directed toward birth in the Pure Land. These features are incorporated in most Pure Land commentaries (*'grel-ba*) and in a variety of Vajrayana texts of a Pure Land orientation that will be discussed in Chapters Five and Six. In fact, the term *bde-smon* is utilized in titles of tantric texts, as in sTag-sham nus-ldan rdo-rje's *sādhana, A Sukhāvatī Prayer* (*bDe ba can gyi smon lam*) (DM 1, 155–158), originally composed by Padmasambhava's consort, Lady mKhar-chen. Many Pure Land Mahayana commentaries are noted for their synthesis of contemplative practices and ethical principles, and they traditionally serve as preliminary training to more advanced Vajrayana methods to realize Sukhāvatī in one lifetime. There exist many independent, yet mutually reinforcing, tantric practices that belong to the Tibetan genre of Pure Land literature and draw authority and inspiration from both sutras and tantras.

We can get a good sense of a wide variety of *bde-smon* texts in the *Anthology of Aspirational Prayers* (*bDe smon phyogs bsgrigs;* hereafter *Anthology*), published in China in 1994 in two volumes. This collection is by no means exhaustive of the variety or volume of Pure Land–oriented texts scattered in Tibet's vast religious literature. It is revealing, nevertheless, in drawing attention to prominent literary trends among affiliates of the rNying-ma and bKa'-brgyud schools.[8]

The first volume of the *Anthology* features fifty-four Pure Land compositions by Tibetan authors, some of which do not strictly belong to one particular Tibetan Buddhist school. Roughly speaking, there are twenty-six Pure Land authors affiliated with the rNying-ma, ten with the bKa'-brgyud, three with the Sa-skya, two with the dGe-lugs-pa, and two with the Jo-nang-pa school.[9] In the first volume we also find a spurious text attributed to the Indian master Nāgārjuna, as discussed at the end of Chapter

One. The second volume of the *Anthology* contains a selection of Pure Land commentaries. Three are authored by rNying-ma scholars, Glag-bla bsod-nams chos-'grub (1862–1944), Mi-pham 'jam-dbyangs rnam-rgyal (1846–1912), and dPal-sprul o-rgyan chos-kyi-dbang-po (1808–1887), and one by Tsong-kha-pa (1357–1419), the founder of the dGe-lugs school.

The *Anthology* also includes passages from Indian Mahayana texts. The following list is suggestive of Indian scriptures that contributed to the interpretation and development of the Tibetan genre of Pure Land literature: 1) the long and short *Sukhāvatīvyūha* sutras (DM 1, 3–117; 117–131); 2) the *Amitābhadhāraṇīmantra* (DM 1, 131–132); 3) Sukhāvatī prayers from the *Sound of the Celestial Drum* (*'Chi med rnga sgra;* DM 1, 134); 4) the *King of Dedications* (*Yongs su bsngo ba'i rgyal po;* DM 1, 136); 5) instructions from the *Jewel Heap Sutra* (*Ratnakūṭa;* DM 1, 137); and 6) the *King of Prayers* (DM 1, 150).

Eulogies of the dGe-lugs-pa School

The religious and political history of Tibet has been inextricably linked with the formation and consolidation of its monastic institutions, which are traditionally divided into the Old School of the rNying-ma, and the New (gSar-ma) Schools of the dGe-lugs-pa, the bKa'-brgyud, the Sa-skya, and the bKa'-gdams. In contrast to the claims of imperial antiquity put forth by the Old School, the New Schools trace the lineages of their scriptures and teachings to the translation of Indian tantras (*gsang-sngags gsar-ma*) dating from the eleventh century onward. These comprise texts that were translated by or after Smṛtijñānakīrti in the East, and by or subsequent to Lo-chen rin-chen bzang-po (985–1051) in the West.[10] Sectarian differences between the schools of Tibetan Buddhism have surfaced over the centuries, notably in polemical literature (*dgag-lan*), yet never to the extent of causing a schism between monastic traditions that share many Buddhist scriptures while distinguished on the basis of their traditional affiliations to individual lineages of teachers and tutelary divinities.[11]

The dGe-lugs-pa, the School of the Virtuous (*dge-ba*), traces its foundation to Tsong-kha-pa (1357–1419) and his immediate disciples. This school is also known as the New Kadampa (bKa'-gdams gsar), because of its self-perception as a revival movement of the original bKa'-gdams tradition.[12] From the fifteenth century onward and not long after its formation, this school came to dominate the political and religious life of Tibet. The spiritual and secular leader of Tibet, the Fifth Dalai Lama, recognized Paṇ-chen blo-bzang chos-rgyan (1567–1662), his foremost dGe-lugs teacher and seat-holder of bKra-shis lhun-po Monastery in gTsang, as an incarnation of Buddha Amitābha. This incarnation-line of the Lord of the Lotus Family (Amitābha) rapidly became one of the most powerful lineages in the dGe-lugs-pa school, second only to the Dalai Lama's own incarnation-line of the celestial bodhisattva Avalokiteśvara, the patron deity of the Tibetan state.[13]

In the following sections we will review representative works of the *bDe-smon* genre authored by Tsong-kha-pa, the Paṇchen Lama, and lCang-skya dbang blo-bzang chos-ldan, three towering monastic figures of the dGe-lugs-pa school. Drawing from hagiographical sources, we will introduce these authors in the Tibetan traditional manner before surveying their contributions to Tibetan Pure Land tenets and practices.

Tsong-kha-pa blo-bzang grags-pa (1357–1419)

Tsong-kha-pa was born in the sixth sexagenarian cycle (*rab-byung*) of the fire-bird year in the Tsong-kha region of Amdo, in Eastern Tibet.[14] He was inclined toward monasticism from an early age, taking Buddhist vows (*upāsaka*) from the Fourth Karmapa Rol-pa'i-rdo-rje (1340–1383) when he was three. Four years later he received novice ordination vows from Chos-rje don-grub rin-chen-pa, who gave him the Buddhist name Blo-bzang grags-pa. He studied medicine and exerted himself diligently in the study of Buddhist philosophy and in the Vajrayana root texts and commentaries with at least fifty-five different teachers, mostly of the bKa'-gdams, Sa-skya, and bKa'-brgyud schools.

By the age of thirty-three, Tsong-kha-pa was an established scholar, engaging vigorously in scholastic debates and composing many works on Buddhism. His prolific output in his *Collected Works* comprises about nine volumes devoted to Vajrayana, and nine on Mādhyamika, Vinaya, Prajñāpāramitā, Vajrayana rituals, epistles, and lecture notes collected by his disciples. Among his renowned books are the *Great Treatise on the Stages of the Path to Enlightenment* (*Lam rim chen mo*) inspired by Atiśa's *Bodhipatha-pradīpa* (*Byang chub lam gyi sgron ma*) and the *Essential Explanation of Intentional and Definitive Meaning* (*Drang nges legs bshad snying po*), a later work focusing on the debate about definitive (Skt. *nītārtha*) versus intentional (Skt. *neyārtha*) meaning in Buddhist scriptures. He is also the author of several influential tantric commentaries on prominent Anuttarayoga Tantras such as the *Guhyasamāja-tantra* and the *Cakrasaṃvara-tantra*, and his *Great Treatise on the Stages of the Secret Mantra* (*sNgags rim chen mo*) is still consulted as a major compendium of the stages of Vajrayana.[15]

In 1408–1409, at the age of fifty-two or fifty-three, with the patronage of Grags-pa rgyal-mtshan and his minister Ne'u nam-mkha' bzang-po, Tsong-kha-pa inaugurated the Great Prayer Festival (*smon-lam chen-mo*) at the Jo-khang temple in Lhasa. The festival, lasting for three weeks, was held annually thereafter the first day of the first month of the Tibetan New Year.[16] A shorter version of his long prayer to Sukhāvatī was recited annually at the Great Prayer Festival in Lhasa.[17]

Not long after the inauguration of the Great Prayer Festival, Tsong-kha-pa's students, concerned about their master's health, requested that he cease traveling and founded dGa'-ldan Monastery for that purpose. A good number of his disciples became prominent dGe-lugs-pa hierarchs and scholars on their own right. Notable among them are 'Jam-dbyangs chos-rje bkra-shis dpal-ldan (1379–1449), who founded 'Bras-spungs (Drepung) Monastery in 1416; and Byams-chen chos-rje shakya ye-shes (1354–1435), who founded Se-ra Monastery in 1419. Following his death, rGyud shes-rab seng-ge (1383–1445) established the rGyud-smad Lower Tantric College in 1433, and rGyal-ba dge'-dun-grub (1391–1474), who was posthumously named the First Dalai Lama, inaugurated bKra-shis lhun-po Monastery in 1447.

Tsong-kha-pa had many mystical visions during his life, especially of the bodhisattva Mañjuśrī, of whom he was considered an emanation.[18] In a mystical encounter, Mañjuśrī is said to have handed him an extraordinary aspiration prayer to Sukhāvatī, which Tsong-kha-pa wrote down in 1395 at the rDzing-phyi Temple.[19] This work, titled *Prayer for Birth in Sukhāvatī: Opening the Door to the Sublime Field,* exerted great influence in the *bde-smon* genre and was held in high esteem by the dGe-lugs masters dPal-'byor lhun-grub (1561–1637) and Blo-bzang rta-mgrin (1867–1937), who composed commentaries on it.[20] Scholars of other Buddhist schools also studied Tsong-kha-pa's eulogy, including the rNying-ma scholar dPal-sprul o-rgyan 'jigs-med chos-kyi-dbang-po (1808–1887), who authored a short commentary to the prayer.[21] Tucci remarks that Tibetan Pure Land literature is broken up into different trends; the most important, or at least the one most extensively followed, is that of the dGe-lugs school that through the *Lotsāba* Ba-ri and the Sa-skya Paṇḍita "finds an outlet in Tsoṅ k'a pa's treatise . . . which codifies by developing the theories of the Sukhāvatīvyūha" (1949, 365).

Tsong-kha-pa's short *Prayer to Sukhāvatī,* which was recited annually in the Great Prayer Festival, is divided into sixteen distinct Mahayana petitions, according to Kajihama (1991, 298–299):

1. To be born in Sukhāvatī
2. To receive Mahayana teachings

3. To accomplish the activities of bodhisattvas
4. To lead all beings to the Pure Path
5. To attain enlightenment
6. To attain a healthy body and remember past lives
7. To be formally ordained and become like Bhikṣu Akṣobhya[22]
8. To receive the excellent *dhāraṇi* and acquire confidence
9. To accomplish various kinds of concentration
10. To attain different kinds of wisdom and their perfection
11. To become like Avalokiteśvara
12. To become like Vajrapāṇi
13. To become like Śākyamuni
14. To become like the Sugata, King of Medicine (Medicine Buddha)
15. To become like Amitāyus
16. To be accepted with proper rituals as a disciple of a spiritual master.

Tsong-kha-pa's *Collected Works* include other minor Pure Land compositions.[23] His *Praise to the Protector Amitābha: Opening the Door to the Sublime Field* is an emotive eulogy written in aureate language that expresses deep devotion, faith, and gratitude in Amitābha's redeeming qualities and celebrates the realization of the Buddha's path.

Praise to the Protector Amitābha: Opening the Door to the Sublime Field

Homage to Śrī Gu-ru Mañjughoṣā!
Sukhāvatī is praised by all the Sugatas!

Victorious King and Protector, Instructor of Gods and Humans, Powerful Conqueror of the Pure Land (*rnam-dag zhing*) Amitāyus, spare living beings from death!

In this world, there is a multiform infinity of appearances, which are like the reflection of the moon, unhindered by clouds, in clear water. [Likewise,] your body manifests countless apparitions for many fortunate beings.

The perfect meaning of your steady words uncovers the "eyes of intellect" and cuts instantly through a web of doubts—countless are those fortunate to be converted! Your mind and signs of accomplishment are unwavering. The power of your wisdom and compassion offers protection and appeases our fears of cyclic existence.

Across the five states of existence, infinite wisdom relies on compassion and radiates into everything worth knowing.

Like the sun on the path of the gods (*lha-yi-lam*), your boundless brilliance [illuminates] infinite lands and provides a feast for the eyes of this fortunate one!

Like the enchanting cooing in the heart of a peacock that imparts supreme bliss (*bde-ba'i mchog*) when it is merely heard, your celestial voice possesses five aspects and sprays nectar to the [attentive] ear.

Like a group of clouds dissolving in the sky's expanse, the knower enters into the sphere of emptiness.

The mind of enlightenment overpowers all appearances and quells the phenomena of this world. It dissolves all discursive points of reference [upheld by] the mind. Just as one cannot locate the end of the teachings of the Victorious Ones (buddhas) across infinite time, the amassing of your virtues goes beyond my explanations. You are a treasure of inexhaustible qualities devoid of the slightest seed of error. There is no teacher equal to you. Protector (Amitābha), you are the sole refuge of beings, for even the word "suffering" is not heard in your exalted land because of your immeasurable aspirations.

When the appearances of this life begin to fade, may I behold your form and, soothed by your voice, be born in the middle of a flower, free of obstructions, in the womb of a thousand-petaled lotus. And having received from you, Protector, the instructions of the Excellent Vehicle (Mahayana), may I practice the same activities as Avalokiteśvara and Mahāsthāmaprāpta and liberate those sinking in the mud of cyclic existence.

Colophon: The so-called *Praise to the Protector Amitābha: Opening the Door to the Excellent Pure Lands* was composed by the learned vagrant Blo-bzang grags-pa at the snow mountains of 'O-de gung-rgyal's Lhasa and Zhol (greater Lhasa).[24]

Paṇchen Blo-bzang chos-kyi-rgyal-mtshan (1567–1662)

The First Paṇchen Lama, Blo-bzang chos-kyi-rgyal-mtshan, was born in the fire-mouse year of the tenth sexagenarian cycle in Lhan at the border of gTsang-rong.[25] From a very young age he showed exceptional ability to recite and memorize religious scriptures. He ordained under the name Blo-bzang chos-rgyan by mKhas-grub sangs-rgyas ye-shes (1590 or 1591), and by the age of twenty-two he was fully ordained by Paṇchen dam-chos yar-'phel as a Buddhist monk.

He excelled in debate and displayed mastery over many traditional Buddhist subjects. In 1601, he ascended to the spiritual throne of bKra-shis lhun-po Monastery and was invited to the monastery of 'Bras-spungs to ordain the young Fourth Dalai Lama, Yon-tan rgya-mtsho (1589–1617), serving thereafter as his main teacher.

Blo-bzang chos-kyi-rgyal-mtshan showed impartiality toward other Buddhist schools. He traveled across Tibet several times, but he especially liked to visit the southern regions, where he granted many teachings and initiations. At the age of forty-eight he became the throne holder of Se-ra and 'Bras-spungs Monasteries, presiding for many years over the Great Prayer Festival in Lhasa. His extraordinary accomplishments, however, are not limited to the realm of religion. When the Mongolian forces invaded Byang-rgyab, he was called to mediate and gained the trust of the Mongol aristocracy. At the age of seventy-five he undertook the construction of dBen-dgon Temple, which he completed in seven months, depositing a golden Kanjur in its premises.[26] Before passing away at the advanced age of ninety-five, he left behind five volumes of writings and many learned disciples.

The First Paṇchen Lama is the author of the *Swift and Unobstructed Path to Sukhāvatī.* The work demonstrates a masterful synthesis of sutra and tantra perspectives on Sukhāvatī.[27] It shares tantric visualizations of Amitābha found in Sakya Paṇḍita's well-known *Meditation on Amitābha* and in Tsong-kha-pa's *Prayer for Birth in Sukhāvatī: Opening the Door to the Sublime Field.* The Paṇchen Lama utilizes the same quotations from the OKG used by Tsong-kha-pa in his lengthy aspirational prayer. In the colophon to the *Swift and Unobstructed Path to Sukhāvatī,* he acknowledges that his work was based on the instructions (*man-ngag*) of Jetāri (rDze-tā-ri) and Bla-ma rdo-rje gdan-pa.

The *Swift and Unobstructed Path to Sukhāvatī* stands out as a classic representative of the genre, full of lucid examples and marked by erudition. It lays out contemplative instructions and contains clarifications on subtle points not found in other Pure Land works of its kind.

It prescribes cultivating mindfulness of Buddha Amitābha and his Pure Land by using a *thang-ka* or a statue of Amitābha, together with whatever one has to offer, and visualizing his place as the actual abode of Sukhāvatī (fol. 733). In the absence of an image of the Buddha, one may envision one's root guru possessing the same essence as the Protector Amitābha. In all cases, the Pure Land aspirant should not nourish a self-serving mind that neglects others but earnestly work for all beings, being skillful in all methods and not remaining ignorant of the ways to bring benefit to others (fol. 737). In the Pure Land he will be able to guide many beings residing in impure lands (*ma-dag zhing*) through his emanations (*sprul-pa*) (fol. 736). Furthermore, he should methodically train to infuse all daily activities with a Pure Land orientation—i.e., when sitting, he should envisage being in the presence of the Teacher in Sukhāvatī; when walking, anticipating that he heads toward the feet of Buddha Amitābha. In short, one should generate oneself as Amitābha during all daily activities and at all times (fol. 738).

In this work, Blo-bzang chos-kyi-rgyal-mtshan draws from the traditional discourse of the four causes, which he reframes as the four powers required to take birth in Sukhāvatī—namely, 1) the power of root virtues accumulated by "three doors" (mind, speech, and body), 2) the power of all good actions performed by ordinary and *ārya* beings in the three times (past, present, and future), 3) the power of the truth in Amitābha's unchangeable vows, and 4) the inconceivable power in the totality of all *dharmas*, the immaculate *dharmadātu* (*chos kyi dbyings*) (fol. 735). For Blo-bzang chos-kyi-rgyal-mtshan, relying on these four powers will ensure that soon after the arising of the appearances of the intermediate state (*bar-do*) the devotee will be accompanied by eight victorious sons (*rgyal-sras brgyad*) to Sukhāvatī.

The Swift and Unobstructed Path to Sukhāvatī

Outline of Contents

1. Salutation to Guru Mañjughoṣā and homage to Buddha Amitābha
2. Statement of intention
3. The stages of practice for those aspiring to be born in Sukhāvatī
    - 3.1. Relying on continuous mindfulness
        - 3.1.1. Visualization of Buddha Amitābha and his retinue
        - 3.1.2. Accumulation of root virtues
        - 3.1.3. Generation of *bodhi*-mind
        - 3.1.4. Dedication of root virtues and aspiration prayer
    - 3.2. Applying the teachings
        - 3.2.1. Meditation in this life
            - 3.2.1.1. Meditation on Amitābha during all activities and at all times
            - 3.2.1.2. Dream-yoga meditation on Amitābha
                - 3.2.1.2.1. Visualization of the white mantra syllable in one's heart
                - 3.2.1.2.2. Tantric visualization of Amitābha utilizing breathing
                - 3.2.1.2.3. Self-generation into Amitābha
                - 3.2.1.2.4. Clear-light meditation
                - 3.2.1.2.5. Waking-up meditation
                - 3.2.1.2.6. Contemplating inseparability with Amitābha at all times

3.2.2. Meditation when death omens occur
 3.2.2.1. Developing no attachment toward one's body, wealth, friends, relatives, and so on
 3.2.2.2. Accumulating merit and purifying past infractions
 3.2.2.3. Recovering broken vows and pledges
 3.2.2.4. Generating joy
 3.2.2.5. Going for refuge and generating *bodhi*-mind
 3.2.2.6. Practicing guru-yoga meditation
 3.2.2.7. Praying in earnest to be born in Sukhāvatī
 3.2.2.8. Offering ritual cakes to the *ḍākiṇīs* and the Dharma Protectors
 3.2.2.9. Applying ritual substances to the crown of one's head
 3.2.2.10. Practicing tantric visualizations in isolation
4. Concluding verses
5. Lineage of the teachings
6. Publisher's colophon

lCang-skya ngag-dbang blo-bzang chos-ldan (1642–1714)

Hagiographers recount that the First lCang-skya was born on the tenth day of the eleventh month in the water-horse year of the eleventh sexagenarian cycle in Yi-dge rta-phyug village near Tsong-kha.[28] As a child he was recognized by Tshul-khrims rgya-mtsho, the abbot of Ring-bo Monastery, and by Paṇchen blo-bzang chos-rgyan as the reincarnation of Grags-pa 'od-zer, who had died in 1641.[29] At the age of twenty he took ordination vows from the Fifth Dalai Lama and received the name Blo-bzang chos-ldan. He studied at 'Bras-spungs Monastery for eight years with the *ācārya* Ngag-dbang blo-gros rgya-mtsho and continued to train with several dGe-lugs-pa masters, studying the works of Tsong-kha-pa and the Paṇchen Lamas. He graduated as a Geshe with the highest distinction, Larampa (*dge-bshes lha-rams-pa*), and attained great fame as the head of the abbey of dGon-lung in 1688.

At the age of forty-six lCang-skya accompanied Ngag-dbang blo-gros rgya-mtsho to Beijing and had two meetings with the Chinese emperor, who bestowed gifts upon him and sought his spiritual counsel.[30] He was reinvited to China to serve as the emperor's religious guide, granting him empowerments and instructions in the *Guhyasamāja, Cakrasaṃvara,* and *Bhairava Tantras.* In 1697, he was sent to Central Tibet with a golden letter from the emperor for the enthronement of the Sixth Dalai Lama. He traveled to

Mongolia and propagated the teachings of the dGe-lugs school. In 1711, with the emperor's support, he founded Pā-dur-jin Monastery in Beijing.

lCang-skya's legacy combined political astuteness and charisma conjoined with a large scholarly production. Two of his works are dedicated to Sukhāvatī: *The Lamp That Illuminates the Quick Path to Sukhāvatī* and *Opening the Door to the Sublime Fields: A Collection of Stages to Visualization,* which was written when he was residing in Beijing.[31]

As noted by Kajihama (2002b), these works largely lack originality. They are a collage of lengthy passages taken verbatim from the First Paṇchen Lama's *Swift and Unobstructed Path to Sukhāvatī* and Tsong-kha-pa's *Prayer for Birth in Sukhāvatī: Opening the Door to the Sublime Field,* stitched together with passages from the OKG also quoted by Tsong-kha-pa in his *Prayer for Birth in Sukhāvatī.* The manner of their composition suggests that they were composed in haste, perhaps at the request of some prominent patrons.

The bKa'-brgyud Yogis of Sukhāvatī

According to traditional Tibetan sources, Mar-pa chos-kyi-blo-gros (1012–1099) was a formidable translator of Indian Buddhist texts and the founder of the bKa'-brgyud school.[32] He was born in Southern Tibet and studied Sanskrit under 'Brog-mi lo-tsā-ba (992–1072) at the hermitage of dPal myu-gu-lung.[33] Having mastered Sanskrit, he went to Nepal and India, where he trained for many years with several Vajrayana masters—most notable among them Nāropa, with whom he studied the Hevajra cycle and received instruction in the tantras and the hidden precepts of the *Sampannakrama;* and Maitrīpa, who transmitted to him the precepts of Mahāmudrā.[34]

On his return to Tibet Mar-pa took many disciples, the most famous being the yogi Mi-la ras-pa (1052–1135), a striking religious figure whose life exemplifies the trials and accomplishments of the Tibetan *siddha* tradition. During the time of the illustrious Buddhist scholar and physician sGam-po-pa (1079–1153), the school established a monastic foundation known as the Dwags-po bKa'-brgyud, which branched out in four main lineages: the Tshal-pa bKa'-brgyud, the Karma bKa'-brgyud, the 'Ba'-rom bKa'-brgyud, and the Phag-mo gru-pa, with eight smaller branches.[35]

The cult of Sukhāvatī was especially popular with the bKa'-brgyud masters, beginning with sKyob-pa 'jig-rten mgon-po rin-chen-dpal (1143–1217), a famous disciple of Phag-mo gru-pa and the founder and abbot (1179–1217) of 'Bri-gung-mthil byang-chub-gling Monastery. His aspirational prayer to Sukhāvatī is imbued with fervent devotion and longing.[36]

Another bKa'-brgyud devotee and promoter of Pure Land was the renowned Pad-ma dkar-po (1527–1592), a scholar and systematizer of the Drug-pa bKa'-brgyud lineage and founder of gSang-sngags chos-gling Monastery in Byar-po.[37] He authored two aspiration prayers, a short work titled *Sukhāvatī Prayer from the Twenty-fourth Chapter* and a longer *Sukhāvatī Prayer* composed at Lo-gro rong-ljon that draws from the OKG.[38] Pad-ma dkar-po's longer *Sukhāvatī Prayer* served as a model for Karma chags-med's celebrated *Aspiration Prayer,* and it remains a core text for obligatory memorization by monks within their respective schools.[39]

Other notable bKa'-brgyud supporters of Pure Land include the Sixth Zhwa-dmar-pa Chos-kyi-dbang-phyug (1584–1630), teacher of Karma chags-med and author of a Pure Land eulogy (*bDe smon;* DM 1, 213–214);[40] the ninth Si-tu Padma nyin-byed dbang-po (1774–1853), author of a short prayer (*bDe smon;* DM 1, 253–253); and 'Jam-dbyangs mkhyen-brtse 'od-zer (1896–1945), who composed the *Excellent Path of Sukhāvatī: Guru Yoga Based on Amitābha* (*sNang ba mtha' yas la brten pa'i bla ma'i rnal 'byor bde chen lam bzang;* DM 1, 253–258). There have also been bKa'-brgyud hierarchs who took interest in Pure Land practices, such as the Fifth Karmapa De-bzhin gshegs-pa (1384–1415), who composed a *Prayer for Birth in Sukhāvatī* (*bDe ba can du bgrod pa'i smon lam;* DM 1, 192–197) at mDo-smad, and the Fourteenth Karmapa Theg-mchog rdo-rje (1798–1868), who authored *Prayers of the Mahāsukhā Kṣetra Sādhana,* included in the celestial Treasure cycle (discussed in Chapter Six).

By and large, the most important champion of Sukhāvatī in the bKa'-brgyud school and all of Eastern Tibet is Karma chags-med, one of the greatest Buddhist scholars and renaissance figures of the seventeenth century.

Karma chags-med (1613–1678)

Karma chags-med (alias Rā-ga a-sya)[41] was born in Zal-mo-gang, a small village near Ri-bo-che in the district of Ngoms. His father, Padma dbang-grags, was a reputable Vajrayana teacher from the ruling lineage of gDong mkha'-spyod. By the age of six Karma chags-med was trained by his father in reading and writing. He studied white and black astrology (*rtsis-dkar-nag*), geomancy, and magic ceremonies for the purpose of averting misfortunes, and received the entire cycle of rNying-ma teachings from his father. He continued his training with the most famous rNying-ma and bKa'-brgyud masters of his time and received ordination at age twenty from the Sixth Sharmapa, Chos-kyi-dbang-phyug (1584–1630), at mTshur-phu Monastery.

Having completed many meditation retreats, at the age of thirty-seven Karma chags-med embarked on strict isolation for thirteen years, during which time he composed many works reported to have been blessed by visions of deities and other miraculous occurrences. His fame as a *mahāsiddha* and learned scholar became widespread. He founded his own school, the gNas-mdo bKa'-brgyud lineage,[42] a branch of the Kaṁtshang or Karma bKa'-brgyud-pa that upholds the bKa'-brgyud and the rNying-ma rDzogs-chen teachings.

His devotion served as an inspiring example for Buddhists throughout Tibet. One account relates that before the statue of Jowo Rinpoche in Lhasa he offered the fingers of his left hand as a butter lamp and took the bodhisattva vows before the sacred statue. Another incident details how he extended one of his fingers as a burning lamp in front of the relics of his root teacher, the Sixth Sharmapa, humbly requesting to realize the teachings of Mahāmudrā.

Karma chags-med had numerous disciples.[43] Among his most notable students was gNam-chos mi-'gyur rdo-rje, whom he recognized as an incarnation and redactor of the celestial doctrines (*gnam-chos*). He also ordained Kun-bzang shes-rab (1636-1698), who later became the throne-holder of dPal-yul Monastery.[44] Karma chags-med was a prolific writer whose mastery of Buddhist philosophy and rituals extended beyond the range of traditional subjects. He often delved into ethnographic research and many of his works deal with the lives of the people of Khams and their popular beliefs and superstitions.[45] In his *Collected Works* it is said that while residing at his hermitage at gNas-mdo he composed sixty volumes of texts on a variety of subjects, including retreat manuals (*ri-chos*), *mdos* rituals, *nāga* (*klu*) rites from Bhutan, rituals for the invocation of the Lion-faced *ḍākiṇī* (Seng-gdong-ma), *sādhana* and ritual offerings to protective deities in the lHa-thog principality of Khams, divination, and so on.[46]

His works illustrate a scholastic and experiential understanding of Buddhism and of a fusion between the rNying-ma and bKa'-brgyud lineages. The most popular among his works is *Buddha in the Palm of Our Hand: Instructions on Dzogchen* (*rDzogs chen gyi khrid sangs rgyas lag 'chang*), which features a blend of Mi-'gyur rdo-rje and Ratna gling-pa Treasure teachings. The synthesis of sutra and tantra is the subject of the author's magnum opus, *Avalokiteśvara's Practical Instructions for Accomplishing the Union of Mahāmudrā and Dzogchen* (*Thugs rje chen po'i dmar khrid phyag rdzogs zung 'jung thos ba don ldan*).[47]

Karma chags-med was passionate about Pure Land practice and was the greatest systematizer of Pure Land ritual literature the Tibetan tradition has ever known. In his hagiographies it was prophesized that his teachings will lead one hundred million sentient beings to Amitābha's Pure Land. Elsewhere we read how he reportedly led his mother, dBon Bla-ma chos-dbang kun-bzang, and his caretakers to Sukhāvatī. In an anecdotal reference, he is reported to have said, "May this old monk Chagme eat shit if his mother doesn't end up in Sukhāvatī."[48]

At the age of sixty-five he had a vision of Buddha Amitābha, who was displeased with him for having taken so long to join him. Karma chags-med understood this to mean that he would soon depart for Sukhāvatī. Soon after this incident, he fell ill but continued, with whatever little strength he had, to grant teachings to his disciples. In the earth-horse year, before wondrous signs, he departed, condensing the heart-drop of his mind in Amitābha's luminous expanse.

Karma chags-med authored many seminal works of the Pure Land genre including eulogies, commentaries, and ritual cycles combining practices and perspectives from the sutra and Vajrayana traditions. In Chapter Six, we will examine some tantric works included in the celestial Treasure cycle revealed by his heart-disciple, gNam-chos mi-'gyur rdo-rje.

Indisputably, his *Aspirational Prayer for the Pure Land Sukhāvatī* is the most widely recited prayer in Tibet and among Tibetan Buddhists in exile. It is rehearsed every year during the bKa'-brgyud Prayer Festival in Bodh Gaya, India. Its beginning is known to many:

> *Emaho!*
> Toward the west from this world,
> Beyond scores of countless worlds,
> In the glorious sphere slightly raised,
> Is the pure realm of the Sukhāvatī.
> Although invisible to my dimmed sight,
> The path to it shines like blazing fire,
> Within the sphere of the self-radiant mind.[49]

Passages from the *Aspiration Prayer for the Pure Land Sukhāvatī* are also incorporated in some of his other works, such as the one he composed for Lama Chos-dbang kun-bsang (DM 1, 232–235). His notable contributions to Tibetan Pure Land literature feature an elaborate commentary, *The Lotus Garland: Commentary to the Aspirational Prayer* (*bDe smon 'grel ba padma'i phreng ba*).[50] This work is faithful to the *bDe-smon* genre and is structured along four causes of birth in Sukhāvatī: 1) recollecting the outer aspects of the Pure Land (*zhing-bkod yid dran-pa*), 2) performing virtuous deeds by reciting the *Seven Limb Prayer* (*tshogs-bsag yan-lag bdun*), 3) generating the mind of supreme enlightenment (*byang-chub mchog tu sems-bskyed*), and 4) performing dedications and aspiration prayers to be born in Sukhāvatī (*bde-ba-can du skye phyir bsngo-ba dang smon-lam 'debs*). The *Lotus Garland* has formed the basis for several Tibetan Pure Land commentaries, including one authored by Glag-bla bsod-nams chos-'grub that is worthy of closer examination.[51]

Glag-bla bsod-nams chos-'grub (1862–1944)

Glag-bla bsod-nam chos-'grup, a native of Nyag-rong in Khams, became an active and influential rNying-ma scholar. He was ordained as a novice in the dGe-lugs tradition by Geshe Blo-bzang tshul-khrims, but in 1883 he left his homeland for the renowned Śrī Siṃha College at Dzogs-chen monastery. There he rose to the rank of Master of Scriptures (*mkhan-po*), refusing a formal appointment at the college. He preferred to continue with his studies and traveled in many districts of Eastern Tibet.[52]

Glag-bla bsod-nam became particularly renowned for his discourses on the *Bodhicaryāvatāra* and the *Guhyagarbha Tantra,* as well as for his pith instructions on the practice of rDzogs-chen. In sDe-dge, he promulgated teachings of the *bDe-smon* genre, and during his life he composed a few works on Pure Land. The most important among these is a landmark commentary on Tibetan Pure Land Buddhism. His opus is a lengthy response to Chags-med's *Aspiration Prayer for the Pure Land Sukhāvatī,* titled *Illuminating the Path of Liberation.*[53] As we can see from an outline of his work below, Glag-bla bsod-nam's comprehensive treatise is divided along the four causes for birth in Sukhāvatī, and includes the Vajrayana preliminary practices of prostration, offerings, and purification. Its structure, divisions, and contents rely heavily on Karma chags-med's Pure Land commentary, *The Lotus Garland: Commentary to the Prayer.* It represents the last lengthy commentary of its kind that integrates the paths of Mahayana and Vajrayana with the Pure Land tradition.

Illuminating the Path of Liberation: Explanatory Commentary on Karma chags-med's Aspiration Prayer for the Pure Land Sukhāvatī

Outline of Text

Offering verses and pledge to undertake this work [1–2]

[The main body of the text explained]

I. First Division: The branches for explaining the doctrine [3]

1. Instructions on how to listen to the Buddhist teachings [3–6]

1.1. The sublime resolve that unites root virtues with skillful means [6–9]

1.2. The main practice of virtue that cannot be lost by [negative] circumstances and [is sustained through] sublime nonconceptual [understanding] [10–20]

1.3. The excellent result of dedicating one's merits to others and increasing virtue [10–22]

II. Second Division: An explanation on the religious objects of hearing [22]

1. Arousing joy from practice [23–24]

2. Commentary on the main part of the Pure Land aspiration [24–25]

3. Explanation on how to enhance understanding of the four causes for birth in Sukhāvatī [25–26]

3.1. First Cause: conceptualizing the field of merit as one's support [26–30]

3.1.1. Meditation on the Pure Land as one's support

3.1.2. Meditation on the Buddha and his retinue as one's support [30]

3.1.2.1. Meditation on the causal characteristics of the Buddha's body [31–33]

3.1.2.2. Meditation on the attributes of the Buddha's mind [34]

3.1.2.3. Meditation on the principal retinue [35–36]

3.1.2.4. Meditation on the other retinue [37–42]

3.2. Second Cause: purifying hindrances to the accumulation of merit [42]

3.2.1. The section on prostrating as a means of overcoming pride [43]

3.2.1.1. Brief explanation [43–44]

3.2.1.2. Expanded explanation [45]

3.2.1.2.1. Meditation on the characteristics of prostration [45–56]

3.2.1.2.2. Apprehending the characteristics of prostration [56–68]

3.2.2. The section on offerings as means of overcoming attachment and miserliness [69]

3.2.2.1. Material offerings [69–70]

3.2.2.2. Mentally produced offerings [71–75]

3.2.2.3. The primordial offering of the practice [75–102]

3.2.3. The branch of confessing faults: the antidote to delusion [102–102]
- 3.2.3.1. Applying the power of confession [103]
  - 3.2.3.1.1. Confessing the faults of committing the ten nonvirtuous actions [103–172]
  - 3.2.3.1.2. Confessing the faults of committing the five offenses that bear grave retribution [173–182]
  - 3.2.3.1.3. Confessing the faults of committing the five offenses that bear immediate retribution [183–190]
  - 3.2.3.1.4. Confessing the faults of abandoning the Dharma [190–195]
  - 3.2.3.1.5. Confessing the faults of depreciating bodhisattvas [195–193]
  - 3.2.3.1.6. Confessing wrong views [203–209]
  - 3.2.3.1.7. Confessing the faults of transgressing vows [209]
  - 3.2.3.1.8. Confessing the faults related to individual emancipation [209–211]
  - 3.2.3.1.9. Confessing the faults related to bodhisattvas [211–213]
  - 3.2.3.1.10. Confessing the transgression of Vajrayana vows [213–215]
  - 3.2.3.1.11. Confessing hidden transgressions that are inherent downfalls [215–221]
  - 3.2.3.1.12. Confessing downfalls which have been recognized [221–223]

3.2.4. The power of disenchantment with further wrongdoing [223–224]
- 3.2.4.1. The power of restoration [224–225]
- 3.2.4.2. The power of support [225–228]

3.2.5. The branch of rejoicing: the antidote to jealousy [228]
- 3.2.5.1. Instructions on the benefits of eliminating jealousy [228–229]
- 3.2.5.2. Rejoicing in contaminated positive mental factors [229–230]
- 3.2.5.3. Rejoicing in the positive aspects of Mahayana [230–231]
- 3.2.5.4. Instructions on the ten virtues, such as protecting life, etc. [231–240]

3.2.6. The branch of requesting the Buddhist teachings: the antidote to renouncing the Dharma [241–242]

3.2.7. The branch of requesting the buddhas not to pass into nirvana; the antidote to wrong views [242–243]
3.2.8. The branch of dedicating merits; the antidote to doubt [243]
3.2.8.1. Dedication of merit for the enlightenment of all sentient beings [243–244]
3.2.8.2. The resolve to establish the benefit of others [245–250]
3.3. Third Cause: Generating the mind of enlightenment [250–252]
3.4. Fourth Cause: The secondary cause of dedicating all root virtues of [one's] pure aspirations, for the purpose of birth in Sukhāvatī for oneself and others [252–252]
3.4.1. The resolve to meet Amitābha at the moment of death [253–257]
3.4.2. The resolve to sever one's desire for samsara; an impediment for taking birth in Sukhāvatī after death [257]
3.4.2.1. Comprehending the proliferation of suffering when causing harm [257–263]
3.4.2.2. A detailed explanation of the suffering of humans and gods [263–273]
3.4.2.3. The ways to reach Sukhāvatī; cutting fixation on attachments [273–274]
3.4.3. The resolve to attain good qualities and break away from samsara [274–279]
3.4.4. The resolve to accomplish the Dharma and meet many buddhas and bodhisattvas in other pure lands [279–280]
3.4.5. The resolve to go to other pure lands [280–282]
3.4.6. The resolve to educate those in impure lands [282–287]
3.4.7. The resolve to meditate on transferring to the Pure Land [288]
3.4.7.1. General explanation [288–289]
3.4.7.2. The good qualities of the earth as pure receptacle [289–289]
3.4.7.3. The good qualities of wood [290–291]
3.4.7.4. The good qualities of lotus and water [291–292].
3.4.7.5. The good qualities of essences [292–297]
3.4.7.6. The resolve to uphold and serve the teachings: meditating on the good qualities of the principal pure realm [297–301]

III. Third Division: Conclusion
1. The benefits of apprehending the characteristics of a buddha [301–309]
2. The accomplishment of aspiration prayers through the blessings of the secret mantra [310–317]

Commentaries from the rNying-ma School

The Tibetan school of the rNying-ma is distinguished from the New Schools in its claim to have inherited the forms of Buddhism introduced to Tibet by the Indian Tantric master Padmasambhava during the reign of the Tibetan emperors—that is, during the earlier spread (*snga-dar*) of Buddhism in the eighth and ninth centuries CE. While rNying-ma lineages claim to date back to the imperial period, they only emerged as a distinct, organized religious school in the eleventh century, when they came under attack by the adherents of the New Schools that questioned the authenticity of their teachings, especially those of the Great Perfection.[54]

The religious literature of the rNying-ma emphasizes a controversial corpus of indigenous scriptures known as Treasure literature, or *gter-ma.* As we will see in Chapter Six, Tibetan Pure Land aspirations are systematically ritualized in several influential rNying-ma Treasure texts. In the following sections we will briefly introduce three Pure Land commentaries composed by notable rNying-ma representatives from Eastern Tibet: dPal-sprul o-rgyan 'jigs-med chos-kyi-dbang-po (1808–1887), Mi-pham 'jam-dbyangs rnam-rgyal (1846–1912), and the Third rDo-grub-chen 'jigs-med bstan-pa'i-nyi-ma (1865–1926).

dPal-sprul o-rgyan 'jigs-med chos-kyi-dbang-po (1808–1887)

dPal-sprul 'jigs-med was recognized by the first rDo-grup-chen 'jigs-med phrin-las 'od-zer (1745–1821) as the reincarnation of dPal-dge bsam-gdan phun-tshogs.[55] He learned reading and writing without difficulty at a very young age while residing at sDe-dge rdza chu-kha. From the founder of dGe-mang Monastery, rGyal-sras gzan-phan mtha'-yas, and other rNying-ma masters, such as rDo-bla 'jigs-med skal-bzang and 'Jigs-med ngo-mtshar, he received instruction on the *Trilogy of Natural Ease* (*Ngal gso skor gsum*), the *Bodhicaryāvatāra,* and the root *Guhyagarbha-tantra* among other Buddhist scriptures and commentaries. He learned the preliminaries (*sngon-'gro'i lam*) of the Klong-chen sNying-thig tradition from 'Jigs-med rgyal-ba'i- myu-gu. Without sectarian prejudice, he mastered many exoteric and esoteric subjects and confined himself for many years in meditation retreats in isolated caves and in monasteries.

At the age of thirty, having attained a profound understanding of the Buddhist doctrines, he began instructing a group of disciples and imparted many teachings on a number of subjects, such as Mādhyamika, Abhidharma, the *Five Treatises of Maitreya*, the *Bodhisattva's Way of Life*, the *Ma ni bka' 'bum*, and the *Yon tan mdzod*, among others. dPal-sprul's fame spread widely across Eastern Tibet, and he is still remembered as a great teacher in the Sa-skya, dGe-lugs-pa, and bKa'-brgyud schools. He continued to compose many influential works until his death in the fire-pig year.

dPal-sprul was known for his nonsectarian orientation (*ris-med*), which is evident in the commentaries he composed on two of the most influential Pure Land prayers ever to be authored in Tibet.[56] His commentaries on the bKa'-brgyud and dGe-lugs prayers of Karma chags-med and Tsong-kha-pa are noted for their brevity and mastery of the *bDe-smon* tradition.

Commentary to Tsong-kha-pa's Prayer

Summary of Text

dPal-sprul's commentary starts with a brief explanation of what is meant by the opening phrase "supreme deeds" (*phul-byung mdzad-pa*) in Tsong-kha-pa's *Aspiration Prayer.* He recounts the story of Buddha Amitābha, who generated the aspiration for enlightenment before the Buddha Lokeśvarāja and accumulated immeasurable merit for the period of two *kalpas*. dPal-sprul comments that one should generate the mind of enlightenment, just as Amitābha had done, motivated by great compassion as explained by Tsong-kha-pa in his stanza on refuge and *bodhicitta.* Each Pure Land aspiration session should contain all four causes required for effecting birth in Sukhāvatī. The first cause is to set one's mind on remembering the field (*zhing*), Sukhāvatī, and the teacher (*ston-pa*), Amitābha. The second cause (*rgyu gnyis-pa*) is to cultivate countless root virtues that can be amassed by reciting the *Seven Limb Prayer.* The third cause is to generate the mind of enlightenment (*bodhicitta*) by exerting great effort, by going for refuge, taking pledges, rejoicing, and meditating as explained in the *Bodhicaryāvatāra.* The fourth cause is to dedicate all of one's root virtues for taking birth in Sukhāvatī. At the end, dPal-sprul recommends abridged sections of the prayer for one to recite.

Mi-pham 'jam-dbyangs rnam-rgyal (1846–1912)

The highly learned and gifted rNying-ma scholar, also known by his family lineage name Ju mi-pham, was born in the fourteenth cycle in the male-fire-horse year in Ya-chu ding-chung, in the district of sDe-dge.[57] The epithet Ju relates to his family having originally descended from a sky-rope (*gnam gyi 'ju-thag*) from the realm of the gods of clear light (*'od-gsal lha yi yul*).

His paternal uncle dPon bla-ma padma dar-rgyas gave him the name Mi-pham rgya-mtsho. At the age of ten he had mastered reading and writing in Tibetan and started composing works of his own. Two years later he was admitted to the rNying-ma monastery of gSang-sngags chos-gling.

His root teacher was the prolific scholar and Treasure discoverer 'Jam-dbyangs mkyen-brtse'i-dbang-po (1820–1892), and he studied at the feet of many masters, including dBang-chen dgyes-rab rdo-rje (1832–?), dPal-sprul 'jigs-med chos-dbang (1808–1887), *dGe-bshes* Ngag-dbang 'byung-gnas (1788–?), the Sa-skya master Blo-gter dbang-po (1847–1914), and gSol-dpon pad-ma, among others. He excelled in all common and uncommon subjects, gaining mastery in the ten sciences and in the oral, Treasure, and Pure Vision (*dag-snang*) lineages of the rNying-ma school. His fame as a great scholar spread throughout dBus, gTsang, and Khams.

When he was seventeen he traveled with nomad camps to mGo-log dressed like them and sharing their simple diet of black tea, roasted barley flour (*rtsam-pa*), and cheese. It is said that he answered carefully any question posed to him, even those about the most mundane aspects of worldly life.

The teacher of many worthy disciples, Mi-pham composed more than a thousand texts. Most of these are in the private possession of those who requested their composition. Xylographs of some of his works were carved in the dPal-spungs and rDzogs-chen monasteries. It is reported that before passing away, he said that he would not return to this impure world but would go to a pure land (*dag-pa'i zhing-khams*) to the north of Śambhala. He died at the age of sixty-seven in the female-water-mouse year of the fifteenth sexagenarian cycle.

The author of many important Buddhist treatises, Mi-pham took great interest in the correct understanding and practice of Sukhāvatī. He composed a lengthy work that is in part philosophical (to the extent that it refutes false views concerning Pure Land doctrines), and in part practice-oriented, insofar as it elucidates the methods to be employed for taking birth in Sukhāvatī.

Training for Sukhāvatī with Luminous Faith: Sun-like Instructions of a Sage was probably followed by a smaller commentary on the four causes (*rgyu-bzhi*), the *bDe ba can du skye ba'i rgyu bzhi'i don ldeb.*[58] The popularity of these texts may have been the reason for composing yet another work on the subject, a practice-oriented summary of the four causes, entitled *bDe ba can du skye ba'i bzhi'i don nyams len* (DM 1, 261–263) at the behest of Lama 'Od-gsal and others.[59] Moreover, two of his students, Zhe-chen rgyal-tshab padma-rnam-rgyal (1871–1926) and Kaḥ-thog si-tu chos-kyi-mtsho (1880–1923 or 1925), continued the tradition by composing Pure Land prayers of their own (DM 1, 267–268; 264–265). Like many scholars before him, Mi-pham quotes several passages from the OKG to enrich his commentary, and does so as a cornerstone to expound on his vast erudition of Buddhist philosophy. His work is an exemplary study of the *bDe-smon* genre that advocates a synthesis between "self-power" (*rang-stobs;* Jpn. *jiriki*) and "other-power" (*dngos-po'i nus-pa,* lit., "power of reality's potency"; Jpn. *tariki*) for the purpose of attaining Amitābha's Pure Land.

Sun-like Instructions of a Sage

Summary of Text

[366] Mi-pham's commentary begins with a salutation to Mañjuśrī and a request from Buddha Amitābha to protect all beings. He recommends offering prayers for birth in Sukhāvatī as an excellent path to nirvana, for it is by the power of Amitābha's aspirations that bodhisattvas take eventual birth there. He enumerates the four causes for birth in Amitābha's Pure Land based on the long *Sukhāvatīvyūha-sūtra:* recollecting Buddha Amitābha, accumulating countless virtues, generating the *bodhi*-mind, and dedicating root virtues toward this goal.

According to the sutra [OKG], those who nourish the four causes will behold Buddha Amitābha and his retinue at the time of their death. Recollecting the Buddha and wishing to take birth in Sukhāvatī are the primary causes to accomplish the aspiration, whereas the collection of root virtues and generation of the mind of enlightenment (*bodhicitta*) are secondary [367]. In brief, faith in Amitābha and a strong aspiration to be born in his Pure Land are essential for taking birth in Sukhāvatī. The sutra says that anyone who remains mindful of the Tathāgata Amitābha and generates the wish for his Pure Land will see him in a dream and go to Sukhāvatī.

[369] Mi-pham quotes from the *Sound of Amitāyus Celestial Drum* (*Tshe dpag med 'chi med rnga sgra*) and emphasizes the importance of having conviction (*yid-ches-pa*) in the Pure Land. "From here to the West lies the Sukhāvatī world-system where the Perfect Buddha, the Tathāgata Amitāyus, presides. Whoever proclaims his name will take birth [in his Pure Land]."

After summarizing the principal causes for birth, he concludes that the manner of acquiring faith in the "structure and inhabitants" of the Pure Land is by recognizing that they are merely emanations of wisdom, and that the prayer to Amitābha should be based on comprehending the superior qualities of the Pure Land [370]. One should generate strong faith and joy upon hearing the qualities of Buddha Amitābha and his field, and abandon having two minds (*yid-gnyis*) (i.e., doubt) about it. Having heard these teachings, one should recognize that faith is the cause for reaching this state. The fruit of Buddhist practice is attained by whoever expresses the aspiration prayer with a yearning that takes all phenomena (*chos-rnams thams-cad*) as its condition (*rkyen*). It is very important to generate faith in this way, for as the Buddha said, "the root of faith lies in all virtuous phenomena."

[371] Mi-pham goes on to discuss in some detail three hindrances that may prevent one from reaching Sukhāvatī that must be cleared away: not understanding, holding wrong views, and dwelling in doubt. Concerning the first, he explains that there are ignorant people coming from a bad lineage who are ignorant and possess no understanding of the qualities of Sukhāvatī and the Teacher (Amitābha), and do not inquire as to their meaning, nor are they interested in understanding what it means to take birth in a buddha field. For this reason, one should receive correct instruction in the qualities of the land [372]. One should listen to the teachings on Sukhāvatī with the Mahayana wish to lead countless sentient beings before the Tathāgata Amitāyus and toward unsurpassable enlightenment.

There is great value in the scriptures, and Mi-pham instructs that one should place great diligence in memorizing, retaining, writing, and meditating on these teachings, and, having perfectly understood them, one should then explain them to others [373]. If after hearing the sermon on Sukhāvatī one cannot generate faith—due to not having previously amassed the accumulations (good karma and merit)—it is as if one holds wrong views like non-Buddhist extremists (*phyi-rol mu-stegs*). The non-Buddhists have not received valid instruction in the Buddha's teachings, and in order to lead them to the perfect meaning of the scriptures they must be tamed gradually by skillful means or reasoning. One should lead nonbelievers to the teachings on the basis of a "threefold scrutiny and examination" (*dpyad-gsum*), pure transmission (*dag-pa'i lung*) of the *Sukhāvatī* sutras, and so on. While certainty arises in the ways of inconceivable wisdom and from prayers to a particular buddha, one should check the validity of the person of the teacher through the path of faultless logic. One must generate conviction in this pure and unmistaken "extremely hidden phenomenon" (*shin-du lkog-gyur*) and "object of valid cognition" (*gzhal-bya*).[60]

Having explained the first two hindrances, Mi-pham notes that there are those who, having heard of the extensive qualities of Sukhāvatī, continue to harbor doubt that ordinary people by merely reciting the name of the Buddha will take birth in his buddha field [374]. For Mipham, this state of doubt falls short of the "great purpose" (*don chen-po*)—namely, enlightenment. Ordinary persons are born in Sukhāvatī by the power of their aspirations and faith. In the *Pramāṇa-vārtikakārikā-śāstra* it says that superior persons (*dam-pa rnams*) should rely on the non-erring instruction concerning the objects of valid cognition that are classified as extremely hidden phenomena. Having the intelligence to acknowledge that pure lands are extremely hidden phenomena, they proceed to engage in the ways of enlightenment. Mi-pham reiterates the story of Dharmākara, who, because of his previous training and activities, fulfilled his bodhisattva prayers and established Sukhāvatī where he now teaches the Dharma. Because of the power of the prayers of this buddha, it is easy to take birth in his land. It is appropriate to recognize that this is in agreement with the great purpose of Buddhism.

[375] Mi-pham quotes verbatim from the OKG the most important passage for all Tibetan Pure Land commentators: the nineteenth vow of Dharmākara, which encapsulates four causes for taking birth in Sukhāvatī.[61] He uses the four-cause theory as a platform to refute yet a different objection, the claim that beings who are not *āryas* (*'phags-pa min-pa*) cannot take birth in Sukhāvatī. He explains that Sukhāvatī is a superior land (*khyad-par 'phags*) because those who are born there possess higher perception (*mngon-par shes-pa*), *samādhi* (*ting-nge-'dzin*), and the power of *dhāraṇī* (*gzungs*). Based on the sutra, if one is willing to accept that beings born in that land must have those qualities ascribed to them, then why should one not accept the same scriptures that expand on the four causes? He concludes this section by saying that these qualities are not based solely on the "ripening force of individual beings" (*sems-can rang-rang gi stobs smin-pa*) but on the power of Amitābha's aspirations (*smon-lam*) and wisdom (*ye-shes*).

[375–376] Mi-pham returns to the contention that merely uttering the Buddha's name and taking birth in his land is "intended for another time" (*dus-gzhan la dgongs-pa*)—that is to say, one must be at the stage of an *ārya* before earning the right to take birth in Sukhāvatī. In response, he states that it is correct to say that in some cases it is not definite that one will be born immediately in the buddha field by merely having uttered the Buddha's name, although it is certain that one will eventually take birth there. At the same time, the scriptures are not mistaken in saying that by the power of faith and so forth some people will transfer immediately to Sukhāvatī. The meaning of the phrase that Sukhāvatī is "intended for another time" can be explained thus: it is the "right time" for birth in the Pure Land if we take into account that a person's karma (*las*), fortune (*skal-ba*), and capacity (*dbang-po'i rim-pa*) are inestimable, like the emanations of the Buddha, which are likewise infinite. According to this apodictic reasoning, it is possible, with the right conditions discussed above, for those who have only heard the name of the Buddha to take immediate birth in his buddha field.

[376] Mi-pham returns to a point that was raised previously. Suppose one was to think that he is able to generate the realization of an *ārya* in his mindstream through meditation and other practices, but having not yet realized that state he is unable to take birth in the land immediately after death. To this Mi-pham responds that there is no doubt that one will transfer to Sukhāvatī if one was to meditate on the *ārya* path in this lifetime and attain its completion. One should not add additional causes to this path, such as hearing the Buddha's name and so on, since birth in the "Pure Land" (*zhing-dag-pa*) is secured [377]. It is stated in the OKG (K 22, 113.3.8) that except for those who have committed heinous crimes or who have abandoned the Dharma, all others will take birth there.

The sutra mentions that those in doubt who have generated some faith after hearing the name of the Buddha will take birth in his land, just as those who have offered prayers to be born there after hearing his name. The way *āryas* take birth in Sukhāvatī is not discussed in the OKG. However, there is no real contradiction between the assertion that through the cause of an ordinary person's prayers he could attain the level of an *ārya* and then take birth in Sukhāvatī, and the sutra's explanation that solely by the power of faith and aspiration one can take birth in the Pure Land. If after hearing Amitābha's name one generates the wish to take birth in Sukhāvatī, due to the power of the Buddha's wisdom and his prayers and by the force of these causes, one will behold an emanation of the Sugata (Amitābha) when one dies. If this objective is held in good faith, with attention, nonforgetfulness, mindfulness, and so forth, due to the power of one's five sense powers, one may be able to generate in a short time the realization of the *ārya* path. Just as a seed planted through a *dhāraṇī* matures quickly, likewise attaining the state of an *ārya* is possible with little effort and in leaps (*thod-rgal*) [377–378].

Those who are divided in their understanding concerning the profound means of the secret Mantrayāna and the subtle qualities of tantric knowledge cannot easily understand the emanations of the Sugata and cannot grasp the greater purpose. Mipham provides examples of such phenomena from the Buddhist scriptures: e.g., a mother and son who at death are born together in the form realm, humans attaining meditative stabilization from the power of suchness during the destruction of an eon, and the attainment of special qualities by buddhas and bodhisattvas who place their hands upon someone's head.

Mi-pham addresses one last contention, that one cannot take birth in Sukhāvatī by offering prayers and so on if one had not previously accumulated a vast amount of merit, since it is explained in the sutra that an infinite collection of merit is the cause for the fulfillment of the prayer. He responds that, generally speaking, accumulating merit is the cause for the fulfillment of the prayer, but the collection of merit differs greatly according to an individual's karma, sense powers, and potential. In any case, if one possesses faith and a strong aspiration, it will be sufficient to be born in that land by the great merit generated in having the conviction and the wish without having to rely upon other causes. Even hearing the names Sukhāvatī and Amitābha is due to a previous accumulation of vast merit [379]. To illustrate this point, Mi-pham quotes from the OKG (K 22, 124.5.6.), where it is said that without previous accumulation of merit one will not hear a teaching like this.

As to the meaning of this instruction, if one inquires into the circumstances of when one heard for the first time the name of the Sugata and so forth—an event that is like a precious treasure and is in itself difficult to obtain—one will come to know with certainty that the cause for this encounter is based on a vast accumulation of merit. The fruit is achieved according to the karma, sense powers, and potential of a person, and therefore by possessing strong faith and aspiration it is not possible to be without good fortune [380]. By generating faith in the leader Amitābha and in Sukhāvatī, one will accumulate extensive merit, for it is said in the OKG (K 22, 119.4.8) that this merit is greater than a land filled with as many jewels as there are particles.

According to the sutra, after hearing the name of the Sugata one will not fall back from the path of bodhi, will possess the power of *dhāraṇī* until enlightenment, will not be born as a woman, will live a pure life raised by a noble family, will attain supreme concentration [381], will rejoice in the activities of the bodhisattvas, encounter root virtues with supreme joy, attain immeasurable qualities, and so on.

For Mi-pham the special qualities of Sukhāvatī are inconceivable and all beings who take birth there will see the Tathāgata sitting in front of the great *bodhi* tree and they will attain the realization and abandonments of an *ārya* without ever retrogressing. Therefore, in order to establish through self-power (*rang-stobs*) the qualities equal to the fortune of this land, it is necessary to have trained previously, for countless eons—whereas those fortunate ones who possess faith and aspiration will be quickly led there through the inconceivable power of Amitābha's previous prayers and wisdom. The fortune of sentient beings and the wisdom of the Buddha are inconceivable phenomena, and thus even a path that is very difficult to practice could be traversed with little difficulty by the power of the mutual interdependence of these two phenomena [382].

The scriptures profess that in these degenerate times, through the path of secret Vajrayana one could obtain the fruition of unity (enlightenment) in one short life. If this is carefully examined, how great and marvelous it is to know that the supreme purpose can be successfully accomplished by the "power of reality's potency" (*dngos-po'i nus-pa*). It is possible to establish this by logical reasoning and attain the great purpose without much difficulty.

For Mi-pham, examining the extensive qualities of Sukhāvatī with faulty reasoning [383] will lead those saturated with foolish nonsense and undeveloped intelligence to misinterpret the meaning of the teachings of the Sugata, without meticulously analyzing the instruction concerning these extremely hidden phenomena. It is important to apply reasoning to the teachings on Sukhāvatī. For even if one has had self-experience (*rang gi nyams*) of these phenomena, if one lacks logical reasoning (*rigs-pa*), he will not come to trust in causality and veer away from the path, and he will develop doubt in the profound methods of the Buddha's wisdom. Mi-pham quotes passages from the OKG (K 22, 124.5.1–124.5.4) to highlight the importance of not entertaining doubt about the wisdom of the Buddha, or disparaging the words of the Tathāgata [384]. Gravely mistaken are those who doubt the unerring instruction, who do not believe that one can be born in Sukhāvatī merely by faith and aspiration, and who entertain that the Sugata's prayer and wisdom have no power. A quote from the OKG (K 22, 124.58) states that those with wrong views will not find faith in the Dharma [385].

Mi-pham reasons that whoever is of a wise disposition and intelligent nature will trust in these words, taking as witness the accumulated wisdom of the victorious buddhas, for this was known and explained by the Buddha himself. Those endowed with fortune to delight in profound topics should know that there are differences in karma, sense power, and capacity among individuals and along the stages of the Buddha's path—all these are indeed incalculable. Therefore, despite major and minor hardships and so forth, in order to accomplish the fruit one should know that the potency of phenomena is unfathomable and unstoppable. He quotes from the OKG (K 22, 118.2.5), where it is said that even if one could approximate the inconceivable means that figure into the composition of karma and its complete ripening, the inconceivable virtues, emanations, and blessings of the Buddha cannot be apprehended or measured by anyone [386]. In other words, it is well established [in the scriptures] that a buddha's objects of cognition are inconceivable. Mi-pham provides examples of Buddhist topics that may be subject to doubt, such as taking birth in Sukhāvatī, the "power of mantras" (*sngags kyi mthus*), and the "potency of perfected substances" (*grub-pa'i rdzas*).

He completes the first section of this work and reiterates that according to the scriptures, birth in Sukhāvatī can be attained by hearing the name of the Tathāgata and generating faith. Moreover, by following the Dharma one gains conviction in the power of the Buddha's reasoning. Those blessed with good fortune are able to generate pure certainty in the inconceivable wisdom, and this is like having eyes as bright as the sun that do not doubt the meaning of the instruction concerning hidden phenomena. By virtue of their immeasurable activities, bodhisattvas attain the state of a buddha. However, those without great wisdom and so on, who find it difficult to put into practice the profound and extensive paths, should know that the best method for accomplishing Samantabhadra's (Kun-tu-bzang-po) deeds is to recite prayers to be born in Sukhāvatī. The reason is [388] that by faith and prayers and through the power of the Buddha's wisdom and aspirations, they can take birth in the Pure Land. Once born there, they will be endowed with faith and so on, and will effortlessly attain the supreme qualities. Without ever straying from the path, they will fully accomplish the deeds of Samantabhadra. It is said in Samandbhadra's prayer, "At the time of my death, having purified all delusions, by directly beholding Amitābha may I swiftly go to the Land of Bliss." It is said that once born there, all prayers without exception are accomplished.

In the second section, Mi-pham turns his attention to instructions for training that he divides into day and night practices. During the day, one should take as "objects of recollection" (*dran-pa'i yul*) the qualities of the Pure Land and its inhabitants as they are described in the sutra. Having done so, one should generate strong faith and have trust in the profound emanations and with pure faith engender longing for Sukhāvatī. By continually visualizing and contemplating the aspects of the buddha field, one should accumulate as much merit as possible and dedicate it with strong determination to obtain in the future birth in Amitābha's Pure Land. Furthermore, on the basis of this instruction one will quickly gather vast merit through the practices of accumulation, purification, and increase, as summarized in the *Seven Limb Prayer*. One should exert diligent effort and recite the name of Amitābha, [389] recite his *dhāraṇī*, and, while offering supplication prayers, invoke his exalted mind. During the night as one is about to go to sleep, without losing mindfulness one should generate a strong desire to see the Sugata and abide in his buddha field.

Concerning day and night practices, one should become familiar with many detailed instructions contained in the Treasures and the teachings of the Old and New Schools. In brief, by reading and understanding the meaning of the scriptures, one is able to take birth in Sukhāvatī and attain the qualities of those born there. One should try to generate faith and dedicate all root virtues for taking birth in the Pure Land continuously day and night.

Mi-pham explains the results of practice based on the capacities of the practitioners. Those of the highest capacity, having seen Amitābha and having received in this life prophetic confirmation of their enlightenment, will attain confidence that they will take birth in Sukhāvatī. Those of middling capacity will receive the blessings of the method, and those of low capacity will dream of aspects of the Teacher and his Pure Land. Even though the signs may not be clear, if one consistently generates faith and nurtures his aspiration, then at the moment of death, by hearing the name of the Buddha, if one so wishes he will undoubtedly take birth in the Pure Land [390].

During the "intermediate state" (*bar-do*) following death, merely remembering the name of the Buddha will become a cause to be born in his buddha field, because the intermediate state is malleable and the power of the Buddha's prayer is very strong. Therefore, it is critical to practice in this life, at the moment of death, and during the intermediate stage. Mi-pham concludes that one should practice diligently and hear and contemplate the teachings with stainless morality, striving with firm faith to accumulate great merit, and meditating in the perfect union (*rdzogs-pa'i rnal-sbyor*). Inspired by the teachings of the precious master who possesses immeasurable kindness, and without any selfish motivation toward his teachings, one should harbor no attachment or aversion toward phenomena and realize that the practice of Sukhāvatī constitutes the immeasurable great purpose.

Mi-pham notes that he exerted effort to compose this text with the motivation that it would bring transcendent virtue to those practitioners who hold subtle hindrances of doubt about the pure lands. He concludes the work by dedicating the virtuous merit to all beings, that they may possess the qualities of sublime faith and be established in the oceanlike wisdom. The colophon [391] to this text informs us that it was composed by Mi-pham in the hermitage of sTag-tshang to repay the kindness of his teacher.

rDo-grub-chen 'jigs-med bstan-pa'i-nyi-ma (1865–1926)

According to his biography, 'Jigs-med bstan-pa'i nyi-ma was the third incarnation of the rDo-grup-chen lineage.[62] He was born at lCags-khung in the Amdo region where the Chinese used to mine iron ore. His family line had a long history of religious affiliation with the rNying-ma school. From childhood he showed great interest in religious subjects and at the age of seven he mastered writing. He studied with O-rgyan 'jigs-med chos-kyid-bang-po and Mi-pham, and received numerous teachings from rNying-ma masters on the subjects of Mahāyoga, Anuyoga, Atiyoga, Phur-ba, the sNying-thig cycle, the bKa'-ma and gTer-ma lineages, as well as Vinaya, Madhyamaka, Logic, and Prajñāpāramitā.

He reports that he went to rDza-stod to receive teachings from O-rgyan 'jigs-med chos-kyi-dbang-po (1808–1887) on Śāntideva's *Bodhicaryāvatāra* but no matter how hard he tried he could not comprehend the meaning of the text and wept in disappointment before going to sleep. One night he was visited in his dreams by mDo mkhyen-brtse 'jigs-med ye-shes rdo-rje, who handed him a scripture. Thereafter, the blessings of the deities caused his wisdom-mind to expand and comprehend all Buddhist teachings.

The third rDo-grup-chen excelled as a great scholar and practitioner, composing many books on several subjects (about ten volumes in all). His extensive and erudite commentary on the long *Sukhāvatīvyūha-sūtra*, entitled *The Bursting Summer Cloud: Instructions for the Field of Bliss—A Eulogy for Increasing the Harvest of Virtue*,[63] is a major contribution to the *bDe-smon* genre. According to the colophon, it was written when he was thirty-seven years of age at the temple of dGe-'phel. A summary of the first three sections of this text with cross-references to the Tibetan long *Sukhāvatīvyūha* and other supporting scriptures have been provided by Kajihama in three separate publications.[64] Following is an outline of the main thematic divisions of this work.

The Bursting Summer Cloud

Outline of Text

Homage and eulogistic verses to Buddha Amitābha [392]

First Section: Fortifying the will to take birth in the Pure Land
1. Generating compassion toward sentient forms [393]
2. Training in the bodhisattva path and relying on Amitābha

3. Performing practices (i.e., prostrations, offerings, and so forth) [394]
4. Supporting conditions for taking birth in the Pure Land (e.g., pleasing one's teacher, meeting noble persons, having bodhisattva friends, and so forth)
5. The disadvantages of impure lands [395]
6. The attributes of Sukhāvatī [395–396]
7. Striving to obtain birth in Sukhāvatī (e.g., pure motivation, dedication, etc.) [397–398]
8. Attaining special powers in Sukhāvatī (e.g., divine seeing, hearing, recollection of past lives, etc.) [398–400]

Second Section: Reducing hindrances that prevent one from taking birth in the Pure Land [400]

1. Scriptural quotations and explanations that non-*āryas* can reach Sukhāvatī [400–404]
2. Clarifying doubts concerning birth in Sukhāvatī
3. The benefits of taking birth in Sukhāvatī according to the sutras [405–406]
4. The beings that have access to the Pure Land [406–407]

Third Section: The causes for taking birth in the Pure Land [407]

1. General explanation on how to obtain the causes of birth [407–408]
    - 1.1. The four causes (e.g., generation of *bodhi*-mind, prayers, visualization, and accumulation of root virtue) [409–411]
    - 1.2. The importance of morality [411–412]
    - 1.3. The consequences of securing the four causes in this lifetime (i.e. seeing Amitābha in a dream accompanied by bodhisattvas at the time of death, etc.)
    - 1.4. The consequences of harboring doubt [413–414]
2. Particular training in faith [415]
    - 2.1. Explanation on how the Pure Land came into existence
        - 2.1.1. Dharmākara's aspiration prayer [415–416]
        - 2.1.2. Dharmākara's bodhisattva activities [417–418]
        - 2.1.3. The result of such actions [418–419]
    - 2.2. Explanation of the benefits of going to the Pure Land
        - 2.2.1. The good qualities of the land (vessel)
            - 2.2.1.1. The earth and the sky [420]
            - 2.2.1.2. The ornaments of foundation and space [420–421]
                - 2.2.1.2.1. Ornaments of the foundation
                    - 2.2.1.2.1.1. Permanent ornaments

A Dream-Yoga to the Pure Land from Sa-skya

Although the Sa-skya (lit., "grey earth") school is traced to the second diffusion of Buddhism in Tibet, it is historically related to the 'Khon clan with roots in the Tibetan empire. Sa-skya Monastery was founded in 1073 by dKon-mchog rgyal-po (1034–1102), who was its throne-holder from 1073 to 1102. The religious order of the Sa-skya was consolidated during Sa-chen Kun-dga' snying-po's (1092–1158) doctrinal reforms and has since been distinguished for its familial succession. Sa-chen kun-dga' and his father, dKon-mchog rgyal-po, who held the abbacy for forty-eight years,[65] saw the need for the rectifications that characterize the Sa-skya collection of Buddhist teachings. These had previously been an amalgamation of diverse traditions—some are said to have been transmitted by Padmasambhava to 'Khon Nāgendrarakṣita (referred to as the 'Khon rNying-ma system), and others, such as the Lamdre (*Lam 'bras;* lit., "path and fruit"), derived from the teachings of the Indian *mahāsiddha* Virūpa and propagated by 'Brog-mi lo-tsā-ba śākya Ye-shes (992–1072).[66]

Heeding the admonition of his master gNam-kha'u-pa, Sa-chen refrained from Buddhist ordination and fathered four sons; two of them, bSod-nam rtse-mo (1142–1182) and Grags-pa rgyal-mtshan (1147–1216), succeeded him as spiritual leaders of the Sa-skya school. His third son, dPal-che 'od-po (1150–1204), became the father of Sakya Paṇḍita kun-dga' rgyal-mtshan (1182–1251), who was to become one of the most famous Sa-skya patriarchs.[67] As we will see, Sakya Paṇḍita was sympathetic to Pure Land practices. According to one biography, he excelled in the study of many Buddhist and secular subjects.[68] These included art, medicine, and Sanskrit grammar, which, along with Logic, Vinaya, Abhidharma, and the sutras, he learned from the Kasmiri *paṇḍita* Śākyaśrī from 1204 to 1214.

Sakya Paṇḍita's scholarly output had a profound effect in the intellectual life of Tibet. His *Treasury of Logic on Valid Cognition* (*Tshad ma rig gter*) and *Discrimination of the Three Vows* (*sDom gsum rab dbye*) are famous to this day and constitute part of the Sa-skya monastic curriculum. Pertinent to our survey of Pure Land literature is Sakya Paṇḍita's short but influential *Meditation on Amitābha,*[69] a dream-yoga meditation (*nyal-bsgom*) on Buddha Amitābha. Drawing from the *Bhadracarīpraṇidhānarāja,* Sakya Paṇḍita's sleep-meditation enumerates visualizations and breathing instructions before going to sleep. This work differs from sutra-based prayers in that it contains tantric meditations conjoined with guru-yoga practices where one trains in the fusion of one's mind with Amitābha.

The *Anthology* contains two Pure Land texts composed by Sa-skya authors. The first, *A Pure Land Eulogy* (DM 1, 204–207), was written by the brilliant scholar Go-rams bsod-nams seng-ge (1428–1489).[70] The second work is a continuation of the "sleep-meditation tradition" composed by the prolific master and founder of rDzong-sar Sa-skya Monastery and College, 'Jam-dbyangs mkhyen-brtse chos-kyi-blo-gros (1896–1959).[71] 'Jam-dbyangs mkhyen-brtse was raised at Kaḥ-thog Monastery by Kaḥ-thog situ, who recognized him as an incarnation of the First mKhyen-brtse, 'Jam-dbyangs mkhyen-brtse dbang-po (1820–1892). Holder of all the major rNying-ma and Sa-skya lineages, 'Jam-dbyangs mkhyen-brtse became known as a nonsectarian master who was sympathetic to the Jo-nang-pa views.[72] A number of his works have been lost, but his *Collected Works*, some 308 texts, are preserved in the rNying-ma Treasure collections, with some additional texts included in the *Treasury of Precious Treasures* (*Rin chen gter mdzod*).

'Jam-dbyangs mkhyen-brtse's *Abridged Sleep-Meditation on Amitābha* (*'Od dpag med kyi nyal bsgom mdor bdus;* DM 1, 275–276) offers a compact summary of the tantric methods described in Sakya Paṇḍita's *Meditation on Amitābha.* Following the completion of preliminary practices, 'Jam-dbyangs mkhyen-brtse recommends attaining mastery of the process of inhalation and exhalation as means of entering into union with Buddha Amitābha while falling asleep in a nonconceptual state.

Abridged Sleep-Meditation on Amitābha

I. Preliminaries

Generate the mind of enlightenment for (the sake of all) sentient beings without exception at the limits of this Sāha world, and go for refuge to the Buddha and the totality of *dharmas*.

(Recite) *oṃ a mi ta bha hrīḥ / sa pa ri wā ra e hye hi badzra sa mā dza / padma ka ma lā ya svāhā.*

With as many suitable offerings perform the *Seven Limb Prayer.*[73]

"I pay homage to the Awakened, Tathāgata, Arhat, and Perfectly Enlightened Buddha Amitābha." Recite with the three signs (body, speech, mind).

II. Visualization

With earnest devotion visualize before you the Buddha Immeasurable Light. From the *hrī* in Amitābha's heart a second *hrī* issues forth. From his right nostril it enters one's own left nostril, [descending to] the center of one's own heart. Light rays radiate [from the heart of Amitābha] purifying evil, defilements, and latent tendencies. Move the wind again together with [the syllables]. From [one's own] right nostril, it enters the Buddha's left nostril and dissolves into the *hrī* [in his heart]. At this point, rest in the nonconceptual indivisibility of one's mind with Amitābha.

III. Concluding Remarks

It is said that, when the manipulation of breath [is performed] in accordance with the visualization, and it is done repeatedly with faith, this [will lead] to the completion of the meditation of fusing Amitābha's enlightened qualities with one's own mind.

This meditation should be done when one is about to go to sleep. While falling asleep one should dissolve his awareness in Amitābha and abide in the nonconceptual state. One should perform the long or short version of this practice as appropriate.

IV. Colophon

This aspiration was written by Chos-kyi-blo-gros at the request of bLa-ma kun-bzang chos-'phel.

Part III

Pure Lands and Pure Visions

Buddha of Infinite Life, Amitāyus

Chapter Five

Tantric Transfer in Sukhāvatī

Pure Lands in the Tibetan Canon

The term "Vajrayana" describes a heterogeneous collection of arcane texts and practices that evolved over time and came to represent the most ritually complex expression of Indian esoteric Buddhism. Tantric teachings are said to have been imparted either by Buddha Śākyamuni or by other enlightened expositors, such as the buddhas Vajradhara, Vajrasattva, Mahāvairocana, and so on, who are sometimes described as tantric manifestations of Śākyamuni.[1] Tantra was at its peak from the eighth to eleventh centuries, but its origins can be traced back to as early as the third century CE, depending on how scholars wish to define the term. In *The Social History of Indian Esoteric Buddhism,* Davidson distinguishes between an early engagement with mantras, *maṇḍalas*, fire sacrifices, and so on and a ritualized Vajrayana corpus that emerged in the second half of the seventh century CE and was adopted by Buddhist monastic institutions in India.[2]

Indian Buddhist tantrism came with a new set of rules, imposing restrictions on the spread of doctrines in a manner not previously witnessed.[3] Institutional esotericism and secrecy flourished in Tibet, embracing a unique body of tantric literature centered on religious cultures that relied on an immutable master-disciple bond, elaborate initiations, covert transmissions, royal acts of consecration, and the use of intricate *maṇḍalas* in which meditators transformed themselves into buddhas.

> [In India p]roponents of the system composed a new class of scriptures that taught the transmission and recitation of mantras. Calling themselves "possessors of mantras or sceptres" (*mantrin/vajrin*), they developed rituals (particularly fire sacrifice) for the purpose of a codified series of soteriological and nonsoteriological acts and ultimately institutionalized this material in Buddhist monasteries where texts were copied, art produced, and rituals performed.[4]

During the second spread of Buddhism to Tibet, an influx of Indian tantric lineages and their esoteric literature gave rise to the foundation of the New Buddhist Schools. The consolidation of new Indian teachings with old texts from Tibetan imperial times formed a widely accepted collection of scriptures, divided into the Kanjur (bKa'-'gyur), the words of the Buddha, and the commentaries, the Tanjur (bsTan-'gyur).[5] The Kanjur and Tanjur contain thousands of religious scriptures; in comparison, texts with a Pure Land orientation constitute a marginal, though representative, section. In addition to the *Sukhāvatīvyūha* sutras in the *mDo* section of the Kanjur, there are some allied works in the Tantra (*rGyud*) division. In Chapter Two we discussed one such text, the *Tshe-mdo* located in the *rGyud* section. In addition to the *Ārya-aparimitāyur-jñāna-nāma-mahāyāna-sūtra* there are other works with Pure Land content preserved in the *gZungs* and *rGyud* sections of the Kanjur, to which we will now turn our attention.

First, there are several *dhāraṇī*-type scriptures that do not center on the principal deities of the Sukhāvatī tradition but nevertheless contain aspirational prayers for birth in Amitābha's Pure Land. For example, a text with a generic Pure Land prayer is the *Cloud of Offerings Dhāraṇī* dating to the time of the Tibetan empire.[6] The *dhāraṇī* assures that its recitation will lead those who die to take birth in Sukhāvatī. As we have seen, it was a commonplace practice in Indian religious literature (and in Tibetan texts of later centuries) to conclude with a Pure Land aspiration and dedication of merit.

There are other *dhāraṇī* sriptures, such as the *Dhāraṇī in Praise of Immeasurable Qualities,* a short canonical text that promotes a number of Mahayana incentives, including an encounter with Buddha Amitābha.[7] Typical of works of this kind, the *dhāraṇī* starts with a short homage to the buddhas and bodhisattvas. It follows with a description of the benefits associated with its recitation (*brjod-pa*). If it is uttered once, it will purify karmic obscurations accumulated over 100,000 eons (*bskal-pa*). If it is repeated three times daily, it will purify one's wrongdoings and reinforce the generation of root virtues. If it is recited twenty-one times, it will cleanse the four transgressions (*ltung-ba bzhi*). If one wishes to come in contact with the buddhas, one must perform 100,000 recitations and will then behold Ārya Maitreya; with 200,000 recitations, one will meet the Lord of the World Avalokiteśvara; and with 300,000 recitations he will attain the *dhāraṇī*'s *summum bonum,* an encounter with the Tathāgata Amitābha.,

Some *dhāraṇī* are included in both the *rGyud* and *gZungs* sections of the Kanjur, like the *Dhāraṇī-Mantra of Amitābha* and the *Recollection of Amitābha,* both of which are listed in Bu-ston's *Collection of Dhāraṇī of the Four Classes of Guhya-Mantra Tantras.*[8] The *Dhāraṇī-Mantra of Amitābha* is similar to the *Dhāraṇī in Praise of Immeasurable Qualities.* Following the proclamation of the mantra, the benefits of its recitation feature the purification of past obscurations. There is no mention, however, of visionary encounters with the buddhas. The text recommends instead the practice of recollecting the Buddha (*sangs-rgyas rjes-su dran-pa;* Skt. *buddhānusmṛti*), but it is not clear if this is equivalent to reciting his mantra or if it entails contemplating the characteristics of the Buddha and his Pure Land, as has been suggested in related literature.

The *Dhāraṇī of the Essence of Aparimitāyus*

The *Dhāraṇī of the Essence of Aparimitāyus* is an influential text translated into Tibetan in the eleventh century. However, a work under a similar title is also listed in the imperial catalogue from Phangthang.[9] It may be, however, a later addition to the *Phangthangma Catalogue,* which remained an open inventory for Buddhist works after the collapse of the Tibetan empire.[10] The earliest known translation of the *Dhāraṇī of the Essence of Aparimitāyus* in Chinese (T. 370) postdates the composition of the *Sukhāvatīvyūha* sutras. It dates between 502 and 557 CE and its author remains anonymous. Two more Chinese translations were made by a Tibetan monk from Dunhuang in the first half of the ninth century (T. 936) and by a monk from Nālandā in the second half of the tenth century (T. 937).[11]

The *Dhāraṇī of the Essence of Aparimitāyus* is an important work in several ways. It provides valuable information on Buddha Aparimitāyus, who by the ninth century (if not earlier) appears in a Tibetan context to have been synonymous with Buddha Amitāyus. Payne (2007) points out that the Aparimitāyus deity belongs to the Indian proto–Pure Land milieu, a statement reinforced by the Tibetan tradition, which continues to read Aparimitāyus as another name for Amitāyus—an identification also found in the *Tshe-mdo,* the *Immeasurable Life and Wisdom Sutra.*[12]

The *Dhāraṇī of the Essence of Aparimitāyus* opens with its title in Sanskrit and Tibetan and a brief homage to all the buddhas and bodhisattvas, followed by the formulaic phrase "thus I have once heard." The narrative part of the text features the Bhagavan Śākyamuni discoursing to a large retinue of monks and bodhisattva-monks, who are listening attentively to his sermon near the banks of the Ganges River. Like the short *Sukhāvatīvyūha-sūtra,* the Buddha praises a world-system (*'jig-rten-khams*) situated in the western direction of our universe, where a perfect Tathāgata resides by the name Buddha Infinite Life (Tshe-dpag-med; Skt. Amitāyus). His world is no other than Sukhāvatī (*bde-ba-can gyi 'jig-rten-khams*), where

Buddha Amitāyus expounds on the inconceivable ways this world-system came to ripen into a perfect world.[13]

During this sermon, Śākyamuni praises Buddha Amitāyus' royal lineage (*rgyal rigs*), comprised of his consort-princess, his son-prince, and principle attendant. He proceeds to instruct his pupils (and readers) that in order to thoroughly apprehend Amitāyus' characteristics, they should recollect the Buddha (*sangs-rgyas rjes-su dran-pa*) and without mental distraction meditate on his field of residence, Sukhāvatī. For this purpose they should constantly recite his *dhāraṇī*, known as the *King among the Sounds of the Drum of Immortality* (*'Chi med rnga sgra'i rgyal po*).

Śākyamuni's advice is to meditate three times a day on the Buddha's sublime characteristics of enlightenment. If one follows these instructions, then at the time of death one will encounter Amitāyus and behold buddhas in all directions. Furthermore, one should thoroughly dedicate all virtues in order to meet the Buddha after death. Having imparted these teachings to his monks, Śākyamuni delivers the *King among the Sounds of the Drum of Immortality*. The audience is advised to have faith in the *dhāraṇī* and recite it out loud for effectiveness. Then one should perform the ritual of offerings. In a thoroughly cleansed place and on an unsoiled cloth, one should make offerings of flowers—the lotus being the best of flowers, as it symbolizes the essence of bodhisattvas—and light incense, as it represents the fulfillment of all that is excellent.

Having thus instructed his monks, Śākyamuni calls upon the "sons and daughters of good lineage" to generate intense devotion and faith to take birth in the Pure Land of Buddha Amitāyus, who resides in his buddha field with Avalokiteśvara and Mahāsthāmaprāpta and a retinue of innumerable bodhisattvas. Those in possession of steady faith in Amitāyus will have no fear of human harm, water (floods), poison, weapons, malignant spirits (*gnod-spyin*), and vampire-like creatures (*srin-mo*). Like many Mahayana sutras, the *Dhāraṇī of the Essence of Aparimitāyus* concludes with a delighted assembly of monks, gods, humans, *asuras*, and *gandharvas* praising the sermon delivered by Śākyamuni.

Aparimitāyus Lineages

In the hundred or so volumes of texts that comprise the entire commentarial tradition of the Tanjur, works with an obvious Pure Land orientation are scarcely represented. The Tanjur contains just a few texts dedicated to Buddha Amitāyus, which nevertheless reveal the kind of Pure Land–oriented tantric works available in India during the tenth and eleventh centuries.

These texts serve as canonical precursors to a later systematization of tantric literature, in which the deity Aparimitāyus is subsumed in the worship of Amitāyus and is associated with tantric rituals for extending life.[14]

The colophons of these Tanjur texts inform us of a male and female transmission line of the Aparimitāyus deity to Tibet. The former was introduced to Tibet by the Indian *acārya* Jetāri dgra-las rnam-par rgyal-ba, and the latter by the wisdom *ḍākinī* (*ye-shes kyi mkha'-'gro-ma*) Grub-pa'i-rgyal-mo. For the Nyingma School that preserves Aparimitāyus scriptures attributed to her lineage, the wisdom *ḍākinī* Mandāravā is known as the "Sole Mother, Queen of *Siddhas*" (Ma-gcig grub-pa'i rgyal-mo) for having attained the *siddhi* of Amitāyus, an immortal body, with Padmasambhava at the Maritika cave in Nepal.

The following Aparimitāyus texts and their colophons are listed in the Narthang Tanjur:

1. *Praise to Aparimitāyus* (*Tshe dpag med la bstod pa;* Skt. *Aparimitāyuḥ-stotra*) (D 2698, fol. 66v–67r)

Narthang, vol. 70, fol. 110r–110v (pp. 219–220). Colophon:

> [This work] was completed by the bodhisattva Jetāri dgra-las rnam-par rgyal-ba. The transmission of the long and short Amitāyus practice by the eminent Jetāri dgra-las rnam-par rgyal-ba was received in Bodh Gaya by Bari lo-tsā-ba, mChims-pa brtson-'grus seng-ge, rGya-nang phug-pa, dBus-pa sangs rgyas 'du ma, Bla-ma gDe-bsdings-pa, and Bla-ma bsam-gtan bzang-po.[15]

2. *Aparimitāyus Fire-Rituals* (*Tshe dpag tu med pa'i sbyin sreg gi cho ga;* Skt. *Aparimitāyur-homa-vidhi-nāma*) (D 2144, fol. 219r–220r)

Narthang, vol. 46, fol. 249v–251r (pp. 498–501). Colophon:

> The fire ritual came to fruition as composed by the *ḍākinī* Grub-pa'i-rgyal-mo (Queen of *Siddhas*). By virtue of this, may all transmigrating beings encounter Amitāyus. This [text] was translated by the Indian scholar Balacandra and Glan Dar-ma tshul-khrims, the translator.[16]

3. *Aparimitāyus Tantric Rituals* (*Tshe dang ye shes dpag tu med pa'i cho ga;* Skt. *Aparimitāyur-jñāna-vidhi-nāma*) (D 2700, fol. 67v-69r)

Narthang, vol. 70, fol. 67v–69r (pp. 134–137). Colophon:

> Composed by Acārya Jetāri dgra las rnam-par rgyal-ba, the son of Brahmin Nam-mkha'-dbyangs. It was translated by the Indian scholar Śrīma-ju and lCe dga'i-ba'i-dpal, the translator.[17]

4. *Aparimitāyus Means of Accomplishment* (*Tshe dang ye shes dpag tu med pa zhes bya ba'i sgrub thabs;* Skt. *Aparimitāyur-jñāna-sādhana-nāma*).

There are four copies with similar titles but variant contents in the N and D Tanjurs (D 2143, fol. 216r–219r; D 2145, fol. 220r–223r; D 2146, fol. 220r–223r; D 2699, fol. 67r–67v).

4-1. Narthang, vol. 46, ff. 226r–229v (pp. 451–458). Title: T*she dang ye shes dpag tu med pa zhes bya ba'i sgrub thabs.* Colophon:

> The so-called *Sādhana* of Bhagavan-Aparimitāyus was composed by the widsom-*ḍākinī* Grub-pa'i-rgyal-mo.[18]

4-2. Narthang, vol. 46, ff. 239v–242v (pp. 478–484). Title: *Tshe dang ye shes dpag tu med pa zhes bya ba'i sgrub thabs.* Colophon:

> It was composed by the Indian scholar Zla-ba bzang-po and the Tibetan translator Glan Dar-ma tshul-khrims.

4-3. Narthang, vol. 84, ff. 200r–204r (pp. 399–407). Title: *Tshe dang ye shes dpag tu med pa zhes bya ba'i sgrub thabs.* Colophon:

> The so-called *Sādhana* of Bhagavan-Aparimitāyus was composed by the wisdom *ḍākinī* Grub-pa'i-rgyal-mo.

4-4. Narthang, vol. 70, ff. 110v–111v (pp. 220–222). Title: *'Phags pa tshe dang ye shes dpag tu med pa zhes bya ba'i sgrub thabs.* Colophon:

> It was composed by the learned preceptor Jetāri dgra-las rnam-par rgyal-ba and translated by the Indian scholar 'Jam-dpa'i-dbyangs and lCe-dga'i-ba'i-dpal, the translator.[19]

5. *Aparimitāyus Maṇḍala Rituals* (*Tshe dang ye shes dpag tu med pa'i dkyil 'khor gyi cho ga;* Skt. *Aparimitāyur-jñāna-maṇḍala-vidhi-nāma*).

There are two variant copies in the N and D Tanjurs (D 2141, fol. 210r–215v; D 2146, fol. 223r–231r).

5-1. Narthang, vol. 46, fol. 229v–239v (pp. 458–478). Colophon:

> It is called "the vessel of ambrosia of deathless wisdom, the Bhagavan-Protector Aparimitāyus rituals of the four empowerments, and related arrangements." It was composed by the widsom *ḍākinī* Grub-pa'i-rgyal-mo.[20]

5-2. Narthang, vol. 46, fol. 242v–249v (pp. 484–498). This text begins by stating that the Bhagavan Aparimitāyus is the same (*rang-bzhin*) as the Buddha Amitāyus (Tshe-dpag-med) in essence/body (*sku*).[21] Colophon:

> The so-called "well-conceived *maṇḍala* rituals of the Bhagavan-Protector Aparimitāyus" are now complete. [This text] was translated by the Indian scholar Zla-ba bzang-po and Glan-dar-ma Tshul-khrims, the Tibetan translator. May this field be purified![22]

Last, the Tanjur contains two short tantric texts related to Buddha Amitābha. The first, of anonymous authorship, is dedicated to Tārā and Amitābha: *'Od dpag med kyi snying po'i rgyud las bcom ldan 'das ma 'phags ma sgrol ma'i rtog pa gsung pa* (Skt. *Amitābha-garbhatantra-bhagavatyā-ārya-tārāyāḥ-kalpoddeśa;* D 3501, fol. 153r–153r). The second lists the Indian scholar Atiśa and the Tibetan translator Prajñāśrījñānakirti: *'Od dpag du med pa'i snying po 'dod chags gshin rje gshed sgrub pa'i thabs* (Skt. *Amitābha-hṛdaya-rāga-yamārisādhana-nāma;* D 1939, fol. 66v–67r).

Amitāyus Longevity Rituals

In his seminal work, *The History of Buddhism in India and Tibet,* the Tibetan scholar Bu-ston makes no reference to the *Sukhāvatīvyūha* sutras or any Pure Land practices in India, but in his section on the biography of the Indian philosopher Nāgārjuna (§II, 123) he narrates that the latter engaged in Amitāyus long-life practices. The precise association of Amitāyus with longevity rituals seems to have its roots in India. In his study of rNying-ma literature, Walter (1980, 319) discusses two Indian alchemical systems presumably dating to before the tenth century, where Padmasambava delivers teachings in the form of Buddha Amitāyus. As we have seen, other texts mention eight immortal magicians that emanate from Amitāyus.

Buddha Amitāyus is supplicated for extending one's life in tantric empowerments (*tshe-dbang bskur*) preserved in the lineages transmitted by the *acārya* Jetāri and the *ḍākinī* Ma-gcig grub-pa'i-rgyal-mo.[23] Thus he is associated with the *tshe-sgrub* genre (Skt. *āyush-sādhana*), as in the longevity-yoga in the liturgical cycle composed by the Second Dalai Lama, dGe-'dun rgya-mtsho (1476–1542), which comprises an Amitāyus long-life *sādhana* and related initiations granted by means of the longevity vase, wine, pills, and the power of truth.[24] He also figures in fasting rituals (*smyung-gnas*) based on the *Aparimitāyur-jñāna-sādhana* (TOH tome 125, no. 6023, tha 1–23).

The Tibetans express their devotion to the cult of Amitāyus in connection with longevity rituals independent of the soteriology of Sukhāvatī. Buddha Amitāyus, not Amitābha, is often included in the triad of long-life deities (*tshe-lha*), where he occupies the center, with White Tārā on his right and Uṣṇīṣavijayā on his left.[25] He is associated with healing rituals in the Tibetan medical tantras and figures as the main deity in a variety of longevity *sādhanas* (*tshe-sgrub*), such as those performed for extending the life of one's Lama (*zhabs-brtan*).[26] His healing powers are also conjured in alchemical processes (*bcud-len;* Skt. *rasāyana*) for extracting vital essences into pills (*ril-bu*), as in the instructions based on the *Aparimitāyur-jñāna-sādhana.*[27]

Tantric Genres and Techniques of Bliss

In Tibetan Buddhism, mortuary rites are the most important rituals to be performed by religious specialists at the end of one's life. The principal purpose of these rites is not merely to dispose the corpse in a dignified way but primarily to secure an auspicious rebirth or liberation from samsara.[28] It is believed that the recently departed will derive great benefit from the performance of certain funeral rites because during the intermediate state following death (*bar-do*), and with the proper guidance, they have a chance to recognize the luminous nature of their mind and reach enlightenment.[29] These soteriological suppositions are known in the West with the translation of the *Liberation through Hearing in the Bardo* (*Bar do thos grol*), better known as the *Tibetan Book of the Dead*.[30] The *Liberation through Hearing in the Bardo* is in fact not a single text but a collection of revealed texts grouped in a liturgical cycle of afterlife doctrines and practices that are especially popular with the rNying-ma and bKa'-brgyud schools. In their original formulation, these ideas are said to go back to the *mahāsiddha* Padmasamhava in ninth-century imperial Tibet, but they were orchestrated in a written collection in the fourteenth century by the Treasure discoverer Karma gling-pa.[31]

Liberation instructions "through hearing in the bar-do" should be read out loud to the dead in the intermediate state for up to forty-nine days following death. It is believed that the awareness of the deceased can be summoned by a ritual specialist and be admonished to recognize the audiovisual experiences (lights, rays, and sounds) that dawn before him in the *bar-do*, as interiorized guides on the path, reflections of his own mind, and thereby attain liberation from samsara. In some traditions, on the fourth day of the intermediate state the dead will encounter a peaceful vision of Buddha Amitābha, and on the eleventh day Amitābha's wrathful aspects will manifest as Padma-Heruka, adorned with skull necklaces and having three heads, six arms, four legs, and open wings like those of the mythical creature *garuḍa*.

In the *Inspiration Prayer for Deliverance from the Dangerous Pathway of the Bardo*, Buddha Amitābha is entreated in his special capacity to guide beings through the bewildering visions of the intermediate state:

> When through intense desire I wander in samsara, on the luminous path of discriminating wisdom, may blessed Amitābha go before me, his consort Pāṇḍaravāsinī behind me; help me to cross the bardo's dangerous pathway and bring me to the perfect buddha state.[32]

While the most prominent rituals associated with Sukhāvatī are mortuary rites, like cremation ceremonies (*ro-sreg*) and inscription rituals for the dead (*byang-chog*), Amitābha and his Pure Land also figure in other tantric genres, such as life-extending rituals (*tshe-sgrub*), guru-yoga visualizations (*bla-ma'i rnal-'byor*), dream-yoga practices (*rmi-lam*), and meditations for transferring one's awareness to the buddha field (*'pho-ba*).

In dGe-'dun rgya-mtsho's longevity *sādhana* (*tshe-sgrub*) the wisdom-beings (*ye-shes sems-dpa'*; Skt. *jñāna-sattva*) in Sukhāvatī are implored in the form of subtle light rays that emanate from the practitioner's body and eventually merge back into it.

> Lights radiate from the *Hūm* at my heart, summoning forth the Wisdom Beings from Sukhavati, the Pure Land of Joy of the Western Realms. These Wisdom Beings, who resemble the Amitayus described above, come and merge into me, the Symbolic Being.[33]

dGe-'dun rgya-mtsho's longevity *sādhana* includes a guru-yoga visualization practice (*bla-ma'i rnal-'byor*) in which one imagines one's spiritual teacher (*bla-ma;* Skt. *guru*) above one's head in the form and attributes of Buddha Amitāyus. During the dissolution stage of the visualization, the transparent form of the deity gradually dissolves into light rays and luminous particles descending down the crown of the practitioner, empowering him with the awakened qualities of body, speech, and mind.

> Lights emanate from the heart of Guru Amitayus, summoning the Bodhisattva Amitayus from Sukhavati, the Pure Land of Joy, who comes from the western heavens. He is surrounded by all the gurus in the lineage of transmission, together with all the Buddhas and Bodhisattvas of the ten directions. These dissolve into Guru Amitayus, who melts into light and dissolves into me. Thus my body, speech and mind become of one taste with the body, speech and mind of Guru Amitayus, and I attain the state of an immortal knowledge holder.[34]

There are several guru-yoga manuals in Tibetan literature that entreat the root teacher in the form of Buddha Amitāyus or Amitābha. These practices are conceptually and technically paired with "*phowa sādhanas*," where the inverse process is enacted during meditation. During the practice of transferring one's awareness to a buddha field, *phowa* (*'pho-ba*), the yogi visualizes his subtle awareness ascending through the subtle channel and exiting from the crown of the head to merge with the Buddha residing in Sukhāvatī.[35] In the devotional prayer of the famous Tibetan *mahāsiddha* Zabs-dkar (1789–1851), Buddha Amitābha and the bodhisattvas that guide the dead to Sukhāvatī are ultimately inseparable from one's lama, who is the unexcelled guide.

> When the time comes for me to die, may you, my guru, come to lead me without hindrance to the Blissful Buddhafield. May we then travel to many Pure Realms, make offerings to all the Buddhas, and return to this impure world to guide all beings![36]

Sukhāvatī features in funeral rites and scriptures dedicated to the ritual care of the dead (*'das-mchod*). The structure and performance of Tibetan death ceremonies varies according to a set sequence of events. Traditionally these may include: 1) gaining the attention of the deceased and alerting them to the fact that they are dead and caught in the intermediate state between death and birth, 2) dispelling negative forces and obstacles that may hinder self-awareness when the *bar-do* visions flood the consciousness of the departed, and 3) transforming the five root delusions into five pure elements. For the duration of these rites, the consciousness of the dead is coaxed into increasing levels of clarity until the time for the ritual transference to Sukhāvatī. Following this, the ritual specialist performs the cremation ceremony that incorporates the basic elements of homa (*sbyin-sreg*) and the disposal of the corpse or effigy in a fire.[37]

Pure Lands are also the subject of dream-yoga meditations (*rmi-lam;* Skt. *svapnadarśana*), which may have evolved out of *buddhānusmṛti* practices, since their aim is the cultivation of lucid awareness during sleep for the purpose of encountering Buddha Amitābha and receiving transmissions directly from him in Sukhāvatī. A short dream-yoga work authored by Karma chags-med details instructions for merging one's awareness with the enlightened qualities of Amitābha during dream time and space.[38] This work is reminiscent of Sakya Paṇḍita's composition that outlines tantric visualizations with the objective of visiting Sukhāvatī.[39]

In Tibetan Buddhism Sukhāvatī underwent conceptual and ritual transformations and formulated the soteriological *raison d'être* for a variety of religious practices and interiorized contemplative methods. A long history of Tibetan ritual innovations and elaborations may account for a conscious aural/scriptural conflation between *bDe-ba-can* (Skt. *sukhāvatī*) and *bDe-ba-chen* (Skt. *mahāsukhā*), or "great bliss," that we encounter in later religious works. This variant spelling and playful variation is noticed for the first time in the corpus of 'Bri-gung skyob-pa (1143–1217) and it may have been influenced by the Chinese translation of Sukhāvatī as "supreme bliss" (Ch. *ji-le*), or simply because in some Tibetan dialects these two words are homonyms.[40] On many occasions, this alternate spelling is inadvertantly reproduced as a scribal error.[41]

Whether this conflation is consciously or mechanically reproduced, it nevertheless fosters a symbolic relation between Amitābha's Pure Land and the overriding emphasis in Vajrayana esoteric exercises to induce mental and physical states of joy. There is a substantial body of Tibetan tantric literature devoted to the interpretation of bliss (*bde-ba;* Skt. *sukha*). Bliss may be the outcome or means of contemplation, exemplified in the irreversible and supreme bliss (*bde-ba chen-po*) of a buddha and in sexual union of the father-mother dyad (*yab-yum*).[42] The identification of Sukhāvatī with *mahāsukhā* ("great bliss") is further reinforced during the Vajrayana technique of transferring one's consciousness to Sukhāvatī, *phowa* (*'pho-ba*). In this practice, the Buddhist practitioner trains to mobilize and localize the subtle principle of her consciousness outside the physical body to a buddha field of her choice. The point of departure is the crown of the head, the circuit of great bliss (*bde-chen gi 'khor-lo;* Skt. *mahāsukha-cakra*) according to subtle body anatomy.[43]

Similar techniques are employed during the generation of inner fire (*gtum-mo;* Skt. *caṇḍālī*), a fundamental meditation for many teachings of the esoteric variety, especially the Mother Tantras.[44] During inner fire meditations, the practitioner trains in subtle body operations in a dynamic landscape comprising internal circuits (*'khor-lo;* Skt. *cakra*) and main and subsidiary channels (*rtsa;* Skt. *nāḍī*) traversed by motile energies (*rlung;* Skt. *prāṇa*). The meditation consists of visualizing the image of a thin flame gradually rising from the navel-circuit, which then pierces through the central channel, causing the nucleus of awakening (*thig-le;* Skt. *bindu*) to melt and drip from the *mahāsukha-cakra* down the same channel. The dripping of *bodhicitta* generates a series of four experiential states of bliss. Parallel processes that utilize bliss and emptiness (*stong-nyid;* Skt. *śunyatā*) are triggered in the retention and reversal of semen drawn up the central channel (*bcud-len;* Skt. *vajrolī mudrā*) by a trained yogi during sexual intercourse.[45]

Contemplative techniques resulting in states of bliss (*bde-ba*), clarity (*gsal-ba*), and no-thought (*mi-rtog-pa*) are integral to the philosophy of Mahāmudrā (*phyag-chen*).[46] The eleventh-century yogi Khyung-po rnal-'byor interprets bliss in terms of the three-body (Skt. *trikāya*) doctrine.[47] He explains that during the practice of Mahāmudrā "the body of great bliss" (Skt. *mahāsukhakāya*) results from the indivisibility of the body of reality (Skt. *dharmakāya*), the body of deity (Skt. *saṃbhogakāya*), and the body of emanation (Skt. *nirmāṇakāya*). In all cases, tantric techniques that utilize and employ blissful experiences are not pursued for the sake of physical pleasure but for the purpose of integrating bliss with the awareness of the insubstantial nature of reality.[48]

Transferring Consciousness to a Buddha Field

The *phowa* meditation (*'pho-ba*), or "transference of consciousness," is the most popular postmortem ritual, widely practiced in Tibet and the Buddhist communities of North India, Sikkim, Bhutan, Nepal, and among Tibetan refugees and Buddhist practitioners abroad.[49] This tantric method is meant to be performed at the time of death, by ejecting one's subtle consciousness to a buddha field and resting in a state of union.[50] *Phowa* is also called "buddhahood without meditation" (*ma-sgom sangs-rgyas*).[51] Detailed descriptions of this practice feature in a number of *phowa sādhanas* performed by oneself and on others' account by Tibetan ritual specialists (*'pho-'debs bla-ma*). Tibetan monks and laypeople are familiar with this liturgy, which is still performed on behalf of deceased relatives.[52]

According to the main Buddhist schools of Tibet, the origins of mind-transference go back to Indian tantric lineages. The contemporary dGe-lugs-pa master Thub-bstan ye-shes (1935–1984) writes that the concept of *phowa* can be found in the *Guhyasamāja-tantra,* though this text does not spell out the detailed instructions in the exact form in which it is practiced today.[53] In the same work, Thub-bstan ye-shes notes that mind-transference "belongs to the highest level of tantra, [and] many skillful Tibetan lamas have extracted it from this context and have presented it in terms of the deities of the lower levels of tantra." In fact, this technique, used in the higher tantras, constitutes the lesser of two ways to disconnect the coarse from the subtle levels of mind. Cozort (1986, 98) explains that *phowa* merely separates the coarse and subtle bodies without leading to the realization of the illusory body (*sgyu-lus*). For tantric teachings, the illusory body is attained during the perfection-type meditation known as the final mental isolation (*sems-dben*), which necessitates the intimacy of an actual female partner, a tantric consort known as "action-seal" (*las kyi phyag-rgya;* Skt. *karma-mudrā*). During this time, the tantric adept dissolves his winds in the "indestructible drop" and the "fundamental wind," and naturally rises into an "illusory body." According to subtle body theory, one's awareness manifests in the form of motility (*rlung;* Skt. *prāṇa*) across a plane of a thin, luminous network of conductors and circuits emanating from a trilateral axis visualized in the physical body. The middle axis, called the *avadhūti* (*dbu-ma rtsa*), runs parallel to the cerebrospinal column joining the circuit-of-bliss in the crown of the head with the phallus or vagina. Two channels adjacent to the middle axis run in lateral courses or in a helix. The left (*rkyang-ma*) and right (*ro-ma*) channels bifurcate respectively at the left and right nostrils and join the central channel at the perineum.[54]

In Tsong-kha-pa's *Collected Works* we find a *phowa sādhana* of the wisdom-*ḍākinī* and two additional *phowa* texts that seem to be connected with the *Sampuṭa-tantra.*[55] There are several tantric cycles that promote the ritual practice of deity *phowa*, and this diversity reflects in part the manifold ways this method has been classified by Tibetan Buddhist scholars. The dGe-lugs-pa Gung-thang dkon-mchog bstan-pa'i-sgron-me (1726–1823 or 1824) relates this method not only with Amitābha (nos. 1, 3), but also with Mañjuśrī (no. 4) and Avalokiteśvara (no. 5).[56]

Phowa sādhanas can be classified according to different deities, based on tantric lineages, and on the types of realization following the practice.[57] For the bKa'-brgyud scholar 'Ba-ra-ba rgyal-mtshan dpal-bzang (1310?–1391?), those of the highest capacity train in the superior method of transferring in the clear light (*'od-gsal du 'pho-ba*), followed by the transference to the illusory body (*sgyu-lus kyi 'pho-ba*), a middle-range attainment, and transference to another realm and world (*gling dang skye gnas su 'pho-ba*) for those of lesser capacity.[58] The bKa'-brgyud hierarch, Karma chags-med, arranges the results according to five kinds of meditative techniques: the *phowa* of the three bodies (*sku-gsum 'pho-ba*)—*dharmakāya, saṃbhogakāya,* and *nirmāṇakāya;* the forced *phowa* (*btsan-thabs kyi 'pho-ba*); the routine mind-transference (*tha-mal-pa'i 'pho-ba*); and the forceful entry into another body (*grong-du 'jug-pa'i 'pho-ba*).[59]

In some Tibetan texts there are specific instructions concerning the suitability of place, astrological time, preliminary preparations, and auspicious conditions necessary for the success of transference. The actual method of the liturgy may vary depending on whether it is to be performed for oneself or on others' behalf. When done for others, Sangs-rgyas gling-pa (1341–1396) distinguishes between *phowa* performed for Buddhist practitioners, for ordinary people, for animals, and for those with a sinful disposition.[60]

In the bKa'-brgyud schools, *phowa* is one of the *Six Yogas* taught by the Indian *mahāsiddha* Nāropa (Na-ro chos drug). For the bKa'-brgyud Shangs-pa it is also part of the *Six Yogas* of Nāropa's sister, the *mahāsiddha* Niguma (Ni-gu chos-drug).[61] Their teachings are closely related to each other and include six complementary practices: the yoga of inner heat (*gtum-mo;* Skt. *caṇḍālī*), the yoga of illusory body (*sgyu-lus;* Skt. *māyākāya*), the yoga of clear light (*'od-gsal;* Skt. *prabhāsvara*), the yoga of transference (*'pho-ba;* Skt. *saṁkrānti*), the yoga of the intermediate state (*bar-do;* Skt. *antarābhava*), and dream-yoga (*rmi-lam;* Skt. *svapnadarśana*).[62]

Nāropa's *Six Yogas* were passed on to his Tibetan disciple Marpa, and from there to the lineage of the bKa'-brgyud school. There are two methods of *phowa,* one that includes the forceful projection of one's consciousness to another body (*'pho-ba grong-'jug;* Skt. *parakāyapraveśana*).[63] This lineage is said to have been interrupted with the sudden death of Marpa's son.[64] Karma chags-med asserts that the forceful *phowa* is preserved in the oral teachings (*bKa'-ma*), but there is no living transmission of its practical performance today in Tibet.[65] It seems that the lineage of forceful projection may not have been altogether lost. rGyal-ba rgya-mtsho (1588–1639) is said to have died through this method, and mention of it is certainly not absent from later textual traditions.[66]

The *phowa* manuals prescribe the propitiation of Buddhist deities and in most cases combine the "generation stage" (*bskyed-rim*) and "perfection stage" (*rdzogs-rim*) meditations included in tantric *sādhanas*. During the generation stage the adept visualizes one's lama in the form of a buddha or of the specific deity designated by the ritual.[67] During perfection-stage meditation, the practitioner rests in the lucid emptiness of mind. In tantric theory, there are eight natural apertures (*sgo-brgyad*) in the human body that may serve as exit passages for consciousness at the time of death. There is however, one more door that is usually closed which can be forced open. This unique passage, located at the sagittal suture where the two parietal bones meet, is known as the aperture of Brahmā (Skt. *brahmārandhra*), and serves as a point of entry into Sukhāvatī. It is highly desirable, after the stages of death have been confirmed, for one's consciousness to exit through the central channel and out through the soft spot on the skull, Brahmā's door to liberation.[68]

A typical Sukhāvatī *phowa sādhana* has several steps. It is habitual to start with Mahayana preliminaries: going for refuge in the Three Jewels, reinforcing an altruistic motivation for the performance of the practice, purifying negative mental states and attitudes, accumulating positive potential (merit), and so on. Following these, one visualizes one's body in the transparent form of a Buddhist deity. Amitābha is vividly conceived an arm's length above the crown of one's head. Resonating in that state, one localizes the subtle consciousness in the shape of a tiny sphere of light (*thig-le;* Skt. *bindu*) at the heart and generates strong devotion and yearning to merge with Buddha Amitābha. With a long and deep inhalation, the breath is locked four finger-widths below the navel by tightening the lower muscles of the body. One unleashes the tension stored at the navel by ejecting the syllable-sound *HIK.* The fundamental wind and mind is forced through the central channel out the sagittal suture to unite with the deity. A single session normally concludes with the subtle consciousness brought to descend the central channel along with the recitation of the syllable-sound *KA*.

Tibetan masters and tantric practitioners contend that training in the transference technique produces certain undeniable physiological effects.[69] It is therefore essential that the practice of *phowa* is undertaken only by those who have received detailed instructions from a qualified teacher and have been granted the proper initiations and empowerments into the lineage of the deities. The Tibetan master Sangs-rgyas gling-pa warns that the practice of *phowa* is generally not suitable for people prone to anger and fear; who are in deep grief; who have shortage of breath, distracted minds, or anomalies related to the life-sustaining wind; pregnant women; those who are physically ill or possessed by evil spirits, etc.[70]

It is said that *phowa* should be practiced at least twice a month during the phases of the new and full moon, when it is most effective. According to Tibetan medicine and astrology, an immaterial principle connected with human vitality (*bla*) is in motion inside the human body following the moon's cycle.

> At the new moon (30th and 1st days of the lunar month), the *La* is found in the soles of the feet, on the left or the right according to gender. During the period of the waxing moon, it moves as a luminous letter toward the crown of the head, which it reaches at the full moon (15th day). It then travels through the body again until it reaches its original position.[71]

The irreversible transference should not be performed unless undeniable signs of imminent death have occurred and after the outer breath of the deceased has stopped. To do otherwise is considered a grave transgression, in effect taking one's own life and killing the wisdom deities that abide in the human body (*lha bsad-pa'i ye-shes-pa*). In his commentary to Karma chags-med's *Union of Mahāmudrā and Dzogchen* (*Thugs rje chen po'i dmar khrid phyag rdzogs zung 'jug thos ba don ldan*), Gyatrul Rinpoche, a contemporary Tibetan Buddhist scholar, explains this point.

> Divinations, dreams, and doctors' prognoses are some of the tests used to determine when death is imminent. If so, it is your responsibility to apply any means available to turn death away, by taking medicine, engaging in religious rituals, and so forth. Only when these methods fail is it appropriate to fully engage in the practice of transference. To do so prematurely lead to the great misdeed of killing a deity—the peaceful deities dwell in your heart and the wrathful deities residing inside of your head. Furthermore, your channels are of the nature of *vīras*, and the vital energies that flow through the channels

> are the nature of *ḍākinīs*. Therefore, if you practice the stage of generation and apply the transference teachings prematurely, it is equivalent to killing the deity that is at the core of your practice. If you follow an ordinary practice and apply transference before it is appropriate, the result is the transgression of killing a human being. In either case you have committed a terrible misdeed.[72]

For Tibetan Buddhists, the possibility of encountering Buddha Amitābha can be fulfilled through the technique of transference, which might involve the visualization of a luminous hook attracting one's conscious principle in the form of an incandescent globe projected from Amitābha's heart.

> Out of Amitābha's heart a hook of light is projected, which draws towards itself the devotee's conscious principle, represented by a luminous globe, the size of a grain, residing in his heart; the principle, thus attracted, disappears and is dissolved into the god's heart, with which it is substantially unified; next, it is once again emanated from it, in order to give birth to the new divine incarnation in the center of the lotus miraculously sprung up in front the of the god.[73]

The popularity of *phowa* may explain why Amitābha's descent from Sukhāvatī to meet the pious in the hour of death, a popular theme in Chinese literature and art, occupies a surprisingly subordinate position in Tibetan cultural production.

The Great Drikung Festival and Public Ceremonies of *Phowa*

Sukhāvatī does not figure in *phowa* meditations before the fourteenth century. It is introduced in two texts from Tibet's revealed literature, the Treasure tradition: *The Standing Blade of Grass* (*'Jag tshug ma*), a water Treasure (*chu-gter*) revealed by Nyi-zla sangs-rgyas; and an earth Treasure (*sa-gter*), *Dying without Regrets* (*'Da' ka 'chi brod*), redacted by the rNying-ma master Sangs-rgyas gling-pa.[74] The fact that there are no records of or references to *phowa* liturgies to Sukhāvatī in India and East Asia would suggest that the Sukhāvatī *phowa* synthesis may very well be a unique fourteenth-century contribution of the Tibetan Treasure tradition.

The Standing Blade of Grass (*'Jag tshug ma*) was discovered by Nyi-zla sangs-rgyas in the fourteenth century as a treasure (*gter-ma*) and contains *phowa* practices devoted to Buddha Amitābha and his buddha field.[75] This revealed text is at the core of a major pilgrimage and cultural celebration known in the Tibetan world as the Great Drikung *Phowa* (*'Bri-gung 'pho-ba chen-mo*). The public ceremony of *phowa* was traditionally held once every twelve years; the last observance took place in the area of gTer-sgrom in August 1992, after a hiatus of thirty-six years due to a ban enforced by the Chinese authorities.[76]

The 'Bri-gung (also 'Bri-khung) lineage is based on the teachings of Phag-mo gru-pa rdo-rje rgyal-po (1110–1170) and forms a smaller branch of the bKa'-brgyud school. It was founded by Phag-mo grupa's senior disciple, sKyob-pa 'jig-rten-mgon-po (1143–1217) from the region of Khams, who migrated west and founded his monastery at 'Bri-gung-mthil in the upper regions of the 'Bri-gung valley. 'Jig-rten-mgon-po, reputed to have been an incarnation of Nāgārjuna, was a charismatic teacher known for his Buddhist learning, compassion, and strict adherence to the monastic code. Famous for his writings on Buddhist philosophy and meditation, he came to be regarded in some circles as doctrinally controversial.[77]

The Great Drikung *Phowa* festival was fixed in its modern form by two eminent 'Bri-gung hierarchs, the brothers dKon-mchog rin-chen (1590–1654) and Rig-pa 'dzin-pa chos-kyi-grags-pa (1595–1659). They integrated Rin-chen phun-tshogs' Treasure cycle with Nyi-zla sangs-rgyas' *Standing Blade of Grass,* conferring the oral transmission of the Sukhāvatī *phowa* on a full-moon day.

The Standing Blade of Grass

The history (*lo-rgyus*) of *The Standing Blade of Grass* is recorded by Nyi-zla sangs-rgyas and by Chos-kyi-grags-pa (1595–1695), who composed a text written at the behest of dBon-po Thar-pa gling-pa at Zla-dgon.[78] It may be summarized as follows.

In Vajrayana Buddhism, transferring one's consciousness is the quickest path to enlightenment. According to the history of this extraordinary *phowa* lineage, Padmasambhava was meditating at the Chimpu caves near Samye Monastery when an unexpected tragedy struck Khri Srong-lde-brtsan's minister Nyi-ma. While moving between houses, he had accidentally caused a fire that burned down his residence, killing his parents, thirteen others, and all his livestock. Nyima was inconsolable.

Emperor Khri Srong-lde-brtsan, moved by the suffering of his minister, went to Chimpu to beseech the help of Master Padmasambhava, who in turn traveled to Sukhāvatī to request the advice of Buddha Amitābha. Amitābha transmitted the teachings of *phowa* to Padmasambhava, instructing him to perpetuate them as a single lineage (*chig-rgyud*). He imparted the instructions to Minister Nyi-ma, who renounced all worldly activities and dedicated himself to their diligent practice. It is said that he attained the rainbow body at death, proof that he had successfully accomplished the transfer to Amitābha's Pure Land.

The Standing Blade of Grass was written on palm leaves by Padmasambhava using blood from his own finger and his consort's hair to tie the leaves together. He entrusted the text as a treasure to the *nāga* king gTsug-na rin-chen in Black Mandala Lake[79] and prophesied that in the future an incarnation of Minister Nyi-ma would come to claim it. Several centuries later, Nyi-zla sangs-rgyas was practicing meditation at the mountain of sGam-po dgar when he had a vision of Vajravārāhī, who instructed him to go to Black Mandala Lake and retrieve the hidden treasure. Nyi-zla studied and practiced *The Standing Blade of Grass* and beheld a vision of Vajrayoginī, who advised him that the text should remain a single-lineage transmission for two more generations, after which it could be disseminated publicly.

The following translation is based on an abridged version of *The Standing Blade of Grass* acquired in Bodh Gaya in January 2004. This text is transmitted annually in Bodh Gaya by K. C. Ayang Rinpoche (b. 1942), a Buddhist master from Eastern Tibet, who is currently living in India and is a recognized authority on Pure Land lineages of the rNying-ma and bKa'-brgyud schools. During his annual teachings in Bihar he grants the oral transmission (*lung*), empowerments (*dbang*), detailed instructions (*khrid*), and commitments of the *phowa* practice to residents from the Himalayan regions of India and to Western and Asian Buddhists.

A detailed history of the origins and instructions of this practice can be found in Nyi-zla sangs-rgyas' *On the Profound Path of Phowa Jag-tshug-ma: History with Explanatory Text* and in three commentaries.[80] The version of *The Standing Blade of Grass* used during the *phowa* teachings in Bodh Gaya is a composite text, and the following translation does not include meditation instructions and explanations, which are meant to be passed on orally only by his Eminence Ayang Rinpoche to his students.

The Standing Blade of Grass contains typical Mahayana aspirations (§I–IV; §X–XII; §XIV); a prayer for the lineage masters of *phowa* (§VII) included in Nyi-zla sangs-rgyas' *Instructions on the Profound Path of Phowa Jag-tshug-ma;*[81] recitation of the mantra of Aparimitāyus (Amitāyus) listed in the *Tshe-mdo* (§IX); and Karma chags-med's abridged aspirational prayer to Sukhāvatī (§XIII). Sections on the 'Bri-gung lineage entreaty (§V), invocation verses (§VI), prayers, and the recitation of the Buddha Amitāyus mantra (§VIII; §IX) are not accounted for in Nyi-zla sangs-rgyas' treasure text. They reflect later arrangements by Pure Land exegetes of the'Bri-gung bKa'-brgyud school.

The Standing Blade of Grass

Translation of Text
Repetitions are in italics

I. Mahayana Aspiration

May I swiftly attain the most precious, unsurpassable, and perfect realization, so that I lead all sentient beings equal to the sky to liberation, omniscience, and to a state beyond sorrow, especially those who create obstacles, harbor hate, and wish me harm.

Therefore, until I reach enlightenment, I will use my body, speech, and mind for the sake of virtue. Until I die, I will use my body, speech, and mind for the sake of virtue. From today until tomorrow, I will use my body, speech, and mind for the sake of virtue.

II. Refuge Prayer

From now until my awakening, I go for refuge to the Buddha, the Dharma, and the supreme Sangha.

III. Dedication of Merit

By the merit of generosity and the practice of the [six] perfections, may I attain enlightenment for the benefit of all sentient beings.

IV. The Four Immeasurables

May all sentient beings equal to the sky find happiness and the causes of happiness, may they be free of suffering and the causes of suffering, may they never part from the bliss devoid of sorrow, and [may they] abide in evenmindedness without partiality and prejudice.

V. The Drikung Lineage Prayer

Namo Guru! rDo-rje-'chang (Vajradhara) of the supreme sixth family; Venerable Tilo (Tilopa), source of the family of the buddhas of three times; Eminent Nā-ro-pa, revealer of the three bodies—*I pray that your blessings [permeate] the stream of my mind.*

Mar-pa, adept in languages vast as oceans; fully realized Venerable rJe-btsun mi-la (Milarepa); sGam-po-pa, life-tree of the Buddha's teachings in Tibet—*I pray that your blessings [permeate] the stream of my mind.*

rDo-rje rgyal-mo, chosen Yoginī; Venerable 'Jig-rten gsum-mgon, second Nāgārjuna; Great Abbot Tsul-rdo (Tshul-khrims rdo-rje), elucidator of the Buddhist teachings—*I pray that your blessings* [*permeate*] *the stream of my mind.*

Sangs-rgyas dpon, lord of nonduality; Venerable sPyan-snga, supreme lineage-holder; rDo-rje grags-pa, emanation of Tilopa—*I pray that your blessings* [*permeate*] *the stream of my mind.*

Thog-kha-pa, manifestation of great compassion; Venerable Grags-pa bsod-nams, (standing) beyond the delusion of binary fixation; rDor-rin (rDo-rje rin-chen), sanctioned by Saraha—*I pray that your blessings* [*permeate*] *the stream of my mind.*

rDo-rje rgyal-po, emanation of Padma (Padmasambhava); Venerable Chos-kyi-rgyal-po, expounder of the Buddha's teachings; Don-grub rgyal-po, crown of *siddhas*—*I pray that your blessings* [*permeate*] *the stream of my mind.*

bDag-po dbang, victorious in all directions; Venerable Chos-rgyal ratna, lord of all humans; Ratna dhwadza, emanation of Vajrapāṇi—*I pray that your blessings* [*permeate*] *the stream of my mind.*

Rin-chen chos-kyi-rgyal, emanation of Mañjuśrī; Venerable Kun-dga', unequaled second Victor; rJe-btsun Ratna, holder of two Dharma lineages—*I pray that your blessings* [*permeate*] *the stream of my mind.*

dPal-gyi-rgya-mtsho, treasury of the oral instructions; Venerable Dharma rā-dza, endowed with ceaseless kindness; Grags-pa'i-mtshan (Grags-pa rgyal-mtshan), holder of the Victor's lineage—*I pray that your blessings* [*permeate*] *the stream of my mind.*

Unrivaled guide of the Dwags-po bKa'-brgyud, dKon-mchog ratna, embodiment of the fundamental unity of the three vows and essence of the Buddha's teachings—*I pray that your blessings* [*permeate*] *the stream of my mind.*

Venerable Chos-kyi-grags-pa, tamer of beings, born from the unborn self-liberated state of *dharmakāya* and abiding in the unwavering *sambhogakāya*—*I pray that your blessings* [*permeate*] *the stream of my mind.*

'Phrin-las rnam-rgyal, outwardly holding the Vinaya's banner of victory, inwardly [possessing] *bodhicitta* for all sentient beings as if for one's child, and [secretly embodying] the indivisibility of the two stages—*I pray that your blessings* [*permeate*] *the stream of my mind.*

Venerable 'Phrin-las bzang-po, personification of all objects of refuge, master of all sutras and tantras, and teacher to all—*I pray that your blessings* [*permeate*] *the stream of my mind.*

Don-grub chos-rgyal, guiding all [beings] to the gates of Dharma and to supreme *bodhicitta,* liberating and maturing beings through the secret and profound teachings—*I pray that your blessings* [*permeate*] *the stream of my mind.*

Venerable dKon-mchog bstan-'dzin 'gro-'dul, holder of the White Lotus (Avalokiteśvara) and essence of all Victors, carrying through the four activities (pacifying, increasing, overpowering, destroying) all beings to awakening—*I pray that your blessings [permeate] the stream of my mind.*

Chos-kyi-rgyal-mtshan, quintessence of self-awareness, continuous and incorruptible flow of the subtle and secret tenets of Mahāmudrā—*I pray that your blessings [permeate] the stream of my mind.*

Venerable Chos-kyi-nyi-ma, excellent guide of those born and yet to be born, versed in the ultimate meaning of the profound celestial Dharma—*I pray that your blessings [permeate] the stream of my mind.*

Nirmaṇakāya Padma'i-mtshan (Padma rgyal-mtshan), luminous field of nonduality, unceasing expression of the unborn *sambhogakāya,* self-originated space of *dharmakāya—I pray that your blessings [permeate] the stream of my mind.*

Venerable Dharma dhwadza, fulfilling the desires of all sentient beings through the ultimate, secret, and profound gem of teachings, the extensive lineage of Ratnasambhava's practice—*I pray that your blessings [permeate] the stream of my mind.*

dKon-mchog bstan-'dzin chos-dbang blo-gros, the nature of unceasing and birthless Vajradhara, *sambhogakāya*'s vast luminosity—*I pray that your blessings [permeate] the stream of my mind.*

Dharma-ma-ṇi, peerless magical emanation-display of Mañjuśrī, teaching guide of the conventional and definitive truth of liberation—*I pray that your blessings [permeate] the stream of my mind.*

Thugs-rje'i-nyi-ma, restless emanation of the deity of compassion and quintessence of all objects of refuge, leader of all beings to enlightenment supreme—*I pray that your blessings [permeate] the stream of my mind.*

Mahāsiddha Nus-ldan rdo-rje, Vidyādhara, [emanation of] Śrī-Sing (Śrī-Singha), extraordinary chief of *siddhas* and transmitter of the most brilliant Buddhist teachings to the Land of Snows (Tibet)—*I pray that your blessings [permeate] the stream of my mind.*

rJe-btsun chos-skyabs, heroic master of renunciation, having realized the qualities of the past, present, and future buddhas you kept your nature hidden to tame sentient beings—*I pray that your blessings [permeate] the stream of my mind.*

bsTan-'dzin chos-kyi-blo-gros, all-pervasive lord of the nature of Vajradhara, with wisdom you discern all that exists and witness all objects of knowledge—*I pray that your blessings [permeate] the stream of my mind.*

Zhi-ba'i-blo-gros, destroyer of all mental fabrications concerning life and death, coming and going, you manifest a wondrous birth to inspire all sentient beings—*I pray that your blessings* [*permeate*] *the stream of my mind.*

bsTan-'dzin chos-kyi-'byung-gnas, matchless and compassionate miraculous emanation of 'Jam-mgon bla-ma, bright like the sun, [quintessence] of the theory and practice of the Buddha's words—*I pray that your blessings* [*permeate*] *the stream of my mind.*

Venerable Root Lama, embodiment of self-awareness and of the sacred *maṇḍala* of the yi-dams, the Dharma Protectors and the Ḍākinīs, conferring extraordinary attainments and protection from all dangers—*I pray that your blessings* [*permeate*] *the stream of my mind.*

With one-pointed awareness pray to the root Lama and the teachers of the lineage.

VI. Invocation

Lama, glorious Teacher, please take care of me.

Dwags-po bKa'-brgyud, master of four bodies and crown ornament of all, please take care of me! I pray that you gaze upon me with compassion, leader of sentient beings and guide to the true path, lord of humanity and regent of the Buddha, incomparably kind and unrivaled teacher Vajradhara, great protector of the 'Bri-gung. Grant me your blessings for realizing the two accomplishments (common and extraordinary). Grant me the spontaneous attainment of benefiting (oneself and others). Grant me the fruit (awakening).

VII. Entreating the Lineage Masters of *Phowa*

I pray to the lotus-born from O-rgyan (Padmasambhava)—*grant your blessings that I may realize the profound path of phowa; grant your blessings that I may travel to the celestial realms through the quick path of phowa; grant your blessings that I take birth in Sukhāvatī soon after I die. I prostrate to Buddha Amitābha.*

(The above passage is repeated below after each invocation.)

I pray to Terton Nyi-zla sangs-rgyas . . .
I pray to the Peerless Nam-mkha' rgyal-mtshan . . .
I pray to the Realized Sangha-bha-dra . . .
I pray to Pha-rgod dri-med blo-gros . . .
I pray to the Lord of Dharma Sangs-rgyas rgyal-mtshan . . .
I pray to the Peerless Ma-ti'i-mtshan-can . . .

I pray to the Mentor Phun-tshogs rnam rgyal . . .
I pray to the Great Abbot rNam-'jams phun-tshogs . . .
I pray to the Exalted dKon-mchog ratna . . .
I pray to Vidyadhāra Chos-kyi-grags-pa . . .
I pray to dKon-mchog phrin-las rnam-rgyal . . .
I pray to dKon-mchog phrin-las bzang-po . . .
I pray to Phrin-las don-'grub chos-rgyal . . .
I pray to dKon-mchog bstan-'dzin 'gro-'dul . . .
I pray to the Mentor Chos-kyi-rgyal-mtshan . . .
I pray to bsTan-'dzin chos-kyi-nyi-ma . . .
I pray to the All-pervasive Lord Padma rgyal-mtshan . . .
I pray to the Exalted Dharma dhwadza . . .
I pray to mGar-chen byang-chub dbang-po . . .
I pray to the Great Throne Holder Blo-gros rgyal-mtshan . . .
I pray to Rin-chen bstan-pa'i mdzes-rgyan . . .
I pray to dKon-mchog thugs-rje'i-nyi-ma . . .
I pray to Lho-sprul chos-dbang blo-gros . . .
I pray to O-rgyen nus-ldan rdo-rje . . .
I pray to the Exalted dKon-mchog chos-skyabs . . .
I pray to bsTan-'dzin chos-kyi-blo-gros . . .
I pray to Thub-bstan zhi-ba'i-blo-gros . . .
I pray to bsTan-'dzin chos-kyi-'byung-gnas . . .
I pray to the Kind Root Lama.

VIII. Homage to Amitāyus

I prostrate to Buddha Amitāyus, Lord and leader of this world and protector of the helpless and those who suffer. He who guards us from untimely death!

IX. Mantra of Amitāyus

oṃ na mo bha ga wa te / a pa ri mi ta āyuḥ rdza nyā na su bi ni tsi ṭa te dzo rā dzā ya / ta thā ga tā ya / arha te samyaksaṃ buddha ya / ta dya thā / oṁ puṇye puṇye / ma hā puṇye / a pa ri mi ta puṇye / a pa ri mi ta puṇye dza nyā na saṃ bha ro pa tsi ti / oṃ sarba saṃ ska ra / pa ri shu ḍha dharma te ga ga na sa munga te swa bha va bi shu ḍhe ma hā na ya pa ri vā re swāhā.

(Amitāyus root mantra) *oṃ a mā ra ṇi dzi vanti ye swāhā.*

[Next follows] The dissolution meditation of Amitāyus.

X. Dedication of Merit

Through the virtue of this [practice], may I swiftly actualize Amitāyus and an assembly of deities, and may I come to lead all beings without exception to this state.

By this merit, may I [reach] the all-knowing state and overcome all that is negative and false and may all sentient beings be released from the ocean of existence, the turbulent whirlpool of birth, old age, illness, and death!

Excellent and precious *bodhicitta:* where it is unborn may it arise; where it is born may it not decline; and may it ever increase.

I pray for the teacher's good health, for his great and long life, and for his enlightened activities to spread far and wide. May I never part from him!

May I reach through my training the wisdom of courageous Mañjuśrī and dedicate like Samantabhadra my virtue to all sentient beings. Through the blessings of the Buddha who attained the three bodies, the blessings of the truth of the immutable reality (*dharmatā*), and the blessings of the undivided assembly of the Buddhist community (sangha), may this dedication prayer come to fruition.

XI. Auspicious Prayer

Vajradhara, Ti-lo-pa, Nā-ro-pa, Mar-pa, Mi-la-res-pa, Dharma Lord sGampo-pa, Phag-mo gru-pa, Victorious 'Bri-gung-pa, and bKa'-brgyud Lamas—may there be auspiciousness!

XII. Prayer for Apprehending the Buddhist Teachings

Omniscient Lord 'Bri-gung-pa, master of dependent origination, may we apprehend now and up to our final incarnation the theory and practice of contemplation and meditation, and the unexcelled, precious teachings.

XIII. Short Aspiration to Be Born in Sukhāvatī

E-ma-ho! To the right side of the luminous Buddha Amitābha is the Lord of

Great Compassion (Mahākāruṇika) and on his left side, the Bodhisattva of Powerful Means (Vajrapāṇi), surrounded by immeasurable buddhas and bodhisattvas. Soon after we die, may we take birth in Sukhāvatī, the buddha field of unsurpassed bliss and happiness, and behold the face of Amitābha without passing through the intermediate state. I pray to all buddhas and bodhisattvas in the ten directions; grant your blessings so that this prayer is fulfilled without hindrance.

(Recite the mantra for accomplishing the aspiration)

tadyathā pace dri ya a wa bhodha nā ya swāhā.

XIV. *Bodhicitta* Aspiration

Excellent and precious *bodhicitta:* where it is unborn may it arise; where it is born may it not decline; may it ever increase.

gNam-chos mi-'gyur rdo-rje (1645–1667). Treasure revealer of the rNying-ma School and redactor of the Celestial Dharma (*gnam-chos*). Illustration from Tsering Lama Jampal Zangpo, *A Garland of Immortal Wish-fulfilling Trees*, translated by Sangye Khandro. (Ithaca, NY: Snow Lion Publications, 1988). Reproduced by permission of Snow Lion Publications.

Chapter Six

The Celestial Treasures of Buddha Amitābha

The Treasure Literature of the Ancients

The rNying-ma school divides its unique body of literature into three main lineages: the long lineage of Transmitted Precepts (*ring-brgyud bka'-ma*), the short lineage of Treasure (revealed texts; *nye-brgyud gter-ma*), and the profound teachings of Pure Vision (*zab-mo dag-snang*).[1] While the rNying-ma adheres to a variety of tantric teachings shared, more or less, by all schools of Tibetan Buddhism, its religious canon is altogether distinctive for its large corpus of treasure teachings attributed to the Indian *mahāsiddha* Padmasambhava, who predicted the suitable time of their disclosure, the persons who would reveal them, and the destined recipients who would become holders of the Treasure lineages.

The first Buddhist Treasure discoverer is said to have been Sangs-rgyas bla-ma from Las-stod mtsho in Western Tibet, who lived during the earlier half of Rin-chen bzang-po's lifetime (958–1051). Unfortunately, none of his revealed texts survive, and not until the thirteenth century did the Buddhist Treasure tradition became a widespread religious movement.[2] Arguably, the introduction of treasure texts in Tibet was in response and direct competition to an influx of new Indian tantric scriptures and lineages that were acquiring mainstream status. Behind the post-imperial acquisition of novel teachings, there were guilds comprised of Tibetan translators, Buddhist scholars, lineage-holders, and patrons, which promoted new standards of scriptural authentication that did not necessarily account for older or contemporary tantric systems that fell outside the vested religious interests of a newly formed Indo-Tibetan orthodoxy.

The short lineage of Treasure literature established its legitimization on the premise that its texts were concealed in the past by reputable masters and later revealed, like hidden treasures, by Buddhist adepts. The authenticity and canonical status of these discovered texts were thus retroactively established by their redactors and adherents, not so much as a pledge of marginality but as a reconception and reclamation of a preexisting religious heritage. To their most critical opponents, however, the revealed scriptures were pseudo-epigraphical and an anathema.[3] The need to provide the authenticity of treasure texts was essential for establishing the "soteriological efficacy" of the Treasure tradition, and the apologists of the ancient tantras did not fail to recall Indian antecedents to the phenomenon of revelation, citing Nāgārjuna's retrieval of the Prajñāpāramitā scriptures from the realms of the *nāgas*, or Maitreya's instructions to Asaṅga from the Tuṣita Heaven.[4]

Just as there are arguments for the impact of Indian Buddhism on the development of Tibetan Treasure literature, there are clearly several indigenous factors that contributed to its growth, such as preexisting autochthonous beliefs concerning the guardians of treasures and the soul-treasure of the Tibetan emperor. Moreover, we cannot discount the possibility that some old Tibetan translations of Indian texts had been preserved in the Himalayan border regions of Southern Tibet, Nepal, Sikkim, and Bhutan and were later rediscovered.[5]

The beginnings of the Tibetan phenomenon of Treasure literature are difficult to determine, partly because of rival claims by the Bön and because of different models of revealed literature adapted to various circumstances between the eleventh and fourteenth centuries, despite much observable continuity. The rNying-ma developed various systems of Treasure classification according to the content of the texts, the manner of their concealment, and so on. Nyang-ral nyi-ma 'od-zer (1136–1204 CE), an alleged reincarnation of Emperor Khri Srong-lde-brtsan, was the first Treasure discoverer (*gter-ston*) to systematize Padmasambhava's concealed teachings into "religious treasures" (*chos-gter*) and "wealth treasures" (*nor-gter*), adding to these categories "life-force treasures" (*bla-gter*), "sorcerer's treasures" (*mthu-gter*), and "medicinal treasures" (*sman gyi gter*), among others.[6] Treasure literature is not restricted to religious texts, nor are all such scriptures written in Tibetan. There are a number of secular treasures, such as medical tantras and histories, like the *Maṇi bka' 'bum*, the *Padma thang yig*, and the *bKa' thang sde lnga*, among others, while some treasures claim to be translations into Tibetan not from Sanskrit but from the secret language of the sky-dancers (*ḍākinīs*) written in *ḍākinī*-script (*mkha'-'gro brda'-yig*).[7]

Technically speaking, there is no temporal or geographic limit to the discovery of treasures, and they continue to be revealed today in Tibet and in Tibetan refugee communities.[8] Like pure lands that manifest for a variety of reasons, treasures are said to appear according to the benefit they render to beings and the fruition of past aspirations. But they do not always take the form of letters and texts—they may manifest as material objects, signs, visions, sudden ideas, or anything of essential meaning that was previously hidden. In the words of the Treasure discoverer Ratna gling-pa (1403–1479):

> It is a Treasure because it is concealed. It is a Treasure because it is hidden. It is a Treasure because it is inexhaustible. It is a Treasure because it fulfills needs and wishes.[9]

Celestial Encounters with Buddha Amitābha

There is a class of revealed scriptures that do not deviate in content from other tantric teachings of the rNying-ma school, but they are nonetheless distinguished for their unique mode of origination, having not been hidden previously like treasures. These texts are called Pure Vision Treasures (*dag-snang gter*), although the difference between these and the discovered Treasure modes of transmission can collapse in usage.[10]

During the "pure vision" revelation, the visionary is usually in a "state of meditative absorption (nyams), in the dream state (rmi-lam), or in the 're-ality' (dngos) of the waking state."[11] The source of inspiration may be a buddha delivering a sermon, or a celestial bodhisattva, a deity, a *ḍākinī* (*mkha' 'gro-ma*), a *nāga*, or even a prominent Buddhist master of the past. In the Great Perfection literature on Thögel (*thod-rgal*), the primordial, all-pervasive state of awareness is the foundation for the experience of luminous visions in the form of *maṇḍalas*, spheres of light, and Buddhist deities.[12]

The setting for pure vision transmissions may be worldly or otherworldly, such as a buddha field, but in all cases, lofty visions are not the same as karmic or "impure appearances" (*ma-dag-pa'i snang-ba*) that habitually flood the mind. Arguably, visionary events experienced by yogis originate from the mind, but their source is not the ordinary state of consciousness (*yid/sems*) but rather the awakened mind (*thugs*). Impure appearances that constitute our daily illusions arise due to the power of residual karma. On the other hand, pure appearances dawn "only for those people who are far advanced in their practice, since for ordinary living beings their perception of the world is more or less obscured by their individual karma."[13] According to Gyatso,

> [T]here is a presupposition which draws on the tantric idea that any advanced practitioner with developed "pure vision" would for that reason experience and participate in a pure world. Here "pure" is reminiscent of "Pure Land," where Buddhas live and advanced teachings are given. (1997, 96–98)

For the nineteenth-century Tibetan Buddhist scholars Guru bKra-shis and 'Jam-mgon kong-sprul, Pure Vision literature goes back to the eleventh or twelfth centuries.[14] Western scholars, such as Mayer (1994), trace the origins of Pure Vision and Treasure to much earlier Mahayana texts, such as the *Samādhi of Direct Encounter with the Buddhas of the Present.* He notes similarities with the Indian cult of hidden treasures (Skt. *nidhi*), and concludes that Pure Vision scriptures are "Buddhist developments of Buddhist ideas" worked out "in Tibetan soil."[15] Martin (2001, 23) also cites Indian Mahayana sutras in reference to Indian antecedents to the Tibetan treasure tradition, while Harrison (2003, 125) reports on the *Sarvapuṇya-samuccayasamādhi-sūtra,* which speaks of "endless dharma-teachings in book-form" that have been deposited inside mountains, caves, and trees and came into the hands of bodhisattvas. Vision and its active counterpart "visualization" are at the inception of Mahayana theology, despite later attempts by Buddhist scholars to detach Mahayana philosophy from its visionary roots (Beyer 1977).

In this chapter we will focus on a striking cycle of texts, the Celestial Teachings (*gnam-chos*), redacted by a young rNying-ma yogi, gNam-chos mi-'gyur rdo-rje (1645–1667), with the aid of his main teacher, the bKa'-br-gyud master Karma chags-med (1613–1678), who practiced them in the order of their discovery.[16] The Celestial Treasures are based on visionary encounters with Buddhist deities and are often referred to as Mind Treasures (*dgongs-gter*); technically speaking, however, they are Pure Vision Treasures since they do not derive from teachings previously encoded and concealed by Padmasambhava in the minds of his disciples, a functional definition of Mind Treasure texts.[17]

The Celestial Treasures comprise a distinct category of Buddhist texts which, according to Mi-'gyur rdo-rje's "inner biography" (*nang gi rnam-thar*), have arisen from the aspirations and pure minds of beings (fol. 10). They are classified according to their main principle (*ngo-bo*), definition (*nges-tshig*), cause (*rgyu*), conditions (*rkyen*), and divisions (*dbye-ba*) (fol. 13). They belong to a class of unusual scriptures that feature Buddhist teachings which have: 1) fallen from the sky (*gnam-mkha' nas glegs-bam bab*), 2) been inspired by apparitions of lamas, yidams, and *ḍākinīs* (*bla-ma yi-dam mkha' gro'i tshogs zhal-gzigs nas des gsung*), 3) been assembled from disembodied sounds (*zhal ma-mthong chos kyi sgra*), 4) appeared in the form of emanated letters (*sprul-pa'i yi-ge*), and 5) manifested from scripts forming in the sky (*gnam-yig*) (fol. 15–19).[18]

Furthermore, Mi-'gyur rdo-rje's inner biography classifies the *bKa' gdams glegs bam* (*Collected Works of the bKa'-gdams*) as a Celestial Treasure, while scriptures belonging to each class of Tantra (Kriyā, Caryā, Yoga, Mahāyoga, Anuyoga, and Atiyoga) are cited as examples of texts fallen from the sky. The passage concludes that all tantras are Celestial Treasures (*des na rgyud thams cad gnam chos lags so*) (fol. 16–18).

The Pure Vision of gNam-chos mi-'gyur rdo-rje

gNam-chos mi-'gyur rdo-rje, the son of mGon-po Tshe-ldan and bSod-nams-mtsho, was born in the wood-bird year of the eleventh *rab-byung*, in the area of Ngom in Khams.[19] His spiritual lineage, like that of most rNying-ma Treasure discoverers, is linked to prophecy of incarnations that go back to the Tibetan empire. It was predicted that he would retrieve texts concealed in the earth, a task he was unable to accomplish due to unpropitious circumstances in his life. The Treasure discoverer Ratna gling-pa (1403–1479) and bDud-'dul rdo-rje (1615–1672), whom Mi-'gyur rdo-rje met in Kham at the request of Karma chags-med, had previously predicted that a Treasure discoverer named rDo-rje, distinguished by a mole on his right hand, would be born in Kham and spread Buddhism in Eastern Tibet.

"Liberation narratives" (*rnam-thar*) written about him detail how he was infused with dazzling spectacles during the compilation of the Celestial Treasures.[20] It appears that for most of his short life Mi-'gyur rdo-rje was immersed in mystical visions of buddhas, bodhisattvas, and guardian deities.[21] His "outer biography" (*phyi yi rnam-thar*) reports that he did not learn to read and write like an ordinary child but was taught the Tibetan script by Padmasamhava, who appeared to him in the apparition of Gu-ru Blo-ldan mchog-sred.[22]

At the age of nine, in 1654, he met his teacher Karma chags-med, who realized that the young child entrusted to him was unusually gifted and inclined toward reading poetry and calligraphy, and was especially drawn to esoteric rituals, which seems to have been one of his favorite subjects. Karma chags-med began instructing him in the teachings of the bKa'-br-gyud school and the Treasure traditions of Ratna gling-pa and Karma gling-pa.[23] Mi-'gyur rdo-rje later wrote that he had foreseen meeting the middle-aged scholar-monk in a vision he had at the age of seven.

After completing a three-year retreat at the hermitage of rMugs-sangs, Mi-'gyur rdo-rje began to give teachings and tantric empowerments, attracting a large number of disciples. His popularity brought him repeated invitations from religious leaders and the governors of the principalities of Chab-mdo and sDe-dge in Khams.[24] His reputation as a powerful tantric yogi spread in Eastern Tibet, and several anecdotes relate how he performed miracles and supernatural feats at several places. Karma chags-med recounts that when he was of age to take a female consort—a common prerequisite for successful treasure discovery—he stopped a lunar eclipse by performing the "yoga of seminal reversal."[25]

One of Mi-'gyur rdo-rje's principal disciples, Rig-'dzin kun-bzang shes-rab (1636–1698), authored commentaries on the Celestial Treasures that became integral features of the monastic training and spiritual foundation of the dPal-yul school he founded in 1665.[26] In fact, the Celestial Treasures revitalized the rNying-ma monastic curriculum with novel and fresh teachings and inspired intrareligious affiliations with the bKa'-brgyud school in the formation of jointly shared incarnation lineages.

Attaining the Sukhāvatī Kṣetra from the Celestial Dharma

The corpus of Celestial Treasures contains a unique assortment of ritual practices devoted exclusively to the realization of Sukhāvatī (*zhing-khams sgrub*). The full title of this collection is *The Means of Attaining the Sukhāvatī Kṣetra from the Primordial Treasury of the Celestial Dharma: The Cycle of the Profound Whispered Lineage.*[27] In short, *The Means of Attaining the Sukhāvatī Kṣetra* represents the most original and systematic anthology of Tibetan Pure Land rituals to date, and its influence extends to the rNying-ma and bKa'-brgyud traditions and across the culturally Tibetan areas of the Himalayas. While many scriptures from this collection were revealed to Mi-'gyur rdo-rje by Padmasambhava, Amitābha, and his retinue of Avalokiteśvara and Mahāsthāmaprāpta, some texts are attributed to different authors altogether.[28]

There are currently several editions of *The Means of Attaining the Sukhāvatī Kṣetra* in circulation in Tibet and India. An inventory included in Appendix II lists four editions at the Library of Congress (Washington, DC); one introduced by Kapstein (2004); one published in Gangtok, Sikkim; an edition obtained in Lhasa (1999); and a 'Bri-gung compilation acquired in India (2004). The authority of the collection is attested to in several liturgical and instructional cycles, such as 'Jigs-med gling-pa's (1730–1798) *Klong chen snying thig*, the *gTer gsar* by bDud-'joms gling-pa, and the *rTsib ri spar ma* compilation of instructional material on the practice of the teachings of the bKa'-brgyud and rDzogs-chen traditions.[29]

In the following section we will focus on ritual texts composed over a span of 200 years, including works by gNam-chos mi-'gyur rdo-rje, his teacher Karma chags-med (1613–1678), and the Fourteenth Karmapa

Theg-mchog rdo-rje (1798–1868). With the exception of Karma chags-med's *Aspirational Prayer to Sukhāvatī* (*bDe chen zhing gi smon lam*) included in TRP (vol. 20), the text arrangements in the Gangtok and *rTsib ri spar ma* collections are identical.

Ritual Texts from *The Means of Attaining the Sukhāvatī Kṣetra*

Sukhāvatī Cremation Rituals
Title: *bDe chen zhing gi ro sreg chog ngan song gnas 'dren sdug bsngal mtsho skem gtan bde rab 'bar.*

Phowa to Sukhāvatī from the Celestial Treasures
Title: *gNam chos thugs kyi gter kha las bde chen zhing du 'pho ba'i gdams pa rgyas par bsgrigs pa.* The 'Bri-gung edition features *The Standing Blade of Grass* and not the *phowa* liturgy from the Celestial Treasures.

Sukhāvatī Effigy Rituals from the Celestial Treasures
Title: *gNam chos thugs kyi gter kha snyan brgyud zab mo'i skor las bde chen zhing sgrub gi byang chog thar lam dkar po.*

A Supplement to the Commentary on the Collection Means of Attaining the Sukhāvatī Kṣetra
Title: *bDe chen zhing sgrub zhing sgrub zin bris kyi lhan thabs nyung bsdus.* An abridged supplement to the extensive, middle-length, and concise commentary of instructions on the correct performance of the *bDe chen zhing sgrub* visions.

Invoking and Visualizing the Guardians of Sukhāvatī
Title: *bDe chen zhing sgrub kyi bka' srung gsol mchod 'gris chags su bris pa.* Rituals for the guardians of Sukhāvatī compiled as a supplement to meditation retreats. A translation of this work is included at the end of this chapter.

Distribution of Empowerments in *The Means of Attaining the Sukhāvatī Kṣetra Collection*
Title: *gNam chos bde chen zhing sgrub kyi dbang 'grig chags su bkod na.* Outline of the methods for bestowing initiations in the *bDe chen zhing sgrub* cycle.

The *Mahāsukhā Kṣetra Sādhana Prayers* (*bDe chen zhing sgrub kyi gsol 'debs*) is included in all the listed editions and is part of the *bDe chen zhing gyi sgrub thabs 'don cha* cycle in the Lhasa (5.1) and 'Bri-gung compilations (7.2). The colophon to this text informs us that this slightly abridged prayer for the *sādhana* was written by the Fourteenth Karmapa Theg-mchog rdo-rje (1797-1867) at the behest of the monk Karma chos-ldan.[30]

Mahāsukhā Kṣetra Sādhana Prayers

Na mo Amitabha-ye!

I supplicate the conqueror, luminous Amitābha, in the principal field of the west, the celestial display of the lotus. *Confer upon me the blessings of attainment; bless me that I may realize primordial buddhahood!*

I pray to Avalokiteśvara, the powerful Vajrapāṇi, and the retinue of bodhisattvas, *śrāvakas*, *pratyekabuddhas*, and arhats. *Confer upon me the blessings of attainment; bless me that I may realize primordial buddhahood!*

I pray to the Second Buddha, the lotus-born Padmasambhava, and to an oceanlike gathering of accomplished awareness-holders. *Confer upon me the blessings of attainment; bless me that I may realize primordial buddhahood!*

I pray to Mi-'gyur rdo-rje bdud-'dul rol-pa rtsal, the sublime heart lineage of my glorious teacher. *Confer upon me the blessings of attainment; bless me that I may realize primordial buddhahood!*

I pray to the manifold transformation of peaceful and wrathful emanations and guiding ocean of the *yidam*. *Confer upon me the blessings of attainment; bless me that I may realize primordial buddhahood!*

I pray to Ber-nag-can in union with dPal-ldan lha-mo,[31] the Lion-faced [protectors] in union, and the ocean of oath-bound Dharma protectors. *Confer upon me the blessings of attainment; bless me that I may realize primordial buddhahood!*

According to the blessings of this prayer may the two obscurations (emotional and cognitive), illnesses, negative forces, and hindrances be pacified! May long life and the light of wisdom greatly increase, and may I become inseparable from the enlightenment of the protector Amitābha!

General Preliminaries to the Three Roots is a short text from *The Means of Attaining the Sukhāvatī Kṣetra.* It contains pith instructions transmitted by Padmasambhava to Mi-'gyur rdo-rje in Chu-stod, Eastern Tibet, when he was thirteen years old, the same age that he received the celestial treasures from Buddha Amitābha.[32]

General Preliminaries to the Three Roots

[Recitation]

Homage to the Three Jewels (Buddha, Dharma, and Sangha) and to the Three Roots (lama, *yidam*, protector)! I go for refuge to the sources of refuge. In order to establish all beings in buddhahood, I generate the mind of supreme enlightenment.

[Visualization]

I manifest clearly [in the form of] Avalokiteśvara. From my heart [center] I radiate light and invite the directional protectors, local deities, and elemental spirits to settle in front of the precious *torma*. May it become nectar with the syllables *oṃ āḥ hūṃ!*

"Foundational deities, local deities, and elemental spirits, whether you reside here or came by accident, receive the offering *torma* and render this place suitable for the accomplishment of the 'secret mantra.' Do not yield to malice and jealousy. Supportive and positive forces, create favorable circumstances. Obstructing spirits of the negative world, go elsewhere. If you do not listen and cause harm, the wrath of wisdom will destroy you! Therefore, listen to [my] command!"

(Mantra recitation) *Oṃ sarwa lo ka pā la ba ling ta khā hi khā hi / sarwa bigha nan gatsha gatsha.*

(Seal) *Samaya gya gya gya.*

The generation of auspicious circumstances is an important element for the success and efficacy of many Tibetan rituals. The *Empowerment of the Eight Auspicious Symbols* is performed for the purpose of creating an auspicious environment and is included in most editions of *The Means of Attaining the Sukhāvatī Kṣetra.*[33] It is commonly followed by an empowerment in the seven precious jewels of a *cakravartin.*[34]

At present, it is unclear if collections of Pure Land rituals were systematized prior to the seventeenth century, when they became part and parcel of the Celestial Treasures. *The Means of Attaining the Sukhāvatī Kṣetra* has an undeniable rNying-ma and bKa'-brgyud orientation that resonates with the *Tibetan Book of the Dead* and many of Karma chags-med's works of the *bDe-smon* genre. The composite auctorial character of the collection contains, as we have seen, ancillary practices by the supreme bKa'-brgyud hierarch, the Fourteenth Karmapa.[35] It has been suggested that a first attempt at an original synthesis of Sukhāvatī rituals may go back to the rNying-ma master Kaḥ-thog-pa dam-pa bde-gshegs (1122–1192), who composed a *sādhana* for the visualization of Amitābha in accordance with the Mahāyoga system, which he transmitted to his disciple and regent gTsang-ston-pa (1126–1216). It is said that he "obtained the prophecy that in his following life he would dwell in Sukhāvatī as the bodhisattva Matisāra (Blo-gros snying-po) . . . and that then, in the future, in the aeon called 'Star-like Array,' he would become the Sugata Amitāyus."[36]

Kaḥ-thog-pa's work, the *Perfect Buddha Amitābha,* is a tribute to visionary compositions and accords in this respect with the celestial treasures (DM 1, 159–163). However, it does not structurally resemble later *sādhanas* to Sukhāvatī that commonly utilize the generation and completion stages, as with *Sukhāvatī Realized: Empowerment and Oral Instructions* by Mi-'gyur rdo-rje, discussed in the next section. Kaḥ-thog-pa's text forges links with the cult of Padmasambhava, a feature shared by both bKa'-brgyud and rNying-ma texts of the *bDe-smon* genre, while its innovation lies in its combination of mantra recitation with prayers and explanations that incite faith and confidence in Amitābha and Sukhāvatī.[37] In this respect, Kaḥ-thog-pa's eclectic work may be said to anticipate Karma chags-med's later compositions that harmonize sutra and tantra perspectives and strike a masterful fusion of Pure Land exoteric literature with esoteric ritual practices.

Sukhāvatī Realized: Empowerment and Oral Instructions

There are over a hundred Celestial Treasures listed in Karma chags-med's *Collected Works.* Among the texts related to Sukhāvatī, only two are catalogued in the Migot Collection: the *Compilation of Empowerments for the Means of Attaining the Sukhāvatī Kṣetra* (*bDe chen zhing sgrub kyi dbang 'grigs chags su bgod pa zhes bya ba zhugs so;* vol. 13, fol. 159–195), written in a rNying-ma style of *dbu-med* script, and *Sukhāvatī Realized: Empowerment and Oral Instructions* (*bDe chen zhing sgrub dbang las chogs zhal gdams dang bcas pa;* vol. 1, dza: fol. 5b4–9b2).[38]

We will now turn our attention to the *Sukhāvatī Realized,* an original contribution and an exemplar of the ritually composite organization that characterizes *The Means of Attaining the Sukhāvatī Kṣetra.* According to its colophon, the text was transmitted in its original form to Mi-'gyur rdo-rje by Buddha Amitābha and the deities in his retinue, and was subsequently committed in writing by Karma chags-med and his disciple Mi-'gyur rdo-rje. In this work, as elsewhere, Mi-'gyur rdo-rje's genius is reflected in his ability to consolidate a variety of Buddhist practices and pith instructions in a single ritual work.[39]

Sukhāvatī Realized is a *sādhana*-cum-empowerment (*sgrub dang dbang las chog*) structured in several interrelated layers that presuppose prior training in tantric visualization and related meditations briefly alluded to in the text. The *sādhana* begins with the visualization of the Amitābha triad arranged as in a Tibetan *thang-ka* of Sukhāvatī (fol. 5b–6a). Buddha Amitābha, ruby red in color, is framed in the middle by two standing bodhisattvas who represent the strength of wisdom (Vajrapāṇi) to his left and the power of compassion (Avalokiteśvara) to his right. Many youthful bodhisattva attendants surround the root deity, who is visualized in transparent form facing empty space. During the practice of self-generation (*bdag-bskyed*), the practitioner rises out of a lotus in the semblance of a white Lokeśvara and invites the wisdom-beings while reciting the root mantra of the deity (folio 6b). The chosen *yidam* is supplicated (fol. 7a–7b) to bestow blessings (*byin-rlabs*) for the realization of the supreme *siddhi*, enlightenment itself.

The Sukhāvatī *sādhana* features a unique assortment of Vajrayana-type practices that form independent meditations and are introduced succinctly as part of the *sādhana*'s progression: dream-yoga (fol. 6b), long-life rituals (fol. 6b), and the technique of mind-transference (fol. 7a). At the end of the text we find instructions for the consecration of ritual instruments utilized during the Sukhāvatī empowerment (fol. 8b–9a). The colophon contains pithy oral instructions that recommend to meditate on all places as the Pure Land Sukhāvatī.

Sukhāvatī Realized: Empowerment and Oral Instructions

Index Title: *Sukhāvatī Realized: Empowerment and Oral Instructions*

Manuscript Title: *The Sādhana of the Pure Land Sukhāvatī: From the Primordial Treasury of the Celestial Dharma, the Cycle of the Profound Whispered Lineage*

I. Self and Other Visualizations

(Recitation of tantric refuge) *Guru deva ḍākinī hūṃ.*[40]

(Preparations) This is the *sādhana* of Amitābha. There is no requirement for a *maṇḍala* or a *torma.*

(Visualization instructions)

Self-arise on the flower of a water lotus [in the form of] a white bodhisattva.[41] To your front is Lord Amitābha in meditative equipoise sitting on a moon seat [on top of] a lotus seat. His body is red in color with one face and two arms. He is seated cross-legged holding a begging bowl and wearing the robes of a monk. To his right is the Lord of the World [Avalokiteśvara], white in color with one face and four arms. He is standing on a moon disc on a lotus with palms held together. In his [second] right hand he holds a rosary and in his [second left hand] a lotus. To the left of

[Buddha Amitābha] is Mahāsthāmaprāpta Vajrapāṇi standing on a moon disc on a lotus holding a bell. They are surrounded by a multitude of buddhas, bodhisattvas, *śrāvakas*, and arhats.

II. Invitation of the Wisdom-beings

Light rays emanate from three syllables (*oṃ āḥ hūṃ*), [situated] in three places (head, throat, and heart)[42] of the three principal figures (Amitābha, Avalokiteśvara, Vajrapāṇi) respectively. Meditate that they are extending an invitation to Sukhāvatī.[43]

III. Amitābha's Mantras

Recite these mantras as many times as possible.

First, the extensive root mantra: *oṃ āḥ hūṃ amidhewa āyuḥ siddhi hūṃ.*

Then, the medium-length root mantra: *oṃ amidhewa hrīh.*

Then, the condensed root mantra: *oṃ āḥ hrīḥ svāhā.*

Then, an even more condensed root mantra: *oṃ hrīḥ svāhā.*

Alternatively, the condensed root mantra: *hrīḥ svāhā.*

Then, recite for as long as you are able the most condensed root mantra: *hrīḥ.*

Then, recite a sufficient number of times the mantra: *oṃ bhrūṃ svāhā.*

This is the practice of Amitābha. (Seal) *Samaya gya gya gya.*[44]

IV. Dream-yoga

For the practice of dream-yoga, [train to] apprehend daytime events as a dream. At your throat center [visualize] a red lotus with four petals, on which are arranged [the four syllables] *oṃ āḥ hrīḥ svāhā.* At the center of the syllable *hrīḥ* appears the syllable *oṃ.* Then visualize in your heart center a red lotus flower, on top of which is the Pure Land Sukhāvatī.[45] Imagine it very clearly as if it was there. Concentrate like this while falling asleep and in your dreams you will behold Sukhāvatī. You will also directly see Avalokiteśvara, Amitābha, and Vajrapāṇi. (Seal) *Samaya gya gya gya.*

V. Life-extending Amitāyus

Follow the activities of the long-life *sādhana*—you do not need to change the visualization. The begging bowl (of Amitāyus) is filled with [long-life] nectar.[46] Contemplate that it dissolves into you. Recite: *oṃ bhrūṃ swāhā bhrūṃ* twice or as many times as you wish. (Seal) *Samaya gya gya gya.*

VI. Transference to Sukhāvatī

Next follows the stages of *phowa*. Visualize in your heart center a red [syllable] *hrīḥ*. In the distance visualize the syllable *oṃ* with intensity. From the syllable *hrīḥ* six light rays issue forth that block the doors of the six kinds of rebirth, after which visualize the opening of the aperture of Brahmā on the crown of your head. Next, visualize above the crown of your head Amitābha, as explained before—the Lord and [his] attendants, [these] three. Meditate that your consciousness, a white drop in the shape of the [syllable] *hrīḥ*, is ejected into the heart center of Amitābha. Then, without the slightest doubt, express the aspiration to be born in Sukhāvatī. (Seal) *Samaya gya gya gya.*

VII. Supplication Prayers

The stages of the supplication prayer follow next.

First, the supplication prayer of accomplishment.

E-ma-ho! With one-pointed devotion, recite supplication prayers to the extraordinary Amitābha, Avalokiteśvara, and Vajrapāṇi and to all the innumerable buddhas and bodhisattvas. (Recite) *Confer the supreme siddhi; bestow upon me the blessings to accomplish Amitābha's sādhana.*

Next is the supplication prayer for the dream-yoga practice.

E-ma-ho! One-pointedly, I supplicate the extraordinary Dharmakāya Amitābha, Avalokiteśvara, and Vajrapāṇi. (Recite) *As I travel to Sukhāvatī in my dreams, bless me to meet Amitābha.*

The supplication prayer for the empowerment follows after.

Lama, Protector Amitābha, Lord Avalokiteśvara, Vajrapāṇi, and immeasurable buddhas and bodhisattvas, (Recite) *I supplicate you, confer upon me the empowerments of Vajrayana.*

[Next is the long-life supplication prayer:]

E-ma-ho! With a mind full of devotion, I prostrate, praise, and make supplication prayers to the perfect Buddha Amitābha, Avalokiteśvara, Vajrapāṇi, and to innumerable buddhas and bodhisattvas. *Bestow upon me the siddhi of [long] life.*

Next is the transference-supplication prayer:

E-ma-ho! Single-mindedly, I supplicate the most extraordinary protector

Amitābha, Mahākāruṇika (Avalokiteśvara), and Vajrapāṇi. *Bless me that my awareness transfers to the Land of Bliss.*

(Seal) *Samaya gya gya gya.*

VIII. Aspirational Prayer

Next follows the aspiration prayer. Recite the following:

E-ma-ho! Splendid Buddha Amitābha of infinite light! To your right is the Lord of Great Compassion and to your left the Bodhisattva Lord of Powerful Means, surrounded by countless buddhas and bodhisattvas. In the Pure Land known as Sukhāvatī there is immeasurable joy and happiness. After passing away, there may I instantly take birth after this life and in all my future lives. Once born there, may I meet Buddha Amitābha. Having recited this aspiration prayer, may the buddhas and bodhisattvas of the ten directions bless me to achieve this [supplication] without delay.

(Recite the mantra for accomplishing the aspiration:) *Tadyathā pañcendriya avabhodhanāya svāhā.* (Seal) *Samaya gya gya gya.*

IX. Consecration and Empowerment

After this, take the initiation. Go for refuge in the Three Jewels and then hold the vase in your hands. The vase is one with the syllable *hūṃ*, it is the Pure Land Sukhāvatī of Buddha Amitābha. When placing it above your head you will behold a vision of the Buddha Immeasurable Light. At this time, recite the root mantra as much as you wish. Then hold an image of the deity and announce: *This hūṃ is the Conqueror Amitābha.* By placing it on the crown of your head, you will take birth in Sukhāvatī and behold the Buddha Immeasurable Light face to face.[47] Recite the root mantra as many times as you want. Then pick up the *torma. This hūṃ is the Buddha Immeasurable Light surrounded by buddhas and bodhisattvas.* By placing it on your crown you will take birth in Sukhāvatī and behold Amitābha. Recite again the root mantra as many times as you wish. Then take the *vajra* in your hand. *This hūṃ is the Protector Amitābha surrounded by buddhas and bodhisattvas.* Place it on the crown of your head; having attained the empowerment of Amitābha you will take birth in Sukhāvatī. Then recite the root mantra as many times as you wish. *This hūṃ is Protector Amitābha.* Placing it above the crown of your head, you will take birth in Sukhāvatī and meet Amitābha. Recite like this the root mantra as much as you wish. (Seal) *Samaya gya gya gya. Katham guhya.*

X. Colophon

On the seventh day of Saka Dawa in the gSer-'phyang year, when Tulku Mi-'gyur rdo-rje was thirteen years old (May 20, 1657), during an [experience of an] unfathomable spectacle of light, [he] actually saw Amitābha and his retinue, [their] bodies the size of mountains. Amitābha instructed him thus: "The oral instruction is to meditate on all places as Sukhāvatī."

It will be good if this [teaching] spreads to all migrating sentient beings. If it does not, it is all right. But if it spreads it will be of great benefit. It is not necessary to visualize oneself as Avalokiteśvara. If one meditates so, it is fine as well. It is good if one performs the long-life rituals, the gathering of the essence of the elements, and so on in a different way. If one does not, all is agreeable.

(Seal) *Samaya gya gya gya.*

It is said that once again, in the evening, he had an experience of Buddha Amitābha and his retinue, who transmitted the oral instructions and the dream-yoga supplication prayer.

The Wrathful Protectors of Sukhāvatī

Karma chags-med composed the *bDe chen zhing sgrub kyi bka' srung gsol mchod* as a supplementary text for Buddhist meditation retreats. It is a unique and unusual addition listed in all *The Means of Attaining the Sukhāvatī Kṣetra* editions devoted to the propitiation of Dharma Protectors (*chos-skyong;* Skt. *dharmapālas*), powerful beings who guard the Pure Land teachings and those who follow them. They are ritually supplicated as the black (male) and red (female) Lion-faced Protectors (Seng-ge gdong) who are, according to the text, bound by oath to protect Pure Land practitioners and the doctrines that promote the realization of Sukhāvatī.[48]

The worship of Buddhist Protectors originates in India. It is likely that many of these fierce-looking deities originally belonged to Tibet's indigenous religions, while others were incorporated into Tibetan forms of Buddhism by the tantric master Padmasambhava in the eighth century.[49] In Tibetan iconography, Dharma Protectors are invariably depicted as wrathful entities with fierce eyes, horrific expressions, and protruding fangs. They have black, blue, or red skin and often multiple heads, hands, and feet. Some may manifest in peaceful form but even then they have an unstable nature and "are apt to assume suddenly a ferocious disposition."[50]

Generally speaking, the frightening appearance and forceful ways of the Dharma Protectors serve a cognitive and symbolic function: to avert and neutralize inner and outer obstacles that prevent Buddhist ascetics from securing the necessary conditions for their practice and from gaining spiritual realization. In "Recitations (III)" in the text, the kratophanic powers of the Lion-faced Protectors are conjured and all the "adverse conditions to spiritual practice" are summoned into a ritual cake, a red *torma* (*gtor-ma*).

Protectors are often enlightened beings (*'jig-rten las 'das-pa'i srung-ma*) belonging to the high-ranking deities (of the eighth, ninth, and tenth rank), or they may be worldly protectors within the six spheres of existence (*'jig-rten las 'das-pa'i srung-ma*), like Pe-har and rDo-rje shugs-ldan, who at one time served as protectors for the dGe-lugs-pa school against detrimental rNying-ma influence.[51]

In *Invoking the Guradians of Sukhāvatī* the Lion-faced Protectors are beseeched to perform the four enlightened activities (II), implying that they are not confined to the six spheres of existence in samsara.[52] It may be that they were once malevolent spirits bound by oath to protect the Buddhist teachings. In the Section II we read that formerly in the gaze of a buddha they promised to protect the doctrines of the Buddha. The "gaze of a buddha" may well refer to Padmasambhava, who is acknowledged in the "Homage (I)." The articulation of their oath in Section III to protect the practitioners of Sukhāvatī *phowa* and lead them to the Pure Land is reminiscent of a popular theme in the *Sukhāvatīvyūha* and other sutras, in which bodhisattvas vow to accompany the dead from behind.

The Lion-faced Protectors are addressed as Dharma-protectors (*bka'-srung;* Skt. *dharmapāla*), but more often they are called field-protectors (*zhing-skyong;* Skt. *kṣetrapāla*), an appellation that invokes a definitive sense of place, a physical location (*zhing*). I have translated the latter as "protectors of location" or simply "protectors." In Section III we read that after the ascetic has completed his practice, the Lion-faced Protectors perform three circumambulations around his retreat house and dwell behind him to support his practice. This suggests their supremacy over local deities and spirits of the land.

According to our text (III) The Lion-faced Protectors belong to the demonic class of the *bDud,* semidivine beings that are aboriginal to the Tibetan ancient world. In the *sādhana* they are invoked along with their retinues. For Nebesky-Wojkowitz, many *dharmapālas* have their own "court,"

> which includes the so called *zhang blon*, a "minister of interior" (*nang blon*), and a "minister of external affairs" (*phyi blon*), a commander-in-chief (*dmag dpon*), officers (*las mkhan*), messengers (*pho nya*)—these are frequently animals, called collectively the *spyan gzigs*—and groups of various companions (*ru 'dren pa*), as: fully-ordained priests, black-hat magicians, armed men, black women, and youthful dancers. To the initiated, however, the various "brothers" and "sisters," even the officers, messengers, etc., are nothing more than the manifold reproductions or "emanations" (*sprul pa*) and the "emanations of the emanations" (*sprul pa'i sprul pa*) of the particular *dharmapāla* on whom the priest meditates. They were produced at the own free will of this deity in order to be able to cope with the various tasks which a *dharmapāla* has to carry out. The deity can therefore reabsorb them into its body at any time. (1956, 21)

Cultic practices associated with the *seng-gdong* in the scriptures of the rNying-ma and bKa'-brgyud schools include propitiation and supplication, offering of blandishments in the form of sacrifices and vows, and magical coercion. Their provenance is not altogether clear and they may belong to the retinue of the four-handed mGon-po ljang-khu, having issued forth from the union of a *bdud* and *rākṣasī*.[53] These beings are described in detail:

> The colour of the *dharmapāla* is said to be "black like rainclouds." He has the ferocious head of a lion, with three eyes and out of his open mouth, in which sharp red teeth and the red tongue are visible, comes the roar of a thunder. In his right hand he holds a lance, in his left hand a skull-cup with a *gtor ma* in it. His dress is a wide cloak of black silk and a belt of jewels, from which a bow-case and a quiver are suspended. *bDud mgon seng gdong* is accompanied by his *śakti*, the *bDud mo seng gdong ma*. . . . As indicated by her name, she has the face of a lioness; her body is of a fiery red colour, and her hair is ablaze. She is naked except for a loin-cloth of a tiger-skin. In her right hand *bDud mo seng gdong ma* carries a trident, and in the left hand a human heart. Her mount is a red horse.

In the retinue of mGon-po ljang-khu, the male and female bDud-mgon seng-gdong have their own entourage of eight ferocious acolytes (*stobs ldan pho nya sde brgyad*).[54] There is a no reference to a retinue of eight assistants in *Invoking the Guardians of Sukhāvatī*, which describe the *bam-ro* as helpers to the Protectors in their work (III).[55] The *bam-ro* of the male Seng-gdong is black in color and has the head of a monkey and birdlike talons for hands. From his mouth spring crackling tongues of flame that scorch the opponents and their strongholds. With his birdlike feet he thrusts red *torma* at enemies, eliminating their line for seven generations. Likewise, another *bam-ro*, red in color, aids the female Seng-gdong-ma and has the same attributes.

Invoking the Guardians of Sukhāvatī

(Opening Statement)
Here is an arrangement of the offering prayers to the *dharmapāla*s for the realization of Sukhāvatī.

I. Homage
Homage to Guru Rinpoche!

II. Ritual Preparations
(The Offering)

In a copper vessel place a triangular *torma,* the size of a hand-span, and another triangular [*torma*] the size of a hand's length in front. To the right and left, place two [more *torma*] four inches in size with white and red ornaments.

(Evocation) *Hūṃ! Dharmapāla*s of Amitābha![56]

(Visualization of the *Dharmapāla*s)

The lion-faced *bDud* (class of beings) is dressed in a cloak and has one black face and two black hands. In his right hand he holds a banner, and with his left he fires red torma at enemies. He is riding on a three-legged black horse.[57] His consort is the red lion-faced, holding a trident and a heart. She is riding on a red horse and there is a pair of male and female *bam-ro* to her right and left [sides]. All of these appear clearly.

(Invocation and Offerings to the Protectors of the Field)

Hūṃ! I invite the protectors of location (*zhing-skyong*) with their retinue from Akaniṣṭha and from the great cemeteries, from the Rugged Forest and the Cool Grove, from the eight charnel grounds and the twenty-four places,[58] from the temples and places of Dharma. Take suitable seats so that I may offer you a cloud of outer, inner, and secret offerings, each one of desirable substances. Please be satisfied as you partake of medicine, blood (Skt. *rakta*), and *torma.*

(Mantra Recitation) *oṃ singha mukha hūṃ phaṭ / oṃ sina rama hūṃ phaṭ / tri hring dza hūṃ phaṭ / tri hring dza bed bed / ba lingta khāhi khāhi.*

(Reminding Them of Their Oath)

Hūṃ! Formerly, under the gaze of a buddha you vowed to protect the Buddhist doctrines with boundless powers like the sky. Praise to the

Protectors and their retinue! Partake of the *torma* and of the sacred substances and accomplish the four enlightened activities and the duties entrusted to your heart.

III. The *Sādhana* Practice

(First Visualization)

In the heart of the protector the syllable *hūṃ* stands on a moon disc encircled by the father-male mantra of the deity spinning clockwise. In the heart of his consort on a solar disc the syllable *Bhyo* encircles the mother-female mantra of the deity spinning counterclockwise. At the heart of the female and male *bam-ro* is the syllable *Tri* in reverse, with mantras spinning clockwise and counterclockwise respectively. In a forceful manner, recite the seven-syllable father-male mantra of the deity. The Mother and Father [Protectors] are incited to recall their previous vows.

For the yogis and for those around them, I will clear all obstacles and accomplish all their wishes in accordance with the Dharma. I promise at the time of death, when they are performing the transference to the Pure Land Sukhāvatī, to lead them there and accompany them from behind.

Meditate thus.

(Recitations)

Recite a few rounds (i.e., counting the beads of a *mālā*) of the father mantra. Then, if you wish to offer a *torma*, sprinkle once on a small red *torma.*

(Recite) *Namo! By the truth of the Three Jewels, the* [*truth of the*] *three roots, and* [*the truth of*] *all the deities residing in the Pure Land Sukhāvatī, and by the power of the Mother and Father Protectors, let there be summoned into this great red torma any harm that may come to us, to masters and disciples, to our merit, and any hindrances* [*that may arise*] *for reaching Sukhāvatī in our next life,* [*any*] *obstacles to liberation by human and non-human agents, demons, and from a host of* (negative) *spirits.*

(Recite) *Dza Hūṃ Baṃ Ho Phaṭ.*

(Visualized Offering)

Then cast [the *torma*] into the mouths of the Father and Mother Protectors and their retinue.

(Recite) *Khā Raṃ Khā Hi.*

(Second Visualization)

Hūṃ, the glorious protector with a black body and the head of a lion, holds in his right hand a lance with a flag to strike the foes, and in his left hand the heart of an "enemy monk."[59] He rides on a black horse dressed in a black cloak. To his right there is a black male *bam-ro* with the head of a monkey. His bird talon-like hands press the earth and with their force cause Mount Sumeru to quake and tremble. He angers the gods with his monkey feet lifted to the sky that carry a red *torma* thrown at enemies, eliminating them for seven generations. From his mouth spring crackling tongues of flame that scorch the opponents and their strongholds.

To the left of the lion-faced stands *dzakadza* who has a red body the color of fire. She holds in her right hand a waving banner that brings all phenomena under her dominion. With her left hand she holds a heart that has the power to destroy the enemies and their progeny. To her right stands a red female *bam-ro* with the head of a monkey. Her bird talon-like hands press the earth and with their force they cause Mount Sumeru to quake and tremble. She angers the gods with her monkey feet lifted to the sky that carry a red *torma* thrust at enemies, eliminating them for seven generations. From her mouth spring crackling tongues of flame that scorch the opponents and their strongholds.

(Supplication)

Father, Mother, and retinue, come forth and partake of this decorated *torma*—remove all hindrances! Expel malicious enemies, bandits, and thieves! Repulse harmful vow-breakers, spirits, and hindrances! Banish maledictions [coming] from beyond and invocations of demon sorcery! Divert epidemics, plagues, and infections! Accomplish the activities entrusted to you.

(Conclusion)

At this point the practitioner should repeat the long mantra seven or twenty-one times. Instantly, the principal deities and their retinue, these four, circle three times the trichiliocosm universe and the three realms and vanquish all detrimental influences. Having performed three circumambulations around your retreat house, they come to dwell behind you, supporting your practice.

IV. Colophon

This practice to the *dharmapāla*s of Sukhāvatī was compiled by the monk Raga Asya in the afternoon of the first day of the new rooster year. It was copied by the monk Jinpa. I confess all errors before the *dharmapālas*. By this virtue may the teachings of the Celestial Treasures spread and expand like the Ganges River. This is the profound means of realizing the Lion-faced *dharmapālas*.

The printing blocks were crafted by the donation of Chos-ldan gsangs-skyabs, who gave twenty silver coins, and from Chos-sgrub don-brgyud, who donated twelve silver coins. Through the virtue of this text may the Dharma spread, may the upholders of the teachings have long lives, and may the kingdom prosper (lit., "be filled with all that is good") through conduct in accordance with the Dharma.

May virtue prevail! May virtue prevail! May virtue prevail! This woodblock is located in Śrī Ne'u.

Maṇḍala of Buddha Amitābha (center)
with bodhisattva attendants

Epilogue

From Sukhāvatī to Tibet and Back

The entire world of appearances and possibilities is the field of Sukhāvatī.
bDud-'joms 'jigs-bral ye-shes rdo-rje (1904–1988)

The religious history of Tibetan Pure Land Buddhism spans over a millennium, encompassing a profusion of scriptures and ritual interpretations of Mahayana doctrines not found elsewhere in Asia. For the purposes of reviewing its prevalence, two registers are of relevance here. The first is generic in that it reflects the growth and success of Mahayana traditions beyond India, in part due to their emphasis on ecumenical discourses of salvation, a proliferation of ritual practices, and their inclusive communities of lay followers and monastics. The second register, more specific to place and time, refers to conditions and developments unique to Tibet. For example, Central Tibet in the eighth and ninth centuries witnessed the gradual displacement of ancient mortuary rites and beliefs in divine kingship by Buddhist conceptions of the afterlife and reincarnation, and the importation of Indian Mahayana scriptures alongside the identity of an imperial elite adopting the basic elements of a "Buddhist worldview," attracted in part to its cosmopolitan spirit.

The most original cultic enunciation of Pure Land ritualism in Tibet, to date, is attributed to the rNying-ma school. More than an exposition on creed, litanies, invocations, and intricate meditations were incorporated in tantric *sādhana*s for transferring one's consciousness to Sukhāvatī, reflecting salient innovations of the *bDe-smon* genre in Tibet. *The Standing Blade of Grass* and *Dying without Regrets,* two "revealed texts" compiled by rNying-ma adepts in the fourteenth century, are emblematic of an indigenous syncretism between sutra evocations of the Pure Land and a ritualized exchange between practitioner and deity in the practice of *phowa.* The Sukhāvatī *phowa* is a central feature in the most comprehensive collection of Pure Land rituals ever compiled in Tibet, the *Means of Attaining* *the Sukhāvatī Kṣetra,* included in Mi-'gyur rdo-rje's Pure Vision Treasures (*dag-snang gter*). This seventeenth-century collection exemplifies an intra-religious synthesis of the bKa'-brgyud and rNying-ma genius at work, whose influence can be discerned to the present times in culturally Tibetan regions of the Himalayas. It comprises an assortment of texts and practices that feature a variety of ritual inflections and ways of conceptualizing and relating to the Buddha and his celestial realm, including postmortem rites of passage (*bar-do thos-grol*), cremation ceremonies (*ro-sreg*), inscription rites (*byang-chog*), life-extending rituals (*tshe-grub*), guru-yoga (*bla-ma'i rnal-'byor*), transference of consciousness (*'pho-ba*), dream-yoga (*rmi-lam*), and supplications to the guardians of Sukhāvatī (*bde-chen zhing-sgrub kyi bka'-srung*).

The mystical and devotional character of Tibetan Pure Land rituals appealed to basic religious needs and supramundane aspirations, while reflecting a synthesis of different themes drawn from the bodhisattva traditions of Mahayana sutras and from homological correspondences to the trilateral nexus of deity, guru, and yogi in Vajrayana contexts. Many critical scholars from all Buddhist traditions in Tibet composed stirring aspirational prayers for Sukhāvatī (*bde-smon*) and detailed commentaries (*'grel-ba*) elaborating on the four causes for attaining the luminous sphere beyond death. Tibetan authors incorporated Vajrayana-type techniques, like Paṇchen Blo-bzang chos-rgyan (1567–1662), whose commentary conspicuously draws on self-generation and completion practices and dream- and guru-yoga meditations on Amitābha.[1] In time, Pure Land devotion carried beyond specific moments of worship that gave rise to unique and polysemic interpretations of Sukhāvatī, informed by a tantric identification of the spiritual path with the fruit of practice. In the rNying-ma corpus of the Great Perfection (rDzogs-chen), the "innermost secret reality" of Sukhāvatī became synonymous with the perfect realization of nondual intrinsic awareness (*rig-pa*). Independently of the propitiation of Amitābha, the theorization of Sukhāvatī served as a "metonymic expression for the primordial ground in which the Buddha's gnosis is disclosed."[2]

Sukhāvatī held special attraction for Treasure discoverers of the rNying-ma school. In their works, mythographic and theological elaboration of pure lands found expression within the bounds of sensory imagery and spatial metaphor, lending narrative consistency to the Tibetan phenomenon of revelation. The miraculous birth of the Indian master Padmasambhava (lit., "Lotus Born"), in Pure Land fashion from an open lotus (*rdzus-skyes*) in Lake Dhanakosha, is imparted in several hagiographies of the Treasure tradition.[3] A Treasure text, allegedly hidden by the Indian master in the rock of Zang-zang lha-brag, circumscribes a legend of a terrestrial land (*sbas-yul*) called mKhan-pa-lung, somewhere in the Himalayas, that resembles Sukhāvatī in all its delectable features, while also serving as a gateway to the Pure Land itself.[4] Treasure lore promoted a visionary and ritual interdependence between doctrines of liberation on the one hand and sacred territories on the other—the latter construed both as physical realities on earth and in heaven and also as symbolic referents of the spiritual potency of mind. The oscillation from metaphysical to physical landscapes and back is allied with a conceptual move from abstract worship to the demands of an immediate social situation and toward a more material notion of sacredness, which can then be elaborated functionally, nominatively, and otherwise. Physical sites are assigned soteriological value as a result of a particular set of circumstances, while some of the causes responsible for this phenomenon are not always of a religious nature. The relative passage from the treasure text in question redacted by Rig-'dzin rgod-ldem (1337–1408) is worth quoting in full.

> The King asked: "Teach us the signs of when the time has come to open a hidden land and of how to recognize when that time is at hand."
>
> "To understand when the moment has arrived three conditions are necessary: It must be the year of the male-water-horse, it must be during the second *rme-ba* and the troops of the tribes of the Gar-log and the Hor must have just arrived from the North; the secret land of mKhan-pa lung is southwest from bSam-yas. It is like the Paradise of bDe-ba-can (Sukhāvatī) blessed by Avalokiteśvara, like Po-ta-la. . . .
>
> Arriving there is like arriving in the three hundred places of bDe-ba-can. Everyone who reaches this place will have the reward of long life and will be free of diseases, will have his desires fulfilled, as one who has in his hands the jewel which grants every wish. All who live there will go to bDe-ba-can. In addition they will reach the dimension of bliss. This valley has been blessed before by compassion and so is purified. There is abundant wild vegetation there of fruit trees and medicinal plants. The interior of the valley is spacious and flat, at its center a river flows northeast as straight as a cord. He who arrives there will reach the level of Bodhisattva. He who remains there three years will go to bDe-ba-can. In the future he will be born inside a lotus flower. Let he who has doubts hear this: In the past in the paradisal kingdom of dGal-ldan where the Ārya Avalokiteśvara and Tara Vajra-bhṛkutī (Khro-gnyer-can) [resided] . . . the most powerful of gods, Śakro Devendraḥ (Lha'i dbang-po rgya byin) offered five hundred Utpalam flowers to them. One of the flowers from his bunch settled on the heart of the Ārya, the others were scattered in the heavens towards the south. Then Śakro Devendraḥ asked: "Why, o Ārya, have the flowers I offered you been scattered into space?" The Ārya replied:

> "Hear me, most powerful of the divinities: These flowers will fall to earth towards the south, and wherever they settle there my presence will be manifest and there will be Buddhist disciples. In addition, wherever the flower of Utpalam which rises from my heart should fall, it will be possible to enter the dimension of bDe-ba-can and to overcome the conflicts which arise from the condition of the life and death of the six realms of transmigration."[5]

It is tempting to read signs of collective distress or millennialism in the resurgence of Amitābha's cult in Tibet, especially in accounts of hidden lands that resemble Sukhāvatī, yet we must bear in mind that spatial metaphors describe both physical and semantic space and are just as diachronically appealing as they may be synchronically relevant. Sacred geographies heighten the attractiveness of soteriological theories by giving them immediately graspable and often aesthetically compelling forms, thus increasing their scope and efficacy. In this sense, they enable believers to relate religious concerns to their own environment—that is, to specific loci that may constitute part of their everyday world, as in the case of pilgrimage sites infused with spiritual qualities; or they can constitute an imagined realm of bliss, beauty, and order, as in the case of heavenly realms. Mystical landscapes abound in Indian Mahayana texts, involving adepts and their encounters with deities during deeper levels of meditation. Intimate visual experiences with buddhas and travels to other worlds are commonplace in Pure Land texts of the tantric variety, such as those dealing with dream- and guru-yoga, as well as the method of transferring to Sukhāvatī.[6]

Soteriological missions often become intertwined with descriptions of sacred spaces, which not only reinstate their *raison d'être* from a religious point of view but also provide them with an iconic and sociopolitical identity of their own. Pure Land traditions combined liberation tactics concomitant with more or less appealing cosmographies that could serve as a means to spatially situate, visualize, and project beliefs in the afterlife and reconstitute death as a means of salvation. The cultic development of Amitābha's Pure Land in imperial Tibet was closely linked to other trends, such as the royal sponsorship of sutras and the deification of Tibetan rulers, while it is plausible that Sukhāvatī served as a tangible expression and attractive vision of what lies beyond death, supplanting pre-Buddhist beliefs in the heavens and divine kingship. The colophon to Tsong-kha-pa's *Praise to Amitābha* is a tribute to Tibet's indigenous gods and serves as a reminder of their substitution by Buddhist deities and Mahayana conceptions of the afterlife. His fleeting reference to the forgotten 'O-de gung-rgyal, an early god of heaven and not of earth, anticipates the Buddhist conversion of the land of Tibet by Avalokiteśvara.[7]

There is a plethora of narratives concerning Tibet's conversion to Buddhism, which are inculcated with legends and edified by prophecies, as in those found in an eminent history about Tibet's golden age, the *Clear Mirror of Royal Genealogies* (*rGyal rabs gsal ba'i me long*). This influential work, authored by the scholar-monk bSod-nams rgyal-mtshan (1312–1375), conjoins ancestral worship and Pure Land ideology in a Tibetan national saga detailing the conversion of an Indian Mahayana bodhisattva into Tibet's guardian deity. According to the Tibetan narrative, a long time ago Avalokiteśvara voiced an aspiration prayer (*smon-lam*) to turn the demon-infested country of Tibet into a field of conversion (*zhing-khams*), a pure land.[8] In line with the Mahayana mission, Buddha Amitābha empowered Avalokiteśvara for this task and the latter incarnated as a monkey to prevent a native rock-ogress from causing further harm to the Tibetan people. From their intercourse, the mating of the spiritual and the gross-physical, the race of the Tibetans and their Buddhist kings emerged.

While this tale of ancestral origins may be interpreted in a variety of ways, there is a readiness to countenance Avalokiteśvara not just as a celestial being of an indigenized Indian cult but as the progenitor of the Tibetan people and lord of a transregional and transhistorical domain whose remit transcends the locality of his Indian origins. As pointed out by Schwieger (2000), a recurrent theme in traditional religious histories is that of Tibetans as the "chosen people" entrusted with the sacred mission to preserve the true teachings of the Buddha. Their mission provides them with a sense of collective identity, reinforced by the continuous activity of buddhas and bodhisattvas who shape Tibetan history through a multiplicity of emanations and incarnations that work for the welfare of the Tibetan people. While this ideology served to provide Tibetans with a sense of supranational identity, it also offered legitimizing power to monastic institutions that adopted the role of preserving the "sacred mission" and ensuring the authenticity of the tradition right up to the present day.

Social cohesion, cultural identity, and nationalist sentiments may be the production of a group of people whose participation in a common spiritual heritage is further reinforced through a shared soteriological mission. The political ramifications are evident in states popularizing sacred cosmographies to sanction their territories under the sphere of operation of a specific god, saint, or cultic deity. The governor of Tibet, sDe-srid Sangs-rgyas rgya-mtsho (1679–1703), ingeniously framed the secular authority of the Fifth Dalai Lama, Ngag-dbang blo-bzang rgya-mtsho (1617–1682), by tracing it back to a supernal source, as in the legends of the Tibetan Buddhist emperors. Rooted in the legendary palace built by Srong-brtsan sgam-po in Lhasa, the "place of the gods," the Potala, a terrestrial double of Avalokiteśvara's pure land erected by the Fifth Dalai Lama served as a fortress, temple, and seat of government as well as a national place of pilgrimage.[9] By resorting to Tibetan legends, the sDe-srid certified at once both divine equivalence with the incarnation (*sprul-sku*) of the Dalai Lama and the deity of location, thus elaborating on a hierarchical polity that gave credal and institutional force to both cult and myth.[10]

While these points may not service empirical descriptions of religious history, they are pertinent for reconstructing a conceptual and causal grid that assigns religious meaning to kingship, a phenomenon detected in the earliest vestiges of Indian Buddhism.[11] In Tibet's religious-political history, Pure Land themes enjoyed the prestige of an almost "atemporal antiquity" that reemerged in the strategies of integration of secular and monastic powers (*chos-srid gnyis-'brel*) invested in the institution of the Dalai Lama, the patron saint and living incarnation of Tibet's ancestral bodhisattva.[12]

The above considerations may have particular salience to the interpretation of Tibetan cults and the resurgence of Pure Land literature in rNying-ma redactions of the seventeenth century. From a Peircian semiotic perspective, soteriology may be defined as a system of signs, of an iconic, indexical, and symbolic kind, embodied in the rituals, images, and textual corpora of a religious tradition—and, in the Tibetan case, even projected unto the canvas of nature, society, and state. The rhetorical force of salvation narratives emplaced in Tibetan material culture (natural loci, buildings, scriptures, and iconography) and embodied in ancestral memory reveal a dynamic correlation between institutionalized Mahayana soteriology, Pure Land cosmography, and state building. These overlapping spaces of meaning are generated along successive instances of territorialization of "sacred time and space," as in the case of deities acquiring transhistorical, social, and institutional consistency beyond their scriptural identities and regional worship.

The contemplative elaboration of Buddha Amitābha, his Pure Land, and his cohort deities, in terms of their different functions, was to a large extent informed by religious, monastic, and political conventions, and had concrete and lasting effects in the expression of Tibetan Buddhist sentiments concerning spiritual attainments and the afterlife and in the identity, interpretation, and persistence of Pure Land creeds among all schools of Tibetan Buddhism in the Tibetan plateau and elsewhere.

Appendix I

A Critical Analysis of the Orgyan-gling Gold *bDe-mdo*

The critical analysis of the Tibetan short *Sukhāvatīvyūha-sūtra* follows the guidelines of a diplomatic edition laid out by Schoening (1995, 171–185), who argues that a diplomatic edition "has historical validity," in contrast to a critical edition that often draws upon texts separated by centuries and resorts to an irreproducible methodology, or on conjecture that reconstructs a hypothetical original of the text, which neither reflects any one period in history nor any historically valid text.[1] A diplomatic edition is an accurate transcription of a known historical document, with variant readings that do not infringe upon the text, and without normalizing its orthography. This approach is particularly relevant in the analysis of Buddhist scriptures in Tibetan translation, since the texts in question are often shown to be open recensions.[2]

Furthermore, we do not know if the Tibetan *Sukhāvatīvyūha-sūtra* was a translation based on one or several Sanskrit texts, nor do we know if the "archetype" was composed originally in a language other than Sanskrit. We are equally unclear of the number of Tibetan translations that may have been in circulation prior to the revision and standardization that followed the new official translation rules (*skad gsar bcad*) in ninth-century Tibet. For these reasons, it seems ineffective to standardize and tamper with the Tibetan text—a feature of many critical editions that has been consciously avoided here.

The critical analysis utilizes as its source text what appears to be the oldest manuscript among the Kanjurs consulted. Since no manuscripts of the *bDe-mdo* have been found in Dunhuang or Ta-pho, the best candidate for a text that is presumably older, with the exception of the Lithang xylograph (1609–1614 or 1621), is the golden O-rgyan-gling MS with its use of old orthographical features and faded quality of its medium.[3] At this early stage of our knowledge concerning the origins of the Og MS, we cannot be certain of its chronological relation to O. Since none of the texts of the Og MS have yet been critically studied, the Og *bDe-mdo* stands out in this comparison with other, better-known Kanjurs.

The following critical study complements the findings published by Onoda (2001), but differs in utilizing the Og MS as the root text, and it also includes the O Ms not consulted by Onoda.[4] The groupings of *shad* are noted for reference, though their distributions do not appear to yield any striking patterns.

Source Text: Og = O-rgyan-gling / rTa-dbang gold MS *mDo-sde* (205a1–208b7), vol. Nya. No colophon.

Other Editions

D = sDe-dge edition. *mDo-sde* (195b4–200a2), vol. Ja. Colophon.
Q = Peking Qianlong edition: *mDo-sna-tshogs* (219b8–224a7), vol. Chu. No colophon.
H = lHa-sa edition. *mDo-sde* (307b6–314b2), vol. Ja. Colophon.
N = sNar-thang edition. *mDo-sde* (306a4–313a6), vol. Ja. No colophon.
F = Phug-brag MS *mDo-sde* (94a4–100a4), vol. Na. Catalogue colophon.
O = O-rgyan-gling / rTa-dbang handwritten MS *mDo-sde* (299b6–304b7), vol. Cha. No colophon.
L = London (Shel-dkar) MS *mDo-sde* (196a7–202a2), vol. Zha. Colophon.

Conventions

add: insert (x)	add. /: insert *shad*
om: omit (x)	om. /: omit *shad*
/ : single *shad*	// : double *shad*
capital vowel: inverted *gi gu*	< > ornamental sign (*mgo-yig*)

* *Italicized* words that are not referenced indicate that their textual variants have been recorded earlier in this analysis.

Folio 205a

[D (195b), H (307b), Q (219b), F (94a), N (306a), O (299b), L (196a)]

Line 1: < > / (OgDNFL / : QHO //) rgya gar skad du / a (Og a : DQHNFOL ā) rya su kha (OgDH kha : QNFOL khā) ba ti *byu hā* (OgL byu hā : DH byū ha; QN byu ha; F bu ha; O byung ha) *na ma* (OgFL na ma : DQHNO nā ma) ma hā yā na *su tra* (OgFL su tra : Q sūtra; DOHN sū tra) / bod skad du / 'phags pa bde ba can gyi bkod pa zhes bya ba (OgDQNFL ba : O ba'i) theg pa chen po'i (OgDHNFOL om. / : Q add. /) [Q 220 a] mdo / (OgDQH / : NFOL //) sangs rgyas dang (OgDHFO om. / : QNL add. /) byang chub sems dpa' thams cad la phyag *'tshal lo* (OgDQHNF 'tshal lo : OL 'tshalo; 'OgDH / : QNFOL //) 'di skad bdag

Line 2: gis (OgDQHNOL gis : F gi) thos pa (OgDQHNOL pa : F pa'i) dus gcig na / bcom ldan 'das mnyan *du yod pa na* (OgH du yod pa na : DQNFOL yod na) / rgyal bu rgyal byed kyi tshal mgon myed (Og myed : DQHNFOL med) [H 308a] zas sbyin gyi (OgQDHNFL gyi : O gyis) kun dga' ra ba na / (OgDQHFO / : NL om. /) [L 196b] dge slong stong nyis (OgDQHNFL nyis : O nyi) brgya lnga bcu'i dge slong gi dge 'dun chen po (OgDQHNFL om. / : O //) gnas brtan nyan thos chen po (OgDQHNFL om. / : F add. /) dgra bcom pa sha stag la

Line 3: 'di lta ste / gnas brtan (OgDQHNFL brtan : O bstan) *sha ri'i* (OgFO sha ri : DQHNL shā ri'i) bu dang / *mo'u dgal* (OgO mo'u dgal : Q mood dgal; D mood gal; HN moodgal; F mi'u 'gal; L mo'u dga') [O 300a] gyi bu chen po dang / 'od srung (OgDQHOL srung : NF srungs) [N 306b] chen po dang / *ka tya'i* (OgOL ka tya'i : DN kā tyā'i; QH kā tiya'i; F ka ti'i) bu chen po dang/ *kab pin* (OgHL kab pin : DQN ka pin; F kab phyin; O kab phyin) chen po dang / gsus po che (OgDQHNFO che : L chen) dang / nam gru dang (OgO : om. / : DQHNFL add. /) lam *bstan blun po* (Og bstan blun po : DQHNFO phran bstan; L phran brtan) dang / dga' bo dang / kun dga' bo dang / *sgra gcan* (OgDHNOL sgra gcan : QF sgra can) zin dang / ba lang

Line 4: bdagdang / *bhar dva dza* (OgD bhar dva dza: QHN bha ra dhva dza FL ba ra dva tsa; O ba ra dvā dza) [F 94b] dang / (OgDQHNFO / : L om. /) 'char byed nag po dang / *ba ku la* (OgDHNFOL ba ku la : Q ba kku la) dang / ma 'gags pa dang / de dag dang (OgQHNOL om. / : DF add. /) nyan thos chen po gzhan dag dang / byang chub sems dpa' sems dpa' chen po *mang po* (OgDQHNL mang po : FO om.) la 'di lta ste [D 196a] / 'jam dpal (OgQHNFOL om. / : D add. /) gzhon nur gyur (OgDQHNFL gyur : O om.) pa dang / (OgQHFOL / : DN om. /) byang chub sems dpa'

Line 5: sems dpa' chen po *myi 'pham ba* (Og myi 'pham ba : D mi pham ba; QHNFOL mi 'pham pa) dang / byang chub sems dpa' sems dpa' chen po spos gyi (OgHO gyi : DQNFL kyi) glang po dang (OgDQHNOL dang : F de dag dang) / byang chub sems dpa' sems dpa' chen po rtag tu brtson dang / byang chub sems dpa' sems dpa' chen po brtson ba (Og ba : DQHNFOL pa) *myi 'dor* (OgFO 'dor : DQHN 'dor ba; L 'dod) dang / de dag dang / (OgFOL / : DQHN om. /) byang chub

Line 6: sems dpa' sems dpa' chen po gzhan mang po dag dang / lha'i dbang po brgya byin dang / *myi* mjed (OgDQHNFL mjed : O 'dzed) kyi bdag po tshangs pa dang / de dag dang / (OgFOL / : DQHN om. /) lha bye ba khrag khrig *brgya stong* (Og brgya stong : DQHNFOL 'bum phrag) [H 308b] mang po gzhan dag dang yang thabs gcig (OgQHO gcic : DNFL cig) tu bzhugs te / de nas bcom ldan 'das kyis (OgDQHNOL kyis; om. / : F kyi; add. /) *tshe dang*

Line 7: *ldan pa* (OgDQHNFL ldan pa : O om.) *shi ri'i* bu la bka' stsal pa / *sha ri'i* bu (OgDQNFOL om. / : H add. /) sangs rgyas kyi zhing 'di nas nub phyogs *logs su* (OgDQHNL log su; om. / : FO logsu; add. /) sangs rgyas kyi zhing bye ba khrag khrig *brgya stong* (Og brgya stong : QHNF 'bum; DOL phrag 'bum) [N 307a] 'das pa na / (OgFOL / : DQHN om. /) 'jig rten gyi khams bde ba can zhes bya ba zhig (OgH zhig : DQNFOL om.) yod de / de na de bzhin gshegs pa *dgra bcom pa* (OgDQHNOL dgra bcom pa : F om.)

Line 8: yang dag par rdzogs pa'i sangs rgyas tshe dpag myed pa zhes (Og zhes : DQHNFOL ces) [L 197a] bya ba bzhugs te / (OgFOL / : DQHN om. /) *'tsho zhing gzhes* (OgDHNL 'tsho zhing gzhes : FO 'tsho zhing bzhes; Q mtsho zhing bzhes) te (Og te : DQHNFOL la) chos kyang ston to / (OgDOL / : QHNF //) *sha* ri'i bu (OgDQNFOL om. / : H add. /) *'di la* (OgQ 'di la : DHNFOL 'di ji) snyam du sems / 'jig rten gyi khams de ci'i phyir bde ba can zhes bya zhe na / *sha* ri'i bu (OgDQNFOL om. / : H add. /) 'jig rten gyi khams bde ba can de na (OgDQHNF na : L la; O ni; OgFO / : DQHNL om. /) [Q 220b, O 300b]

Folio 205b

Line 1: sems can rnams kyi lus la sdug bsngal *myed* / sems la sdug bsngal *myed* cing / (OgQFO / : DHNL om. /) bde ba'i rgyu tshad med par (OgDQHNFO par : L pa) yod de / (OgDQHNFL / : O om. /) de'i phyir 'jig rten gyi khams bde ba can zhes bya'o / (OgDOL / : QHNF //) [F 95a] *sha* ri'i bu (OgDQNFOL om. / : H add. /) gzhan yang 'jig rten gyi khams bde ba can ni (OgDQHNL ni; om. / : F gyi; O add. /) kha khyer rim pa bdun

Line 2: dang (OgF om. / : DQHNOL add. /) *shing ta la'i 'phreng ba* (OgQH shing ta la'i 'phreng ba : DNL shing ta la'i phreng ba; F shing rta la phreng ba; O shin ta la'i 'phreng ba) rim pa bdun dang / dril bu g.yer kha'i (OgHFOL kha'i : DQN ka'i) dra ba rnams kyis kun nas yongs su bskor ba (OgDQHNFO om. dang : L add. dang) / *bkra ba* (OgDHNFOL om. / : Q add. /) *blta* (OgDQHOL bkra ba blta : N bkra ta lta; F bkra ba lta) na sdug pa'o / (OgDHNOL / : QF //) *sha* ri'i bu sangs rgyas kyi (OgDQHNFL kyi : O kyis) zhing de ni (OgDQHNFL om. / : O add. /) rin po che sna *bzhi la* (OgDHL bzhi la : QN bdun la; O bzhi'i; FO om. la) 'di lta ste / gser dang / dngul dang / *be du rya* (Og be du rya : D bee dū rya; Q bee tu rya; H bee ṭūrya; N bee ṭūrya; F bee du rya; O bee ḍū rya; L bee ḍū Rya) dang/shel dang / (OgDQFOL / : HNom. /)

Line 3: rnam pa de lta bu'i sangs rgyas kyi zhing gi yon tan bkod pa dag gis legs par brgyan pa'o / (OgDHOL / : QNF //) *sha* ri'i bu (OgDQNFOL om. / : H add. /) gzhan yang 'jig rten gyi khams bde ba can na / (OgFOL / : DQHN om. /) [H 309a] rin po che sna bdun gyi rdzing bu (Og bu : DQHNFOL om.)

yan lag brgyad dang ldan ba'i (OgO ba'i : DQHNFL pa'i) chus *yongs su* (OgDQHNFL yongs su : O yongsu) gang ba / (OgDQHNFO / : L om. /) rin po ce'i (OgHO ce'i : DQFNL che'i) [N 307b] *pad mas* (OgDQF pad mas : HNOL padmas)

Line 4: khebs pa (OgDO om. / : QHNFL add. /) bya rog gis btung (OgDQHNOL btung : F gtung) *du rung bar khad* (OgDQNOL rung bar khad : H rung bar kha da; F rung ba kha dang /) cad (OgQNOL cad : DHF chad) [D 196b] du gyur pa / (OgFOL / : DQHN om. /) gser gyi bye ma bdal ba dag yod de / rdzing *bu* de (OgDQHNFL de : O om.) dag gi (OgDQHNOL gi : F om.) phyogs bzhi kun na (OgDQHNOL ni : F tu; Og / : DQHNFOL om. /) them skas bkra ba / blta (OgDQHOL blta : NF lta) na sdug pa (OgDQHNFO pa : L add. dang; OgDQHNOL / : F om. /) gser dang / dngul dang / *be du rya* dang / shel dang / rin po che sna bzhi las byas pa (OgDQHNO om. / : FL add. /)

Line 5: bzhi (OgDQHNOL bzhi : F rdzing bzhi) bzhi yod do (OgDHFOL do : QN de; OgDQNF / : HOL //) rdzing *bu* de dag gi 'gram na (OgDQHNFO na : L ni; Og / : DQHNFOL om. /) rin po *ce'i* shing ljon pa / (OgFOL / : DQHN om. /) rin po *ce* sna bdun la (OgDQHNOL la : F om.) 'di lta ste / gser dang / dngul dang / *be du rya* dang / shel dang / mu tig dmar po dang / rdo'i (OgDQHNOL rdo'i : F rdo rje'i) snying po dang / spug (OgDHNFOL spug : Q pug) gi shing bkra ba (OgQHL om. / : DNFO add. /) blta na sdug pa dag skyes so / (OgD / : QHNFOL //) [L 197b] rdzing de dag kun nas

Line 6: pad ma (OgDQ pad ma : HNFOL padma) [F 95b] skyes pa 'di lta ste (OgQHNFO ste : DL add. gser dang) / *gser gser gyi kha tog* (Og gser gser gyi kha tog : HO om.; DQNL gser gyi kha tog; F gser gi kha tog dang; O add. gser dang; OgDQHNFO / : L om. /) gser gyi 'od 'byung ba / gser (OgDQHNOL gser : F add. gyi) lta bur ston pa / (OgDQHNFO / : L om. /) sngon po kha dog sngonpo / 'od sngon po 'byung ba / sngon po lta bur ston pa / ser po (OgDQHNOL om. / : F //) kha dog ser po / (OgDQHNF / : OL //) *'od ser po 'byung ba* (OgDQHNOL 'od ser po 'byung ba : F om.) / *ser po lta bur ston pa* (OgDQHNOL ser po lta bur ston pa : F 'od ser po lta bur ston pa) /

Line 7: dmar po (OgDHNFL om. / : QO add. /) [O 301a] kha dog dmar po / (OgDQHNFL / : O //) 'od dmar po 'byung ba / dmar po lta bur ston pa / dkar po (OgL om. / : DQHNFO add. /) kha dog dkar po / (OgDQHNL / : O om. /; F //) 'od dkar po 'byung ba / dkar po lta bur ston pa / (OgDQHNFO / : L om. /) bkra ba (OgFL om. / : DQHNO add. /) kha dog bkra ba / (OgDQHFOL / : N om. /) 'od bkra ba (OgDQHFOL om. / : N add. /) 'byung ba / bkra ba lta bur stonpa / (OgDQNFOL / : H om. /) [H 309b] shing rta'i (OgDQHFOL shing rta'i : N shing ta'i) 'phang lo tsam dag skyes so / (OgDNOL / : QHF //) [Q 221a]

Line 8: *sha* ri'i bu (OgDQNFOL om. / : H add. /) sangs rgyas kyi zhing de ni (OgL ni : DQHNFO na; OL add. /) sangs rgyas kyi zhing gi yon tan (OgDQHFOL om. / : N add. /) [N 308a] bkod pa / (OgL add. / : DQHNFO om. /) rnam pa de lta bu dag gis legs par brgyan pa'o / (OgDO / : QHNFL //) *sha ra dvati'i bu* (Other editions as before. H add. /) gzhan yang 'jig rten gyi khams bde ba can na (OgDQHNL om. / : OF add. /) lha'i sil snyan gyi sgra rtag tu 'byung ngo / (OgDOL / : QHNF //) sa chen po ni gser gyi kha dog lta bu ste / (OgFOL / : DQHN om. /)

Folio 206a

Line 1: < > / (OgDHFOL add. / : QN om. /) nyams dga' ba'o / (OgDFOL / : QHN //) *sha* ri'i bu (OgDQNFOL om. / : H add. /) *sangs rgyas kyi zhing de ni* (OgDQHNFL sangs rgyas kyi zhing de ni : O 'di ji snyam du sems; OgQ add. / : DHNFOL om. /) sangs rgyas kyi zhing gi yon tan bkod pa rnam pa de lta bu dag gis legs par brgyan pa'o / (OgDF / : QHNOL //) *sha* ri'i bu (OgDQNFOL om. / : H //) gzhan yang sangs rgyas kyi zhing de na (OgDQHNFO na : L ni; OgFO / : DQHNL om. /) nyin lan gsum (OgFOL om. / : DQHN add. /) mtshan lan gsum du (OgDQHNOL om. / : F add. /) lha'i me

Line 2: tog *man dar ba'i* (Og man dar ba'i : DF man da ra ba'i; QH mandā ra ba'i; N manda ra ba'i; O mtog man dar ba'i; L man da ra ba'i) lha'i *me tog* (OgDQHNFL me tog : O mtog) gi char 'bab bo (Og om. / : DQHNFOL //) der sems can gang dag skyes pa (OgQHNOL pa : DFba) de dag kyang snga (OgDQHNOL snga : F ma) dro gcig (OgDQHNOL gcig : F cig) bzhin du / (OgQFL add. / : DHNO om. /) sangs rgyas kyi zhing gzhan dang (OgDHN om. / : QFOL add. /) gzhan (OgDQHN gzhan : FOL add. dag) du (OgDQHNFL du : O tu) dong ste / (OgHFOL add. / : DQN om. /) sangs rgyas bye ba *brgya stong* (OgDOL brgya stong : QHN phrag 'bum; F khrag 'bum) la phyag 'tshal zhing / de bzhin gshegs pa re re la yang (OgDQFOL yang : HN l'ang) me tog *skon bu* (OgDHFOL skon bu : QN skun bu) bye

Line 3: ba *brgya stong* (OgDQHNOL brgya stong : F phrag 'bum) mngon bar (OgQHO bar : DNFL par)'thor (OgDHNFOL 'thor : Q mthor) te / (OgDQHNL / : OF //) gtor (OgDQHNFL gtor : O thor) nas nyin mo gnas pa'i phyir / (OgFOL add. / : DQHN om. /) [D 197a] slar 'jig rten gyi khams de nyid du 'dong ngo / (OgDHFOL / : QN //) *sha* ri'i bu (OgDQNFOL om. / : H add. /) sangs rgyas kyi zhing de ni (OgDQHNFL ni : O na; FOL add. /) [F 96a, L 198a] sangs rgyas kyi zhing gi yon tan bkod pa (OgDQHNOL om. / : F add. /) rnam pa de lta bu dag gis legs par brgyan pa'o // (OgQHNFOL // : D /)

Line 4: *sha* ri'i bu (OgDQNFOL om. / : H add. /) gzhan yang 'jig rten gyi khams bde ba can na / (OgFO add. / : DQHNL om. /) ngang pa dang /

(OgDQHNOL add. / : F om. /) khrung khrung dang / (OgDQHNOL / : F //) rma bya dag (OgDQHNFL dag: O om.) *yod de* (OgFL yod de: O yod pa dee; DH yod pa de; QN yod pa; OgQFL / : DHNO om. /) de dag kyang nyin lan gsum (OgFOL om. / : DQHN add. /) mtshan lan gsum 'dus (OgDQHNOL 'dus : F du) nas *glud byangs len te* (Og glud byangs len te : DHO yang dag par 'gro bar byed de; QN yang dag par bgro bar byed de; F yang dag par 'grol bar byed do; L yang dag par 'gro bar byed do; OgDQHNFO / : L //) [N 308b] rang rang gi *sgra skad kyis* (Og sgra skad kyis : DQHNOL skad dag gis; F skad dag gi) [H 310a] smra'o / (OgDFO / : QHNL //) de dag smra ba na (OgDQHNOL na : F dang; L add. /) dbang po dang (OgDNO om. / : QHFL add. /)

Line 5: stobs dang / byang chub kyi yan lag gi sgra dag 'byung ngo / (OgDH / : QNFOL //) [O 301b] sems can gang dag der skyes pa de dag gis (OgDQHNOL gis : F gi) *sgra de* (OgDQHNO sgra de : F om.; L om. de) chos nas / (OgFOL add. / : DQHN om. /) sangs rgyas yid la byed pa skye (OgDQHNFO skye : L skyes; OgDQHNFO / : L //) chos yid la byed pa skye (OgDQHNOL skye : F skyes) / dge 'dun yid la byed pa (OgQHFOL pa : DN par) skye'o / (OgDQHNL / : OF //) *sha* ri'i bu (OgDQNFOL om. / : H add. /) *'di la ji* (OgQH 'di la ji : DNFL'di ji; O om.'di) snyam du

Line 6: sems (Og om. / : DQHNFOL add. /) sems can de dag dud 'gro'i skye gnas su (OgDQHNF gnas su : OL gnasu) gyur pa yin snyam du sems pa *lta na* (OgDQHNO lta na : F add. sdug; L ldan; OgL / : DQHNFO om. /) de ltar *myi blta*'o /(OgD / : QHNFOL //) de ci'i phyir zhe na / *sha* ri'i bu (OgDQNFOL om. / : H add. /) sangs rgyas kyi zhing de na (OgDQHNFL na : O ni; OgL / : DQHNFO om. /) sems can dmyal ba dang / dud 'gro'i skye gnas dang (OgDQHNFO dang : L nas) / gshin rje'i

Line 7: 'jig rten du (OgDQHNFL om. / : O add. /) skye ba'i *mying* yang *myed* do // (OgQHNFOL // : D /) bya'i (Og bya'I : DQHNFOL bya'i) tshogs de dag ni de bzhin gshegs pa tshe dpag *myed* de nyid kyis (OgDQHNOL kyis : F kyi; OgHF / : DQNOL om. /) [Q 221b] chos kyi sgra dbyung ba'i phyir sprul pa dag go (OgDQHNOL go : F gi) / *sha* ri'i bu (OgDQNFOL om. / : H add. /) sangs rgyas kyi zhing di (Og dI : DQHNFOL de) ni (OgDQHNFL om. / : O add. /) sangs rgyas kyi zhing gi (OgDQHNOL gi : F om.) yon tan bkod pa rnam pa de lta bu

Line 8: dag gis legs par brgyan pa'o (OgDQHNOL pa'o : F to; OgDL / : QHNFO //) *sha* ri'i bu (OgDQNFOL om. / : H add. /) gzhan yang sangs rgyas kyi zhing de'i shing (OgDQL shing : HNFO om.) [F 96b] *ta la'i* (OgQHNL ta la'i : D de'i ta la'i; F rta la'i; O ra ta la'i) *'phreng* (OgHO 'phreng : DL phreng; QN phreng ba; F 'phreng ba) de dag dang (OgQ om. / : DHNFOL add. /) dril bu g.yer *kha'i* dra ba de dag *la rlung gis phog cing* (OgDQHNO la rlung gis phog cing : F om.; L add. /) rlung gis bskyod (OgDQHNOL bskyod : F skyod) na / (Og / : DQHNFOL om. /) sgra snyan pa (OgDHNFOL om. / : Q add. /) yid du 'ong ba (OgHFOL om. / : DQN add. /) nyams (OgDQHNFL nyams : O nyam su) dga' ba dag (OgQO dag : DNHFL om.) [L 198b] 'byung ste / *'di lta*

Folio 206b

Line 1: *ste* (OgDQNOL ste : HF om.) dper na / rol mo mkhan gyis (OgDQHNOL gyis : F gi) yan lag bye (OgDQHNOL bye : F bya) ba *brgya stong* (Og brgya stong : DQHNFOL 'bum) dang ldan pa'i lha'i sil (OgDQHFOL om. / : N add. /) [N 309a] snyan blangs pa bzhin no // der *myi* de dag gis sgra de thos nas (OgDQHNFL om. / : O add. /) sangs rgyas rjes su dran pa dang / chos rjes su dran pa dang / dge 'dun rjes su *dran pa lus* (OgDQHNFL dran pa lus : O dran pa dang / lus) la gnas so //

Line 2: *sha* ri'i bu (OgDQNFOL om. / : H add. /) [H 310b] sangs rgyas kyi zhing *de ni* (OgDQHNFL om. / : L add. /) *sangs rgyas kyi zhing* (OgDQHNFL de ni sangs rgyas kyi zhing : O om.) gi yon tan *bkod pa'i* (OgDNF bkod pa'i : QO add. brkyan; H add. rgyan; L bsgod pa'i brgyan) rnam pa de lta bu dag gis legs par brgyan (OgDQHNOL brgyan : F rgyan) pa'o / (OgDF / : QHNOL //) *sha* ri'i bu (OgDQNFOL om. / : H add. /) *'de la ji* snyam du sems / (OgQHNFOL / : D //) ci'i phyir (OgDQHNOL phyir : F add. zhe) de bzhin gshegs pa tshe dpag (OgQNF dpag : DHOL add. tu) [D 197b] *myed* ces bya zhe na / *sha* ri'i bu (OgDQNFOL om. / : H add. /) de bzhin gshegs

Line 3: pa tshe (OgDQHNFO tshe : L 'od) *dpag myed* de'i tshe'i tshad dpag tu *myed* de / de'i phyir de bzhin gshegs pa tshe *dpag myed* ces bya'o / (OgDQHL / : NFO //) *sha* ri'i bu (OgDQNFOL om. / : H add. /) gzhan yang ci'i phyir de bzhin gshegs pa (OgQHFOL pa : DN add. de) 'od *dpag myed* ces bya zhe na / *sha* ri'i bu (OgDQNFOL om. / : H add. /) de bzhin gshegs pa 'od dpag *myed* de'i 'od sangs

Line 4: rgyas kyi zhing thams cad du thogs pa *myed* de / de'i phyir de bzhin gshegs pa 'od dpag *myed* ces bya'o / (OgDHNFL / : QO //) [O 302a] bcom ldan 'das de bzhin gshegs pa 'od dpag *myed* de (OgDQHNO om. / : FL add. /) bla na *myed* pa yang dag par rdzogs pa'i byang chub (OgQNF chub : DHOL add. tu) mngon bar (OgQHFOL bar : DN par) rdzogs par sangs rgyas nas bskal pa

Line 5: bcu lon no / (OgDO / : QHNFL //) *sha* ri'i bu (OgDQNFOL om. / : H add. /) gzhan yang bcom ldan 'das de'i nyan thos kyi dge 'dun dag pa (OgDQHNO om. / : FL add. /) dgra bcom pa sha stag tshad myed (OgDQHNFO om. / : L add. /) de / (OgDQHNFO / : L om./) de dag gi (OgDQHNOL gi : F om.; add. /)

tshad brjod par *sla ba* (OgDQHNOL sla ba : F slar bar) [F 97a] ma *yin no* (OgDQHNFO yin no : L yino; OgDFL / : QHNO //) [N 309b] *sha* ri'i bu (OgDQNFOL om. / : H add. /) gzhan yang sangs rgyas kyi zhing der skyes pa'i sems can dag ni phyir *myi* ldog pa (OgL om. / : DQHNFO add. /) skye ba

Line 6: gcig (OgDQHNOL gcig : F cig) gis (OgDHNFOL om. / : Q add. /) [Q 222a] thogs (OgDQHNFL thogs : O thob) pa'i byang chub sems dpa' dag pa (OgDQHNOL pa : F om.) sha stag go / (OgDQHNFO / : L //) [L 199a] *sha* ri'i bu (OgDQHNOL bu : F add. gzhan yang; H add. /) [H 311a] byang chub sems dpa' de dag gi tshad ni brjod par sla ba ma yin te / gzhan du na (OgDQHNFL na : O om.) tshad *myed* grangs *myed ces bya* (OgDQHNFO ces bya : L om.) ba'i *grangs su* (OgDQHNL grangs su : FO grangsu)'gro'o / (OgD / : QHNFOL //) *sha* ri'i bu (OgDQNFOL om. / : H add. /) sangs rgyas kyi zhing de ni (OgDQHNFO om. / : L add. /) sangs

Line 7: rgyas kyi zhing gi yon tan bkod pa rnam pa de lta bu dag gis legs par brgyan pa'o / (OgDF / : QHNOL //) *sha* ri'i bu (OgDQNFOL om. / : H add. /) de lta bas na / (OgHFO / : DQNL om. /) rigs kyi bu'am (OgDHNO om. / : QFL add. /) rigs kyi bu mos / (Og / : DQHNFOL om. /) sangs rgyas kyi zhing der skye bar bya ba'i phyir / (OgFL / : DQHNO om. /) dge ba'i rtsa ba rnams gus par yongs su bsngo bar bya'o / (OgDN / : QHFOL //)

Line 8: de ci'i phyir zhe na / 'di ltar skyes bu dam pa de lta bu (OgDQHNOL bu : F om.) dag dang phrad par 'gyur ba'i phyir ro / (OgD / : QHNFOL //) *sha* ri'i bu (OgDQNFOL om. / : H add. /) dge ba'i rtsa ba ngan don tsam gyis ni / (OgFOL / : DQHN om. /) bcom ldan 'das de bzhin gshegs pa tshe dpag *myed* de'i zhing du skye bar *myi* 'gyur ro / (OgD / : QHNFOL //) *sha* ri'i bu (OgDQNFOL om. / : H add. /) rigs kyi (Og kyI : DQHNOL kyi; F om.) bu'am (OgDHNFO om. / : QL add. /) rigs

Folio 207a

Line 1: < > / (OgDQHNFL / : O om. /) kyi bu mo gang gis bcom ldan 'das de bzhin gshegs pa tshe dpag *myed* de'i mtshan *thos la* (OgDHFOL thos la : QN om.; FOL add. /) thos nas kyang yid la byed cing / (OgQ / : DHNFOL om. /) [O 302b] nub *gcig* gam (Og om. / : DQHNFOL add. /) nub gnyis sam (Og om. / : DQHNFOL add. /) nub gsum 'am (OgDQFOL 'am : HN mam; DQHNFO add. /) nub bzhi 'am (OgH om. / : DQNFOL add. /) nub lnga 'am (OgH om. / : DQNFOL add. /) [D 198a] nub drug gam (OgH om. / : DQNFOL add. /) nub bdun du / (OgD / : QHNFOL om. /) [N 310a] g.yeng ba *myed* pa'i sems

Line 2: kyis (OgDQHNOL kyis : F kyi) yid la byed na (Og om. / : DQHNFOL add. /) rigs kyi bu'am (OgO om. / : DQHNFL add. /) rigs (OgQHNL rigs : DFO add. kyi) bu mo de 'chi (OgDQHNOL 'chi : F mchi) ba'i dus kyi tshe (OgDQHNFL om.

/ : O add. /) phyin ci log *myed* pa'i sems kyis (OgDQHNOL kyis : F kyi) [F 97b] *'chi ba'i* dus byas nas / (OgFOL / : DQHN om. /) 'chi ba'i (OgDQHNOL 'chi ba'i : F om.) dus byas pa (OgDQHNO pa : FL ba) de (OgDQHNFL om. / : O add. /) de bzhin gshegs pa 'od dpag *myed* nyan thos kyi dge 'dun gyis (Og gyis : DQHNF add. yongs su; OL add. yongsu) [H 311b] bskor cing / (OgHFOL / : DQN om. /) byang chub sems dpa'i

Line 3: tshogs *kyis mdun* (OgDQHNOL kyis mdun : F kyi 'dun) gyis *byas pa'i* (Og byas pa'i : DQHNOL bltas pa; F ltas pa)[5] mdun na bzhugs (OgDQHNOL bzhugs : F zhugs) pa / (OgFOL / : DQHN om. /) bcom ldan 'das de bzhin gshegs pa 'od dpag *myed* de'i sangs rgyas kyi zhing 'jig rten gyi khams bde ba can du skye bar 'gyur ro / (OgD / : QHNFOL //) [L 199b] *sha* ri'i bu (OgDQNFOL om. / : H add. /) de lta bas na don kyi (OgQF kyi : DHNOL gyi) dbang de (OgDHNOL de : QF po) mthong nas / (OgFOL / : DQHN om. /) rigs kyi bu

Line 4: 'am (OgHNO om. / : DQFL add. /) rigs kyi bu mos sangs rgyas kyi zhing der gus par smon lam gdab (OgDQHNL gdab : F btab; O gtam) par bya'o zhes de skad (OgDQFOL skad : HN add. ces) *bshad do* (OgHFOL bshad do : DQN brjod do; OgD / : QHNFOL //) *sha* ri'i bu (OgDQNFOL om. / : H add. /) ji ltar de bzhin gshegs pa ngas da ltar *yongs su* brjod pa de bzhin du / (OgHFOL / : DQN om. /) *sha* ri'i bu (OgDQNFOL om. / : H add. /) shar phyogs na bcom ldan 'das de bzhin gshegs

Line 5: pa *myi* 'grugs (OgQNOL 'grugs : DHF'khrugs) pa zhes bya ba dang / de bzhin gshegs pa lhun po'i rgyal mtshan zhes bya ba dang / de bzhin gshegs pa lhun po *phung po* (OgO phung po : DQHNFL om.) [Q 222b] shes bya ba dang / de bzhin gshegs pa lhun po chen po zhes bya dang / de bzhin gshegs pa lhun por (OgDFOL por : QHN po; DQHN add. chen po) snang ba zhes bya dang /

Line 6: de bzhin gshegs pa 'jam sgra zhes bya ba dang / de bzhin gshegs pa 'jam dbyangs zhes (OgDHNOL zhes : QF shes) bya ba dang / de dag la *stsogs* (Og stsogs : DQHNFOL sogs) [N 310b] pa shar phyogs kyi (OgDQHNFL kyi : O na) sangs rgyas bcom ldan 'das *gang ga'i* (OgFL gang ga'i : DQHNO gangā'i) *klung gi* (OgDQHNOL klung gi : F om.) bye ma snyed dag (OgDQHNFO om. / : L add. /) rang rang gi sangs rgyas kyi zhing rnams

Line 7: ljags kyi dbang pos khebs par mdzad de (OgDQNFOL de : H do) / khye' (OgN khye' : DQHFOL khyed) cag yon tan bsam gyis *myi* khyab pa *yongs su* brjod pa (OgDQHNF om. / : OL add. /) sangs rgyas thams cad kyis (OgDQHNOL kyis : F kyi) *yongs su* bzung ba'i chos kyi rnam grangs 'di la yid ches (OgDQNOL om. / : HF add. /) [H 312a, O 303a] par (OgDQHNFL om. / : O add. /) gyis shig

(OgDQHNOL shig : F om.) [F 98a] ces (OgDQHNO ces : FL shes) *gsung ba* (OgDQHN gsung ba : F gsungs bar; O gsungs ba; L gsungs pa) mdzad do / (OgDF / : QHNOL //) de bzhin du lho

Line 8: phyogs na (OgDQHNFO om. / : L add. /) de bzhin gshegs pa nyi zla'i sgron ma zhes bya ba dang / de bzhin gshegs pa grags pa zhes bya ba dang / de bzhin gshegs pa grags pa'i 'od ces bya ba dang / de bzhin gshegs pa (OgDQHNFL pa : O pa'i)'od 'phro phung po zhes bya ba dang / de bzhin gshegs pa

Folio 207b

Line 1: lhun po'i sgron ma zhes bya ba dang / de bzhin gshegs pa (OgDQHNFO om. / : L add. /) [L 200a] brtson 'grus mtha' yas shes bya ba dang / de dag la *stsogs* pa lho phyogs kyi sangs rgyas bcom ldan 'das *gang ga'i* klung gi bye ma snyed dag (OgDQHNFO om. / : L add. /) rang rang gi sangs rgyas kyi zhing rnams ljags kyi dbang pos khebs

Line 2: par mdzad de / khyed cag yon tan bsam gyis myi khyab pa *yongs su* brjod pa / (OgFL / : DQHNO om. /) [D 198b] sangs rgyas *thams cad* (OgDQHNFL thams cad : O thad) kyis *yongs su* bzung ba'i chos kyi rnam grangs *'di la yid* (OgDQHNFL 'di la yid : O yid la yid) ches par gyis (OgDQHNOL gyis : F gyi) shig ces gsung (OgDQHNOL gsung : F gsungs) bar (OgHO bar : DQNFL ba) [N 311a] mdzad do / (OgDO / : QHNFL //) de bzhin du nub phyogs na de bzhin gshegs pa tshe

Line 3: dpag *myed* ces bya ba dang / de bzhin gshegs pa phung po dpag (OgDQHNOL dpag : F dpag tu) *myed* ces bya ba dang / de bzhin gshegs pa *rgyal mtshan* (OgDQHNL rgyal mtshan : FO rgyal tshab) *dpag myed* ces bya ba dang / de bzhin gshegs pa 'od *chen zhes* (OgDQHNOL chen zhes : F om. chen; add ces) bya ba dang / de bzhin gshegs pa 'od gzer (Og gzer : DQHNFOL zer) snang ba zhes bya ba dang / de bzhin gshegs

Line 4: pa rin po che'i tog *chen po* (Og chen po : DQHNFOL om.) [Q 223a] *zhes* (OgF zhes : DQHNOL ces) bya ba dang/ de bzhin gshegs pa 'od *gzer* dag pa zhes bya ba dang / de dag la *stsogs* pa nub phyogs kyi sangs rgyas bcom ldan 'das *gang ga'i* klung gi bye ma snyed dag (OgDQHNFO om. / : L add. /) rang rang gi sangs rgyas kyi zhing rnams ljags kyi dbang pos khebs par mdzad

Line 5: de (Og om. / : DQHNFOL add. /) [H 312b] khyed cag yon tan bsam gyis *myi* khyab pa *yongs su* brjod pa (OgDQHN om. / : FOL add. /) sangs rgyas thams cad kyis (OgDQHNOL kyis : F kyi) [F 98b] *yongs su* bzung ba'i chos kyi rnam grangs 'di la yid ches par gyis shig ces (OgDQHNFL ces : O om.) *gsung* *ba* (OgDQHNFO gsung ba : L gsungs par) mdzad do / (OgDHF / : QNOL //) de bzhin du byang phyogs na (OgDQHNFO om. / : L add. /) de bzhin gshegs pa 'od 'phro'i *ba'i* (Og ba'i : DQHNFOL om.) [O 303b] phung po

Line 6: chen po zhes bya ba dang / de bzhin gshegs pa *thams cad* sgrol ba'i dbyangs zhes bya ba dang / de bzhin gshegs pa rab tu thul dka' zhes bya ba dang / de bzhin gshegs pa nyi ma 'byung zhes bya ba dang / de bzhin gshegs pa dra ba can gyi (OgDQHNFL gyi : O gyis)'od ces byabadang/de

Line 7: bzhin gshegs pa 'od kyi 'byung gnas zhes (OgDHNFO zhes : Q shes; L ces) [L 200b] bya ba dang / de dag la *stsogs* pa byang phyogs kyi sangs rgyas bcom ldan 'das *gang ga'i* klung gi bye ma snyed dag rang rang gi (OgDQHNFO gi : L gyis) sangs rgyas kyi zhing rnams ljags kyi dbang pos khebs par mdzad de / khyed cag yon

Line 8: tan bsam gyis (OgDQHNOL gyis : F gi) *myi* khyab pa *yongs su* brjod pa / (OgFOL / : DQHN om. /) [D 199a, N 311b] sangs rgyas *thams cad* kyis (OgDQHNOL kyis : F kyi) *yongs su* bzung (OgDQHNFL bzung : O bzungs) ba'i chos kyi rnam grangs 'di la (OgDQHNOL om. / : F add. /) yid ches par gyis (OgDQHNOL gyis : F gyi) shig (Og shIg : DQHNFOL shig) ces gsung ba (OgDQHNFO ba : L par) *mdzad do* (OgDQHNFL mdzad do : O mdzado) // (OgDQHNOL // : F /) *de bzhin du 'og gi phyogs na de bzhin gshegs pa seng ge zhes bya ba dang* (OgDQHNOL de bzhin gshegs pa seng ge zhes bya ba dang : F om.)

Folio 208a

Line 1: < > / de bzhin gshegs pa grags pa zhes bya ba dang / de bzhin gshegs pa grags (OgDQHNL grags : FO om.) 'od ces bya ba dang / de bzhin gshegs pa chos zhes (OgDHNO zhes : QFL shes) bya ba dang / de bzhin gshegs pa chos 'dzin ces bya ba dang / de bzhin gshegs pa chos kyi rgyal mtshan *zhes* (OgDQHNF zhes : OL ces) *bya ba*

Line 2: *dang /de dag la stsogs pa 'og gi phyogs kyi sangs rgyas bcom ldan 'das gang ga'i klung gi bye ma snyed dag* (OgDQHNFO gi : L add. na; add. /) *rang rang gi sangs rgyas kyi zhing rnams ljags kyi* (OgDQHNOL zhes bya ba . . . ljags kyi : F om.) dbang pos khebs par mjad de (OgDQHFO de : N do; L om.) / khyed cag yon tan bsam gyis (OgDQHNOL gyis : F gi) *myi* khyab pa *yongs su* brjod pa / (OgFOL / : DQHN om. /) [Q 223b, H 313a] sangs

Line 3: rgyas *thams cad* kyis (OgDQHNOL kyis : F kyi) *yongs su* bzung ba'i chos kyi rnam grangs 'di la yid ches par gyis shig ces *gsung pa* (OgDQNFO gsung pa : L gsungs par; H gsung ba) mdzad do (OgDQHNFO do : L om.) // (OgDQHNOL // : F /) de bzhin du steng gi phyogs na (OgDQHNFO om. / : L add. /) de bzhin gshegs pa tshangs (OgDQHNOL tshangs : F add. ces bya ba dang / de dag la sogs pa 'og gi phyogs kyi sangs rgyas bcom ldan gang ga'i bye ma snyed dag rang rang gi sangs rgyas kyi zhing rnams ljags kyi) pa'i dbyangs zhes (OgDHNO zhes : QF shes; L ces) [F 99a] bya ba dang / de bzhin gshegs pa skar ma'i rgyal

Line 4: po zhes bya ba dang / de bzhin gshegs pa spos mchog ces bya ba dang / de bzhin gshegs pa spos (OgDQHNFL spos : O om.) [O 304a] 'od ces bya ba dang / de bzhin gshegs pa spos kyi phung po zhes bya ba dang / de bzhin gshegs pa rin *cen* me (OgDQHNO me : FL om.) tog shin tu rgyas pa'i rigs zhes (OgDHNOL zhes : QFshes) bya ba dang /

Line 5: de bzhin gshegs pas *la'i* (OgQOL la'i : DHN sā la'i; F sa la'i) [N 312a] dbang po'i *rgyal po* (OgDQHNOL rgyal po : F om.) zhes bya ba dang / de bzhin gshegs pa rin chen *ut pa la'i* (OgDQFOL ut pa la'i : HN utpa la'i) dpal zhes bya ba dang / de bzhin gshegs pa mthong ba don yod ces bya ba dang / de bzhin gshegs pa ri rab lta bu zhes bya ba dang / de dag la *stsogs* pa

Line 6: steng gi phyogs kyi sangs rgyas bcom ldan 'das *gang ga'i* klung gi bye ma snyed dag rang rang gi (OgDQHNOL gi : F gis) sangs rgyas kyi zhing rnams ljags kyi dbang pos khebs par mdzad de (OgDQHNFO de : L om.) / khyed cag yon tan bsam gyis *myi* khyab pa *yongs su* brjod pa (OgDQHNOL pa : F do; OgDQHNOL / : F //) [H 313b] sangs rgyas

Line 7: *thams cad* kyis (OgDQHNOL kyis : F kyi) *yongs su* bzung ba'i chos kyi rnam grangs 'di la yid ches par gyis shig ces *gsung ba* mdzad do / (OgDO / : QHNFL //) [L 201a] *sha* ri'i bu (OgDQNFOL om. / : H add. /) *de la ji* snyam du sems / (OgDQHNOL om. de : F add. de) ci'i phyir chos kyi rnam grangs 'di sangs rgyas *thams cad* kyis (OgDQHNOL kyis : F kyi) *yongs su* bzung ba zhes bya zhe na /

Line 8: *sha* ri'i bu (OgDQNFOL om. / : H add. /) rigs kyi bu'am (OgDHNO om. / : QFL add. /) rigs kyi bu mo gang dag chos kyi rnam grangs 'di dang / sangs rgyas bcom ldan 'das de dag gi mtshan thos par gyur pa dang (OgL om. / : DQHNFO add. /) [D 199b, N 312b] thos pa dang / (OgQFL / : DHNO om. /) thos par 'gyur ba de dag *thams cad* sangs rgyas bcom ldan 'das rnams (OgDQHNOL rnams : F om.) kyis [F 99b]

Folio 208b

Line 1: *yongs su* bzung bar 'gyur ro // (OgQHNFOL // : D /) *sha* ri'i bu (OgDQNFOL om. / : H add. /) *sems can* (OgDQHNFL sems can : O sen) gang dag bcom ldan 'das de bzhin gshegs pa 'od dpag *myed* de'i sangs rgyas kyi zhing 'jig rten gyi khams bde ba (OgDHNFOL om. / : Q add. /) [Q 224a] can du sems *kyis* smon par byed pa'am (OgDQHFOL pa'am : N pa 'am) / byas pa'am (OgDQHFOL pa'am : N pa 'am; OgQFOL / : DHN add. byed pa'am; OgDQNL / : HFO om. /) byed par

Line 2: 'gyur ba de dag *thams cad* bla na *myed* pa yang dag par rdzogs pa'i byang chub las phyir *myi* ldog go // (OgQHNFL // : DO /) phyir ma log (OgDQHNFL log : O ltog) go // (OgNFL // : DQHO /) phyir *myi* ltog par 'gyur ro // (OgQHNFOL // : D /) *sha* ri'i bu (OgDQNFOL om. / : H add. /) ji *ltar da da ltar* (OgQHL ltar da da ltar : D om.; Nltar da ltar; F ltar na; O lta rang da ltar) sangs rgyas bcom ldan 'das de dag gi yon tan bsam gyis *myi* khyab pa *yongs su*

Line 3: brjod pa de bzhin du / (OgDQHNOL / : F om. /) *sha* ri'i bu (OgDQNFOL om / : H add. /) [H 314a] sangs rgyas bcom ldan 'das de dag kyang nga'i yon tan bsam gyis (OgDQHNOL gyis : F gyi) *myi* khyab pa *yongs su* brjod do // (OgQHNFOL // : D /) *sha* ri'i bus gsol pa / bcom ldan 'das *shag kya* (Og shag kya : D shā kya; QHNFOL shākya) [O 304b, L 201b] thub ba (OgDQNFOL om. / : H add. /) *shag kya'i* rgyal pos bskal pa'i snyigs ma dang / nyon mongs

Line 4: pa (Og pa : DQHNFOL pa'i) snyigs ma dang / *sems can* snyigs ma dang / lta ba (Og ba : DQHNFOL ba'i) snyigs ma dang / tshe'i snyigs *ma de'i tshe* (Og ma de'i tshe : DQHNFOL ma'i tshe; OgQNFOL / : DH om. /) 'jig rten gyi khams *myi* mjed du / (OgFOL / : DQHN om. /) [N 313a] bla na *myed* pa yang dag par rdzogs pa'i byang chub (OgDQHNOL chub : FO add. tu) mngon bar (OgDQHOL bar : NF par) rdzogs par sangs rgyas te / 'jig rten *thams cad* dang (OgDQHNFO dang : L om.) *myi* mthun (OgQHNFOL mthun : D'thun) ba'i (OgDQOL ba'i : HNF pa'i) chos

Line 5: bstan pa ni ngo mtshar (OgDQHNOL mtshar : F tshar) to (Og to : DQHNL lags so; FO lagso) // bcom ldan 'das kyis bka' stsal pa / *sha* ri'i bu (OgDQNFOL om. / : H add. /) snyigs ma lnga'i tshe (OgDQHNOL om. / : F add. /) 'jig rten du ngas (OgDQHNFL ngas : O nga) gang 'jig rten gyi khams *myi* mjed du (OgDQHNFO du : L om.; OgFOL / : DQHN om. /) bla na *myed* pa yang dag par rdzogs pa'i byang chub (OgDQHNL chub : FO add. tu) mngon *bar* rdzogs [F 100a] par (OgDQHNLO om. / : F add. /) *sangs rgyas* (OgDQHNFL sangs rgyas : O pra sadyas) te / 'jig rten

Line 6: *thams cad* dang (OgDQHNFL dang : O dnga) *myi mthun* ba'i (OgQOL ba'i : DHNF pa'i) chos *bstan pa* (OgDQHNOL bstan pa : F stan pa) de ni mchog tu dka' ba byed pa'o // bcom ldan 'das kyis (OgQHNFOL om. / : D add. /) [D 200a] de skad ces bka' *stsal pa dang* (Og stsal pa dang : DQHNFL scal nas; O stsal nas; OgQFOL / : DHN om. /) tshe dang ldan pa *sha* ri'i (Og ri'I : DQHN-FOL ri'i) bu dang / nyan thos chen po de dag dang / byang chub sems dpa' de dag dang / lha dang (OgDNFOL om. / : QH add. /) *myi* dang (OgDNL om. / : QHFO add. /) lha

Line 7: ma yin dang / (OgDQHNOL / : F //) dri zar bcas pa'i 'jig rten (Og rten : DQHNFOL add. yi rangs te; QFOL add. /) bcom ldan 'das *kyis* gsungs pa la *yid rangs te* (Og yid rangs te : DQHNFOL om.) [H 314b] mngon par bstod do / (OgDNL / : QHFO //) 'phags pa bde ba can gyi bkod pa *zhes bya ba* (OgDQHNOL zhes bya ba : F om.) theg pa chen po'i mdo / (OgDQHNOL / : F //) [L 202a] *rd-zogs so* (OgDHNF rdzogs so : QO rdzogs sho; L rdzog soha) //

Appendix II

The Means of Attaining the Sukhāvatī Kṣetra: Editions and Liturgical Texts

List of Editions

I. *gNam chos bde chen zhing sgrub kyi las byang skor.* An impression from blocks preserved at mTho-mthong Monastery in Solu, Nepal, 1972, 56 pp. (Library of Congress: 78902132).

II. *gNam chos bde chen zhing sgrub kyi las byang skor.* An impression from blocks preserved at Me-tog dpag-yas in Solukhumbu, Nepal, 1971, 44 pp. (Library of Congress: 78902104).

III. *gNam chos bde chen zhing sgrub dang kar gling zhi khro'i tshor chung skor dang chos rgyal rdo rje'i nor lha zam dkar bcas.* Edited by Nu-bri chos-kyi-nyi-ma rin-po-che. Kathmandu: Kenpo Shedup Tenzin and Lama Thinley Namgyal, 2005, 917 pp. (Library of Congress: 2005385935).

IV. *gNam chos thugs kyi gter kha snyan brgyud zab mo'i skor las bde chen zhing gi sgrub thabs.* Delhi: Chos spyod dpar skrun khang, 2000, 172 pp. (Library of Congress: 2003305623).

V. *gNam chos thugs kyi gter kha snyan brgyud zab mo'i skor las bde chen zhing gyi sgrub thabs 'don cha.* Copy obtained by the author in Lhasa, 1999, 152 fol. No publishing house listed.

VI. *gNam chos bde chen zhing sgrub.* Xylograph obtained from the old 'Ja'-sa temple of Solu district, Nepal, 103 fol. Kapstein 2004, 49, n. 64.

VII. *Drikung Compilation* adapted by 'Bri-gung Lama K. C. Ayang Rinpoche. Drikung Kagyu Meditation Centre, Washington D.C. Personally acquired in Bodh Gayā, 2004.

VIII. *Means of Sukhāvatī* texts in the *rTsib ri spar ma,* vol. 21, 1978–1985. Collected and arranged into a coherent structure and carved onto xylographic blocks at La-stod rtsib-ri from 1934 to about 1958, by 'Khrul-zhig padma chos-rgyal. Darjeeling: kargyu sungrab nyamso khang.

IX. *gNam chos bde chen zhing sgrub kyi skor*. Xylographic print from blocks preserved at Burmiok ('Ba'-nyag) House, Gangtok, Sikkim, 1972, 235 pp.

List of Texts

Library of Congress Edition, no. IV

4.1. *bDe chen zhing sgrub kyi gsol 'debs*

4.2. *rTsa gsum spyi'i sngon 'gro*

4.3. *dKar gtor (gNam chos thugs kyi gter kha gu ru zhi ba'i skor las dkar gtor)*

4.4. *bDe chen zhing sgrub kyi 'don cha las byang*

4.5. *'Od chog bsngo ba*

4.6. *bDe chen zhing sgrub kyi bka' srung gsol mchod*

4.7. *Tshogs mchod byin rlabs char 'bebs*

4.8. *bDe chen zhing sgrub kyi byang chog thar lam dkar po*

4.9. *bDe chen zhing gi ro sreg cho ngan song gnas 'dren sdug bsngal mtsho skem gtan bde rab 'bar*

4.10. *bDe chen zhing du 'pho ba'i gdams pa rgyas par bsgrigs pa*

4.11. *bDe chen zhing sgrub kyi zin bris*

4.12. *Zin bris lhan thabs nyung bsdus*

4.13. *bDe chen zhing sgrub dbang bsdus*

4.14. *rTags brgyad dbang*

Lhasa Edition, no. V

5.1. *gNam chos thugs kyi gter kha snyan brgyud zab mo'i skor las bde chen zhing gyi sgrub thabs 'don cha* (13 fol.)

5.2. *Zhing sgrub zin bris kyi lhan thabs nyung bsdus* (5 fol.)

5.3. *bDe chen zhing sgrub kyi bka' bsrung gsol mchod bkrigs chags su bris pa* (4 fol.)

5.4. *Tshogs mchod byin rlabs char 'bebs* (6 fol.)

5.5. *bDe chen zhing sgrub kyi byang chog thar lam dkar po* (12 fol.)

5.6. *gNam chos thugs kyi gter kha las bde chen zhing sgrub kyi zin bris* (12 fol.)

5.7. *bDe chen zhing gi ro sreg cho ga ngan song gnas 'dren sdug bsngal mtsho skem gtan bde rab 'bar* (21 fol.)

5.8. *gNam chos thugs kyi gter las bde chen zhing du 'pho ba'i gdams pa rgyas par bsgrigs pa* (23 fol.)

5.9. *gNam chos bde chen zhing sgrub kyi dbang 'grig chags su bkod* (21 fol.)

5.10. *bKra shis rtags brgyad kyi dbang* (2 fol.)

5.11. *mKhas grub rā ga sya mdzad pa'i rnam dag bde chen zhing smon lam* (23 fol.)

Kapstein Edition, no. VI

6.1. *bDe chen zhing sgrub kyis* (sic) *gsol 'debs* (1 fol.)

6.2. *gNam chos thugs kyi gter kha snyan brgyud zab mo gu ru zhi ba'i skor las rtsa gsum spyi yi sngon 'gro* (1 fol.)

6.3. *gNam chos thugs kyi gter kha snyan brgyud zab mo'i skor las bde chen zhing gyi sgrub thabs 'don cha* (10 fol.)

6.4. *bKra shis gtso bo rdzas brgyad* (1 fol.)

6.5. *Zhing sgrub zin bris kyi lhan thabs nyung bsdus* (5 fol.)

6.6. *bDe chen zhing sgrub kyi bka' bsrung gsol mchod bkrigs chags su bris pa* (4 fol.)

6.7. *Tshogs mchod byin rlabs char 'bebs* (6 fol.)

6.8. *bKra shis rtags brgyad kyi dbang* (2 fol.).

6.9. *gNam chos thugs kyi gter kha snyan brgyud zab mo'i skor las bde chen zhing sgrub kyi byang chog thar lam dkar po* (12 fol.)

6.10. *bDe chen zhing gi ro sreg cho ga ngan song gnas 'dren sdug bsngal mtsho skem gtan bde rab 'bar* (16 fol.)

6.11. *gNam chos bde chen zhing sgrub kyi dbang 'grig chags su bkod na* (17 fol.)

6.12. *gNam chos thugs kyi gter kha las bde chen zhing sgrub kyi zin bris* (10 fol.)

6.13. *gNam chos thugs kyi gter las bde chen zhing du 'pho ba'i gdams pa rgyas par bsgrigs pa* (17 fol.)

6.14. *dBang bsdus* (2 fol.)

Drikung Compilation, no. VII

7.1. *'Bri gung 'pho ba chen mo 'jag tshugs ma zhes bya ba* (18 fol.)

7.2. *gNam chos thugs kyi gter kha snyan brgyud zab mo'i skor las bde chen zhing gyi sgrub thabs 'don cha* (4 fol.)

7.3. *gNam chos thugs kyi gter kha snyan brgyud zab mo gu ru zhi ba'i skor las rtsa gsum spyi yi sngon 'gro* (2 fol.)

7.4. *Zhing sgrub jin bris kyi lhan thabs nyung bsdus* (6 fol.)

7.5. *Tshe 'gugs tshe sgrub* (5 fol.)

7.6. *bDe chen zhing sgrub bka' srung gsol mchod dkrigs chags su bris pa* (4 fol.)

7.7. *Tshogs mchod byin rlabs char 'bebs* (6 fol.)

7.8. *mKhas grub rā ga a syas mdzad pa'i rnam dag bde chen zhing gi smon lam* (11 fol.)

***rTsib ri spar ma*, no. VIII**

8.1. *Tshig bdun gsol 'debs / byang zhus yin na ltung bshags / bde chen zhing sgrub kyi gsol 'debs*

8.2. *gNam chos thugs kyi gter kha snyan brgyud zab mo gu ru zhi ba'i skor las rtsa gsum spyi yi sngon 'gro*

8.3. *gNam chos thugs kyi gter kha snyan brgyud zab mo'i skor las bde chen zhing gi sgrub thabs 'don cha*

8.4. *Zhing sgrub zin bris kyi lhan thabs nyung bsdus*

8.5. *bDe chen zhing sgrub kyi bka' srung gsol mchod 'gris chags su bris pa*

8.6. *Tshogs mchod byin rlabs char 'bebs*

8.7. *gNam chos thugs kyi gter kha snyan brgyud zab mo'i skor las bde chen zhing sgrub kyi byang chog thar lam dkar po*

8.8. *bDe chen zhing gi ro sreg cho ga ngan song gnas 'dren sdug bsngal mtsho skem gtan bde rab 'bar*

8.9. *gNam chos bde chen zhing sgrub kyi dbang 'grig chags su bkod pa*

8.10. *Zhing sgrub dbang bsdus*

8.11. *bKra shis rtags brgyad kyi dbang*

8.12. *gNam chos thugs kyi gter kha las bde chen zhing sgrub kyi zin bris*

8.13. *gNam chos thugs kyi gter kha las bde chen zhing du 'pho ba'i gdams pa rgyas par bsgribs pa*

Gangtok Edition, no. IX

9.1. *Tshig bdun gsol 'debs byang zhus yin na ltung bshags bde chen zhing sgrub kyi gsol 'debs*

9.2. *gNam chos thugs kyi gter kha snyan brgyud zab mo gu ru zhi ba'i skor las rtsa gsum spyi yi sngon 'gro*

9.3. *bDe chen zhing gi sgrub thabs 'don cha*

9.4. *Zhing sgrub zin bris kyi lhan thabs nyung bsdus*

9.5. *bKa' srung gsol mchod dkrigs chags su bris pa*

9.6. *Tshogs mchod byin rlabs char 'bebs*

9.7. *bDe chen zhing sgrub kyi byang chog thar lam dkar po*

9.8. *bDe chen zhing gi ro sreg cho ga ngan song gnas 'dren sdug bsngal mtsho skem gtan bde rab 'bar*

9.9. *bDe chen zhing sgrub kyi dbang 'grig chags su bkod pa*

9.10. *dBang bsdus*

9.11. *bKra shis rtags brgyad kyi dbang*

9.12. *bDe chen zhing sgrub kyi zin bris*

9.13. *bDe chen zhing du 'pho ba'i gdams pa rgyas par bsgribs pa*

9.14. *mKhas grub ra ga a syas mdzad pa'i rnam dag bde chen zhing gi smon lam*

Appendix III

An Anthology of Pure Land Texts from the Treasure Tradition

In Chapter Five we mentioned two Treasure texts that played a seminal role in the ritual development of Pure Land practice in Tibet—*The Standing Blade of Grass* and *Dying without Regrets.* In the *Anthology of Aspiration Prayers,* a contemporary compilation of Tibetan Pure Land literature, we find a variety of revealed texts of the *bDe-smon* genre (i.e., prayers, *sādhanas*, guru-yoga, etc.) dating from the fourteenth to twentieth centuries. They are identified as Treasure texts on the basis of their colophons and/or by the use of orthographical Treasure signs (two circles with a crescent moon), and by inclusion of the ending phrase *sa ma ya rgya rgya rgya.*

1. *Sukhāvatī Prayer: The Powerful Supplements of the Profound Path* (*bDe ba can gyi smon lam zab lam dbang gi cha lag*), by Rig-'dzin rgod-ldem (1337–1409). This Pure Land Treasure was extracted from the Western Red Copper Treasury (*nub zangs-mdzod dmar-po*) (DM 1, 181–184).

2. *Sukhāvatī Prayer* (*bDe ba can gyi smon lam*) by sTag-sham nus-ldan rdo-rje (1655–?). This *sādhana* was originally composed and hidden by the consort of Padmasambhava, Lady mKhar-chen, Ye-shes mtsho-rgyal (DM 1, 155–158).

3. *The Display of the Field of Great Bliss: Instructions to Transform Iron into Gold* (*bDe chen zhing gi bkod pa lcags khams gser du 'gyur ba'i gdams pa*) by O-rgyan bstan-'dzin-pa (1701–1727) (DM 1, 270–272).

4. *Aspiration Prayer of Kun-bzang gzhan-phan* (*Kun bzang gzhan phan gyi bde smon*) by Kun-bzang gzhan-phan (1745–1821), rDo grub-chen the first (DM 1, 272–273).

5. *Aspiration Prayer of mChog-gyur bde-chen gling-pa* (*mChog gyur bde chen gling pa'i bde smon*) by O-rgyan mchog-gyur gling-pa's (1829–1870). This terma was extracted from a rock at mDo-khams and written down by 'Bangs mkhyen-brtse dbang-po (DM 1, 258–261).

6. *Aspiration Prayer: Three Manifest Sayings* (*mThas mngon gsum gsungs pa'i smon lam*) by Khrag-'thung bdud-'joms rdo-rje, alias bDud-'joms gling-pa (1835–1904). A pure-vision *terma* (*dag-snang gter*) (DM 1, 273–274).

7. *Three Bodies Guru-Yoga on Buddha Amitābha* (*Sangs rgyas snang ba mtha' la bsten pa'i sku gsum bla ma'i rnal 'byor*) by bDud-'joms 'jigs-bral ye-shes rdo-rje (1904–1988). This text is based on a mind-*terma* (*dgongs-gter*) (DM 1, 277–278).

8. *An Amitābha Sādhana: Vajra Speech from the Profound and Vast Treasury of Mantra* (*sNgags mdzod zab rgya las gsung rdo rje snang ba mtha' yas kyi sgrub thabs*) by rDo-rje bde-chen gling-pa (nineteenth–twentieth centuries) (DM 1, 302–304).

Prayers for Birth in Sukhāvatī and the *Abode of Padmasambhava on the Glorious Copper-colored Mountain* (*Zangs-mdog dpal-ri*) form part of the regular liturgical cycle of rDo-rje-brag Monastery and all its satellites that follow the Northern Treasures (Byang-gter) tradition, stemming from the fourteenth-century revelations of the *gter-ston* Rig-'dzin rgod-ldem. Such prayers, however, play their most important role in the series of mortuary rituals of this school, associated with the tantric cycle of Avalokiteśvara called *'Gro ba kun grol, Liberation for All Beings.*[1]

The *Anthology of Aspiration Prayers* includes several Pure Land texts that are not designated as Treasure texts per se but are nevertheless composed by notable rNying-ma Treasure discoverers. These include an *Aspiration Prayer* by the visionary Jigs-med gling-pa mkhyen-brtse 'od-zer (1729 or 1730–1798) of the *Klong chen snying thig* cycle; *Opening the Gate to Amitābha: A Sukhāvatī Prayer* written at dPal-chos-rdzong by Ratna gling-pa (1403–1479); an *Aspiration Prayer* by bDud-'dul rdo-rje (1615–1672), a famous Treasure discoverer from Eastern Tibet who opened the hidden land (*sbas-yul*) of Padma-bkod; and a visionary work by the founder of Kaḥ-thog Monastery, Ka-thog-pa dam-pa bde-gshegs (1122–1192), entitled in short *An Aspiration Prayer and Practice of the Perfect Buddha Amitābha.*[2]

A small number of texts listed in the *Anthology* are affiliated with larger cycles of teachings, such as three short *Aspiration Prayers* from the celestial Treasures of gNam-chos mi-'gyur rdo-rje (1645–1667);[3] an *Aspiration Prayer for Birth in Pure Sukhāvatī* from the *Mi tra snying thig* attributed to Guru Mi-tra dzo-ki (ca. late twelfth–thirteenth centuries);[4] and *Opening the Door to Liberation: An Aspiration Prayer for the Sukhāvatī Field* from the *Sangs rgyas dgongs 'dus* cycle.[5]

Notes

Introduction

1 These observations were first noted by Fujita (1996, 3), known for his landmark 1970 study on the formation and development of early Pure Land Buddhism, *Genshi Jōdo shisō no kenkyū* (*A Study of Early Pure Land Buddhism*). His 1996 article draws from this earlier work.

2 Concerning Western attitudes, scholarly and popular, toward Buddhism, see Lopez 1996, 1998; Amstutz 1997; Almond 1988; Conze 1997, 206.

3 According to Gombrich, "there is plenty in the Pali Canon about faith. The word most used is *pasāda,* which indicates emotion as much as belief, a calm and happy confidence that something is so. In the *Sutta-vibhanga,* the canonical commentary on the *pātimokkha* which constitutes about half the Vinaya Piṭaka, Wijayaratna has counted 409 occasions on which the Buddha criticises conduct on the grounds that 'it is not going to instil faith (*pasāda*) in those who lack it or increase the faith of those who have it.' Calm and happiness are themselves 'profitable', 'skilful' states of mind, little steps along the path to nibbāna" (1998, 119).

4 Ritual and scholastic interpretations of Amitābha's Western paradise have been anything but simple or naïve. Chappell has shown that there is nothing simplistic about Chinese Pure Land scriptures—in fact, the efforts of Buddhist thinkers to interpret pure lands "in the light of other Buddhist doctrines have generated rather intricate and complicated theories" (1977, 23).

5 "Transferring to the Land of Bliss: Among Texts and Practices of Sukhāvatī in Tibet," DPhil thesis, University of Oxford, 2006.

Chapter One: Indian Mahayana Origins and Departures

1 The term "soteriology" expresses any theory, doctrine, or system of salvation that aims toward the *soteria* (Greek, "salvation," "liberation") of the individual. The term is widely used in relation to Abrahamic religions and especially Christianity (redemption through Christ), but it also applies to other religious systems, including Buddhism. The aim of Buddhist soteriology is liberation from the fetters of causality that bind one to compulsive repetitions of suffering, illness, death, and rebirth. Ruegg reflects similar concerns:

> [A]nalytical distinctions are of course highly important for the historian of Buddhist religion and philosophy, for they relate to the distinction between

> spiritual practice and philosophical position as understood in Buddhism. This distinction between mahāyāna as a set of teachings or texts and mahāyāna as spiritual practice and intellectual penetration appears to echo in part two established uses of the term dharma, namely (i) a verbalized teaching . . . and (ii) ethical practice and intellectual understanding. (2004, 29)

Arguably, soteriology represents the main *raison d'être* of the world's major religions. The formation of soteriological doctrines appears as a relational process that often leads religious movements to distinguish themselves from their rivals and develop their own identity. There appears to be a direct correlation between the degree of diffusion and the level of attractiveness of a soteriological system on the one hand, and the success of an emerging religion on the other.

2 In Mahayana scriptures the bodhisattva's supreme and perfect "awakening" (Skt. *bodhi*) is ranked highest among spiritual accomplishments, followed by that of *pratyekabuddhas* and *śrāvakas*, who attain the *pratyeka-bodhi* and *śrāvaka-bodhi* respectively; see Dayal 1932, 9–18. Nattier (2003, 180) notes the name arhat in a Mahayana list as one of the ten epithets of Buddha Śākyamuni. This designation recurs in many sutras that feature an audience of *śrāvakas* and where Śākyamuni is often referred to as a Tathāgata and Arhat—a label that demonstrates continuity between his own achievement and that of his bodhisattva followers.

3 In the Pāli Tripiṭaka, ten perfections (*dasa pāramiyo*) are listed; see the *Successive Lives of the Buddha* (*Buddhavaṃsa*). Ruegg notes that Mahayana came to be widely known as the Pāramitāyāna (*phar-phyin gyi theg-pa*), the "Vehicle of the Perfections," "even though pāramitās are recognized also within the Śrāvakayāna and although the Mahāyāna may on occasion embrace in addition the Vajrayāna or 'Adamantine Vehicle'" (2003, 5–6).

4 The conception of the term "bodhisattva" (Pāli bodhisatta) originates in Śrāvakayāna Buddhism. In the *Ariyapariyesana-sutta,* for example, the Buddha, in reference to his life prior to his enlightenment, refers to himself as bodhisatta; Trenckner 1889; *Majjhimanikāya* 1.163. For a seminal survey of buddha fields in Mahayana literature, see Rowell 1935 and 1937; and for a discussion of their prominence in the chiliocosms of Indian cosmology, see Kloetzli 1983, 6.

5 Nattier 2003, 184.

6 Compare for example the "wheel of existence" (Skt. *bhavacakra*) displayed for instructional purposes in the porch of every Tibetan Buddhist temple. The presence of a similar painting in Cave 18 at Ajantā suggests that such a practice was well established in Indian Buddhist settings; see Snellgrove 1987, 14.

7 For example, the *Mahāvastu-Avadāna* contains numerous references to buddha

fields: Vol. II, pp. 9, 276, 283, 298, 299, 302, 304, 318, 326, and 342; Vol. III, pp. 135, 262, 265, 337, and 340; see Jones 1949. There are also references to buddha fields in the *Buddhāpadāna* of the Pāli Tripiṭaka. Bechert (1992, 102–104) has cautioned that this text accepted by the Mahāvihāras was composed roughly at the same time as the *Sukhāvatīvyūha* sutras (first–second centuries CE), and therefore is a fully fledged Mahayana text that stands out from all other works in the Pāli Tripiṭaka.

8 Fujita 1970, 19. In conjunction with rudimentary notions of pure abodes in Pāli sources, we ought to mention the idea of the *suddhāvāsa* (lit., "pure abode"), a heaven where "non-returners" can converse and meet with the Buddha. This heaven could be seen as an early antecedent to later Mahayana developments. The large *Sukhāvatīvyūha-sūtra* compares the inhabitants of Sukhāvatī to beings born in the highest heavenly abode of the desire realm (§71–78).

9 Williams 1989, 216.

10 Lamotte 1994, 276–277. Lamotte notes that certain recensions of the *Saṃdhinirmocana-sūtra* list eighteen excellences of pure *buddha-kṣetras* (i.e., their color, shape, dimensions, and so forth), and employ a whole stock of formulae to describe a pure universe as "pleasant, charming, most lovely to see, thoroughly pure, flourishing, rich, wholesome and fertile" (1994, 278).

11 Fujita 1987, 91.

12 Lamotte 1994, 279–280.

13 For a detailed discussion of the *Akṣobhyavyūha-sūtra,* see Nattier 2000. The antiquity of this sutra is confirmed with the discovery of a related text in 1999 amid birch-bark scrolls in the ruins of a Buddhist monastery in the Bajaur area of Pakistan. It was disseminated in Gāndhārī language sometime in the first–second centuries CE, and it is the only Indian original of the sutra written in Kharoṣṭhī script to have survived (albeit in fragments). It does not seem to have been closely related to the *Akṣobhyavyūha-sūtra* in the form known to us through the Chinese and Tibetan translations of the text. Arguably it can be traced back to a common narrative or text; see Strauch 2008.

14 Williams 1989, 233.

15 Murakami 2008, 137, 139.

16 Murakami 2008, 142.

17 The seventh great vow (Skt. *mahā-praṇidhāna*) of bodhisattvas is to purify and cleanse all the buddha fields; for a discussion of the nine vows, see Dayal 1932, 66. Nattier addresses evidence for some confusion between the "Prakrit forms of *vyūha* 'array,' *śubha* 'auspicious' and *(vi)śuddha* 'pure.'" She suggests that these words may be synonyms if understood in a Middle Indic language as "a reference to the purified quality (**viśūha,* interpreted as a form of *viśuddha* 'pure') of a buddha-field" (2007, 391). This has important implications for the

development of the idea of "purifying a buddha field," seen already in Zhi Qian's early third-century translations of the *Vimalakīrtinirdeśa.* The notion of the purification of buddha fields is found in a number of Mahayana sutras, including the *Aṣṭasāhasrikā Prajñāpāramitā,* the *Saddharmapuṇḍarīka,* the *Gaṇḍavyūha,* and the *Daśabhūmika;* see Fujita 1998, 34. In the *Vimalakīrtinirdeśa-sūtra* we read: "[T]he Bodhisattva who wishes to purify his Buddhakṣetra should, first of all, skillfully adorn (*alaṃkartum*) his own mind (*svacitta*). And why? Because to the extent that the mind of a Bodhisattva is pure is his Buddhakṣetra purified" (VN I, §14).

18 Advocates of the bodhisattva ideal had to reconcile a number of issues for promoting such an extremely difficult path, among them an unimaginable amount of time required for its completion, and the belief that only one buddha can appear in the world at a time; see Nattier 2003.

19 For Dayal, "*praṇidhāna* is both the cause and the result of the thought of Enlightenment and it is of three kinds: that which relates to happy births; that which aims at the good of all beings; and that which is intended to purify the buddha-fields" (1932, 66). Precursors are not absent in early Buddhism; in the *Path of Purification* (*Visuddhimagga*), Buddhagoṣa follows the tripatriate system distinguishing buddha fields as: "*jātikkhetta* ("birth field"), i.e., the realm that quakes on the occasion of the birth of a future Buddha; *āṇākkhetta* ("field of authority"), i.e., the realm where the recitation of *paritta*s is effective; and *visayakkhetta* ("field of objects"), i.e., the realm in which the respective Buddha potentially knows whatever he desires to know" (Bechert 1992, 102).

20 This narrative is recounted in several sūtras, such as the *Bhaiṣajyaguru,* the *Vimalakīrtinirdeśa,* the *Mañjuśrībuddhakṣetraguṇavyūha,* the *Akṣobhyatathāgatasyavyūha,* the *Saddharmapuṇḍarīka,* the *Avataṃsaka,* and the long and short *Sukhāvatīvyūha* sutras.

21 For a related discussion, see Nattier 2003.

22 Harrison 1978, 55, argues along the same lines.

23 The VN reserves an instructive passage listing the conditions for accessing the pure lands (IX, §18). In I, §13 the six *pāramitā*s and their respective fields of giving, patience, vigor, meditation, and wisdom are described as the *buddha-kṣetra* of the bodhisattva.

24 Compare with the *Akṣobhyavyūha,* where a great amount of merit is required for attaining birth in the Abhirati pure land; see Nattier 2003, 193–194. Similarly, in the Tibetan version of the short *Sukhāvatīvyūha-sūtra* Śākyamuni warns Śāriputra that "by inferior root virtue one will not be born in the field of the Tathāgata Amitāyus" (D 197b).

25 Bodhisattvas must fulfill eight conditions to reach, safe and sound, a pure *buddha-kṣetra:* 1) be of benefit to all beings, but not expect the slightest benefit from them; 2) bear the suffering of all beings and grant them all the good roots

that they have gained; 3) maintain toward all beings an even sameness of mind and not feel any aversion; 4) see all bodhisattvas and delight as if they were the master; 5) not reject texts that they have heard or not yet heard; 6) be without jealousy in the gain of others and without pride in their own gains; 7) discipline their own minds and examine their own failings and calm the flows of others; 8) delight in heedfulness and collect all the good virtues (VN IX, §18).

26 "A Bodhisattva establishes his world according to the beings who are to be taught and disciplined" (VN IX, §18).

27 The *Śūraṃgamasamādhi-sūtra* was one of the very first Mahayana sutras to be transmitted in China; the first translation of it appeared in 186 CE; see Lamotte 1998, 107.

28 According to Skorupski, the transfer of merit is "fully endorsed and constitutes one of the essential elements of Mahāyāna and tantra practices" (2001, 140). Although it is an unresolved issue in the texts of Śrāvakayāna Buddhism, transfer of merit is practiced and observed in Theravāda countries. Thomas cites a Pāli Jātaka story (no. 109) "of a sea-spirit (*nāga*) who saved a shipwrecked disciple, but who refused to save his companion until the disciple allowed him to share in the merit of his having kept the commandments" (1933, 258). Schopen's analysis of many early inscriptions confirms that it was well established in Śrāvakayāna Buddhism and its present practice in Theravāda countries does not seem to stem out of the Mahayana. For a discussion of Theravāda mortuary rituals in relation to the transfer of merit, see Gombrich 1988, 124–127. For a brief analysis of problems concerning its interpretation, see Ruegg 2004, 52–53.

29 There are a good number of Mahayana sutras with votive formulas attached to their colophons; see Murakami 2008, 131–132. Pure Land dedications can be found in inscriptions accompanying mural paintings. This is the case with Tibetan-style murals executed in 1966 at the Shish Mahal Palace in Rampur-Bashahr, as indicated by the inscription: "[This inscription] has been composed by the painter of the sacred images, Ne sang Ca Ras Sherab Senge. May we swiftly encounter benefit and in the next life, take birth in Sukhāvatī"; see Halkias 2009b.

30 Tanaka 1990, 21.

31 Ruegg explains, "The idea of salvific activity, exercised by the Buddha or by a Bodhisattva, which benefits a collectivity inasmuch as this activity exercised by them, and marked by their highly expert use of the appropriate salvific devices (*upāya*), does not take as its object any single, individualized beneficiary of compassion. Essential to this kind of activity appears to be on the one side the ethical and spiritual autonomy of its numerically unlimited beneficiaries and on the other side the soteriological action of the Buddha and Bodhisattva as agents of this 'interpersonal'—but none the less universalized and non-objectifying—activity" (2004, 54).

32 For the identity of Nāgāhvya, see Ruegg 1981, 56–57.

33 Lopez 1996, 26.

34 The relation between Nāgārjuna and Pure Land doctrines is discussed at the end of this chapter.

35 *Madhyamakakārikā* 24, 18. Nāgārjuna's exact dates cannot be determined and he is usually placed somewhere between the first and second centuries; for relevant scholarship, see Mabbett 1998.

36 Williams (1989, 61) shows how this concept has evolved for some philosophical schools in Tibet in which "dependent origination" came to mean "dependent upon a designating mind." Interpreted in this way, entities do not exist essentially from their own side but are imputed by the mind, including the terms "mind" and the concept of "emptiness."

37 Conze 1957, 72.

38 Conze 1979, 487.

39 Lamotte 1998, 113.

40 Rowell 1937, 138–139.

41 All references and translations of passages from the LV in this text are from Gómez 1996.

42 Watanabe 2004, 99.

43 Griffiths 1998, 213. Italics added.

44 Tucci 1958, 102–103. Harrison suggests that we get a different understanding of the long *Sukhāvatīvyūha-sūtra* and other similar texts if we read them not as "descriptions of something already existing, but as blueprints for something which is to be constructed in the mind, and then engaged with, just like the Buddha in the *pratyutpanna-samādhi*" (2003, 122).

45 It would seem that the phenomenal relationality of pure lands on the one hand and their devotional reification on the other belong to different and distinct levels of analysis. The emptiness of buddha fields do not preclude faith in the practice of recollecting Amitābha and visualizing Sukhāvatī. Payne identifies telling correspondences between Yogācāra psychology and methods of contemplative transformation, such as visualization. The cosmological and ontological status of *buddha-kṣetras* may be doctrinally disputed, but their psychological duration and epistemological resilience is directly visible "in the sense that in the absence of a living Buddha of our own realm, one is able to enter into the actual presence of another Buddha, Amitābha for example, and hear the [D]harma directly" (2003, 265).

46 See Gómez 1996 for a discussion, translation, and comparison of the contents and themes of the Chinese and Sanskrit recensions of the long and short *Sukhāvatīvyūha* sutras.

47 Nattier (2007, 382, n. 90) cautions that a Sanskrit transcription of the title in the Tibetan text does not guarantee that this was the actual name of the Indian source text. In the case of the *Amitābhavyūha-sūtra,* we can be fairly certain that the Sanskrit reconstruction is accurate, since both *'od-dpag-med* and *bkod-pa* are given with these Sanskrit equivalents in the *Mahāvyutpati* (nos. 85 and 520).

48 Fujita 1996, 10–11. On linguistic grounds, Boucher (1998) cautioned against a common assumption that many of the early Chinese Buddhist translations derive from originals written in Northwest Middle Indic. Lamotte (1988, 575), relying on Ashikaga's studies, classified the sutras as works in which the verse is in mixed Sanskrit and the prose in Sanskrit; see Ashikaga 1952, 1953.

49 Nattier 2000, 72, and Payne 1997, 24. For a comparison between the early and later Chinese translations of the LV, see Nattier 2003, 188–193.

50 See Hirakawa 1990, 288; Pas 1995, 10–11; Gómez 1996, 226, n. 1. This issue is too involved to be settled here. Fujita (1996, 22) argues for descriptions peculiar to later recensions that support the antiquity of the SV. We may bear in mind Ruegg's critique that "a shorter, or simpler, version of a text is not necessarily and invariably older than a longer, or more elaborate, version" (2004, 23).

51 Fussman 1999.

52 Gandhārī is a Prākrit language of Northwest India and Central Asia that was popular from the third century BCE to the third century CE; see Lamotte 1988, 568–572; Tanaka 1990, 3–4. Recently Karashima (2007, 339) suggested that there are transliterations in the oldest Chinese translation of the long *Sukhāvatīvyūha,* the *Amituo jing* (T. 362), which may indicate Middle Indic developments. Recent evidence has been analyzed in Nattier 2006, 2007.

53 The earliest known fragments of the long *Sukhāvatīvyūha* in Indic languages are located in the Schøyen Sanskrit collection; see Braarvig 2002, 180–182.

54 Harmatta 1964, 1.

55 Gaulier 1976, 2.

56 Salomon 199, 5. Interestingly, Luoyang had been a stronghold for Chinese Pure Land Buddhism. According to Chen (1964, 342), the earliest devotees of Sukhāvatī in China were Jue Gongze (265–274), his disciple Wei Shidu, and Wei's mother, all of whom lived in the trading capital of Luoyang.

57 Gaulier 1976, 2. The *Ancient Sogdian Letters from Dunhuang* (composed ca. fourth century) provide vivid evidence of the life of Sogdian settlers in China; see Marshak 1996, 256. These early Chinese translations were thought to be the oldest known editions of Mahayana literature in the world, until the identification of Gāndhārī Buddhist manuscripts in Kharoṣṭhī script dating from about the first half of the first century CE, which makes them the oldest Buddhist manuscripts yet to be discovered. See Harrison 1987 for a discussion of this comparatively small body of texts (eleven in all), which presents

the oldest literary evidence for the Mahayana. For details on the Kharoṣṭhī collection, see Salomon 1999. The manuscripts in the Schoyen and Gilgit collections are discussed in Dietz 2007, 69.

58 T. 310 (5), 360, 361, 362, and 363. For a summary of the five extant Chinese translations and related issues of translatorship, see Fujita 1996, 6–11; 1970, 10–12. The titles of the seven lost Chinese translations of the LV have been reconstructed from the *Kai yuan shi jiao lu gai gen shakkyō roku* (T. 2154), compiled by Zhisheng some time after 730; see Blum 2002, 148. For the Sanskrit LV manuscript see Müller 1883; Ashigaka 1992–1993. For introductions and English translations of the Sanskrit and Chinese versions of the LV see Inagaki 1995; Gómez 1996.

59 Blum 2002, 147; Kudara 2002, 104; see also Chapter Two in this volume.

60 Corless 1995, 250.

61 According to Nattier (2003, 189), this would mean that the most popular Chinese version of the long *Sukhāvatīvyūha* would date from approximately the same time as Kumārajīva's translation of the short sutra.

62 Corless 1995, 251.

63 Fujita 1970, 13.

64 Kudara 2002, 104. This evidence suggests that Amitābha's Pure Land gained popularity among the Uighurs. This is substantiated by a Dunhuang painting of Sukhāvatī that shows coloring and stylistic details comparable to Uighur Manichaean art; see Whitfield 2004, 317.

65 The popularity and impact of this text on the development of East Asian Pure Land Buddhism was considerable. Tanaka writes, "From the Sui to Sung period, at least forty commentaries of the *Kuan ching* are known, most of which were compiled prior to year CE 800. Nine have survived, and two more have been partially restored" (1990, xvii); see also Silk 1997.

66 For a discussion of other Pure Land sutras considered apocryphal, see Tanaka 1990, xvi–xvii.

67 For the Central Asian origins of this text, see Tanaka 1990, 38–42. Recently, Yamabe (1999) argued that Turfan is a likely place for the sutra's composition, based on his examination of the mural paintings of Toyok Cave 20; see also Chapter Two in this volume. In his study, Silk argues for the Indian origins of the first part of the prologue section of the sutra and concludes that "as a whole [it] cannot be an Indian product . . . it is most likely a work initially composed in the Chinese language, perhaps in Central Asia" (1997, 219). For Nattier (2003, 189) there is no sufficient evidence for the sutra's Central Asian origins.

68 This being said, the *Meditation on Amitāyus* and later Tibetan Pure Land literature emphasize the importance of Pure Land visualizations. Sukhāvatī *sādhanas* and other tantric works of the Tibetan variety, as well as Pure Land

commentaries composed by Tibetan scholars, valorize the importance of visualizations as an expedient means of Pure Land practice; see Wilson 2006; Chapters Five and Six in this book.

69 For a detailed discussion on the origins and contents of this text, see Fujita 1990; Pas 1977; Silk 1997. For a summary of current views, see Blum 1985. Silk (1997, 234, n. 2) notes that the text's authenticity was questioned by Dōgen, a view that may have been prevalent in Japan at the time.

70 In Śrāvakayāna Buddhism, Sahā generally refers to a universe of beings that are subject to transmigration; see Wong 1998–1999, 67. It is a world-system cosmologically located in the south quarter of our universe that falls within Śākyamuni's field of spiritual influence. For the etymology of the term *sahā,* see Kloetzli 1983, 6, n. 1.

71 Hirakawa 1990, 290. For a recent assessment of evidence see Nattier 2006, 2007.

72 Amstutz 1998, 45. The Japanese denominations are known as the Jōdo-shū, or Pure Land sect, founded by Hōnen (1133–1212), and the Jōdo Shinshū, the True Pure Land sect, founded by his most gifted disciple, Shinran (1222–1282). The *Sukhavatīvyūha* sutras are listed in the Korean canonical collections of Buddhism; see Lancaster 1979. The cult of Sukhāvatī in Korean Buddhism is traced to the Chinese lineages of Huiyuan (523–592), Xuanzang (596–664), and Kuiji (632–682); see Tanaka 1990, xviii. Tanaka writes, "[T]hese Silla Pure Land commentaries directly and vitally participated in the development of Japanese Pure Land doctrine during the Nara and early Heian periods" (1990, xviii). For the development of the Sukhāvatī cult during the Silla dynasty, see Minamoto 1991, 131–168; Walter 1994.

73 Machida 1988, 3.

74 Nattier 2003.

75 According to Payne, "[I]n the milieu of Buddhist India in which these figures came into prominence, there was a single Buddha—Amitābha—and not two different Buddhas having distinct characteristics and hence separate names. Rather, the process of interpretation inherent in translation and scribal emendation led to a form in Chinese being created that meant 'immeasurable life' and which then created the appearance of a second Sanskrit name, Amitāyus" (2007, 284).

76 LV §29/5. A brief description of the names Amitābha and Amitāyus can be found in SV §§14, 15.

77 For an examination of evidence, see Nattier 2007b, 391.

78 Fujita 1996, 15. Nattier (2007, 389–390) argues on philological grounds that there is no evidence that Amitāyus might refer to Amitābha, or that Amitāyus may be a variant of Amitābha in a Middle Indic form, in any of the translations during the Han period.

79 For Tibetan *mtha'-yas,* "infinite"; *snang-ba,* "luminosity," "manifestation," "vision," or "appearance." The name sNang-ba mtha'-yas is not found in the Tibetan *Sukhavatīvyūha* sutras but the antiquity of its usage is widely attested to in numerous Dunhuang Tibetan MSS, such as Pel.Tib. 6, 49, 57, 99, 158, 245, 252, 253, 266, 288, 75; see also Lalou 1939.

80 Machida 1988, 7.

81 Inagaki argues that the *Pratyutpannasamādhi-sūtra* played a vital role in the establishment of Pure Land Buddhism in China. He explains: "Hui-yüan, the founder of Chinese Pure Land tradition, formed the White Lotus Society on Mt. Lu in the early fifth century with a view to practicing the Buddha-Recollection Samādhi, presumably based on this sutra. Further, a seventh-century Pure Land master, Chia-ts'ai, mentions his sutra in the list of twelve sutras and seven discourses of Pure Land Buddhism. This list is quoted by Genshin (942–1017) of Japan in his *Ōjoyōshū*. Shan-tao (613–681), a great exponent of Pure Land Buddhism, quoted this sutra extensively in his works, especially the *Kuan-nien-fa-mên,* to explain the method of meditation on Amitabha and the Pure Land. All this indicates the authentic position of the *Pratyutpanna-samādhi Sūtra* in Pure Land tradition" (1981, 194).

82 The Tibetan title of this work is *'Phags pa da ltar gyi sangs rgyas mngon sum du bzhugs pa'i ting nge 'dzin ces bya ba theg pa chen po'i mdo* (D 133). It is listed in the *Phangthangma Catalogue* in the Ratnakūṭa section. For an insightful discussion on the relation of this sutra to Pure Land scriptures, see Harrison 1990, 1978.

83 For evidence of Pure Land worship in Chinese biographical records, see Zürcher 1995, 10. Harrison postulates, "it is quite clear from other passages in the sūtra that he [Amitāyus] is employed only as an example, and that the object of the samādhi can be any Buddha or number of Buddhas, in whatever direction their buddhakṣetras may lie" (1978, 43).

84 Harrison 1990, 31–32; 36–37.

85 Harrison 1978, 215. For a comparative study of *buddhānusmṛti* in India, China, and Tibet, see Chen 2007. *Meditating on the Buddha* is attested to in the Pāli Nikāyas as one in a series of recollections (Pāli *buddhānussati*). In seventh-century Tang China (618–907), *buddhānusmṛti* was predominantly practiced as the oral recitation of the Buddha's name—a method not singled out in the *Sukhāvatīvyūha* sutras. For a summary of arguments on whether Pure Land aspirants in India made a distinction between "recollecting the Buddha" and "chanting his name," see Moriyama 2005, 242–249. According to the Tibetan Treasure tradition (*gter-chos*), *buddhānusmṛti* is one of "six liberations" (*grol-ba drug*), following seeing, hearing, tasting, wearing, and touching; see Gayley 2007, 463. The practice of buddha invocation (Ch. *nianfo*) is recommended in a curious manuscript from Dunhuang, entitled *Methods of Contemplation of the South Indian Meditation Master Bodhidharma* (*Nantian zhuguo Putidamo chanshi guanmen*), that combines Chan esoteric Buddhism and Faxiang; see Sørensen 1998, 33.

86 For examples, see Schopen 1977. The practice of deity-recollection at the moment of death is not restricted to Buddhist literature, however. The Hindu deity Kṛṣṇa says in the *Bhagavadgītā*, "whoever at the time of death, when he casts aside his body, bears me in mind (*smaran*) and departs, comes to my mode of being: there is no doubt about this" (Beyer 1977, 333).

87 A similar observation was made by Lusthaus 2002, 62–63.

88 Mukherjee 1979. Schopen (1987) takes 78 CE as the beginning of the Kaṇiṣka era and reads the twenty-sixth year to be 104 CE Murakami (2008, 127), following Ghirshman's theory that 144 CE marks the starting date, concludes that the inscription dates to 171 CE

89 Murakami 2008, 127. Italics added.

90 Murakami 2008, 127.

91 Schopen 1987, 123.

92 Murakami (2008, 127–131) sides with Brough (1982) and argues against Schopen and Salomon (2002).

93 Tanaka 1990, 13. This seminal work for the development of Yogācāra philosophy, no longer extant in Sanskrit, survives in four Chinese translations (T. 1592, 1593, 1594, 1596) and one Tibetan version, the *Theg pa chen po bsdus pa* (D 4048), translated by Jinamitra, Śīlendrabodhi, and Ye-shes-sde.

94 For the relevant passage, see Tanaka 1990, 12. The *Mahāyānasaṃgrahabhāṣya* does not survive in Sanskrit. It is preserved in three Chinese translations (T. 1595, 1596, 1597) and one Tibetan translation (with lacunae), the *Theg pa chen po bsdus pa'i 'grel pa* (D 4050), translated by Dīpaṅkaraśrījñāna and Tshul-khrims rgyal-ba. Moriyama (2005, 237) maintains that Vasubandhu the Elder was the author of the *Mahāyānasaṃgrahabhāṣya.* For a discussion of two persons by this name, the younger and elder Vasubandhu, see Frauwallner 1951; Bhikku Pasadika 1991, 15–21.

95 Griffiths (1989, 35) remarks that Amitābha worship appears to have gained some popularity before Asaṅga's times in an arising movement that championed the cult of Śākyamuni over Pure Land devotional practices.

96 Yamada 1968, 88–89.

97 For an analysis of these issues, see Barber 1999.

98 Barber 1999, 196.

99 Hazra 1983; Tanaka 1990, 3.

100 The discovery of 1,000 documents in Kharoṣṭhī-Gāndhārī in the ruins of abandoned oasis cities of the southern Tarim basin point out that Gāndhārī was the administrative language of the oasis states of the Southern Route, presumably as a result of trade and political developments in the vast empire of the Kuṣāṇas. The Kuṣāṇa empire, with its extensive trading networks and multicultural constituents, fostered the conditions for the spread and establishment

of Buddhism outside India. Buddhist monasteries across the Kuṣāṇa empire have been identified in Afghanistan, Kashmir, present-day Turkmenistan and Uzbekistan, the Ferghana valley, and around the Amu-darya (Oxus). Inscriptions from Greater Gandhāra attest to the presence of the Buddhist schools of the Kāśyapīyas, Dharmaguptakas, Sarvāstivādins, and Mahāsāṃghikas in the region; see Zurcher 1999, 12; Dietz 2007, 62; Snellgrove 1987, 330; Litvinsky and Vorobyova-Desyatovskaya 1996, 432.

101 Beckwith 2000, 84–85.

102 Snellgrove 1987, 330; Vorobyova-Desyatovskaya 1996, 432.

103 The Mauryan emperor Candragupta, Aśoka's grandfather, signed a treaty with the Greek king Seleucos Nicator and sealed it with marital rites between Indians and Greeks. Thereafter, the Seleucids maintained an ambassador to the Mauryan court at Pāṭaliputra. Woodcock (1966, 17) entertains the possibility that Aśoka's bloodline may have been in part Greek.

104 The Greeks within Aśoka's kingdom and in neighboring Bactria occupied prosperous zones and engaged in successful trading activity at the crossroads of the great east-west caravan that linked the Mauryan capital Pāṭaliputra with Asia Minor and mainland Greece. Trade passed through the Ganges valley to the Panjab, Taxila, Pushkalavati, and Alexandria ad Caucasum. From Alexandria it crossed over the Hindu Kush to Hellenistic Bactria and continued onward to Persia and the Mediterranean Sea.

105 For an introduction and English translation of Aśoka's Greek edicts from Alexandria of Arachosia, see Halkias, forthcoming.

106 It is clear from Edict XIII that Emperor Aśoka was keenly aware of the strategic importance of Greek communities and had accurate knowledge of the Greek rulers far beyond the political sphere of influence of the Mauryas. He dispatched diplomatic missions to the Greek kings of Syria, Egypt, Macedonia, Cyrene, and Corinth (or Epirus); for a translation and discussion of the edict, see Vassiliades 2004, 142–144. The Pāli Sutta Piṭaka, the *Chronicle of the Island* (*Dīpavaṃsa*), the *Great Chronicle* (*Mahāvaṃsa*), and Aśokan edicts III, V, and IX contain overt references to the Greeks (Pāli *yona;* Skt. *yavana*), who appear to have been an important target for Buddhist missions; see Halkias, forthcoming.

107 Harmatta 1964, 4.

108 The Dharmarājikā stupa at Taxila presents archaeological evidence for an early institutional presence of Buddhism in Gandhāra. Recent scholars date this site to the second century BCE; see Glass 2004, 132. Harmatta argues that the introduction of Buddhism to the Tarim basin (and China) coincides with Indo-Chinese commerce initiated during the times of the Greco-Bactrian kingdom. He writes:

> [T]here cannot be any doubt that the Graeco-Bactrian kings, who proved their political discernment on several occasions, have clearly realized the

role of essential importance for their own country of commerce between Indian and China, these great and rich states, with a developed commodity production and, on account of the highly centralized state organization, disposing over large supplies of goods. It is not an exaggeration to say that one of the main raisons d'être of the Graeco-Bactrian Kingdom, the Indo-Scythian State, and the Kuṣāṇa Empire as a political power including North Western India and Inner Asia, was exactly the pursuance of commerce between India and China (as well as the West). (1964, 12)

109 Litvinsky and Vorobyova-Desyatovskaya 1996, 432.

110 The Kuṣāṇas utilized Greek literacy for the administration of their own empire and the Greek alphabet to write the Bactrian language. Concerning the finds at Khalchayan, beside the Greek winged Nike and the Greco-Kushan Zeus/Ahura Mazda, the Hellenistic Mithra represents the third type of Greco-Iranian syncretism; see Harmatta, Puri, Lelekov, Humayan, and Sircar 1994.

111 See Hazra 2009, 61; there is special emphasis on the development of Buddhism during the reign of the successor of Kadphises II, Emperor Kaniṣka (78–101 or 102 CE).

112 Harmatta, Puri, and Etemadi 1994, 491.

113 For a discussion of Near Eastern influences, see Karetsky 1997; Fujita 1996, 8–9. Gómez repudiates this assertion on the ground that "there are enough precedents for light imagery and the association of light with spirituality within the Indian tradition to account for the symbolism of light in the two sutras without assuming an exclusively Iranian origin" (1996, 35–36).

114 This has been dismissed by Hirakawa (1990, 290), who argues that faith in Pure Land Buddhism has elements in common with devotion to the Hindu god Kṛṣṇa. However, the Sanskrit term *bhakti* ("devotion") does not appear in the *Sukhāvatīvyūha* sutras and did not become a significant force in Indian culture before the Gupta period (fifth–seventh centuries CE). Machida (1988, 5–6) quotes Ogiwara Unrai, who puts forth an intriguing argument that the term *amita* is a vernacular form of the Sanskrit *amṛta*. Therefore, *amṛta* as the "nectar of immortality" has many links with the cultic use of consuming soma in the *Ṛg-Veda* that brings health and immortality. Since *soma* is identical with the sun in Vedic mythology, the author theorizes how it may have influenced both the idea of Amitāyus (measureless life) and Amitābha (measureless light). In Ruegg's assessment, even though "certain areas of Mahāyāna have shared features of the *bhakti* movement with other Indian religions . . . this movement is not confined exclusively to one or two traditions and appears almost pan-Indian, a fact overlooked in many publications on the subject" (2004, 31).

115 Fujita 1970, 15.

116 Interestingly, the earliest known reference to Buddha Lokeśvararāja is found in a Bactrian text in praise of various buddhas written in Greek script; see Braarvig

2002, 275–277. The number and contents of Dharmākara's vows vary across the extant editions of the long *Sukhāvatīvyūha-sūtra.* The Tibetan translation of the sutra, which dates to the early ninth century CE, lists forty-nine vows roughly divided into three categories: those concerning Dharmākara's future awakening as Buddha Amitābha, the purification of Sukhāvatī, and the inhabitants of the Pure Land. The Sanskrit text lists forty-seven vows and the Chinese recensions have twenty-four, thirty-six, or forty-eight vows; see Fujita 1996, 16. For a comparative table of the vows between the Sanskrit version and Chinese translation attributed to Saṃghavarman, see Gómez 1996, 264–265. The so-called eighteenth vow based on the Saṃghavarman translation has been the most important for the Shinshū sect of Pure Land Buddhism in Japan; see Nakamura 1987, 205. Fujita (1970, 385) offers a discussion of each vow. Hirakawa (1990, 290) notes that some of Dharmākara's pledges are cited in the *Karuṇāpuṇḍarīka-sūtra* (T. 157), a text that may share a historical affinity with the LV.

117 As we have examined earlier in this chapter, bodhisattvas may formulate their vows according to the needs of those who will receive benefit. For example, Bhaiṣajyaguru's buddha field arises from aspirations to aid those who are ill, have deformities, or who have no doctor or medicine, and so on. Likewise, Akṣobhya's buddha field is attractive to women and childbearing mothers; see Williams 1989, 243–250. On the other hand, Sukhāvatī is easily accessible to all who aspire to take birth from a lotus and not a womb. Neumaier elaborates on the theme of an "all-male" birth in a Freudian light: "An all male birth obliterates the possibility of an Oedipal dilemma arising, where the brothers not only kill the father due to their sexual desire for their mother but also attempt to destroy each other to enjoy the mother for themselves. As a consequence, the all male birth frees an all male society from carnal yearning and potential violence. It becomes the cornerstone of religions that strive for a mystic transmutation of the self, that is, Buddhism as well as Christianity" (2007, 235). For a critique of the exclusion of women in Sukhāvatī, see also Young 2004, 219–222.

118 These narratives are mentioned by Inagaki 1999, 12.

119 Gómez (1996, 35) discusses some of these issues. Some time ago, Przyluski (1927) called attention to parallels between Amitābha's Pure Land and Mesopotamian descriptions of sacred seven-walled cities. But as Mus rightly noted in response:

> [I]t is not only the Mahāyānist traditions which are affected by this comparison, but also certain passages of the Pāli scriptures and even a large and ancient group of Brāhmanical materials. The whole of Buddhism, and even India in its entirety, has been influenced by this idea. One would not therefore expect to find in it one of the specific components, itself at the same time specifically extra-Indian, of the Great Vehicle. (1998, 12)

120 Machida 1988, 13. According to Tucci (1949, 350), we cannot tell if iconographic depictions of Sukhāvatī have ever been very popular in India, as there are no trustworthy documents on the subject. For an insightful presentation of the interplay of Buddhist mythology and contemplation in the Pāli and Central Asian versions of the *Mahāsudassana-sutta* in relation to the *Sukhāvatīvyūha-sūtra,* see Gethin 2006.

121 Fujita 1998, 39.

122 Hirakawa's thesis contains some compelling points, but it has not been without its share of criticism; see Hirakawa 1990, 339–340; Chappell 1977, 24–25. In defense of Hirakawa's thesis, there is one Amitābha Jātaka tale that foretells of a bodhisattva called Brilliant Ensign who made a pilgrimage to all the stupas throughout the universe and led many pilgrims to visit and practice around them. This bodhisattva later became Buddha Amitābha; see Inagaki 1999, 13. Legends that link Buddha Amitābha with the origins of the Svayambū stūpa among the Newār traditions of Kathmandu valley have been noted by Lewis (1996).

123 Dutt 1962, 222.

124 Fujita 1996, 21. *Sukha* is contrasted with suffering (*duhkha*), the defining characteristic of samsara in Buddhism.

125 LV §136. Avalokiteśvara, the bodhisattva regent of Sukhāvatī, is commonly portrayed holding a lotus flower in the form of Padmapāṇi (lit., "Lotus-holder").

126 Rhi 2003, 168.

127 Beer 2003, 8. The lotus opens and closes with the sun, and for the ancient Egyptians the sun was believed to rise from an eastern lotus at dawn and set into a western lotus at sunset. The lotus was also a symbol of the sun in India and the sun god Sūrya is known as "Lord of the lotus, father and king"; Ward 1952, 136.

128 Cleary 1993, 976.

129 Rhi (2003, 169) identifies the meritorious practice of making buddha images on lotuses for the sake of *upapāduka* in the *Sumatidārikāparipṛcchā, Vimaladattāparipṛcchā,* and the *Bhadrakalpika-sūtra.*

130 Book VII, Ch. 2; Book IV, Ch. 8; translation from T. W. Rhys Davids 1894.

131 For examples, see Beer 1999, 37; Ward 1952, 138. Rhi quotes an instructive passage from the *Dazhidu lun* (*Mahāprajñāpāramitopadeśa*) that sheds light on the significance of the lotus seat: "Why does the Buddha necessarily sit on the lotus while he could sit on a mat? [That is because] the mat is a conventional seat for the ordinary people in the world. The lotus is tender and pure, and the Buddha wishes to show his supernatural power by sitting on it without breaking it off. Also he wishes to adorn the seat of the lotus of fine dharma. Also all other

flowers are small and not comparable to a lotus in fragrance, purity and size" (2003, 168).

132 Young 2004, 220.

133 The similarity between birth from a lotus in Sukhāvatī and buddhas or bodhisattvas depicted or visualized on lotuses suggests the transposition and popularization of themes. Beer comments on the significance of the lotus as a synonym for the female vagina, soft and open. He writes that the "union of vajra and lotus is a sexual metaphor for the union of form and emptiness, compassion and wisdom, blissfully uniting in divine embrace. The inner symbolism of sexual union refers to the psychic winds entering and ascending the central channel of the subtle body, and piercing the 'lotuses' of each channel-wheel and causing them to open" (1999, 37).

134 Tucci notes that sometimes Amitābha is portrayed in a golden color, a convention "justified by literary tradition, although in the *maṇḍala* the color belonging to him is red" (1949, 288).

135 Bhattacharya 1985, 1.

136 Fremantle and Trungpa 1987, xix.

137 Dalton (2002, 41–42) identifies the introduction of the five buddha families as a central development of the *Mahāvairocana-abhisambodhi-tantra* from around the mid-seventh century, and the *Sarva-tathāgata-tattva-saṃgraha-tantra* from the end of the seventh century.

138 See Fremantle's (1990, 101–114) discussion of Chapter VII of the *Guhyasamāja-tantra*. Amitābha features in many esoteric contexts without any reference to the soteriology of Sukhāvatī, as in the ancillary tantric pledges pertaining to each of the five buddha families. The pledge of Amitābha is to be faithful to the higher and lower tantras and to the three vehicles; see Beyer 1978, 406. In the *Five Mahāyoga Tantras* (*rTsa rgyud sde lnga'i nang tshan*) pure lands acquire a tantric dramatization:

> Ghanavyūha is the place [where] Vairocana taught the tantra of the enlightened body. Sukhāvatī is the place where Amitābha taught the tantra of enlightened speech. Abhirati was the place where Akṣobhya taught the tantra of enlightened mind. Ratnapurī is the place where Ratnasambhava taught the tantra of enlightened qualities. Sukarmasiddhi is the place where Amoghasiddhi taught the tantra of enlightened activity.

See Butters 2005, 314.

139 In a *Guhyasamāja* ritual performed at the tantric college of bKra-shis lhun-po, the practitioner visualizes in his body a *maṇḍala* of thirty-two subtle deities, among them Amitābha, located between the hairline and the throat. In the *Hevajra-tantra*, Amitābha is supplicated during the tasting of nectar; see Beyer (1978, 72).

140 This tantric practice is mentioned by Bentor (1996, 292, n. 304) and Tucci (1949, 310–311); Tucci notes that during the liturgy of consecration and vivification of sacred objects, Amitābha's syllable, a red *āḥ* that corresponds to the verbal plane, is employed.

141 Getty 1978, 37–39. The imagery of buddhas in sexual intimacy symbolizes the union between skillful means (*thabs;* Skt. *upāya*) and wisdom (*shes-rab;* Skt. *prajñā*), the male (*yab*) and female (*yum*) principles of enlightened awareness.

142 Tucci 1949, 540.

143 See, for example, Blo-bzang rgya-mtsho's (1617–1682) *sādhana* that features Amitābha with Avalokiteśvara; *gSung 'bum dkar chag* (1990, vol. Tha, 45. 1 fol.). Traditionally speaking, Avalokiteśvara, Padmasambhava, Hayagrīva, Kurukulla, Bhrikuti, and certain forms of Tārā are members of the Lotus Family, and in Tibetan paintings it is common to find some of these deities next to Amitābha; see Beer 2003, 236. However, Tārā is also included as a member of the Karma Family; see Wilson 1986, 21; 376, n. 22.

144 The matter-of-fact inclusion of Tārā and Padmasambhava in Karma chags-med's *Aspirational Prayer for the Pure Land Sukhāvatī* suggests a case of Tibetan innovation. The relevant section reads: "Dharmakāya Amitābha is the Lord of the Lotus Family; [visualize] from the palm of his right hand light rays radiating in the semblance of Avalokiteśvara, further refracting and emanating 100 million powerful Avalokiteśvaras. From the palm of his left hand light rays radiate in the form of Tārā, further refracting and emanating 100 million Tārās. From his heart light rays radiate in the form of Padmasambhava, further refracting and emanating 100 million of Orgyens" (Tibetan text: *chos sku snang ba mtha' yas rigs kyi bdag / phyag g.yas 'od zer las sprul spyan ras gzigs / yang sprul spyan ras gzigs dbang bye ba brgya / phyag g.yon 'od zer las sprul sgrol ma ste / yang sprul sgrol ma bye ba phrag brgya 'gyed / thugs gyi 'od zer las sprul padma 'byung / yang sprul u rgyan bye ba phrag brgya 'gyed*).

145 Kapstein 2004, 17.

146 Sørensen 1994, 104.

147 Shakya 1994, 87. The same author (1999, 90) reports on depictions of Dharmadhātu-Vagishvara, a multi-armed esoteric form of Mañjuśrī, that show him crowned with Buddha Amitābha.

148 The emblematic headdress and the *dhyāna-mudrā* are Amitābha's distinct features before the Gupta period; see Handa 1994, 215; Saunders 1960, 230. In Nepalese traditions current from the eighth century onward, or perhaps earlier, Buddha Amitābha is represented in stupas along with the directional buddhas Akṣobhya in the east, Ratnasambhava in the south, and Amoghasiddhi in the north (Snellgrove 1978, 177). Along with his bodhisattva attendants, Amitābha was the subject of devotion for the Newār Buddhists of Nepal. A Licchavi inscription from Patan, dated 610 CE, illustrates: "I praise Amitābha,

the best, dispeller of illusion by the light of great *prajñā;* the light, victor who lives in Sukhāvatī with Lokeśvara, the destroyer of the fear arising in the world, bearer of the lotus, and Mahāsthāmaprāpta, the affectionate-hearted one" (Lewis 1996, 6).

149 Lewis 1996, 6.

150 This symbolism continued, as shown in the triple-point crown that adorns an unusual standing statue of Avalokiteśvara from the early *phyi-dar* period; see Heller 2008.

151 Huntington 1980. Tucci (1988, 85) notes the iconographic tradition of the triad in the *Karuṇāpuṇḍarīkasūtra,* where Araṇemi, who reigned during past cosmic eras, became Buddha Amitābha, while his two eldest sons became the bodhisattvas Avalokiteśvara and Mahāsthāmaprāpta. In the preface to Tucci's work, Lokesh Chandra argues that in Northwest India the triad of Śākyamuni, Brahmā, and Indra were later replaced by Amitābha, Avalokiteśvara, and Mahāsthāmaprāpta.

152 The eight bodhisattvas are the Mahayana counterparts of the eight *śrāvakas*, or disciples of Buddha Śākyamuni; see Chandra 1987, 55–56. They are Maitreya, Avalokiteśvara, Nīraraṇaviṣkambhin, Samantabhadra, Vajrapāṇi, Ākāśagarbha, Mañjuśrī, and Kṣitigarbha. In the *Aspiration Prayer for the Pure Land Sukhāvatī,* Karma Chags-med refers to eight bodhisattvas accompanying Amitābha. This reference resembles a passage from the sutra of the Medicine Buddha where a dying person is likewise accompanied by eight bodhisattvas; see Skorupski 1995, 210.

153 The Vairocana cult in imperial Tibet produced an iconography that resembles depictions of Amitābha with his acolytes. Heller (1997, 387–388) notes that Vairocana is commonly surrounded by eight bodhisattvas, while the literature of the *Vairocanābhisambodhi* cycle stipulates that Vairocana is accompanied by Vajrapāṇi and Avalokiteśvara. According to a Dunhuang manuscript (Pell. Tib. 240), the octad may include eight female attendants; four of them are "offering goddesses, while the other four are the *yum* (consorts) of the tathagāta"; see Heller 1998, 139. Yoritomi (1990, 325) writes: "In thankas and wood-block prints the eight Bodhisattvas are almost always depicted with Amitābha as the central figure. In this case 'Od-dpag-med in Tathāgata form or Tshe-dpag-med in magnificent Bodhisattva form are depicted as especially large inside a holy building. Amitābha is sometimes seated on a pedestal with a peacock (*māyūra*) and at other times is seated on a lotus which has sprung forth from the lotus pond of Paradise. The eight Bodhisattvas flank Amitābha, four on each side, and most often the figures are seated."

154 Walter (1980, 319) writes:

> Let us first look at the system in Padmaist literature. Our examination reveals that it is almost completely oriented around the extraction of

essences (rasas) from the physical elements of the universe. . . . Padmasambava delivers these teachings as a mediator for, or is to be evoked as a form of, Amitāyus. There are also several texts which mention the conjuring of eight immortal magicians which emanate from Amitāyus.

155 Tucci (1988, 82) notes that a vessel with a narrow base and wider at the top can be traced back to ancient rituals from which the water of life gushes out.

156 Getty (1978, 39) is clearly mistaken in writing that Amitāyus is never represented with a consort.

157 See Himalayan Art (http://www.himalayanart.org), accessed on October 2009. Jeff Watts describes the painting as follows: "The floor of the palace is divided into four colours, blue, yellow, red and green, decorated with eight gold vases. The square enclosure is composed of five walls of different colours. The four doors are indicated with 'T' shaped structures topped with four steps, two deer and a Dharma wheel. Various ornaments of banners, vases and standing arrows adorn the roof of the palace. Outside of that are a ring of multicoloured lotus petals, a ring of gold vajras and the multi-coloured fires of pristine awareness."

158 Tucci 1988, 84. The Tibetans, unlike the Chinese and Japanese, do not confuse their forms nor do they conflate their distinctive symbolisms.

159 Tucci notes, "the same uncertainty remains also in the Vajrayāna. . . . In the *maṇḍala* described by Advayavajra, the West is occupied by Amitābha; in the Guhyasamāja, Amitāyuḥ (Amitāyurvajra) predominates over Amitābha, but there is no allusion to a difference between the two" (1949, 349).

160 Pandey 1971, 77.

161 Pugachenkova 1994, 378.

162 Pandey 1971, 88–89. He notes that the *Aṅśumadbhedāgama* treatise prescribes the color red for the garment of the sun (p. 126), while images showing the sun god standing on a lotus flower have also been discovered in many parts of the country (p. 91). In the village of Paikore in Bīmrbhū District, Bengal, the sun god is seated on a lotus flower carved on the pedestal of a sun image (p. 105). For references to relevant studies concerning the influence of solar cults on the development of Amitābha, see Karetzky 1997, 8.

163 Pandey 1971, 125. The prevalence of sun worship during the time of the Buddha is confirmed in the *Brahmajāla Suttanta;* see T. W. Rhys Davids 1899, 24.

164 Upasak 1990, 161. Horse motifs in India are common in relation to worship of the sun god, who is often depicted on a chariot drawn by horses. A tantric emanation of Amitābha is the wrathful Hayagrīva (rTa-mgrin), a ferocious horse-headed totemic deity also worshiped in Japan (Jpn. Bato Kannon) and in Hinduism; he belongs to the "wrathful lineage" (*khro-bo'i-rgyud*) of the Lotus Family. The capacity of buddhas and bodhisattvas to emanate themselves in

different forms is a well-known theme in Mahayana sutras and in Vajrayana narratives. Bhattacharya (1924, 15–17; 53–60) draws from the *Sādhanamālā* and other cognate Buddhist tantric texts and enumerates Amitābha's variable emanations: two varieties of Mañjuśrī, Vāk and Dharmadhātu-Vāgīśvara; and in addition to Mahāvala and Saptaśatika-Hayagrīva, the goddesses Kurukullā, Bhṛkuṭī, and Mahāsitavatī. Among the earliest Tibetan texts dedicated to this deity is the *rTa mgrin dregs pa zil gnon,* a rNying-ma treasure text revealed by Sangs-rgyas blama (ca. 1000–1080), who is regarded as the first Buddhist treasure discoverer (gter-ston).

165 Shinran, the founder of the Japanese Jōdo Shinshū school and chief proponent of "other-power" (Jpn. *tariki*), lists seven patriarchs: Nāgārjuna, Vasubandhu, Tanluan, Daochuo, Shandao, Genshin, and Hōnen; see Kajiyama 1989, 137, n. 1.

166 For a critique of these texts see Harrison 1978, 55, n. 5; Williams 1989, 257.

167 Inagaki 1998, 8. Lindtner (1982, 14, n. 26) suggests that this work is authentic.

168 Inagaki 1998, 36.

169 Tanaka 1990, 12.

170 For a translation and study of the *Sukhāvatīvyūhopadeśa,* see Kiyota 1978.

171 Moriyama 2005, 241. Inagaki (1998, 8–9) explains that the Chinese master Tanluan (476–542), in his commentary on Vasubandhu's *Sukhāvatīvyūhopadeśa,* paid special attention to Chapter IX of the *Discourse on the Ten Stages.* He made it the basis of his distinction between easy (other-power) versus difficult (self-power) approaches to Buddhist practice. This concept was elaborated by his successor Daochuo (562–645), who simplified the ten stages in two gates to enlightenment: the path of sages and the path of Pure Land devotion.

172 A recent compendium of Tibetan Pure Land literature, the *Anthology of Aspirational Prayers* (*bDe smon phyogs bsgrigs,* vol. 1), contains one short prayer to Sukhāvatī attributed to Ārya Nāgārjuna (pp. 151–155). Unfortunately, the Tibetan editors of the *Anthology* make no reference to the origins and means of acquisition of this prayer, which may be of Tibetan authorship.

Chapter Two: Pure Lands and the Tibetan Empire

1 Bushell 1880, 439.

2 Pan 1992, 117–118.

3 Pan notes that "before the An Lushan rebellion, there had been two Tang-Tibetan treaties, the treaties of 706 and 732, and each time it was the Chinese who violated the treaty first, while after the rebellion, when Tang was in a weakened positions vis-à-vis Tibet, five were concluded and each was broken off by the Tibetans first" (1992, 148–149).

4 Beckwith 1987, 30.

5 For Chinese sources on the military strategies and tactics used by the Tibetans against the Tang, see Ren Shumin 1991; for Tibetan sources, see Thomas 1951.

6 Beckwith writes that the first phase of Tibetan colonialism in the Tarim basin ended in 692. For a history of the Tibetan empire's involvement in the western regions, see Beckwith 1987, 37–54.

7 Pan 1992, 124.

8 An Lushan was of Sogdian-Turkish descent and served as the Tang governor of three defense forces in the northeast. Aware of efforts by other political factions to remove him from power, he rose in revolt with some 150,000 troops on December 16, 755. He crossed the Yellow River and cut off all supplies to the imperial court from the south. A year later the Tang government was forced to withdraw troops from the southern borders to confront the rebellion. Taking advantage of this opportunity, some local populations rebelled and threw off the yoke of Chinese rule.

9 Benn 2004, 13.

10 Dotson explains that "there appear to have been eight or nine such colonial military governments, each of them coming into existence at different times following a major conquest, with a new *khrom* sometimes replacing older *khrom.* Their chain of command was military in nature, with a general at the top, and below him two prefects (*rtse-rje*) who governed the larger settlements or cities. These colonial military governments were full of subordinate units such as ten-thousand-districts (*khri-sde*), thousand-districts, sub-thousand-districts, units of fifty households (*tshan*), and smaller *tshan* units" (2009, 41).

11 According to the south inscription of the Zhol Pillar in Lhasa, the Tibetan campaigns against China made the Chinese emperor Suzong offer a perpetual yearly tribute of fifty thousand rolls of silk. It was only when the next emperor, Daizong, ceased paying the tribute that the Tibetans launched an attack on Chang'an (Richardson 1985, 13).

12 In Beckwith's assessment, following the An Lushan Rebellion among the most serious losses for the Tang "were the circuits of the northeast centering on Hopei, which had been the main silk-producing region of the empire before the Rebellion; and the horse pastures in the circuits of Long-yu and Ho-hsi" (1991, 186). In fact, the Tang dynasty was in constant need of silk to purchase mounts for its cavalry and to maintain its postal service and public roads. The Uighurs had taken advantage of the situation and sold horses to the Chinese on credit for up to forty pieces of silk per horse. This added to a massive national debt. For a reconstruction of the events that brought the Tang dynasty into debt, see Beckwith 1991. The Tang emperor Wuzong, who assumed the throne in 840, took drastic measures to save the dynasty from its crippling deficit. With the implicit support of Daoist sects, in 842 he launched a persecution of Buddhism and all other "foreign faiths" such as Manichaenism,

Zoroastrianism, and Nestorian Christianity. By 845 he had closed 4,600 monasteries and 40,000 smaller chapels and shrines. As stated by Benn, "the real motive for the proscription was economic, not ideological. The state was short of revenues, and the defenseless Buddhist church provided easy pickings. The government seized its slaves, cash, silk, and grain to pay the salaries of its officials. It expropriated all metal statues and bells, converting those of bronze into coins, those of gold and silver into ingots that found their way into the public purse, and those of iron into farming tools" (2004, 16).

13 Compare with the beginning of the Sino-Tibetan Treaty of 783: "Tang possesses all under heaven; wherever the footprints of Yu extended, as far as boats and chariots can go, there is no one that does not obey. Under the renewed brilliance of successive sovereigns, it continues year after year to all eternity, throwing luster on the great kingly inheritance, and spreading holy teachings within the four seas. With the Tibetan *btsan-po* (Emperor) it has made matrimonial alliance generation after generation. It has firmly bound itself in the neighbourly friendship, forming a common body in peace and danger, and forming nephew-and-uncle countries for nearly two hundred years" (Pan 1992, 155).

14 Translation of the east inscription in Richardson 1985, 111 (italics added). For the problematic use of the word "barbarian" in reference to Central Eurasian peoples, see Beckwith 2009, 320–362. The *Jiu Tangshu* reads, "As for what is presently under control of China, Tang is the sovereign, and as for the whole region of the western frontiers, Great Tibet is the ruler"; see Pan 1992, 157. Richardson's translation of the west inscription similarly reads, "Both Tibet and China shall keep the country and frontiers of which they are now in possession. The whole region to the east of that being the country of Great China and the whole region to the west being assuredly the country of Great Tibet, from either side of that frontier there shall be no warfare, no hostile invasions, and no seizure of territory."

15 Pan 1992, 147.

16 Beckwith 1987, 169–171.

17 As we will see, the mid-eighth century coincides with the time the Tibetans started to translate Mahayana canonical texts into their language. Legendary references to King lHa-tho snyan-btsan are invariably suggestive of an earlier (ca. fourth century) Tibetan encounter with a Buddhist mission, probably from Central Asia. King lHa-tho snyan-btsan was residing at the Palace of Yum-bu bla-sgang when he received several "Buddhist texts and sacred objects" from heaven that he couldn't decipher; see Francke 1926, 81; the *Yar lung chos 'byung* (p. 48), the *bDud 'joms chos 'byung* (p. 122), and the *dBa' bzhed* (p. 25).

18 Davidson 2002a, 153. Central Asia in this context refers to a large area extending west of the Pamirs that includes the ancient regions of Chorasmia,

Sogdiana, and Serindia proper, and the regions traversed by the ancient Silk Road north and south of the Taklamakan desert and eastward to Dunhuang.

19 For a detailed discussion of the artifacts from the Ördek's Necropolis in Loulan, see Hansen 2004, 281–285. The peoples of the Silk Road also participated in funeral clubs and made donations to a funeral fund; see Whitfield 2004, 323.

20 Machida 1988, 1–2.

21 For a discussion of these texts, see Walter 2006, 34–61.

22 Tremblay 2007, 103–104.

23 Tokharian manuscripts from the monastery of Yurpishka in Shorchuk, west of the Lop desert, refer to Kucha as a major center for copying Buddhist texts in the first half of the seventh century. These were for the most part written in Tokharian-A. Monastery records, names of donors, and administrative and commercial correspondence were written in Tokharian-B; see Litvinsky and Vorobyova-Desyatovskaya 1996, 447.

24 Buddhism does not appear to have taken root in Sugdh itself, and it must have been Central Asian Sogdian monks recorded in Chinese sources from the second through seventh centuries. The *Biographies of Eminent Monks* (Ch. *Gao-seng-zhuan*), composed in 519 CE, mentions Sogdian Buddhists from merchant families as the first translators of Indian Buddhist texts into Chinese, but the records of the translations themselves show that the Yuezhi were the first Central Asians to translate Buddhist texts into Chinese; see Chandra 2002; Vaissière 2004, 21; Tremblay 2007, 93. During the Tang dynasty, Sogdian merchants from Samarkand are reported to have settled permanently in Turfan, some receiving allocations of land according to the equal-field system while others "opted for a nonresident status that allowed them to move from oasis to oasis with their goods and rendered them subject to commercial taxes;" see Hansen 1999, 26.

25 Gaulier 1976, 22. The cult of Maitreya, shared by Śrāvakayāna Buddhists and Mahayana followers, was widespread in Kucha. The *Sutra on the Meditation on Bodhisattva Maitreya Born in Tuṣita Heaven* was composed in Kucha or Turfan; see Hikata 1985, 29–30.

26 Supposedly, "the worshipers could only afford a single statue between them, but when they arrived in the temple the statue doubled itself to enable each one of them to make an offering" (Gaulier 1976, 24–25). Gaulier explains that the same motif is found on a banner on hemp in Turfan region dating to the ninth century. A statue of a two-headed buddha has been discovered in Karakhoto and is now in the Hermitage Museum in Leningrad.

27 Gaulier 1976, 25.

28 Hansen 1999, 24.

29 Beal 1906, xxiv.

30 Puri 1987, 77–79. From the 1,586 documents found at the cemeteries of Astana and Karakhoja north of the ancient city of Kocho, "403 dated from the period when the Ch'ü family ruled the Kocho kingdom and 1,020 from the Tang period" (Zhang Guang-du 1996a, 307).

31 From the Tang census conducted at the time, we learn that the city comprised 37,000 people and 4,300 horses in 8,000 households; see Hansen 1999, 25. Hansen notes that "Kaoch'ang was well-known for the size of its Buddhist community, and the Kao-ch'ang state, unlike central Chinese governments, taxed the Buddhist religious community, presumably because it was so large" (1998, 58).

32 The king of Turpan (Turfan) sent 500 bolts of damask and plain silk and two cartloads of fruit to the most powerful king, the Yabgu khan of the Western Turks. In addition to these gifts, he also provided Xuanzang with gold, silver, and all kinds of silk clothes, plus 500 bolts of damask and plain silk to support his travels. Xuanzang needed thirty horses and twenty-five laborers to carry all these gifts and treasures. By the time he reached northern India, Xuanzang had donated all the silks to Buddhist stupas and establishments along the route (Liu Xinru 1995, 30).

33 Hansen 1995. Recovered manuscripts from the Astana tombs included Confucian classics, but also books on history, some poems, and children's readers in Chinese, including the *Book of One Thousand Characters* (*Qian zi wen*) and the *Elementary Book of Chinese Characters* (*Ji jiu zhang*); see Zhang Guang-du 1996a, 310.

34 The Kuṣāṇa Zhiqian, credited with the first Chinese edition of the *Teachings of Vimalakīrti* and the oldest canonical translation of the long *Sukhāvatīvyūha-sūtra,* allegedly also translated the *Sutra of Seven Daughters* (Ch. *Qi nü jing*) from Sanskrit; see Paul 1985, 11, 12–14.

35 Even though this text cannot be dated with certainty, it reflects the kind of Buddhist literature that was available to the residents of Turfan. Hansen explains that "the text does not actually condemn those funeral practices or advocate cremation, which few Chinese practiced" (1998, 51). The aim of the *Sutra of Seven Daughters* was to caution its readers that funeral observances can do nothing to lessen the effects of death.

36 Soper 1959, 215–216.

37 Yamabe 1999 argues in this respect. Although there are good reasons to suppose that the *Guan wu liang shou jing* was of Central Asian origin and possibly from Turfan, Yamabe (1999) does not offer any compelling evidence that excludes the possibility that it was composed in a neighboring settlement and therefore equally deprived of canonical authority.

38 Gaulier 1976, 25.

39 Kudara 2002, 104.

40 Dietz 2007, 52. Annexed by the Northen Wei in 445 CE, Miran was largely deserted by the Tang by the eighth century. Sir Aurel Stein's excavations in the area failed to produce Chinese manuscripts but brought to the surface an abundance of Kharoṣṭhī and Tibetan texts.

41 Some seals from Niya featured the Greek deities Pallas Athena, Eros, and Heracles; see Stein 1933. For a discussion of the spread of Nestorian communities in Eastern Turkestan and across Central Asia, see Comneno 1997; Zhang Guang-da 1996a, 298–299.

42 Puri 1987, 67–68; Whitfield 2004, 15.

43 There is an abundance of Tibetan wood slips that were recycled into knives, spoons, spatulas, and even toilet "paper," suggesting that they were originally used as tallies, soldiers' tablets, tags, and military dispatches. The evidence confirms that there was frequent postal communication between Tibetan units and other city-colonies. Messages were carried day and night by couriers, while silver and turquoise scripts were used in records to differentiate between different army brigades; see Takeuchi 2004, 50; Thomas 1951, 408.

44 MS Or. (15000/501) and MS Or. (15000/434–437) respectively; Takeuchi 1998.

45 The aesthetic qualities of jade, its symbolic and monetary prestige, and its religious and medicinal attributes were an integral part of Chinese culture since post-Neolithic times, when Khotan was the principal, and perhaps even the only, Chinese source for the consumption of nephrite. For an informative study of jade in Chinese sources, see Michaelson 2004, 44.

46 Zhang Guang-du 1996a, 284–285.

47 Some legends trace the introduction of Buddhism to Vairocana, who allegedly came to Khotan from Kashmir to meditate. For an overview of Buddhist and secular narratives concerning the founding of Khotan, see Skjaervø 1999, 279–280.

48 The Khotanese history *Prophecy of Khotan* dates to the mid-ninth century and was translated from Khotanese into Chinese and Tibetan. It draws from the *Prophecy of Saṃghavardhana* (*Dgra bcom pa dge 'dun 'phel gyi lung bstan pa*) located in the Tanjur; see Thomas 1935, 42–52.

49 Thomas 1935, 102. This passage from the *Annals of Khotan* (*Li yul gyi lo rgyus*) is often included as part of the *Prophecy of Khotan* (located in D, no. 3701, vol. 182, fol. 536v–567r). The founding legends of Khotan are all linked with Buddhism. Khotanese names and terms indicate that the *Prophecy of Khotan* was originally translated from Khotanese or written by someone with direct access to Khotanese sources; see Hill 1988, 179. The Tibetan version shares an anecdote of the Chinese princess carrying the secret of sericulture to Khotan: "On hearing of this, the queen, being unable at that time to explain it to the king with knowledge, extracted some of the silk-worms and reared them in secret. Afterwards, having produced *kha-cher-dar* and floss (*srin-bal*), she wove silk (*dar*) and *men-dri,* and showed them to the king" (Takeuchi 1994, 582).

50 Based on the accounts of the Chinese pilgrim Faxian; see Beal 1906, xxv–xxvii. The *Annals of Khotan* list seventeen monasteries and seventeen nunneries and enumerate sixty-eight monasteries inside and outside the fort. Furthermore, a total of 3,688 minor chapels, temples, and stupas are recorded; see Thomas 1935, 108–134.

51 Thomas 1951, 311.

52 According to the colophons of texts discovered in Dunhuang, a number of Khotanese monks originally came from western India; see Whitfiled 2004, 165. Faxian reports that he stayed in Khotan for three months in order to witness a special Buddhist ceremony conducted in the spring and lasting for two weeks. He gives details of a lively procession of sacred Buddhist images sent from fourteen monasteries that were paraded on enormous carts through the city.

53 Skjaervø 1999, 274.

54 Stein (1907, 120) notes that, according to a legend reported by Xuanzang, the founding king of Khotan was without an heir. He prayed at the Vaiśravaṇa Temple and a boy emerged from the statue's head.

55 Stein 1907, 120. The Hoernle collection contains Sanskrit manuscripts discovered on the Northern and Southern routes; see Hartmann 1999.

56 Puri 1987, 110. Litvinsky and Vorobyova-Desyatovskaya assert that Sanskrit versions of sutras in circulation in Khotan were "adopted as the basis of Chinese, Tibetan, Tangut, Uighur and Mongol Buddhism" (1996, 448).

57 Zhang Guang-du 1996a, 293. A Sanskrit-Khotanese bilingual scroll discovered in Dunhuang records the conversation of a Khotanese monk on his way to China to visit Wutaishan, carrying books of Sutra, Abhidharma, Vinaya, and Vajrayana he had acquired from India; Chandra 2002, 96.

58 Chandra 2002, 92.

59 Whitfield 2004, 165.

60 Bailey 1961, 16. Among the most important Mahayana sutras brought to China from Khotan and translated in Chinese are the *Gandavyūha-sūtra,* the *Mahāparinirvāna-sūtra,* the *Saddharmapuṇḍarīka-sūtra,* and the *Laṅkāvatāra-sūtra;* see Hikata 1985, 41.

61 Dalton 2007, 13.

62 The discovery of a significant portion of the *Book of Zambasta* (207 out of 440 folia), the longest native Buddhist composition extant in Old Khotanese, played a crucial role in deciphering the Khotanese language. Harold Bailey named this untitled work the *Book of Zambasta* because it was compiled at the request of an official named Ysaṃbasta (pron. Zambasta). It draws from several Indian Buddhist sources, such as the *Bhadramāyākāravyākaraṇa,* but it is not a translation of any one Indian Mahayana text. In chapter III of the text, Buddha

Śākyamuni counsels Maitreya on the necessity of love and the understanding of emptiness: "Then one should so think: That these things are all empty. Little have I meditated upon love with my mind. The empty, as empty, cannot cause obstruction. Selfless are beings, without self all the Buddhas. I have the *kṣetras* of the three times in every single particle of me. The beings of the three times are all in every single *kṣetra* of mine. . . . The *kṣetras* are infinitely varied, purified, pure" (Emmerick 1968, 71). The *Book of Zambasta* ends in typical Mahayana fashion with a dedication of merit. The colophons preserve two versions. The first wishes that the copyist and all beings attain awakening (Skt. *bodhi*), and the second is dedicated to the patron of the text, the official Zambasta, so that he may soon awaken as a buddha; see Skjaervø 1999, 292.

63 Litvinsky and Vorobyova-Desyatovskaya 1996, 448.

64 Skjaervø 1999, 314.

65 Fragments of twenty-five Mahayana sutras have been discovered; see Emmerick 1992, 1995. For a list of Khotanese texts from Khotan and Dunhuang, see Kumamoto 1999, 358–359.

66 Bailey 1961, 14

67 Bailey 1974, 18.

68 Skjaervø 2002, lxv. According to Takeuchi (1994, 578), Khotan was under Tibetan occupation from 790–ca. 850.

69 Takeuchi 1994, 578. The Khotanese king was subordinate to a Tibetan official in charge of Khotan (*li'i-blon*), while high Khotanese officials answered to a Tibetan town prefect (*rtse-rje*) who was probably stationed at the Mazār-tāgh fort, the administrative headquarters to the north of Khotan; see Takeuchi 2004, 55.

70 Takeuchi 2004, 54.

71 Thomas 1951, 184–185. Post stations were established a hundred *li* from each other, and housed a station master (who was always Tibetan), an assistant master, post messengers, and cooks. Messages to be delivered were classified into different categories and those considered urgent had to be delivered on time; the speed for urgent delivery was 500 *li* in twenty-four hours; see Ren Shumin 1991, 145.

72 Such as the Pod-kar thousand-district; see Takeuchi 1994, 580.

73 MS (IOL Khot 50[4]); translation by Skjaervø 2004, 36.

74 Khotanese architects were invited during the reign of Khri lDe-srong-brtsan and during the reign of Emperor Khri lDe-gtsug-brtsan (712–ca. 754), also known as Mes Ag-tshoms (lit., "old and hairy"). Seven Buddhist monasteries were said to have been built to house Khotanese Buddhist monks at the behest of Khri lDe-gtsug-brtsan's wife, Kimshing Kongco, the Chinese princess of Jinzheng; see Tremblay 2007, 101; Gaulier 1976, 3; Laufer 1918, 46.

75 *Dri ma med pa'i 'od kyis zhus pa* (D, 168); see Thomas 1935, 139–258.

76 Thomas 1935, 254.

77 Dunhuang MS P. 5007; Lien 2009, 38.

78 Chandra 2002, 90.

79 Xinjiang 2004, 60.

80 van Schaik 2002, 137. Sa-cu is a Tibetan transcription of the Chinese name Shazhou. There were stationed two "one-thousand districts" (*stong-sde*), known as sTong-sar and rGod-sar, which were in direct communication with the Tibetan garrisons positioned in Miran. In other documents the Snying-tsoms, Spyitshogs, and Tshas-stobs divisions in Sa-cu are mentioned; see Thomas 1951, 40.

81 Whitfield 2004, 259.

82 Okazaki 1977, 29; Sørensen 1998, 29. Eighty new caves were built in the Sui period and another hundred during the first half of the Tang dynasty. While the bulk of Buddhist scriptures at Dunhuang are Mahayana sutras, there are a number of esoteric texts dedicated to Avalokiteśvara, scriptures of Daoist-Buddhist contents, Chan meditation manuals, and prayers to the heavenly King Vaiśravana, among others.

83 Sørensen 1998, 32–35.

84 Perhaps inspired by references to 1,000 buddhas in the *Gaṇḍavyūha-sūtra,* in 366 CE the monk Lozun had a vision of 1,000 buddhas floating above the valley of Dunhuang. In the following centuries, almost 500 cave temples were hewn out of the mountainside, connected to each other by a series of wooden porches, galleries, and stairs. Their walls were painted and they were furnished with Buddhist sculptures. In 422 CE the complete collection of the *Avataṁsaka* sutras were translated by Buddhabhadra and Śikṣānanda between 695–699 CE, with an imperial preface written by Empress Wu Zetian, who sent a special envoy to Khotan in search for the Sanskrit original; see Chandra 2002, 93.

85 Okazaki 1977, 29. On the basis of different trends of Dunhuang esoteric paintings, Tanaka (1992, 277) argued that there were two schools of Esoteric Buddhism prevalent in Central Asia: Chinese Esoteric Buddhism introduced by Śubhākarasiṃha, Vajrabodhi, and Amoghavajra; and Tibetan Esoteric Buddhism introduced by Padmasambhava, Vimalamitra, and Vairocana.

86 The first wall paintings and statues date from the latter half of the fifth century, and the last from the end of the thirteenth century; see Whitfield 2000, 82. McIntire explains, "For much of the history of Chinese Buddhism, 'Pure Land' was not a distinct entity with a self-conscious lineage. When the concept of rebirth in Buddhist paradises was first introduced in China, Chinese devotees did not view Amitābha's Sukhāvatī as the only desirable destination for rebirth. There may have been specific brief periods when Amitābha was the

focus of popular movements, but exclusive devotion to Amitābha and his Western Paradise was by no means sustained as an independent, continuous tradition. Judging from the evidence that survives at Dun-huang, Chinese Buddhist devotees of the seventh century viewed many paradises as worthy destinations of rebirth" (2000, 87).

87 Members of the Zhai family had served as officers in the Tang military campaigns against Turfan and concerns about wounded or recently departed members of the family may have inspired the production of Pure Land murals. These paintings served as healing rituals for the family and for the accumulation of merit for the departed Zhai. Illustrations of infants and children in Amitābha's Pure Land are an indication of families reuniting after death in Sukhāvatī; see Qiang 2004.

88 For example, Cave 146 contains a wall painting depicting Amitābha and fifty bodhisattvas. Other representations in Dunhuang include paintings based on the *Meditation on Amitāyus Sutra* in Cave 139a; Amitābha accompanied by eight bodhisattvas in his Pure Land, showing some Tibetan influence, in Cave 17; a popular Chinese configuration of a woman being led after her death to Amitābha by Avalokiteśvara in Cave 17; illustrations on the north wall the *Meditation on Amitāyus Sutra* in Cave 45; and Caves 127, 148, and 320 contain portrayals of Sukhāvatī; see Wong 1998–1999; Whitfield 1990, 2004.

89 Thomas and Clauson 1927.

90 Sørensen 1998, 35.

91 Giles 1935, 819.

92 Giles 1937, 6.

93 Giles 1937, 8–9. In most cases it was placed as an appendix to the short *Sukhāvatīvyuha-sūtra.*

94 Zwalf 1985, 219.

95 The Tibetan emperor Khri Srong-lde-brtsan (756–ca.797) sponsored Buddhist temples at the "center and borders" (*dbung mthar*) of his empire and those erected in Dunhuang are listed by name; see Thomas 1951, 88–91. According to Xinjiang (2004, 57), the Tibetans remained in control until 848, when a Chinese loyalist landowner, Zhang Yichao, led a popular uprising and expelled the Tibetans from the region. The dates of the Tibetan occupation of Dunhuang are in dispute; see Dalton 2007, 18, n. 29. In the Chinese sources, Lijifu reports that the Tibetans conquered Dunhuang in the second year of the Jianzhong reign (781) under the Tang emperor Dezong. Yueshi dates the Tibetan conquest near the end of the Tianbao reign (742–756) and records that the Tang court reclaimed its sovereignty over Dunhuang in 851, a date on which the two standard histories of the Tang dynasty agree. One Dunhuang manuscript shows the year to be 848; see Lien 2009, 21.

96 Sørensen 1998, 37.

97 Sørensen 1998, 38–39. Buddhist texts included the *Prātimoksa*, the *Brahmajāla-sūtra*, the *Vajracchedikā*, the *Vimalakīrti-sūtra*, the *Prajñāpāramitā-hṛdaya-sūtra*, and so on. Apparently, the Tibetan councilors ordered the *Prajñāpāramitā* to be copied in Tibetan in eight sections and in 600 chapters in Chinese; see Thomas 1951, 75–78. MS Pel. Tib. 999, which we will examine in the next chapter, bears witness to joint Pure Land ventures between Chinese and Tibetan families in Dunhuang.

98 The colophons of many Tibetan sutras record the names of Chinese scribes (Ch. *jingsheng*) at Dunhuang who were able to write in Tibetan; see Dalton 2007, 11. A document from Dunhuang refers to a major translation enterprise employing eighty scribes (*yi-ge-pa*) and twenty editorial revisors (*zhu-chen*); see Thomas 1951, 77. These may have been monks, officials, or common people.

99 Thomas 1951, 80. The duties of the superintendent and the scribes' obligations are described thus: "The scribes must complete at once the supplies of paper entrusted to them; until completion has been made, their cattle, property, and so on of twice the value should be taken as security and deposited with the *rub-ma-pa*. If the person in charge be not equal to the opposition or should not have collected the allotments, the *li-ceng* should punish him by whipping at the rate of ten lashes per roll (*yug*) of paper" (Thomas 1951, 82).

100 The earliest archaeological records for Mahayana Buddhism in the Tarim basin may be a third-century wooden tablet discovered by Sir Aurel Stein at Niya. It tells of a local governor with the title "advanced to the Mahayana religion"; see Murakami 2008, 124. Sanskrit manuscripts found in Central Asia amount to at least seven different versions of the Sūtrapiṭaka relating to different Śrāvakayāna schools. Fragments of the Vinayapiṭaka of the Sarvāstivāda, Mūlasarvāstivāda, and Dharmaguptaka schools have been discovered; see Litvinsky and Vorobyova-Desyatovskaya 1996, 442–443.

101 Other exotic and high-valued articles transported along the Tarim basin included "jade from Khotan, turquoise from Iran, lapis lazuli from Afghanistan, tortoiseshell and ivory from India, coral from Sasanian Iran, glassware from the eastern Mediterranean and bronze mirrors, tricoloured pottery and lacquerware from China . . . Byzantine gold coins and large amounts of Persian silver species"; Zhang Guang-da 1996a, 291–292.

102 Liu Xinru shows that it is possible "to identify [in Eurasia] trends concerning its circulation, the origins of its supply and demand, and the relationship between silk transactions and social institutions, especially religious institutions" (1995, 26–27).

103 It has been suggested that the acquisition of religious merit gave rise to professional woodblock printing in medieval China. Between 972 and 983 woodcarvers from Sichuan were commissioned to produce the first large-scale

printing project in the world, the reproduction of the Buddhist Tripiṭaka; see Whitfield 2004, 300–301.

104 Liu Xinru (1995, 33–34) argues that in the Tang dynasty Buddhist relics became objects of worship and generated a great deal of wealth for monasteries in China and India. She relates that in 661 the Tang emperor Gaozong dispatched Wang Xuance with 4,000 bolts of silk to obtain a precious parietal bone from Kapisa in Northwest India, while a monk called Huigong donated 3,000 bolts of silk to the relics.

105 Wang 2004, 27–32.

106 Thomas 1951, 88.

107 Whitfield 2004, 259.

108 Hansen 2004, 279.

109 Agrawala 1954; Whitfield 2004, 259. Hansen (2004, 293) reports a case where a member of the Buddhist clergy (called a *śramaṇa* in the documents) gave his daughter in marriage to another monk, who in turn married his own daughter to yet another monk.

110 Zurcher explains that in "its original context this obviously referred to closely interrelated regional languages or dialects, and eventually also to Sanskrit. However, it is an important fact that the propagation of Buddhism was fully accepted and practiced long before Buddhism spread beyond the Indian subcontinent" (1999, 8).

111 Chinese manuscripts comprised educational exercises, multiplication tables, and textbooks; see Whitfield 2004, 251. In Central Asia there were also followers of Daoism, Manichaeism, Nestorian Christianity, Iranian Mazdeism, and Turkic "täŋrism." In fact, the Manichaean textual and artistic corpus from Turfan is the largest extant accumulation of Manichaean works of art (eighth–eleventh centuries) and illuminated manuscripts; see Gulácsi 1997.

112 Nattier 1990, 211–212. Buddhist patrons in Turfan included Chinese settlers from the eastern regions or local rulers following the example of Chinese rulers to the east; see Hansen 1998, 37.

113 Hansen 1998, 40.

114 This periodization scheme follows bCom-ldan ral-gri's (1227-1305) classification of three migration phases of Indian Buddhism to Tibet. For alternate Tibetan historiographical traditions, see Cuevas 2006. Schaeffer and van der Kujip (2009, 61) suggest that the *bar-dar* (intermediate) propagation of Buddhism commenced with the arrival of Smṛtijñānakīrti in Tibet (ca. 970–980) and ended with the death of Atiśa around 1054. For a discussion on the process of indigenization see Mayer and Cantwell 2008.

115 Regal dating follows Dotson 2009.

116 Laufer 1918, 34–35. According to Chinese sources, the Tibetan *btsan-po* also requested silkworm eggs, stone crushers, presses for making wine and paper, and ink makers—all of which was granted by the emperor together with the almanac; see Rockhill 1891, 191; Bushell 1880, 446.

117 Dotson 2007, 6; *Old Tibetan Chronicle,* Pel. Tib. 1287.

118 Laufer 1918, 37.

119 Uebach 2008, 64.

120 Walter 2009, 3. Uebach (2008, 65) asserts that either Buddhism influenced the introduction of paper in the Tibetan administration, or that the introduction of paper influenced the spread of Buddhist scriptures; in fact, these two scenarios are not mutually exclusive.

121 While details in the Tibetan accounts vary, the principal elements of the story are identical in historical works and grammatical treatises; see Laufer 1918, 35. In this work and elsewhere (1914), Laufer demonstrated that the theory held uncritically by Hoernle (1916)—that the Tibetan script originated from the Tarim basin and especially Khotan—is completely unfounded. Walter (2009, 39–40, n. 4) expresses doubt that Sambhoṭa devised by himself the Tibetan script and points to similarities between the Tibetan lettering and a seventh-century Gupta inscription from Gopālpur. The Bön tradition claims Iranian and Central Asian origins for the Tibetan script; see van Der Kuijp 1996, 431.

122 Skilling 1997a, 87–89. It is said that when the gifted minister returned to Lhasa he formed two Tibetan alphabets, one "with heads" (*dbu-can*) derived from the Lāñcā script, and another "headless" (*dbu-med*) fashioned out of the Wartula characters. Furthermore, Sambhoṭa trained Tibetan translators and scribes and reintroduced to Tibet texts supposedly dating to the time of King lHa-to-tho-ri, namely the *Saddharma Cintamaṇi* (*Dam chos tsin dha ma ṇi*); the *Lotus Sutra* (*Snying rje padma dkar po*); the *Nānānadī Sutra** (*Chu klung sna tshogs rol pa'i mdo*); and the *Mūlanadī Sutra** (*Chu klung ba tsha'i mdo*); see the *Pillar Testament* (*Bka' chems ka khol ma*), p. 106.

123 Walter 2009, 4.

124 Buddhist narratives describe how at the age of thirteen Srong-btsan-sgam-po was enthroned in a grand ceremony initiated by Samantabhadra, while the form of Buddha Amitābha arose on the top of his head. The walls of the Khra-'brug temple in Yar-lung, founded by Srong-btsan-sgam-po, depicted the initiation scene. Srong-btsan-sgam-po's portrayal as a bodhisattva-king was inflated by post-dynastic narratives, such as the *Mani Kabum* (*Maṇi bka'-'bum*) collection attributed to him; see Kapstein 2000, 144–155. For a recent discussion see, Neumaier 2007.

125 For Srong-btsan-sgam-po's posthumous title, see Beckwith 1987, 25. Walter suggests that the bestowal of this title "was reinforced by the position of Tibet, to the west of China, which made it easy to consider it Amitābha's paradise,

which also fit considerations of the place of the Chinese Emperor in a *maṇḍala*" (2009, 265, n. 10). The *Prophecy of Khotan* also refers to Srong-btsan-sgam-po as a bodhisattva who took birth as a king; see Thomas 1935, 79.

126 Dotson 2006, 4.

127 Dargyay (1991, 1988) discusses Tibetan narratives of the bodhisattva-king theme.

128 For a related discussion, see Halkias 2006b. In Ahmad's translation, the Fifth Dalai Lama Blo-bzang rgya-mtsho narrates: "In accordance with the praise bestowed by such clear prophesies, [Srong-btsan sgam-po] was born as the son of his father King gNam-ri Srong-btsan and his mother sPong-bza' 'Bri-ma Thod-dkar, 1508 years after the all knowing Ādityamitra (the Buddha) has attained nirvana. . . . In his thirteenth year he was consecrated as a mighty wheel-turning king on the fearless lion-throne of his father. At that time, a thought occurred in the mind of the King: 'Would that I was consecrated (king) in order to do good to the people of Tibet!' At that time when he thought this, the glorious Samantabhadra washed his body with a precious pitcher filled with the water of divine nectar. The god Amitābha consecrated the king by touching him on the head" (2008, 13).

129 Ahmad 2008, 31–32.

130 Following the reign of Srong-btsan-sgam-po, the Buddhist sangha continued to gain the support of the *btsan-po* and of noble families, except during a short period marked by a ministerial conspiracy to suppress Buddhism following the death of Khri lDe-gtsug-brtsan in 755–756.

131 Richardson 1985, 29–31. Walter and Beckwith (2010, 303–304) have argued that unlike other so-called "imperial inscriptions," this is a genuine marker that dates to the time of the Tibetan empire.

132 Dotson 2007, 2.

133 Wangdu and Diemberger 2000, 56.

134 For a discussion of politics in Tibetan historiography, see Dotson 2006, 9–11. The antiquity of the inscription has been challenged. Walter and Beckwith (2010, 305–309) argue that the sKar-chung derives from the bSam-yas Inscription, but there is nothing in the inscription to indicate that it was produced by Khri lDe-srong-brtsan, or during the Tibetan empire for that matter.

135 Richardson 1985, 77.

136 MS Pel. Tib. 999; see the *Ārya-aparimitāyur-jñāna-nāma-mahāyāna-sūtra* section in this chapter.

137 For a discussion, see Walter 2009.

138 Walter (2009, 52–53) speculates that natural disasters may have been responsible for the negative appraisal of Emperor Glang dar-ma who, therefore was unable to extend the same support to Tibetan monastics as had his predecessors. Karmay (1996) and Richardson (1989) have addressed this issue at

some length, and Yamaguchi offers a compelling argument that "since he reigned for only one year, the assertion that a 'persecution of Buddhism' was conducted by him becomes virtually untenable" (1996, 243). The *Phangthangma Catalogue* lists a Madhyamaka commentary attributed to Emperor 'U'i-dum-brtan (Glang dar-ma), an inclusion that adds weight to a growing body of work that calls into question his supposed opposition to Buddhism; see Halkias 2004, 57–58.

139 See Ruegg 1989 for a seminal study on the philosophical implications of the bSam-yas debate. Chinese perspectives on the debate are provided in Demiéville 1952; a review and translation of Tibetan and Sanskrit sources are found in Tucci 1958 and Houston 1980. Bretfeld (2004) elaborates on the Tibetan cultural mythos surrounding the interpretation of the debate.

140 The *Testimony of Ba* is one of the oldest texts recounting the circumstances leading to the establishment of Buddhism in Tibet, and it is cited by later historiographical traditions as an authority on events during this time. There are several versions of this text and each gives a slightly different account. A recent discovery of a fragment of the text in Dunhuang testifies to its antiquity; see van Schaik and Iwao 2008. For concerns regarding its historical accuracy, see Kapstein 2000, 23–37. All Tibetan passages quoted in this section are from Wangdu and Diemberger 2000.

141 Richardson 1998, 203. The PT (§XXXI, no. 877) lists a work attributed to Queen Byang-chub-ma, the rGyal-mo-btsan of the 'Bro clan. She was apparently a devoted follower of the Chinese Buddhist master Hva-śang, and authored a *pranidhāna* (*smon-lam*) that could have read like the inscription cast by the Chinese monk Rin-chen on her behalf on a heavy bronze bell she donated to the Khra-'brug temple; see Richardson 1985, 83.

142 According to a Dunhuang document (Pelliot chinois 4646), the queen invited Hva-śang to Lhasa; see Demiéville 1952, 29. Khri Srong-lde-brtsan appears to have taken an active interest in the *dhyāna* meditation traditions of the Chinese faction; two minor works of the genre listed in the *Phangthangma Catalogue* are attributed to him: the *bSam gtan gyi dgos pa brgyad bstsal bal ha btsan pos bkas bcad pa,* 1 sl. (§XXVII, no. 675) and the *Theg pa chen po'i bsam gtan gyi man ngag lha btsan pos mdzad pa dang de'i brjed byang,* 1 sl. (§XXXI, no. 842).

143 *Dba' bzhed* 2000, 88.

144 Demiéville (1952, 253–255) narrates an account of Hva-śang leaving Central Tibet after the debate and becoming a pillar of the Tibetan administration.

145 Tibetan Chan treatises from Dunhuang have been discussed in Dalton and van Schaik 2006, and some have been studied by Ueyama (1983). There is a marked increase in the number of Tibetan translations of Chinese sutras in the last imperial register from Phang-thang, suggesting that the bSam-yas debate did not have adverse consequences for the credibility of Chinese Buddhism as a

whole. The *Phangthangma Catalogue* also provides indirect iconographic evidence for "a milieu far more permissive of the 'simultaneist' than that depicted in later Tibetan Buddhist historiography" (Dotson 2007, 6, n. 24). Dotson's comment is in reference to a captioned illustration of "Hwa-shang ma-hwa-ya-na" on the first page of the *Phangthangma Catalogue.* The unknown redactor of the catalogue states that the original manuscript contained illustrations of Nāgārjuna, Asaṅga, Vasubandhu, Candrakīrti, Śāntarakṣita, Kamalaśīla, Vimalamitra, Pad-ma 'byung-gnas (Padmasambhava), and the "great Chan teacher Hwa-shang ma-hwa-ya-na (*bsam gtan gyi mkhan po chen po hwa shang ma hwa ya na*)"; *Dkar chag 'phang thang ma,* p. 2; see Halkias 2004, 58–60.

146 Bretfeld (2004) discusses how the bSam-yas debate, recounted in religious histories (*chos-'byung*) and in later doctrinal polemics, plays an integral and important role in Tibet's cultural memory.

147 Lamotte 1998, 182, n. 200. The existence of innumerable buddha fields is basic to the philosophy of the *Śūraṅgamasamādhi.* Several buddha fields are mentioned by name, but the only one known from other sources is the pure land of Buddha Akṣobhya. The *Vimalakīrtinirdeśa-sūtra* (Chap. CXV) was also invoked as a scriptural authority during the bSam-yas debate.

148 Tibetan text, pp. 280–281. Tucci explains that during the tenth "stage" (*sa;* Skt. *bhūmi*), the bodhisattva (now technically a buddha) "possesses a peculiar knowledge which leads to the maturity of beings through magical creations and therefore the perfection of knowledge here predominates. Since the teaching of the Law is like a rain cloud which showers truth over all the worlds, this stage is called Dharmameghā, 'The Cloud of the Law'" (1958, 491–492).

149 Lamotte 1998, 123. Kamalaśīla's commentary to the *Vajracchedikā Prajñāpāramitā* follows Vasubandhu's reading of the same text. The purity of buddha fields is listed as one of the six kinds of accomplishments peculiar to the realization of a buddha; see Tucci 1958, 135. It is a misconception to strive after buddha fields as long as one has not realized that all *dharmas* are without substantial existence; see Vasubandhu's analysis of the *Vajracchedikā;* Tucci 1958, 164–165. Ultimately, even the view that buddha fields are objects of purification is likewise mistaken; see Diṅnāga's commentary on the *Prajñāpāramitā;* Tucci 1958, 115.

150 In his *Bstan pa rgyas pa rgyan gyi nyi 'od,* bCom-ldan ral-gri lists approximately 1,094 titles of texts translated during the early spread of Buddhism to Tibet; see Schaeffer and van der Kujip 2009, 62. Translations of some secular works also found their way into the Tibetan Tripiṭaka; see Roesler 2002; Ruegg 1995; Pathak 1974.

151 Halkias (2004, 74–76) discusses the editorial process in the compilation of the *Phangthangma Catalogue* that entailed comparing titles (*mtshan-byang*) with gZhon-nu snying-po's register and with two older registers (*dpe-rnying*). which may be in reference to the *Denkarma* and *Samye* imperial catalogues.

152 In this book the chronological sequence of the three catalogues (*dkar-chag*) is in agreement with Bu-ston (1988, 314), who may have been indebted to bCom-ldan ral-gri, and with testimonies preserved in the *Yar lung chos 'byung*, p. 65, and the *mKhas pa'i dga' ston*, p. 417; see also Tshul-khrims skal-bzang khang-dkar (1985, 95; 2003, 87). Si-tu paṇ-chen advocates an alternative Tibetan tradition that places the *dKar chag 'phang thang ma* first among the three Tibetan catalogues; see Schaeffer and van der Kujip 2009, 55. Herrmann-Pfandt (2008) argues for the tradition followed by Si-tu paṇ-chen.

153 Khri lDe-srong-brtsan's rule (ca. 798–ca. 800) was interrupted by his brother Mu-rug-brtsan (ca. 800–ca. 802), who seized the throne after their father's death and died two years into Khri lDe-srong-brtsen's second reign; see Dotson 2007. The *Denkarma Catalogue* is located in the Tanjur with the title *Pho brang stod thang ldan dkar gyi chos kyi 'gyur ro cog gi dkar chag* (D 4364). The dates 812 and 824 have been put forth for its composition; see Herrmann-Pfandt 2008; Rabsal 1996; Lalou 1953; Yoshimura 1950.

154 The *dKar chag bsam yas mchims phu ma* was compiled during the reign of Khri lDe-srong-brtsan at the court of Mchims-phu ('Chims-phu) in bSam-yas. This region allegedly served as a repository of Buddhist texts since the times of Emperor Srong-btsan-sgam-po and Mes Ag-tshom (712–ca. 754); see *rGyal rabs gsal ba'i me long*, p. 196.

155 An extant version of the *Phangthangma Catalogue* was published in China in 2003. According to the estimation of its editor, this catalogue was the last of the three; see *Dkar chag 'phang thang ma*, p.3. It continued to be used and augmented during the second spread of the teachings to Tibet; see Halkias 2004.

156 Most Tibetan translations fall in the sutra and *śāstra* sections and a dozen or so scriptures are listed in different categories as translations from Chinese. The Tantras of the Old School (*rNying ma'i rgyud bum*) that claim imperial antiquity and a good number of Tibetan scriptures from Dunhuang are not listed in the LK and PT. According to the introduction to the *sGra byor bam po gnyis pa*, Khri lDe-srong-btsan's edict prohibited the translation of tantras without prior official permission. Bu-ston (1988, 197) records that during the reign of Emperor Khri gTsug-lde-btsan (ca. 815–841) it was prescribed that the Hinayana scriptures, other than those accepted by the Sarvāstivādins, and the tantras were not to be translated. Karmay (1988, 5–6) also notes that during the reign of Khri gTsug-lde-btsan, the Buddhist Council took up the question of the suitability of the tantras as a teaching fit for the Tibetans. The translation of certain types of texts, particularly the Mother Tantras (Ma-rgyud), was forbidden; see Snellgrove 1987, 456; Panglung 1994, 165; Germano 2002.

157 Verhagen writes, "The creation of this translation-literature, consisting of several thousands of translations generally of high quality, reliable and consistent in terminology demanded that the Tibetan translators be thoroughly competent in and acquainted with the intricacies of Sanskrit language and

literature. This in turn led to the development of a tradition of Sanskrit linguistic studies within the Tibetan monastic curriculum. Sanskrit studies covered such diverse topics as grammar, poetics, metrics and lexicography. A high level of proficiency in these disciplines was attained in the Tibetan tradition" (1994, 2).

158 Walter (2009, 16) notes that Newari artisans and teachers served the Tibetan kings and they may have been an important foreign influence in the Tibetan court. There were also scholars from Khotan, and a few of their works are included in the Tibetan Buddhist Tripiṭaka: the *Gośṛṅgavyākaraṇa* translated from the language of Khotan and "Śīladharma, a Bhikshu from Khotan," who collaborated in the translation of the "Kanjur work no. 242.43" are mentioned by Laufer (1918, 46). For the contributions of Nepalese scholars in Tibet, see Lo Bue 1997, 629–658.

159 *sBa bzhed* 2000, 90.

160 See Scherrer-Schaub 1999; 2002. In the PT we can glimpse some information about the process of revision. Texts that were in the process of inclusion are listed in the category of "Scriptures of sūtras and *śāstras* in the process of revision, remaining translations" (§XXVIII). Here we find twenty-four texts apportioned in four subdivisions: 1) unrevised sutras and commentaries on sutras, 2) incomplete translations of sutra and vinaya texts, 3) unrevised *śāstras*, and 4) incomplete translations of texts on logic; see Halkias 2004, 73.

161 Scherrer-Schaub 2002, 306–307. The *Vyutpatti Treatises* featured authoritative rules for word-by-word translation and exact equivalences for Sanskrit-Tibetan terms. They also offered definitions of Buddhist tenets and practical advice on grammatical matters. Three *Vyutpatti Treatises* are known in Tibetan literature: 1) the *Bye brag tu rtogs byed chen po* (Skt. *Mahāvyutpati*); 2) the *Bye brag tu rtogs byed 'bring po,* commonly known as the *sGra sbyor bam po gnyis pa* (Skt. *Madhyavyutpatti*); and 3) the *Bye brag tu rtogs byed chung ngu* (Skt. *Alpavyutpatti/Svalpavyutpatti*), no longer extant; see Uray 1989, 3. Verhagen (1994, 12–13) lists three Tibetan grammatical treatises from the same time, said to have been composed by the Tibetan translator lCe khyi-'brug: the *gNas brgyad chen po'i rtsa ba;* its commentary, the *gNas brgyad kyi 'grel pa;* and a linguistic treatise of unlisted authorship, the *sGra'i rnam par dbye btsan pa.* Another text, perhaps related to the codification of religious terminology, is the *Chos skad gtan la dbab pa,* listed in the PT (§XXXI, no. 876).

162 Vostrikov (1970, 205) was the first historian to ascertain the value of Tibetan catalogues as historical documents for their evident importance as summaries of the kinds of Buddhism that were adopted in Tibet.

163 bCom-ldan ral-gri lists among his text inventories those compiled by the *lotsā-ba* (translators) Rin-chen bzang-po (968–1055), Nag-tsho, Tshul-khrims rgyal-ba (1011?–ca. 1170), and rNgog blo-ldan shes-rab (1059?–1109?), neither of which have been seen to date; see Schaeffer and van der Kujip 2009, 57.

164 Herrmann-Pfandt notes that out of the 735 texts included in the *Denkarma Catalogue,* the first 445 texts were later put into the Kanjur, and the rest, "so far as they have survived, were mostly to become Tanjur texts" (2002, 135).

165 Apropos, Snellgrove writes concerning the Great Revision, "[B]y the ninth century high standards of competence in this most difficult of translating work was achieved. In this respect, the best known figure must be the Chinese scholar Fa-ch'eng, known in Tibetan as Chos-grub with the equivalent meaning 'Perfect in Religion.' Active in Dun-huang from the early 830's onward, he received from the Tibetan administration the title of 'Great Translator-Reviser of the Kingdom of Great Tibet' (Bod chen-po'i chab-srid-kyi zhu-chen gyi lo-tsa-ba), producing translations of Buddhist works subject to the sympathetic interest of a Tibetan district commissioner who was himself a fervent Buddhist" (1987, 445).

166 It is acknowledged that Sanskrit manuscripts were copied, reproduced, and translated in Khotan, and we know of at least one copy of the long *Sukhāvatī-vyūha-sūtra* that was translated probably from Sanskrit into Khotanese; see Bailey 1961, 14. Hoernle (1916) notes the dearth of Sanskrit texts of the *Sukhāvatīvyūha* in Central Asia.

167 The colophon of the DKG reads: *bsgyur cing gtan la phab pa.*

168 LK (§III, no. 29). The divisional headings and number references to specific texts in the LK and PT are from Lalou (1953) and Halkias (2004) respectively.

169 When the size of texts is recorded in the catalogues, the largest unit of length is the *bam-po* (bp.) and the smallest the *sloka* (sl.). Dung-dkar (1997, 338) explains that each *bam-po* contains 300 *śloka* (*sho-lo-ka*) and each *śloka* is subdivided into eight syllables (*tsheg-bar brgyad*). For further discussion on these measurements, see Scherrer-Schaub 1992, 218–20; *Lo pan bka'i thang,* pp. 357–358.

170 A table of listings is published in the supplement to the rNying ma sDe-dge bKa'-'gyur and bsTan-'gyur, Tarthang Tulku 1980; see also Géza 1982, 18.

171 See Tarthang Tulku 1980; Géza 1982, 28.

172 The Tabo collection of manuscripts is the only Tibetan canonical compilation known to me that does not include the short *Sukhāvatīvyūha-sūtra.*

173 In the *Phangthangma Catalogue* he is addressed as "*zhu chen gyi lo tsha ba chen po bandhe*"; see Halkias 2004, 63.

174 Another important Pure Land text, the *Bhaiṣajyaguru-sūtra* (*'Phags pa bcom ldan 'das sman gyi bla baiḍurya'i 'od kyi sngon gyi smon lam gyi khyad par rgyas pa zhes bya theg pa chen po'i mdo;* D 504) was also translated by them. Along with the Indian scholar Śīlendrabodhi, they also translated the *Sutra on the Merits of the Fundamental Vows of the Seven Buddhas* (*'Phags pa de bzhin gshegs pa bdun gyi smon lam gyi khyad par rgyas pa zhes bya ba theg pa chen po'i mdo;* D 503). In the *Phangthangma Catalogue* Jinamitra is addressed as "*rgya gar gyi pandi ta mkhas pa chen po*"; see Halkias 2004, 63.

175 Klu'i-rgyal-mtshan's title as *"don sgyur gyi lo tsha ba chen po"* is given in the *Phangthangma Catalogue;* see Halkias 2004, 63.

176 There is no colophon to the Phug-brag edition of the sutra. Nevertheless, the Phug-brag catalogue lists the translators Prajnāvarma, Surendrabodhi, and Ye-shes-sde, and remarks that this translation of the short *Sukhāvatīvyūha-sūtra* does not vary from the translation executed by Dānaśīla and Ye-shes-sde. Tibetan text: *dkar chag tu pra dznyā varma dang / su rendra bo dhi dang / ye shes sdes bsgyur bar bshad kyang / dā na shī la dang / ye shes sdes gnyis kyis bsgyur ba de rang las bsgyur khyad mi 'dug;* see Samten 1992, 51.

177 Dānaśīla is known as the Kashmiri (Kha-che) sByin-pa'i nang-tshul. He authored books on logic, but his most notable contribution is the *Pustakapāṭuhopāya, Glegs bam bklag pa'i thabs* (D 4252), translated into Tibetan by the author himself. The Tibetan historian Tāranātha makes him a contemporary of Mahīpāla of Bengal in eastern India; see Niyogi 2001, 28. The Indian scholar-monk Jinamitra was a Vinaya preceptor and served as a spiritual guide to the king (*rgyal-ba'i bshes-gnyen*). Hence, he must have held a prominent position in the Tibetan court and was actively involved in the clarification of Tibetan grammar and in the compilation of the *sGra sbyor bam po gnyis pa* (Skt. *Madhyavyutpatti*); see *Dus rabs*, p. 2.

178 *dBa' bzhed* 2000, 96, n. 380. Zhang sNa-nam Ye-shes-sde, i.e., belonging to the family of sNa-nam; see Karmay 1988, 28–29, 149.

179 Śāntarakṣita's writings on Madhyamaka were very popular among the Tibetans; four lengthy commentaries on his *Ornament of the Middle Way* (*Madhyamakālṃkāra*) are catalogued in the PT under Madhyamaka *śāstras*, along with a very long summary of this text that is ten *bam-po* long; see Halkias 2004, 72.

180 For a discussion of the *lTa ba'i khyad par* (D 4360), see Ruegg 1989; Karmay 1988. The PT features another work by the same author that may have been used for teaching Buddhist tenets to beginners; see *lTa bai' bye brag gi brjed byang* (PT §XXI, 769).

181 *Nges pa'i don dbu ma* (PT §XXXI, no. 823). Blezer (1997, 87–88) notes that he is mentioned in relation to a search party composed of Vimalamitra and sKa-ba dpal-brtsegs, who sought out rDzogs-chen manuscripts.

182 *The lTa ba'i rim pa bshad pa;* see Tucci 1958, 447–451. He also collaborated with the Indian preceptor Vidyākaraprabha in the Tibetan translation of the *Vimuttimagga* from Pāli; see Skilling 1993, 135–140.

183 *dBu ma rgyan gyi brjed byang slob dpon bkra shis kyis mdzad pa,* 10 bp. (PT §XXXI, no. 786).

184 *bTsan po dba' dun brtan gyi dbu ma'i bka' bcad bshad pa dang bcas pa,* 60 sl. (PT §XXXI, no. 828).

185 Halkias 2004, 66–67.

186 For Davidson (2009a), the rationality surrounding *dhāraṇī* draws from encapsulating the Mahayana scriptural or doctrinal essence, which was encoded into a concentrated form and was thus inherently powerful in conferring mastery of the scriptures through recitation.

187 Davidson 2009a, 135–136.

188 The *dhāraṇī* of Avalokiteśvara enjoyed wide circulation in the Tarim basin. For a discussion of Dunhuang sources, see van Schaik 2006. Future studies could examine the relation between the cults of Amitābha and Avalokiteśvara in pre–eleventh-century Tibet and assess the extent to which they influenced and reinforced each other.

189 Halkias 2004, 66.

190 Halkias 2004, 67–68.

191 See Inagaki 1999. *'Phags pa sgo mtha' yas pas bsgrub pa shes bya ba'i gzungs* (D 914); MS IOL Tib J 307, Pel. Tib. 407, Pel. Tib. 408.

192 Nattier 2007, 370–371.

193 An annotated translation of Jñānagarbha's commentary (D 2696) is in Inagaki 1999.

194 Nattier 2007, 371.

195 Davidson 2009a, 139–140.

196 The LK lists: 1) *Anantamukha-nirhāra-dhāraṇī* (*sGo mtha' yas pa sgrub pa'i gzungs*) 260 sl. (§VI, no. 178); 2) *Extensive Commentary on the Anantamukha-nirhāra-dhāraṇī* (*sGo mtha' yas pa sgrub pa'i gzungs kyi rgya cher 'grel pa*), 4 bp. and 115 sl. (§XX, no. 550); 3) *Explanation on the Anantamukha-nirhāra-dhāraṇī in sections* (*sGo mtha' yas pa bsgrub pa'i gzungs kyi rnam par bshad pa'i chig le'ur byas pa*), 190 sl. (§XX, no. 551). The PT lists: 1) *Anantamukha-nirhāra-dhāraṇī* (*sGo mtha' yas pa*), 210 sl. (§V, no. 169); 2) *Extensive Commentary on the Anantamukha-nirhāra-dhāraṇī* (*sGo mtha' yas pa sgrub pa'i gzungs kyi rgya cher 'grel pa*), 4 bp. (§XIX, no. 497); 3) *Explanation on the Anantamukha-nirhāra-dhāraṇī in sections* (*sGo mtha' yas pa bsgrub pa'i gzungs kyi rnam par bshad pa'i chig le'ur byas pa*), 190 sl. (§XIX, no. 498); 4) *Explanation on the Ārya-Anantamukhanirhāra-dhāraṇī in eighty verses* (*'Phags pa sgo mtha' yas sgrub pa'i gzungs kyi tshig brgyad bcu bshad pa*) (§XXX, no. 740).

197 LK: *Aparimitāyur-jñāna-hṛdaya-nāma-dhāraṇī** (*Tshe dpag tu med pa'i gzung*), 110 sl. (§XIV, no. 350); and Amitāyus, unspecified (*Tshe dpag tu med pa*) (§XIV, no. 381). PT: Ārya-Aparimitāyus, unspecified (*'Phags pa tshe dpag tu med pa*), 120 sl. (§XV, no. 334).

198 These works are listed with the following titles and sizes: The long and short *Aparimitāyur-sādhana* (*Tshe dpag tu med pa'i sgrub thabs che chung gnyis*) (§XXXII, no. 916) and Vairocanarakṣita's recitation of the names of Amitābha (*A tsa rya Bai ro tsa na sang shi tas mdzad pa'i snang ba mtha' yas kyi mtshan brjod pa*) (§XXXI, no. 879). These works may be of a later date; see Halkias 2004.

199 See, for example, *Invocation Mantra to Amitābha* [1.5]; text on sNang-ba-mtha'-yas [6.1]; Beginning of a fragment of the *Bodhipraṇidhāna* [46.3]; *Dhāraṇī of sNang-ba-mtha'-yas* [49.1]; the qualities of sNang-ba-mtha'-yas and his buddha field [67.2]; Sanskrit formula of the *Amitāyur-jñāna-dhāraṇī* [75]; fragment of the *Ratnakūṭa* that ends with the *Amitāyurvyūhanirdeśa-sūtra* [96]; text on sNang-ba-mtha'-yas' buddha field [99.3]; fragment on the good qualities of Amitābha [158]; Vajrayana ritual of magical syllables to Amitābha [241]; *gTorma* ritual related to sNang-ba-mtha'-yas [245]; fragment of formulas to sNang-ba-mtha'-yas [252]; reference to Amitābha in a Vajrayana ritual [254]; fragment addressing Amitābha [256]; reference to Amitābha in a ritual [266]; reference to Amitābha [268]; description of sNang-ba-mtha'-yas [288]; homage to Amitāyus [317]; fragment with reference to Sukhāvatī [556]; fragment of the *Aparimitāyur-jñāna-nāma-mahāyāna-sūtra* [558]; description of Sukhāvatī [562]; fragment on the cosmology of Sukhāvatī [563]; the *Amitābha-sūtra* [758]; text that ends with a praise of the qualities of sNang-ba-mtha'-yas [759]; and homage to Amitābha [760].

200 Ducor 1988, 110.

201 The foundation of De-ga g.yu-tshal Temple (*gtsigs kyi gtsug-lag-khang*) and execution of its murals may have taken place during the reign of the Tibetan emperor Khri gTsug-lde-brtsan to commemorate the council and subsequent peace treaty between Tibet, China, the Uighurs, and possibly Nanzhao; see Kapstein 2004; 2009, 21–71. In another work, Kapstein explains that the icon of Buddha Amitābha was one of three primary images installed in De-ga g.yu-tshal and that this buddha was in no way exalted above Vairocana and Maitreya, the other two in the trio (2003, 20).

202 Kapstein 2003, 20.

203 Kōshō Akamatsu (1988, 195–220) edited some Dunhuang Tibetan texts of the Pure Land variey; see Silk 1993, 12.

204 Williams 1989, 146–147.

205 See Halkias 2004, 70–71; Kapstein 2000, 60–65; Heller 1998, 139–140; 1997, 387–388; Richardson 1998, 177–181.

206 The last dated manuscript discovered in cave 17 dates to 1002 and suggests that the famous library was sealed shortly thereafter, possibly in fear of Tangut invaders or the Muslim Karakhanids who had taken Khotan in 1006; see Whitfield 2004, 16–17. There are two studies and translations in French of Pel. Tib. 999; see Scherrer-Schaub 1991; Imaeda 1998. The Tibetan version of Pel. Tib. 999 is available online at IDP and OTDO.

207 The latter seems to have worked closely with Zhang Yichao during the expulsion of the Tibetans in 848 CE; see Chandra 2002, 94.

208 Similar practices prevailed in China up until the eighteenth century. Rawski writes, "Records from 1796, after the Qianlong emperor had abdicated in favour

of his son, show that two thousand Tibetan lamas were employed in chanting the 'The long life sutra' (*Wangshoujing*) at the Hongrensi for the four days leading up (and including his birthday). The sutra recitation which was repeated annually through the year after his death, cost over 1,758 taels of silver each year. That this became customary practice for every new emperor is suggested by the staging in 1799 and 1820 of the same recitation at the Hongrensi for the Jiaqing and Daoguang emperors on their birthdays" (1998, 273).

209 In Stein (1912) there is a full account of his second expedition. Van Schaik (2002, 133, 136) reports that out of the 212 Tibetan scrolls preserved in the Dunhuang collection at St. Petersburg, 202 contain the *Aparimitāyur-sūtra*, while the great majority of Dunhuang manuscripts in China are copies of the same sutra.

210 The Central Asian, Tibetan, and Sanskrit editions of the *Aparimitāyur* were published by Hoernle in 1916. In the same year, Walleser published a critical edition and German translation of the Sanskrit text based on a manuscript he obtained from Nepal.

211 Takeuchi (1998, xv) notes that some rolls of the *Aparimitāyur-nāma-mahāyāna-sūtra* deserve special notice because their paper is of a better quality than other manuscripts in the collection. He suggests that they were copied on special occasions in relation to prominent patrons who may have sponsored them.

212 For the editors of the Tibetan and Chinese Tripiṭakas this is an esoteric text; see Payne 2007, 275. Silk (1993, 16) disagrees with Akamatsu that this work belongs to tantric literature.

213 Payne (2007, 285) explains that the Chinese translators often rendered phonetically both Amitāyus and Aparimitāyus as Amitou, and notes that this conflation occurs in the Tibetan use of Tshe-dpag-med and Tshe-dpag-tu-med-pa.

214 See Schopen 1975. The *Sarvadurgatipariśoshana-tantra*, described by Bjerken as an exemplary royal work, played an important role in the conversion of Tibet to Buddhism: "those who write, or copy it, or those who have it copied, will become like powerful kings, to whom the various gods pledge willing submission as their servants" (2005, 834).

215 Payne (1997, 23) notes that in the *Immeasurable Life and Wisdom Sutra* the reference to birth in Sukhāvatī is a later emendation to the Sanskrit text, similarly to the Chinese translation of the sutra, which contains no such indication. This reference is also lacking in the Nepalese manuscript consulted by Walleser (1916).

216 For a discussion, see Payne 2007.

217 Hoernle 1916, 289–295. Walleser's 1916 translation and critical edition of the Sanskrit text offers a valuable context for comparison between the two editions. The Tibetan and Sanskrit translations diverge in a number of ways that have been addressed by Payne 2007.

218 I refrained from translating a Dunhuang version of the *Tshe-mdo* and opted for the Derge edition, burdened by the formidable task to select one representative Central Asian edition among hundreds of versions available in the UK, China, and Russia.

219 A commonplace supposition has been to date Tibetan texts from Dunhuang as early as the ninth century, assuming that most of the works were left there during the period of Tibetan occupation. However, more recent studies have demonstrated that the Tibetan language continued to be used in Dunhuang after the collapse of the Tibetan empire. A large number of manuscripts, including most of the tantric texts discovered, have been dated between the mid-tenth and early eleventh centuries; see Dalton and van Schaik 2006.

220 The Tibetan text reads *mtshan,* which literally means "name" or "characteristic," but in the context of this text, as rightly suggested by Payne (2007), it refers to the syllables of the *dhāraṇī.*

221 A lengthier version of the *dhāraṇī* is reconstructed here from the Sanskrit MS (Wallaser 1916) and a variant Derge recension (no. 855). Versions of the *dhāraṇī* from Dunhuang display variations that do not correspond with the Derge edition or the Sanskrit MS; see, for example, Pell Tib 3500; IOL Tib 310.1208.

222 The beginning of the Tibetan edition of the sutra equates the world-system of immeasurable qualities with Sukhāvatī. However, this identification may very well be an interpolation that was added sometime during the history of its transmission to Tibet. It is not found in all Tibetan versions; see for example Derge no. 855; Pell Tib 3500; IOL Tib 310.1208. Payne (2007) notes that there is no mention of Sukhāvatī in the Sanskrit MS edited by Wallaser (1916). The Tibetan text of our edition reads: *de shin phos nas de bzhin shegs pa tshe dang ye shes dpag tu med pa'i sangs rgyas kyi zhing 'jig rten gyi khams bde ba can yon tan dpag tu med pa la sogs par skye bar 'gyur ro* (p. 133).

223 The Tibetan reads *bjug-pa,* "to resolve, allow." Wallaser (1916) translates "establish as many as 84,000 dharma-groups"; Payne 2007, 294.

224 The Tibetan text reads: *spyin pa'i stobs kyis sangs rgyas yang dag 'phags // mi yi seng ge spyin pa'i stobs rtogs nas // snying rje can gyi grong khyer 'jug pa na // spyin pa'i stobs kyi sgra ni grag par 'gyur* (p. 439). The "compassionate city" (*snying-rje-can gyi grong-khyer*) may be in reference to Amitābha's Pure Land. Although not fully supported by the Tibetan syntax, one is tempted to read this passage in less ambiguous ways: "Through the power of generosity of the pure exalted buddhas, the lions of men, having internalized the power of generosity, enter the city with compassion and make the message of generosity heard."

225 Tucci 1973, 63.

226 Tucci acknowledges two stages to this process of collective recollection: the first is marked by an ancestral descent from heaven, and the second arises

"from the entry into Tibet of a conquering aristocracy whose ideas were still firmly anchored to aristocratic traditions, but who gradually amalgamated with the autochthonous belief which continued to exist side by side" (1955, 204). Walter challenges Tucci's "conquering aristocracy" and argues that the creation of an imperial authority in Tibet was the result of the "superimposition of a small outside group, with a leadership structure built around an inspirational warrior leader, the *btsan-po,* on a set of tribal aristocracies brought under his often unsteady control" (2009, 23). As we will see in the Epilogue, a popular Tibetan legend assigns to the Tibetans half-divine origins from the union of Bodhisattva Avalokiteśvara, who descended from Sukhāvatī, and a mean ogress. The Bön preserve an alternative narrative to the bodhisattva-ogress story that may be considerably older. It traces the beginning of the world to two eggs that spontaneously arose, one white and the other black. From the white egg came the beneficent father (*phan-byed*) and from the black the maleficent one (*gnod-byed*)—"the former is luminous and is therefore called the 'luminous appearance,' *snang-ba 'od-ldan,* or simply the 'one of light,' *'odzer-ldan*"; see Tucci 1955, 204.

227 Kapstein 2000, 5–7. This crisis was probably instigated as the result of Tibet's encounter with Central Asians and Indians, making the royal court susceptible to influences from foreign religious systems that challenged their own belief structures about the afterlife.

228 Imaeda 2007, 173. Bjerken argues that the *Sarvadurgatipariśoshana-tantra* and the *Tale of the Cycle of Birth and Death* "share more than a concern with transforming the deceased by means of mantras and mandalas, for they both present stories that feature the death of a god. The death of a god motif was a common missionary strategy used to subvert the cult of local deities found in pre-Buddhist traditions" (2005, 826).

229 Imaeda 2007, 133–134.

230 Kapstein 2000, 7–8. Kapstein (2003, 20) points out that this tradition differs to some degree with what is taught in the *Tibetan Book of the Dead,* which emphasizes to avoid both divine and infernal realms and search only for liberation.

231 Narratives of divine kingship and ancestral tomb worship figured in Central Asia, Tibet, and China, and among the Kuṣāṇas. This is reflected in the titles they assigned to their rulers: Tibetan "Son of God" and "Divine Emperor" (*lha-sras* and *lha-btsan-po*), Kuṣāṇa "Son of God" (*devaputra*), and Chinese "Son of Heaven (*tianzi*). Chen (2002) argues that the Kuṣāṇa use of the term *devaputra* (rarely seen in Sanskrit manuscripts) is a translation of the Chinese "Son of Heaven." However, the concepts of "heaven" and "son of heaven" are not quite native Chinese notions. These royal titles reflect deep-rooted traditions of divine kingship shared by Altaic and Indo-Iranian cultures, and may suggest a

common origin. Walter (2009, 21–22) reconstructs possible Scythian-Tibetan encounters through the discovery of Scythian-like artifacts in Tibet and in a Scythian royal legend from ancient Uḍḍiyāna that details methods for pacifying the Nāgarāja to avoid drought.

232 Beckwith 2009, 127, n. 51, identifies as Tibetan features of the Central Eurasian Culture Complex "the ruler and his heroic companions, the comitatus as the pinnacle of society; the burial of the ruler together with his comitatus, horses, and personal wealth in a great tumultus; and a strong interest in trade."

233 For a discussion of the evidence, see Dotson 2008; Stein 2010, 2007. Current research has revealed much about the competition between Buddhists and other ritual specialists vying for royal patronage; see also Lalou 1952; Imaeda 2007. Useful analogies can be drawn between archaic Tibetan notions of "rule by divine descent" and their eventual substitution with "rule by incarnation" regimes that populated the political life of post-imperial Tibet.

234 As illustrated in Rowell's pioneer study, "Asaṅga interprets purification in intellectual terms because in his system there is nothing to be purified except the mind—all things being 'originally pure'" (1935, 391).

235 Fujita 1987, 20, 90. The Chinese term *jingdu* appears many times in the first chapter of the Chinese translations of the *Vimalakīrtinirdeśa-sūtra* (T. 14) and the *Sukhāvatīvyūha-sūtra* (T. 12). Apparently, Tanluan (476–542) was the first among the masters of Pure Land Buddhism in China to have used it; see Kajiyama 1989, 137.

236 This work is cited in K (6018, 38.4.1–38.5.6), and in the *Collected Works of Tsong Kha Pa* (vol. Kha, 85a–100a, part 69 of Work 2; Lhasa Edition). In Mi-pham 'jam-dbyangs rnam-rgyal's (1846–1912) *Training for Sukhāvatī with Illuminating Faith,* we find the term *zhing-dag-pa* and other laudatory epithets for Sukhāvatī, such as, the "buddha field of the nobles" or "noble buddha field" (*'phags-pa'i zhing-khams*); see DM 2, 366–391; Mi-pham's *Collected Works,* vol. 7, pp. 223–251.

237 I am grateful to Professor Silk for identifying MS IOL Tib J310.1207 as a portion of the manuscript Pelliot tibétain 761, preserved in Paris and studied by him in 1993. The interjection *a myi ta pur* also occurs in MS IOL Tib J724 where the opening sentence reads *amyi ta phur gyi yon tan bcu la* in reference to Amitābha's ten qualities.

238 The manuscript is available online from IDP (IOL Tib J310.1207). The text employs the *ma-ya-btags* (*ya* attached to *ma*), final *'a* suffix, the *gi-gu-rlcg* (reverse *gi-gu*), and the mid-line *tsheg.*

239 Practicing in cemeteries is one of the thirteen *dhutanga* (Pāli) practices undertaken by forest monks, a set of optional ascetic rules said to have been established during the Buddha's time. According to Buddhagoṣa's *Path of Purification* (*Visuddhimagga*), the aim of *dhutanga* is to perfect the qualities that arise from contentment with a renunciant lifestyle (Caroline A. F. Rhys Davids 1975, 83).

Chapter Three: The Dharma That Goes against the Ways of the World

1 The Bön refer to their canonical collection of texts as Kanjur, but the contents of the two collections significantly differ. For an introduction to the Bön Kanjur, see Kvaerne 1974. Strictly speaking, the Kanjur and Tanjur are not the "sole canons" of Tibetan Buddhism, in that they are not fixed collections nor representative of all canonical collections of Buddhist texts in Tibet.

2 The manuscripts of the old Narthang Kanjur came from different libraries and required the expertise of many Buddhist scholars. For example, the contents of the *mDo* section drew from numerous sutra collections (*mdo-mangs*) from the monastic "libraries of Sa skya, gTsang gCu mig ring mo, Shog chung, sPun gsum, Zha lu, and other monasteries, together with those held at sNar thang itself" (Harrison 1996, 77). The Peking-line Kanjurs form an exception and list the three main divisions in reverse order; Eimer 2002b.

3 Samten (1994) asserts that the Li-thang ('Jan-sa-tham) edition, dated 1609–1614, is the earliest printed Kanjur currently available to scholars.

4 Bethlenfalvy (1982) provides a description of the Them-spangs-ma (Them-dpang-ma) catalogue. According to Skilling (1994, 768), by the seventeenth century at the latest, Tibetan scholarship recognized two main Kanjur lineages—as represented in the *Record of Teachings* (*gsan-yig*) of Jayapaṇḍita Blo-bzang 'phrin-las and 'Jam-dbyangs bzhad-pa'i rdo-rje. Contrary to Harrison (1996, 1994) and Silk (1994), who argued that the old Narthang Kanjur is a common ancestor for the Tshal-pa and Them-spangs-ma lineages, Skilling (1994a, 769; 1994b, xliii) acknowledges the relation between Tshal-pa and Narthang, but finds no convincing evidence for an ancestral affiliation between the Them-spangs-ma line and the old Kanjur from Narthang. In his estimation, the Thems-spang-ma drew from local sources available to the Chos-rgyal of rGyal-rtse in the early fifteenth century.

5 Harrison explains that the Tibetan canonical tradition is "implicitly open, non-unitary, and prone to contamination from the very outset" (1992, xlvi).

6 Skilling 1994a, xxxvii–xl. There exist a number of independent Kanjurs, such as the Newark, an incomplete Kanjur (fifteen volumes in the Sutra division) from Batang in Khams dating from the fifteenth and sixteenth centuries. The readings of the *Mahāsūtras* suggest that it belongs to an old and independent textual transmission; see Skilling 1997b, 193.

7 Eimer 2002, 4. The term "recension" refers to a consciously written version of a text.

8 The sigla are based on a list drawn at the Seventh Seminar of the International Association for Tibetan Studies (IATS) in 1995; see Harrison and Eimer 1997, xi–xiv.

9 Samten 1994, 396–397. At the time of my visit in summer 2005, Jampa Samten,

the director of the Central Institute of Higher Tibetan Studies (CIHTS), was working on compiling an index for the contents of the rTa-dbang MSS.

10 Samten theorizes that after the destruction of the temple by Lajang Khan's campaign, all its valuable "religious possessions, statutes, scriptures and silver stūpas were handed down to the Tawang monastery, the dGa'-ldan rnam-rgyal lha-rtse, which was founded in 1680 as the spiritual and administrative centre of the Gelukpa government in Monyul" (1994, 393–394).

11 lHa-sras gtsang-ma was the first member of the Tibetan imperial family to be ordained as a Buddhist monk, but according to the *Religious History of the Mon,* this did not deter him from fathering progeny not long after his arrival in Mon-yul; see Sperling 2008, 234.

12 Nanda 1982, 71. She relates the following popular tradition concerning the foundation of rTa-bang Monastery:

> [B]efore the Tawang monastery was built in the 1680's the Monpas of Monyul were Nyingmapa Buddhists of the Red Sect. . . . Gelukpa Buddhism came to the fore only with the establishment of the Tawang gonpa which was built under the inspiration and leadership of a persistent and devoted monk called Mera Lama. . . . While young he went as a lama to Tibet and studied in the famous Yellow Sect monasteries of Tashi Lumpo and Drebung. . . . While he was meditating in a cave he had a vision of a white horse sleeping. The next morning as he scrambled out of the cave he noticed the hoof-marks of his horse leading down in a south-western direction. Following them he found the horse sleeping on the grassy mount which he had seen in his dream and thus he sited his gompa which was named Tawang, or the place chosen and blessed by the horse. The gompa was completed during the reign of the 5th Dalai Lama who was asked to send his blessings.

13 This observation has been made by Eimer 1997–1998, 424.

14 Samten 1994, 394–397.

15 Edited by Daisetz Teitaro Suzuki (1955–1961).

16 Skilling 1994, xxxiii–xxxv.

17 The Derge edition has been catalogued in Ui, Suzuki, Kanakura, and Tada 1934.

18 Samten 1987, 18–19.

19 Eimer 2002, 5.

20 See RKS for relevant groupings.

21 Skilling 1994, xl. The editors of the Lhasa collection consulted the Narthang Kanjur, comparing it with the Derge edition whose readings they sometimes adopted. It has been listed in Takasaki 1965.

22 Harrison 1996, 82. It is listed in Nagashima 1975; Takasaki 1965. Harrison maintains that with the information to hand at present, "the sNar-thang carries

Them-spangs-ma derived texts in most if not all of the 'Dul-ba section, some of the Sher-phyin, some of the Dkon-brtsegs, a few texts at the end of the Mdo section and some of the Rgyud" (1992, xxx, n. 58).

23 See Eimer 1988; Samten 1992, ii. A copy of the Phudrag MS at the Library of Tibetan Works and Archives in Dharamsala, India, has been catalogued in Samten 1992. For a location list of the texts of the microfiche edition in the Institute for the Advanced Study of World Religions at Stony Brook, New York, see Eimer 1993.

24 See Silk 1994, 26; Eimer 1997–1998. Paul Harrison (1992) has questioned Phudrag's independent status based on his text-critical study of the *Druma-kinnara-rāja paripṛcchā-sūtra.* He discovered that it shares variants with the old Narthang-derived Kanjur editions from London and sTog Palace and not with the Tshal-pa-derived Kanjurs. He notes that for the *Śālistamba-sūtra* the situation is reversed. Schoening (1995, 168–169), on the other hand, argues that the Phudrag Kanjur is an independent collection that did not descend from the old Narthang Kanjurs, because it does not consistently agree with either the Tshal-pa or Them-spangs-ma groupings, while many of its unique readings may be simply corruptions. He concludes that the Phudrag copy of the *Śālistamba-sūtra* is closely connected with the Dunhuang manuscripts and the classical editions.

25 See Harrison 1994, 295; and RKS. This has also been confirmed by Schoening's (1995) analysis of the *Śālistamba-sūtra.* It is listed in Grinstead 1967; catalogued in Pagel and Gaffney 1996.

26 According to Gómez (1996, 126), it is still popular in China, Taiwan, Korea, Vietnam, and Japan.

27 Three Sanskrit manuscripts of the sutra were discovered and published in Japan in 1773 and 1797; see Ducor 1989, 141–149. See also Müller and Bunyū 1880; 1883. Another Sanskrit edition of the SV is found in Kimura 1943.

28 Pagel notes that the conventional usage of a "Sanskrit original" is misleading, "since the Indic versions themselves were often subject to interpolation, re-arrangement or shortening" (1995, 328).

29 As noted by Thomas, "The names and numbers of these Buddhas vary greatly. The short *Sukhāvatīvūyha* puts five or six at each point. The *Lotus* has a list of sixteen, two at each point, except that there is one at the N.E. and Śākyamuni in the centre" (1933, 185).

30 I have opted for the Derge edition because it is most commonly consulted for its accuracy by Tibetan and non-Tibetan scholars. For a critical edition of the DKG, see also Onoda 2001; for the OKG, see the *Zoyaku muryojukyo ihon kogohyo (kobon),* Kagawa 1999.

31 *bCom-ldan-'das* (Skt. *bhagavān*) is a usual epithet for Śākyamuni Buddha; Bhagavan means "conqueror," and here it is also used as an adjective for

Buddha Amitābha. The Tibetan term literally means "the subduer who has gone beyond." In this translation, *bcom-ldan-'das* is rendered as "Awakened," since the verb *bcom-pa* means "to conquer or subdue," and refers to those who have subdued their mental afflictions and are thereby awakened to the true nature of reality.

32 Concerning the Jeta Grove, Handa (1994, 44) explains that Buddha Śākyamuni had to perform before the king a miraculous feat at Śrāvastī, the capital of the Kośala kingdom. He created multiple representations of himself rising seated on a thousand-petaled lotus to the highest heaven. He then preached the Dharma before the king, who thereafter became a lay disciple of the Buddha and extended his patronage. It was near Śrāvastī that the merchant Anāthapiṇḍada commissioned a *saṃghārāma* in a pleasure garden he purchased in exchange for the gold acquired from Prince Jeta.

33 The term *sems-dpa' chen-po* (Skt. *mahāsattva*) translates "great bodhisattvas."

34 In this passage, the Tibetan *mi-pham-ba* serves as an epithet for Maitreya, and it is unlikely that it refers to the Elder Ajita, who should have been included in the previous list.

35 Literally, "the giver of one hundred sacrifices" (*brgya-byin;* Skt. *śakra*); an epithet for the god Indra, who resides in the Trāyastriṃśa heaven. According to a legend, he became the guardian of Buddhism because Śākyamuni transmitted to him the *Aparimitāyus dhāraṇī* when he was about to die, after which his life was extended significantly; see Shakya 1994, 128.

36 Both the Tibetan and Sanskrit texts list large numbers of enumeration. These superlative notations do not represent an exact number, but are meant to express vast quantities.

37 Śāriputra was the son of a brahmin, and is depicted as one of the two chief disciples of the Buddha, along with Mahā-Maudgalyāyana. While he is positively portrayed in the Pāli Tripiṭaka, in some Mahayana sutras he came to represent the inferiority of early Buddhism as compared with the bodhisattva path of the Mahayana.

38 The term "buddha field" translates the Tibetan *sangs-rgyas kyi zhing* (Skt. *buddha-kṣetra*); "world-system" translates *'jig-rten gyi khams* (Skt. *lokadhātu*); see Chapter One.

39 The phrase *blta na sdug pa* is idiomatic, meaning "beautiful to behold."

40 The eight qualities of water are: 1) sweet (*mngar-ba*), 2) cool (*bsil-ba*), 3) smooth (*jam-pa*), 4) light (*yang-ba*), 5) clear of sediments (*dvangs-pa*), 6) clean (*gtsang-ba*), 7) pleasing and soothing to the throat (*mgrin-pa sang-song bde-ba*), and 8) beneficial to the stomach (*lto-ba la phan-pa*).

41 The Tibetan *spug* may refer to any precious gem. In this translation it is rendered as coral, commonly listed as one of the "seven precious substances." Liu Xinru notes that "the concept of the seven-treasures as the formula of the

Buddhist paradise and the ideal donation for Buddhist deities was a major part of these texts. It seems that the [Chinese] translators were uncertain about what items the Sanskrit names of the seven treasures actually designated. Even translations of the same text give different lists of the seven treasures" (1988, 161).

42 *Erythrina variegata* (syn. *E. indica Lam., E. variegate*) is an ornamental tropical tree that produces scarlet-colored flowers. Its association with the subtropical island Socotra (the "Island of Bliss") on the Arabian Sea suggests the transmission of elements taken from itinerant accounts and travelers' descriptions.

43 The Sanskrit manuscript reads *krauñca,* which translates as curlew or heron.

44 The five faculties are: 1) faith (*dad-pa*), 2) perseverance (*brtson-'grus*), 3) mindfulness (*dran-pa*), 4) meditative stabilization (*ting-nge-'dzin*), and 5) discriminative awareness (*shes-rab*). The five powers are intensifications of the five faculties to be developed along the Buddhist path of training. The seven branches of awakening are: 1) mindfulness (*dran-pa*), 2) discrimination of phenomena (*chos kyi rnam 'byed*), 3) perseverance (*brtson-'grus*), 4) joy (*dga'-ba*), 5) equanimity (*btang-snyoms*), 6) meditative stabilization (*ting-nge-'dzin*), and 7) pliancy (*shin-sbyangs*). In the *Sadharmapuṇḍarīka-sūtra* we can identify references to Buddhist teachings issuing forth from unusual sources: "[W]ithout ceasing the sounds of Dharma come from birds, trees, light, rays, and even from space" (Martin 2001, 22); and in verse thirty-seven of the tenth chapter of the *Bodhicaryāvātara:* "May all embodied beings hear the sounds of Dharma without cease from birds, trees, and from the lights and sky" (Martin 2001, 22, n. 15).

45 The Dharma recitals in Sukhāvatī may represent specific social arrangements, for example monastic settings. Harrison notes, "In this way, as in many others, the fantastic vision of Sukhāvatī is the product of a specific embodied experience and specific social arrangements. The former aspect of it—the experience of hearing the dharma being constantly recited around oneself in the forest environment—is completely consistent with the word of the *Dharmasaṅgīti-sūtra* quoted in the Śikṣāsamuccaya" (2003, 142, n. 51).

46 It corresponds with Dharmākara's first and second vows (LV §28, 1; §28, 2). His second vow reads: "Blessed One, may I not awaken to unsurpassable, perfect, full awakening if living beings, once they have been born in my buddha field, should die to be reborn in the hells, or as animals, or among the hungry ghosts (*pretas*), or as members of the host of *asuras*." The "realm of *pretas*" (insatiable beings) should follow the series of the three lower births, but here a substitution is made for Yama, the king of death, who traditionally rules over the realm of pretas; see Shakya 1994, 129.

47 The reference to "good family" is reminiscent of Brahmanical texts, which nevertheless do not include women. Hirakawa argues that the designation "sons and daughters of a good family" (1963, 69–73) were used by Mahayana

writers to address their followers. However, there is not much known about this group, "but there are frequent references made to a bodhisattvagana, suggesting that they formed a group (*gana*) significantly different from the saṅgha of monastic, sectarian Buddhism. It is unclear, however, whether the bodhisattva-*gana* included only bodhisattvas who were renunciants or also included lay bodhisattvas"; see Fujita 1996, 11.

48 Amitāyus and Amitābha are used interchangeably in the Tibetan text.

49 This "legalistic" section of the sutra consists of authoritative testimonials by buddhas residing in the eastern direction and proceeding clockwise.

50 'Jam-sgra may translate as Mañjusvara. This name is not available in the MV.

51 The Sanskrit and Tibetan versions literally say that the Buddha "covers with his tongue the buddha field and reveals it"—in other words, he gives expression to it (Skt. *nirveṭhanaṃ kurvanti*).

52 The Tibetan version duplicates the name of this Tathāgata who also presides in the southern direction.

53 In both the Sanskrit and Tibetan versions this Tathāgata presides in the south.

54 This section maybe linked with the concept of *vyākaraṇa* (*lung-bstan-pa*), or a prediction by a buddha concerning the future enlightenment of a bodhisattva. It is well-known tradition that a bodhisattva must declare his *praṇidhāna* in the presence of a living buddha, who then predicts his future success in attaining enlightenment; see Dayal 1932, 67.

55 The Tibetan text provides the title of the sutra at the beginning and end of the text, while in the Sanskrit version it is customary for the title of the text to be given at the end.

Chapter Four: Tibetan Pure Land Commentaries

1 The Tibetan text reads: *bcom ldan 'das gal te bdag byang chub thob pa'i tshe / sangs rgyas kyi zhing grangs ma mchis pa dpag tu ma mchis pa dag na / sems can gang dag gis bdag gi ming thos nas / sangs rgyas kyi zhing der skye bar bgyi ba'i slad du sems gtong zhing / dge ba'i rtsa ba rnams kyang yongs su bsngo bar bgyid na / mtshams ma mchis par bgyid pa dang / dam pa'i chos spong ba'i sgrib pas bsgribs pa'i sems can rnams ma gtogs par de dag tha na sems bskyed pa'i 'gyur ba bcus sangs rgyas kyi zhing der skye bar ma gyur pa de srid du bdag bla med pa yang dag par rdzogs pa'i byang chub mngon par rdzogs par 'tshang rgya bar mi bgyi'o* (K vol. 22, 3.8.113).

2 The Tibetan text reads: *kun dga' bo sems can gang dag kha cig de bzhin gshegs pa de rnam pas yang dang yang yid la byed pa dang dge ba'i rtsa ba mang po dpag tu med pa bskyed pa dang / byang chub tu sems yongs 'jig rten gyi khams der skye bar smon lam 'debs pa de dag 'chi ba'i dus nye bar gnas pa na / de bzhin gshegs pa dgra bcom pa yang dag par rdzogs pa'i sangs rgyas 'od dpag med dge slong gi tshogs du mas yongs su bsgor zhing mdun gyis bltas nas bzhugs par 'gyur de* (K vol. 22, 5.9.119).

3 *'Phags pa bzang po spyod pa'i smon lam gyi rgyal po* (D 1095). This Mahayana text is widely used in Tibetan tantric rituals for similar purposes.

4 The Tibetan text of the *Seven Limb Prayer* reads: *phyag 'tshal ba dang mchod cing bshags pa dang / rjes su yi rang bskul zhing gsol ba yi / dge ba cung zad bdag gis ci bsags pa / thams cad bdag gis byang chub phyir bsngo'o* (*'Phags pa bzang po spyod pa'i smon lam gyi rgyal po;* 2000, folio 7).

5 The Tibetan text reads: *rgyal ba'i dkyil 'khor bzang zhing dga' ba der / padmo dam pa shin tu mdzes las skyes / snang ba mtha' yas rgyal bas mngon sum du / lung bstan pa yang bdag gis der thob shog / der ni bdag gis lung bstan rab thob nas / sprul ba mang po bye ba phrag brgya yis / blo yi stobs kyi phyogs su rnams su yang / sems can rnams la phan pa mang po bgyis shog* (DM 1, 150).

6 The Tibetan text reads: *bzang po spyod pa'i smon lam bsngos pa yis / bsod nams dam pa mtha' yas gang thob des / 'gro ba sdug bsngal chu bor bying ba rnams / 'od dpag med pa'i gnas rab thob par shog* (*'Phags pa bzang po spyod pa'i smon lam gyi rgyal po;* 2000, folio 23).

7 This unique collection of Tibetan scriptures is part of a broader genre of *smon-lam* used in daily rituals, recited as an ornament at the end of a practice, or for reinforcing dedications with aspirations. Cabezón and Jackson note that there is no Tibetan term that conveys exactly the sense that "genre" does in the West. "There are, of course, 'typology' words, such as *rigs* ('kind'), *sde* ('class') or *rnam pa* ('aspect'), but none of these seems to be used consistently to refer to an abstract notion of literary type in the way that 'genre' does" (1996, 20–21).

8 For example, this collection does not include a diversity of tantric texts, funeral and *bar-do* rituals, Amitābha Jātakas, and so forth, which should be included as part of the *bDe-smon* genre.

9 The Pure Land inclinations of Dol-po-pa shes-rab rgyal-mtshan (1292–1362) have been discussed elsewhere; see Halkias 2009a, 259–275.

10 Smith 2001, 15.

11 Richardson 2003, 139.

12 The bKa'-gdams tradition originates with the founding of Rwa-sgreng Monastery (1056–1057) by Atiśa's most prominent disciple, 'Brom-ston rgyal-ba'i-'byung-gnas (1005–1064). I have not been able to locate any texts exclusively dealing with Sukhāvatī in the works of the bKa'-gdams, who nevertheless held Amitābha in high esteem. As noted by Kapstein, Khyung-po rnal-'byor (ca. 1140), himself a Sukhāvatī devotee, identified his preceptor Glang-ri thang-pa rdo-rje seng-ge (1054–1123), an important figure in the early bKa'-gdams order, as an emanation of Amitābha (2004, 21). For historical introductions on the bKa'-gdams movement, see Davidson 2005; Roesler Ulrike and Hans-Ulrich 2004; Roerich 1946.

13 Concerning the blending of secular and spiritual interests in Tibet, see the Epilogue and Halkias 2006b, 121–151. The religious and political eminence of the Paṇ-chen Lama's incarnation lineage is attested to by the disruption of his lineage by the Chinese authorities and subsequent disappearance of the eleventh Paṇ-chen Lama in 1995.

14 There are several traditional biographies on the life and works of Tsong-kha-pa, written by Tibetan scholars from different Tibetan schools. The following biographical information is taken from the *gSung 'bum dkar chag* (1990, 12–13); the *mKhas dbang tshe brtan zhabs drung gi dpyad rtsom mkho bsdus* ('Jigs-med-chos 'phags-kyis-bsgrigs 1994, 122–144); Thurman 1985, 372–382; 1982, 3–47.

15 For selections from the *sNgags rim chen mo* and an introduction to the subject by the Fourteenth Dalai Lama, see Hopkins 1987.

16 Shakabpa 1967, 85. This important annual festival was discontinued soon after the Chinese invasion of Tibet in 1950. Richardson (1993, 22–26) reports that in the twentieth century about 20,000 monks from all over Tibet and especially from 'Bras-spungs, Se-ra, and dGa'-ldan Monasteries would stream into Lhasa to conduct regular day-long praying sessions accompanied by short, although occasionally longer, debates between candidates competing for advanced religious diplomas.

17 *bDe ba can gyi zhing du skye ba 'dzin pa'i smon lam zhing mchog sgo 'byed* (DM 1, 334–365). This work is located in the Peking edition of the Tibetan Tripitaka: *rGyal ba tsong kha pa chen po'i bka' 'bum* (K vol. 153, 87b6–102a1). The short prayer is located in Tsong-kha-pa's *gSung-'bum* (vol. 2, kha, p. 367). It comprises sections taken from the *bDe ba can gyi zhing du skye ba 'dzin pa'i smon lam zhing mchog sgo 'byed* (87b6–87b8, 96b3–99b1, 101b3–101b8). For an English translation and discussion, see Kajihama 1991, 300–321; Thurman 1982, 207–212.

18 For the dGe-lugs-pa school the *gcod* teachings have their origins in pure vision encounters with the celestial bodhisattva Mañjuśrī; Gyatso 1985, 337. See Chapter Six for a discussion of Pure Vision Treasures.

19 Thurman 1982, 18.

20 The *bDe ba can gyi zhing du skye ba 'dzin pa'i smon lam zhing mchog sgo 'byed ces bya ba'i rnam bshad dngos grub 'byung gnas* by dPal-'byor lhun-grub was scanned from a microfilm copy of a blockprint of unknown origin listed at TBRC (W1CZ1111). Blo-bzang rta-mgrin's *bDe smon zhing mchog sgo 'byed kyi 'don 'grigs 'khyer bde gnad tshang rnam dag zhing du bgrod pa'i nye lam* is in his *Collected Works* (TBRC W13536).

21 Tsong-kha-pa's *Prayer to Sukhāvatī* and the *Thog mtha' ma* are two of the eight prayer books used regularly by the dGe-lugs-pa school; see Kajihama 1991, 294–295.

22 This stands for correction. The phrase *dge-slong mi-'khrugs-pa* in the text does not refer to Buddha Akṣobhya but more generally to an "imperturbable monk."

23 The *mGon po 'od dpag med kyi bstod pa zhing mchog sgo 'byed* is cited in the Peking edition of the Tibetan Tripitaka: *rGyal ba tsong kha pa chen po'i bka' 'bum;* no. 6018, 38.4.1–38.5.6; and in *Asian Classics, Collected Works of Tsong Kha Pa* (vol. Kha, 85a–100a, part 69 of work 2; Lhasa Kanjur). Four short eulogies and petitions to Amitābha are found at 38.5.6, 39.1.6, 39.2.1, and 39.2.5.

24 'O-de gung-rgyal, evidently the same as 'O-de spu-rgyal, was the primeval king of Lhasa. According to the inscription from Lhasa and on the pillar erected on the Yarlung tomb, he was a god who descended from heaven upon earth to become the first king of Tibet; Tucci 1955, 199.

25 According to variant systems of reckoning, Paṇ-chen blo-bzang chos-kyi-rgyal-mtshan was the fourth in an incarnation line with mKhas-grub rje as the first; see Smith 2001, 119, n. 390. The following biographical information draws from the *gSung 'bum dkar chag* 1990, 98–99; Khetsun Sangpo 1973, 464–495.

26 He is known to have collected many editions of the Kanjur and published a new canonical edition known as the *sKya pod chen po ljags zhud ma bka' 'gyur.*

27 The *Bde ba can gyi zhing du thogs pa med par bgrod pa'i myur lam* is listed in Paṇchen's *gSung 'bum dkar chag* (vol. Nga, fol. 729–742).

28 The following biographical information is taken from the *Gangs can mkhas grub rim byon ming mdzod* (1992, 526–529) and the *gSung 'bum dkar chag* (1990, 235–237). Detailed information on his life can be found in his autobiography, listed in *lCang skya bka' 'bum* (K no. 6234, 159.2.8–172.1.7).

29 Smith (2001, 146, n. 470) notes that Grags-pa 'od-zer was born at lCang-skya and served for a short time (from 1630 to 1633) as the abbot of dGon-lung. However, in the biographies of the successive abbots of dGong-lung there is no mention that Ngag-dbang blo-bzang was the successor of Grags-pa 'od-zer.

30 Rawski (1998, 273) reports on longevity rites and chanting of Pure Land sutras during the Chinese emperors' birthdays. Among the Tibetan clergy who performed these rites lCan-skya was the highest dignitary in Beijing during Qianlong's reign. The relevant passage reads:

> The Daoguang emperor's birthday had not only the monks of Hongrensi, but other high-ranked Tibetan monks entering the palace to chant the Amitāyus sutra in the Yangxindian and the Zhongzhengdian. Sutra recitation was also a feature of birthday celebrations for empress dowager. At the Yanshousi (extended long life temple), which he had erected for his mother seventieth and eightieth birthday, the Qianlong emperor had the highest Tibetan dignitary in Peking, the lCang skya khutukhtu, lead a thousand lamas from various temples in chanting the Sukhāvatīvyuha or Amitāyus sutra, designed to ensure rebirth in the Pure Land. He bestowed a set of nine Buddhas and a complete set of Amitāyus figures on his mother for her sixtieth birthday; for her seventieth birthday, she received over nine thousand statues of Buddhas, bodhisattvas, Amitāyus, tar, and lohans,

in multiples of nine (nine being a homophone for eternity, i.e., long life). Ten thousand Amitāyus statues, signifying wishes for long life and rebirth in the Western Paradise, were made for Hongli's own sixtieth birthday. Funds for these 'birthday presents' were contributed by the court: one the emperor's seventieth birthday, the princes and officials clubbed together to present a total of 2,233 Amida Buddhas costing over 321,000 taels of silver.

31 These are: the *bDe ba can gyi zhing du bgrod pa'i myur lam gsal bar byed pa'i sgron me* (K no. 6226, 146.1.2.–159.1.5) and the *Zhing mchog sgo 'byed kyi dmigs rim mdor bsdus* (K no. 6225, 142.1.3–147.4.5), respectively.

32 Smith (2001, 40) remarks on the inaccurate yet nonetheless conventional use of the term "bka'-brgyud" to encompass both the Shangs-pa and Mar-pa sects and their offshoots.

33 Roerich 1946, 399.

34 Roerich 1946, 399.

35 Smith 2001, 41–46.

36 *bDe smon,* DM 1, 171–172; translation in Kapstein 2004, 27.

37 Smith 2001, 82.

38 These works are entitled respectively as the *Padma dkar po'i le'u nyer bzhi pa las byung ba'i bde smon* (DM 1, 135) and the *bDe smon* (DM 1, 207–211).

39 Kapstein 2004, 26.

40 Douglas and White (1976, 147) report that in the male-iron-horse year when the Sharmapa felt seriously ill, his close disciples requested him to postpone his death until the arrival of Karma chags-med, who had yet to receive some very important teachings.

41 Karma chags-med is the first in a series of seven incarnations. The present gNas-mdo throne-holder of bKra-shis chos-gling Monastery is Karma bstan-'dzin 'phrin-las kun-khyab-dbal bzang-po. The biography of the first Chags-med is based on the following sources: *gTer ston brgya rtsa'i rnam thar* (513–516); *mKhas grub karma chags med rin po che'i gsung 'bum gyi dkar chag* (Introduction); Tsering Lama 1988, 35–44; Chagmé 1998, 7–11.

42 For a brief history on the gNas-mdo lineage, see *Shes bya kun khyab mdzod* (fol. 16, 186, 193).

43 Students listed in his biography include Drung-ram kun-'phel, Drung-ram 'phel-rgyas, Drung-ram shes-rab, Karma dbang-po, Chos-dbang kun-bzang, bKa'-bcu mkha'-mnyam, 'Brug-pa dbu-mdzad, Chos-ldan rab-'byor, Kun-drag bla-ma padma of Zur-mang, Padma dbang-drag, rDzogs-chen padma rig-'dzin, Skyo-thu bla-ma, 'Gyur-med rdo-rje, lHo-pa sprul-sku, Chos-rgyal rin-chen rnam-rgyal, 'Ja'-mo sku-skye, Sa-skya snga-ma, 'Brug-bla dge-'phel, the renunciant of sTag-lung, O-rgyan the *siddha* from mNga'-ri, the cotton sage Kha-ba dkar-po, and others.

44 For a history of the dPal-yul rNying-ma lineage, see Tsering Lama 1988.

45 Chophel 1982, 86.

46 Karma chags-med's *Collected Works* contain many works on divination and folk rituals. For an English translation of the *Kun rdzob gya sel me long,* see Chophel 1982. Machine prints of his collected works in Chengdu (Khrin-tu), China, averaged forty to forty-eight volumes.

47 We may also discern a synthesis between Ratna gling-pa's revelations on the *zhi-khro* (peaceful and wrathful deities) and the celestial Treasures of Mi-'gyur rdo-rje is forged in Karma chags-med's *gNam chos thugs kyi gter kha snyan brgyud zab mo'i skor las zhi khro dam pa rigs brgyu'i sgrub pa* (GB vol. ba, fol. 187–190), *gNam chos thugs kyi gter kha'i zur rgyan zhi khro bsams gtan cho ga* (GB vol. ba, fol. 587–590), and *gNam chos dang bka' ma dang gter kha gsar rnying gang la yang sbyar rung ba'i zhi khro'i dbang tshang ma* (GB vol. ba, fol. 591–616).

48 Tibetan text: *a ma bde ba can du ma 'khyol na / ban rgan chags med skyag pa zos pa yin* (Gu-ru bkra-shis, 630). The devotion shown by adepts to their mothers is reminiscent of the story of the Buddha going to Tuṣita heaven to instruct his mother. Zabs -dkar (1997, 499) has his own story to share:

> One night I dreamt that I came to a place said to be the Paradise Arrayed in Turquoise Petals (*g.yu lo bkod pa'i zhing;* the buddha field of Tārā)—a vast and even plain, perfect in all aspects, ringed with different kinds of trees with beautiful leaves, flowers, and fruits. In the middle of the plain stood a lofty three-story pavilion entirely made of jewels, the beauty of which was enhanced by a glittering golden dome, just like paintings of Buddhafields. As I arrived on the path that encircled the pavilion, there came three young maidens doing circumambulations. One of them kept on looking at me and asked, 'Don't you recognize me?' 'No,' I said, 'I don't.' She continued, 'Son I am your mother! After I died, I came here. It has been many years since I've seen you. It is good that we've met again. You've grown old, my son.' The image of my mother in her old age was vivid in my mind and I cried. My mother, too, could not hold back her tears. Then I asked, 'Who are these two girls?' and she mentioned the names of two old women of our village who were always reciting prayers to Drolma. The girls, too, looked at me and cried. When I recalled the faces of the two old grandmothers, more tears filled my eyes. 'It is really good you are all happy now! But where do you usually stay?' I asked. 'We live in the Western Blissfu Buddhafield; we came this morning to circumambulate and offer prostrations to Jetsun Drolma. For the moment, you must continue benefiting beings; later we will meet again, in whichever Buddhafield you attain.' With that, the three girls continued their circumambulations. As I was thinking myself to do some, I woke up.

49 English translation of the opening to the *rNam dag bde chen zhing gi smon lam* (DM 1, 217–231) by Skorupski 1995, 224. There are at present several copies of

Karma chags-med's *bDe chen smon lam* in circulation in Tibet and the Indian subcontinent. For a critical edition and annotated German translation of the prayer, see Schwieger 1978. For an introduction and English translation, see Skorupski 1995.

50 The copy of the text in my possession is courtesy of Kundreul Ling Monastery, France.

51 Pure Land works inspired by Chags-med's *bDe chen smon lam* include Thugs-rje gzhan-phan dpal-bzang's nineteenth-century commentary, *rNam dag bde chen zhing gi smon lam gyi 'byed 'grel bde chen zhing du bgrod pa'i them skas bzang po* (TOH, tome 212, no. 7019, 1–82); dPal-sprul o-rgyan 'jigs-med chos-kyi-dbang-po's (1808–1887) *dPal sprul rin po ches mdzad pa'i chags med bde smon gyi sa bcad* (DM 2, 447–451); O-rgyan bstan-'dzin nor-bu's nineteenth-century *bDe smon gyi spyi bshad byang chub sems dpa'i myur lam;* and *mKhas grub karma chags med kyis mdzad pa'i rnam dag bde chen zhing gi smon lam gyi 'grel bshad thar lam snang byed* by Glag-bla bsod-nams chos-'grub (1862–1944), a student of O-rgyan bstan-'dzin nor-bu.

52 Also known as bShad-sgrub bstan-pa'i-rgyal-mtshan, more popularly, rMe-ri dge-slong. The information provided in this short introduction is taken from Kapstein's (1997, 1–8) preface to the *gSung-'bum* of Glag-bla bsod-nams-chos-'grub.

53 This work is also located in the TRP, vol. 20, 27–541, and in Gla-bla's *gSung-'bum*, vol. 5, 25–562. In the final volume of his *gSung-'bum* we also find an associated ritual for the realization of Amitābha's Pure Land (pp. 563–568) and Gla-bla's own abbreviated version of the *bDe smon* and his commentary on it (pp. 569–626).

54 Kapstein 2000, 164.

55 The biographical information is taken from a short biography of rDza dpal-sprul written by his disciple 'Jigs-med bstan-pa'i-nyi-ma (1865–1926); see *Khams grul mkhas dbang rnams kyi snyan ngag dper brjod phyogs bsgrig* 1987, 10–16.

56 These works are titled *dPal sprul rin po ches mdzad pa'i chags med bde smon gyi sa bcad* (DM 2, 447–451) and *Tsong kha pas mdzad pa'i bde smon zhing khams sgo 'byed 'grigs* (DM 2, 452–454). They are listed in dPal-sprul O-rgyan 'jigs-med chos-kyi-dbang-po's *Collected Works* (vol. 2, 403–407 and vol. 4, 82–84, respectively).

57 'Jam-mgon mi-pham's short biography draws from the following two sources: *'Ju mi pham rgya mtsho'i gnas tsul thor bu,* published in sBrang-char 3, 74; Khetsun Sangpo, vol. 4, 531–547.

58 The *Bde ba can gyi zhing spyong ba'i dad pa gsal bar byed pa drang srong lung gi nyi ma zhas* (DM 2, 366–391) is also located in Mi-pham rgya-mtsho's *Collected Works,* vol. 7, 223–251. The shorter commentary on the four causes can be found in Mi-pham's *Collected Works,* vol. 6, 417–423.

59 This work appears in DM 1 under the title *Mi pham bde smon.* The title above is from the opening paragraph in the text (p. 261).

60 Amitābha's Pure Land is classified neither as an evident (*mngon-gyur-ba*) nor a slightly obscured (*lkog-pa*) phenomenon. It is an extremely obscure phenomenon that can only be cognized by a valid inferential cognition that relies on conviction (*yid-ches*). A threefold scrutiny establishes the validity of Sukhāvatī doctrines if they cannot be invalidated by 1) perception, 2) inference, and 3) contradiction with other propositions derived from scriptural sources.

61 See LV §28–19; K vol. 22, 113.3.8.

62 The following biographical material is excerpted from *rDo grub chen 'jigs med phrin las 'od zer gyi rabs rnam thar*, fol. 21–36.

63 *bDe ba can gyi zhing las brtsams pa'i gdam dge ba'i lo tog spel byed dbyar skyes sprin chen glal ba'i sgra dbyangs* (DM 2, 392–446). This work is also located in the *Collected Works* of the third rDo-grub-chen (vol. 4, pp. 307–376).

64 See Kajihama 1994, 1996, 2002a. rDo-grub-chen draws mainly from the OKG to frame his extensive commentary. Kajihama (1996, 950–951) notes that he quotes from the following sutras, *śāstras*, and *dhāraṇīs*: *Ārya-Karuṇāpuṇḍarīka-sūtra, Ārya-tathāgata-jñāna-mūdra-samādhi-sūtra, Ārya-mahāpariṇāma-rājasamantraka, Buddhāvatṃsaka-nāma-mahāvaipulya-sūtra, Mahāyānottaratantra, Deśanā stava, Ārya-adhyāśaya-saṃcodana-sūtra, Ārya-samādhirāja-sūtra, Ārya-karaṇḍa-vyūha-sūtra, Ārya-saptatathāgata-pūrva-praṇidhāna-viśeṣa-vistara-nāma-sūtra, Ārya-aparimitāyur-jñānahṛdaya-nāmadhāraṇī, Ārya-sarva-tathāgatoṣṇīṣasitāta-patrā-nāma-aparājitā-pratyaṃ-gira-mahāvidyārājñī*, and the *Sarvatathāgatoṣṇīsa-vijyaya-nāma-dhāraṇī-kalpa-sahitā*. There are also two references to the DKG (*zhing bkod kyi mdo chung ba*) concerning Sukhāvatī's attributes (DM 2, 423).

65 Smith 2001, 99–100.

66 Kapstein 1996, 277. The Lamdre system of meditation is characteristic of Sa-skya oral esoteric instructions based on the Hevajra Tantra and related tantric scriptures that dKon-mchog rgyal-po received from 'Brog-mi lo-tsā-ba along with the *Vajrapañjara* and *Sampuṭa* Tantras; see Smith 2001, 100.

67 Stearns 1997, 190.

68 Biographies on Sakya Paṇḍita include: 1) a versified version, composed in 1579 by the Rin-spungs-pa Prince Ngag-dbang 'jig-rten dbang-phyug (1542–1625?), and 2) A-mes-zhabs ngag-dbang kun-dga' bsod-nams' (1597–1659) biography, which is contained in his well-known history of the leading families of Sa-skya of 1629; see van der Kuijp 1993, 530, n. 12; 13. The biographical information above is taken from a short biography on Sakya Paṇḍita found in the *Gangs can mkhas dbang rim byon gyi rnam thar mdor bdus* (1996, 45–55).

69 *sNang mtha' yas bsgom don* is located in *The Complete Works of the Great Masters of the Sa skya Sect of Tibetan Buddhism* (*Sa skya pa'i bka' 'bum*; vol. 5, 406), and in the *Sa paṇ kun dga' rgyal mtshan gyi gsung 'bum* (vol. 3, 520–521). This work is translated in Kapstein 2004, 28.

70 Sakya Paṇḍita's treatises have become canonical in the Sa-skya school. His *Distinguishing Views* (*lTa ba'i shan 'byed*) is taken as the ultimate exegesis for the orthodox Sa-skya doctrinal position defined as the real Middle Way beyond extremes (*mtha'-bral*) that refutes the views of Dol-po-pa as eternalistic (*rtag-mtha'*) and those of Tsong-kha-pa as nihilistic (*chad-mtha'*); see Stearns 1999, 207, n. 69.

71 Kapstein writes that the sleep-meditation tradition of Amitābha continues to be transmitted among the Sa-skya and other orders, "while a number of important doctrinal authors have written texts explaining it, and liturgies for its practice, that remain popular at the present time" (2004, 28–29). In 1918 and 1919 respectively, 'Jam-dbyangs founded an important Sa-skya monastery in the vicinity of sDe-dge and seat of the rDzong-sar mkhyen-brtse line of incarnations, and an adjacent college, known as the rDzong-sar khams bye grwa-tshang; see TBRC (P 733).

72 According to his secret autobiography, he had a dream vision of Tāranātha who bestowed on him the Kālacakra initiation, after which he composed a guru-yoga text on Dol-po-pa; see Stearns 1999, 77, n. 136; 215.

73 As we have seen in the introduction to this chapter, this prayer includes prostrating to the Three Jewels, confessing negative actions, making offerings, rejoicing in the virtue of others, requesting the buddhas to turn the wheel of Dharma, beseeching them not to pass into nirvana, and dedicating the merit for the liberation of all sentient beings.

Chapter Five: Tantric Transfer in Sukhāvatī

1 Gyatso 1993, 101, n. 9.

2 Davidson explains that by the late eighth century CE, even the "most extreme Vajrayāna scriptures, the *yōgīṇī* tantras, had begun to be integrated into the ritual curricula in the great monastic centers of North and Central India" (2002b, 338).

3 For Davidson, the "primary domains of secrecy were meditative ideology and ritual performance rather than philosophical or doctrinal development, even while the tantras made significant contributions to the latter." He infers that secrecy may have been a "powerful psychological tool for group integration and an equally powerful method of proselytization" (2009b, 60, 63).

4 Davidson 2002b, 116–117.

5 For an informative discussion on how the Kanjur was conceived as an open canon by different Tibetan Buddhist schools, see Mayer 1996, 14–21. Schaeffer and van der Kujip (2009, 10) bring forth evidence that suggest that the designations Kanjur/Tanjur date from the second half of the thirteenth century. In the imperial *Phangthangma Catalogue* we see that a growing body of Buddhist

literature was allocated across categories reserved only for commentaries, i.e., *bstan-bcos, 'grel-ba, bstan-bcos kyi ṭīkā,* and *ṭīkā.*

6 The *mChod pa'i sprin shes bya ba'i gzungs* (Skt. *Pūjāmegha-nāma-dhāraṇī*) is not listed in the *Phangthangma Catalogue* (at least not by the same title). It is preserved in the Kanjur (D 538) and its colophon names the translators Śilendrabodhi, Jinamitra, Ye-shes De, and others. It concludes: *'di nas shi 'phos nas yang 'jig rten gyi khams bde ba can du skye bar 'gyur te.* There are other works that promote similar aspirations, such as the *bDe ldan snying po gzhungs* (D 680), which concludes: *di nas shi 'phos nas kyang bde ldan gyi 'jig rten du skye bar 'gyur ro.* Another work of this kind is the *Yongs su bsngo ba'i rgyal po las byung ba'i bde smon* (D 810).

7 The *'Phags pa yon tan bsngags pa dpag tu med pa zhes bya ba'i gzungs* (Skt. *Ārya-aparimitāguṇā-muśaṁsā-nāma-dhāraṇī*) is listed in the *rGyud* and *gZhungs* sections (D 678 and D 857). There are no translators listed for this text, which is also recorded in Bu-ston's *Collected Works* (no. 290).

8 See the *Dhāraṇī-Mantra of Amitābha (sNang ba mtha' yas kyi gzungs sngags;* D 676 and D 870) and the *Recollection of Amitābha (sNang ba mtha' yas rjes su dran pa;* D 677 and D 873). The latter is a three-line mantra without a Sanskrit title. Bu-ston's *Collected Works,* vol. Ma (Chandra 1965) lists forty-one genealogies of the transmission of various tantric traditions along with 355 mantras culled from several tantras. Text nos. 24, 229, 230, 231, 242, and 290 are related to Amitābha.

9 The *'Phags pa tshe dang ye shes dpag tu med pa'i snying po shes bya ba'i gzungs* (Skt. *Ārya-parimitāyur-jñāna-hṛdaya-nāma-dhāraṇī*) is preserved in the Tibetan Tripiṭaka and dates from the New Translation period. It is listed in the *gZhungs* (D 856) and *rGyud* (D 675) sections, translated by Puṇyasambhava and Pa-tshab Nyi-ma grags. It is also recorded in Bu-ston's *Collected Works* (no. 231). A text with a similar title, *'Phags pa tshe dpag tu med pa'i snying po shes bya ba'i gzungs* (36 sl.), is located in the PT under the category "Miscellaneous Dhāraṇī of Various Sizes" (§XV, no. 365).

10 Halkias 2004, 77–79.

11 Payne 1997, 24.

12 See Chapter Two. The Tibetan translations do not seem to distinguish between Amitāyus (Tshe-dpag-med) and Aparimitāyus (Tshe-dpag-tu-med-pa). Similarly, the Chinese translators seem to render phonetically both Amitāyus and Aparimitāyus as Amitou; see Payne 2007, 17.

13 In light of the Tibetan and Chinese material, we could reexamine Schopen's claim that there is "no evidence, either internal or external . . . that would vaguely suggest" (1977, 200) a connection between Aparimitāyus and Amitābha.

14 A Tanjur text, the *Aparimitāyus Maṇḍala Rituals* (*Aparimitāyur-jñāna-maṇḍala-vidhi-nāma*) unequivocally states that Amitāyus and Aparimitāyus are one deity in essence. This identification does not exclude divergences in their respective

iconographic depictions and functions; compare for example Tibetan depictions of Amitāyus and Amitābha, who are nevertheless representations of a single buddha. Tucci similarly notes, "The cult of Ts'e dpag med, as a distinct entity goes back to Indian masters, namely to Ti p'u (Te p'u) who taught its revelation to Ras c'uṅ grags pa, who in his turn spread his worship in Tibet. This Ts'e dpag med is called Ts'e daṅ ye öes dpag med, 'infinite life and gnosis,' the theological opinions of the schools are reflected upon him" (1949, 349).

15 The list of translators is in agreement with the Peking edition. Tibetan text, Narthang Tanjur, TBRC (W227043320, p. 220): *byang chub sems dpa' dze ta ri dgra las rnam par rgyal bas mdzad pa'o/ 'di'i rgyud pa ni tshe dpag med / grub pa brnyes pa'i snying po zhabs / dze ta ri dgra las rnam par rgyal ba / rdo rje gdan pa che chung gnyis / pa ri lo tsā ba / mchims brtson 'grus seng ge / rgya nag phug pa / dbus pa sangs rgyas 'du ma / bla ma dge bsdings pa / bla ma bsam gtan bzang po'o.*

16 Tibetan text, Narthang Tanjur, TBRC (W227043297, p. 501): *sbyin bsreg las kyi 'bras 'byin 'di // mkha' 'gro grub pa'i rgyal mos b[r]tsams // dge ba 'di yis 'gro ba kun // tshe dpag med pa rnyed 'gyur shog // rgya gar gyi mkhan po wa la tsaṇḍa bla ma dang / lo tsā ba glan dar ma tshul khrims kyis bsgyur ba'o.*

17 Tibetan text, Narthang Tanjur, TBRC (W227043321, p. 137): *slob dpon dze ta ri dgra las rnam par rgyal pas / bram ze nam mkha' dbyangs kyi bu'i ched du mdzad pa rdzogs so // rgya gar gyi mkhan po shri ma dzu dang lo tsā ba lce dga' ba'i dpal gyis bsgyur pa'o.* Jetāri, also Jitāri, or Guhyajitāri (Dgra-las-rnam-rgyal or Dgra-las-rgyal-ba-gsang-ba) may have been a native of Bengal and teacher of Atiśa. He is the instigator of a major Amitāyus lineage in Tibet, for there are many works attributed to him including: the *Nine-deity Maṇḍala of Amitāyus according to the System Transmitted by Ācārya Jetāri* (*Tshe dpag med lha dgu slob dpon dze ta ri'i lugs kyi dkyil 'khor*) located in the Rgyud sde kun btus (vol. 2, 113–210); the *Ritual Text of Abhiseka of Long Life* (*Tshe chog bdud rtsi'i chu gter*) in the Tāranātha's *Collected Works* (vol. 12, 793-832); the *Contemplation of Amitāyus according to Jetāri tradition* (*Tshe dpag me dze tā ri'i lugs kyi bsgom bzlas tshe dpal ye shes kun 'grub*) in Kun-dga' blo-gros' *Collected Works* (vol. 4, 107–112); and a *Ritual Text for the Abhiṣeka of Long Life according to Jetāri* (*Chi bslu'i zur 'debs*) in the *Collected Works* of Ngag-dbang bstan-'dzin 'phrin-las, 749–758.

18 Tibetan text, Narthang Tanjur, TBRC (W22704–3297, p. 458): *bcom ldan 'das tshe dang ye shes dpag tu med pa zhes bya ba'i sgrub thabs // ye shes kyi mkha' 'gro ma grub pa'i rgyal mos mdzad pa rdzogs so.*

19 Tibetan text, Narthang Tanjur, vol. 70, TBRC (W22704–3321, p. 484): *slob dpon mkhas pa dze ta ri dgra las rnam par rgyal bas mdzad pa rdzogs so // rgya gar gyi paṇḍi ta / 'jam dpa'i dbyangs dang / lo tsā ba lce dga'i ba'i dpal gyi bsgyur ba'o.*

20 Tibetan text, Narthang Tanjur edition, p. 478, TBRC (W22704–3297–462): *bcom ldan 'das mgon po tshe dang ye shes dpag tu med pa'i dbang bzhi bskur ba'i cho ga'i las khrigs 'chi med ye shes bdud rtsi'i bum pa zhes bya ba / ye shes kyi mkha' 'gro ma grub pa'i rgyal mos mdzad pa rdzogs so.*

21 Tibetan text, Narthang Tanjur edition, p. 484, TBRC (W22704-3297-488): *bcom ldan 'das tshe dpag tu med pa la phyag 'tshal lo // rang bzhin tshe dpag med pa'i sku.*

22 Tibetan text, Narthang Tanjur edition, p. 498, TBRC (W22704-3297-488): *bcom ldan 'das mgon po tshe dpag tu med pa'i dkyil 'khor gyi cho ga bzang po yongs bzung zhes bya ba rdzogs so // rgya gar gyi paṇḍi ta zla ba bzang po dang / bod kyi lo tsā ba glan dar ma tshul khrims kyis bsgyur zhing zhus te dag par byas so.* There is an identical version in the Narthang Tanjur, vol. 84, ff. 204r–211r (pp. 407–421) with the same colophon.

23 *Aparimitāyur-jñāna-abhiṣeka-vidhi* (TOH tome 142, no. 6303, kha 1–15). See also dKon-mchog 'jigs-med dbang-po's (1728–1791) instructions on Amitāyus long-life empowerment rituals based on the lineage of Ma-gcig grub-pa'i-rgyal-mo (NAR no. 2189, vol. 29, Ta 1–18b). There are several important ritual cycles focusing on longevity rites attributed to her lineage, such as (in short) the *Amitāyus System based on Grub-pa'i-rgyal-mo* (*Grub pa'i rgyal mo'i lugs kyi tshe dpag med lha gcig bum gcig gi byin rlabs dbang bskur gyi cho ga 'chi med bdud rtsi'i grol thigs*), in 'Jam-mgon kong-sprul blo-gros mtha'-yas, *Bka' brgyud sngags mdzod* (vol. 1, 213–240); *Amitāyus Deity-yoga based on Grub-pa'i-rgyal-mo* (*Tshe dpags med grub rgyal lugs kyi bskyed rdzogs zab khrid*), in 'Jam-mgon kong-sprul blo-gros mtha'-yas, *Rgya chen bka' mdzod* (vol. 5, 543–595); *Amitāyus System of Rituals and Empowerments based on Grub-pa'i-rgyal-mo* (*Ma gcig grub pa'i rgyal mo'i lugs kyi tshe dpag med kyi dbang chog*), in Mkhyen-brtse'i dbang-po, *Sgrub thabs kun btus* (vol. 1, 327–362); *Aparimitāyus Oral Instructions for Meditation by Grub-pa'i rgyal-mo* (*Tshe dang ye shes dpag tu med pa'i khrid dmigs grub pa'i rgyal mo'i zhal lung*), in Kun-dga' grol-mchog, *Gsung thor bu* (vol. 2.); among several other works in the collected works of Kun-gzigs chos-kyi-snang-ba (1768-1822), Ngag-dbang blo-bzang bstan-pa'i rgyal-mtshan (1770-1845), and others.

24 Mullin 1986, 149–172. The Fifth Dalai Lama is also the author of an Amitāyus longevity *sādhana*, the *'Chi med dwangs ma chu 'dren,* said to have been revealed as a pure-vision Treasure (*dagsnang gter*); see Thondup 1986, 90. There are many Amitāyus practices in the Treasure tradition; see the *Rin chen gter mdzod,* vols. 29–32.

25 For example, the *Tshe lha rnam gsum gyi mngon rtogs* by the dGe-lugs-pa master Gung-thang dkon-mchog bstan-pa'i-sgron-me (1726–1823 or 1824) relies on the visualization of Amitāyus, Uṣṇīṣavijayā, and Tārā (NAR no. 2313, vol. 39a, ja 1–2b).

26 For more on the *zhabs-brtan* genre, see Cabezón 1996, 344–357. Long-life *sādhanas* are not exclusive to Amitāyus. They are found in association with other deities, including Tārā, the Medicine Buddha, Cakrasaṃvara, and so on. An innovative Amitāyus long-life *sādhana,* the *Light Rays of the Red Drum: Amitāyus Life-extending Practices,* follows a fourfold esoteric schematic common to many genres, including hagiographies—the outer *sādhana* (*phyi-sgrub*) of Amitāyus (ka 11–12), the inner *sādhana* (*nang-sgrub*) (ka 12–13), the secret

sādhana (*gsang-sgrub*) (ka 13), and the innermost secret *sādhana* (*yang gsang-sgrub*) of Amitāyus (ka 13–14); *Tshe dpag med kyi rgyud tshe chen 'od zer rnga dmar zhes bya ba* (NC vol. 1, ka 5–14).

27 The *bCud len gyi ril bu bsgrub nas spyod tshul* by Dharmabhadra (1772–1951) (TOH tome 142, no. 6305, Kha 1–4). Among Dharmabhadra's works there is an abridged explanation of the *Aparimitāyur-jnāna-sādhana* with the aim of obtaining long life; see *Tshe sgrub thun mong dang thun mong ma yin pa zab gnad can 'khyer bde kun phan* (TOH tome 142, no. 6302, kha 1–3). Walter writes that the interpretation of *rasāyana* (*bcud-len*) rests on "the 'extraction of the essence' of elements, spiritual beings, etc., outlined in early tantric materials, such as the sixth- or seventh-century Bhūtaḍāmara tantra, and later elaborated upon" (2003, 23). Alchemical practices for extracting vital essences into pills (*bcud-len gyi ril-bu*) may supplicate the Medicine Buddha or Cakrasaṃvara; see for example dByangs-can grub-pa'i-rdo-rje, Dharmabhadra's disciple, describing a method for empowering longevity pills by propitiating Srīcakrasaṃvaraśukla (TOH tome 148, no. 6449, kha 1–4).

28 Skorupski 2001, 137.

29 For a historical discussion concerning early Pāli references to the intermediate state (*antarābhava*) and later developments in Indian, Tibetan Buddhist, and Bön traditions, see Blezer 1997.

30 Liberation through the sense of hearing is one of six kinds of liberation. The other five are usually given as liberation through wearing blessed vestments, seeing and remembering sacred items, and tasting and touching sacred substances. For English translations of the *Bar do thos grol*, see Evans-Wentz 1927; Freemantle and Trungpa 1987. Lopez 1998 offers an engaging discussion of its reception in the West. The long and intricate history of this text has been discussed in Cuevas 2003.

31 For Germano (1997, 458), the fullest development of the concept of the intermediate state (*bar-do*) finds expression in the *Seminal Heart* (*sNying thig*), a series of rNying-ma works composed from the eleventh to fourteenth centuries.

32 Germano 1997, 458.

33 Mullin 1986, 157.

34 Mullin 1986, 163.

35 For a detailed study of the practice of *phowa*, see the last sections of this chapter. An example of guru-yoga practices centered on Sukhāvatī is the *Excellent Path of Sukhāvatī: Guru-Yoga based on Amitābha* (*sNang ba mtha' yas la brten pa'i bla ma'i rnal 'byor bde chen lam bzang*; DM 1, 253–258), composed by the bKa'-brgyud master 'Jam-dbyangs mkhyen-brtse 'od-zer (1896–1945). See also *Relying on Buddha Amitābha: Guru Yoga on the Three Bodies* (*Sangs rgyas snang ba mtha' la bsten pa'i sku gsum bla ma'i rnal 'byor*; DM 1, 277–278). For guru-yoga meditations on the Amitāyus deity see dByangs-can dga'i-ba'i-blo-gros' collection of

guru-yoga *vidhis*, in which the teacher is systematically meditated upon in the form of Amitāyurjñāna (TOH tome 154, no. 6590, kha 1–6); Blo-bzang thub-bstan chos-kyi-nyi-ma's (the sixth Paṇ-chen) guru-yoga instructions for relying on one's own Lama, Amitāyus, and Kurukulle (NAR no. 1743, vol. 1, kha 1–7b); and guru-yoga instructions centered on Amitāyus (NAR no. 1745, vol. 1, kha 1–4a).

36 Zabs-dkar 1997, 488.

37 Mullin 1986, 194–195.

38 *rMi lam bzung ba'i bde smon* (GB vol. Ga, ldeb 1, fol. 65–66). See also Karma chags-med's *rMi lam du bde chen zhing mjal thabs* (NCG text 8, fol. 1b–3a).

39 See Chapter Four. Karma chags-med is the author of several works focusing on Buddha Amitābha and Sukhāvatī, including 1) Sukhāvatī, Amitābha, and Amitāyus empowerments, *bDe chen zhing sgrub* (GB vol. Ga, ldeb 17, fol. 239–272), *gNam chos bde chen zhing sgrub kyi dbang khrigs chags su bkod pa* (GB vol. Ga, ldeb 12, fol. 273–296), and *gNam chos snang mtha' tshe dbang* (GB vol. Ga, ldeb 12, fol. 273–296); 2) transmissions of the new Sukhāvatī deities, *bDe ba can gyi zhing bkod gsar pa'i lha ngo sprad pa bsdus pa* (GB vol.Ga, ldeb 5, fol. 365–374); 3) a Pure Land *sādhana, gNam chos thugs kyi gter kha snyan brgyud zab mo'i skor las: bDe chen zhing gi sgrub thabs zab mo* (GB vol. Ga, ldeb 5, fol. 166–174); and 4) prayers to the protectors of the Sukhāvatī teachings, *Zhing skyong gi bde smon* (GB vol. ji, ldeb 1, fol. 549–550).

40 Kapstein 2004, 49, n. 63.

41 The conflation of these terms is noticeable in the literature of the rNying-ma and bKa'-brgyud schools, and it is common in the fourteenth-century work by Nyi-zla sangs-rgyas and in the seventeenth-century cycle, the *bDe chen zhing sgrub,* both of which will be examined in the following sections. In their study of the *Phur pa Myang 'das,* Cantwell and Mayer identified a similar scribal confusion between *can* and *chen* in other compounds too, such as *skal-chen* for *skal-can,* and *sdig-chen* for *sdig-can* (private correspondence, 2006).

42 A text in the *rGyud* section of the Tanjur refers to "great bliss" (*bde-ba chen-po*) in terms of the "generation" (*bskyed-rim*) and "completion" (*rdzogs-rim*) stages of the secret mantra practice (*gsang-sngags kyi tshul*); see the *Mahāsukha-prakāśa* (*bDe ba chen gsal ba;* D 2239), translated by Avadhūtapāda Śrī Advaya-vajra (gNyis-su med-pa'i-rdo-rje), Vajrapāṇi, and rMa-ban. Other Vajrayāna texts include the *Mahāsukhāmṛtaprabhā-nāma* (*bDe ba chen po'i bdud rtsi'i 'od ces bya ba;* D 1343) by Yes-shes rin-po-che (Śrī Jñānaratna), the *Mahāsukha-mudropadeśa-nāma* (*bDe ba chen po phyag rgya'i man ngag shes bya ba;* K 4767), and the *Mahāsukha-sādhana* (*bDe ba chen po'i sgrub thabs;* K 5118).

43 In tantric physiology there are five main "circuits" (*rtsa-'khor*) intercepting the central channel that runs horizontally in the physical body: the circuit of great bliss at the crown of the head with thirty-two petals, or subtle channels emanating outwardly from the center; the circuit of enjoyment at the throat,

with sixteen petals; the circuit of phenomena at the heart, with eight petals; the circuit of emanation at the navel, with sixty-four petals; and the circuit of sustaining bliss at the secret region, with thirty-two petals; see Lati Rinbochay and Hopkins 1979, 65.

44 For the relation between the Mother Tantras and the yoga of inner fire, see Stoddard 1999. For a discussion of the inner fire meditation, see Bentor 1995; Evans-Wentz 1935.

45 This practice is discussed in Davidson 2005, 37. In the biography of the *mahāsiddha* Babhala the technique is described thus: "In the lotus *maṇḍala* (vagina) of your partner a superior, skillful consort, mingle your white seed (semen) with her ocean of red seed. Then absorb, raise and diffuse the elixir and your ecstasy will never end. Then to raise the pleasure beyond pleasure, visualize it inseparable from emptiness" (Dowman 1985, 216).

46 Gyatso 1999, 119. These states are the result of the successful practice of four Mahāmudrā yogas (*phyag-chen rnal-'byor bzhi*) namely: single-pointed concentration on the nature of mind (*rtse-gcig ma'i rnal-'byor*); freedom from conceptual elaboration (*spros-bral gyi rnal-'byor*); the yoga of one taste between mind and its forms (*ro-gcig gi rnal-'byor*); and the yoga of no more meditation (*sgom-med kyi rnal-'byor*).

47 Kapstein 2000, 9.

48 In her study on meditative experiences in Tibetan Buddhism, Gyatso encapsulates that "in order for the realization of the empty nature of one's bliss to take place, one needs to have some bliss, and have it in focus" (1999, 122).

49 For studies conducted in Nepal, see Mumford 1990; for a survey of rites in the Nubri valley, see Childs 2004; for Newari Buddhism, see Lewis 1996, 2004. For a study of *phowa* ceremonies to Sukhāvatī in Ladakh, see Brauen-Dolma 1982.

50 Mei notes that mind-transference is a very important aspect of Tibetan funeral rites that "has never received the same attention either among ordinary readers or in the scholarly circles. Even the fundamental question like the developmental history of *'pho-ba* practice remains regrettably unknown" (2004, 47). Mei's 2009 doctoral study provides an informative study of the origins and development of *phowa* texts and practices in the bKa'-brgyud school. While the goal of *sādhanas* may be mundane (Cozort 1996, 334), the aim of *phowa sādhanas* is the attainment of buddhahood in the shortest time possible.

51 For the great Buddhist teacher sGam-po-pa (1079–1153), *phowa* is a technique to arrive at enlightenment without meditation; see Guenther 1963, 197. This characterization of *phowa* is repeated in Nyi-zla sangs-rgyas' *'Pho-ba 'Jag tshug ma*.

52 Brauen-Dolma (1985) interprets the popularity of *phowa* among Tibetan refugees in Switzerland as the result of a crisis of millenarianism. However, her assessment should be read cautiously against a traditional context. Although she may be right to deduce a case of millenarianism in the search for

"hidden lands" (*sbas-yul*) that resemble Amitābha's Pure Land, this is clearly not the case with Tibetan followers of *phowa* in Switzerland. As much as in Tibet as elsewhere, Tibetans would tend to follow the public teachings of a charismatic Buddhist master.

53 Yeshe Thubten 1991, 1.

54 Cozort (1986, 65) explains that during the "perfection stage" one is transformed into the deity one has visualized during the "generation stage," and arises in a body made of subtle wind and mind (illusory body). During the complete dissolution of the winds into the central channel and into the seminal heart-drop, the meditator experiences an irreversible union of bliss and emptiness and overcomes all obscurations to liberation and omniscience.

55 *Ye shes mkha' 'gro'i sgrub thabs 'pho ba bka bsgo bcas;* TBRC (W 488). See also *'Pho khrid kyi rtsa tshig brtag pa brgyad pa'i rab byed;* TBRC (W 569) and its commentary, the *rNam shes gong du'pho ba'i rgya cher bshad pa;* TBRC (W 5570).

56 Five texts are found in his *mGon po 'od dpag med la brten pa'i 'pho khrid sogs 'pho khrid kyi skor dag zhing du mar bgrod pa'i myur lam* (NAR no. 2285, vol. 38, ca 1–12a): 1) *mGon po 'od dpag med la brten pa'i pho ba'i nyams len mdor bsdus* (1b–5a), 2) *gShin po la 'pho ba dang bsngo ba byed tshul dmigs kyis bkar ba* (7a–7b), 3) *mGon po 'od dpag med kyi thugs kar 'phos pa'i dmigs pa* (7b–9a), 4) *'Jam dbyang kun gzigs la brten pa'i 'pho ba* (9a–10a), 5) *'Phags pa thugs rje chen po dang 'brel ba'i 'pho ba byed tshul* (10a–12a).

57 Result-oriented classifications of *phowa* are briefly discussed in Evans-Wentz 1935, 246–247; Guenther 1963, 198–199.

58 Mei 2004, 49–50.

59 Skorupski 2001, 145–146. Rang-byung rdo-rje (1284–1339) offers an alternate scheme. He divides transference techniques into those that do not require a foundation or a base (*rten-med du 'pho-ba*) and those requiring a physical support or body (*rten-can du 'pho-ba*). The first division includes transference in luminosity (*'od-gsal la 'pho-ba*), also known as *dharmakāya phowa;* in an illusory body (*sgyu-lus la 'pho-ba*), *saṃbhogakāya phowa;* and in the body of a deity (*lha-sku la 'pho-ba*), *nirmāṇakāya phowa;* see Mei 2009, 70.

60 Mei 2009, 185. Pure Land prayers for animals are not uncommon. Zabs-dkar's hagiography contains the following aspiration: "To the west is the Buddha-field called Blissful Realm. By the power of whatever merit I possess, may my faithful friend, the duck who was killed today, not be reborn within samsara, but be reborn in the Blissful Realm" (1997, 165).

61 Mei (2009, 81–87) examines Niguma's and Sukhasiddhī's *Six Yogas* in the Shangs-pa bKa'-brgyud school.

62 There exist alternate listings that may include the yoga of entering a corpse (*'pho-ba grong-'jug*) and the yoga of the state of union (*zung-'jug*).

63 It is part of the *Ārya-Catuṣpīṭha-tantra;* see Lauf 1975, 9. For the history of this practice, see Evans-Wentz 1935, 254–259. Milarepa's query concerning the practice of forceful projection inspired Marpa to search for explanatory treatises on the subject among his Indian manuscripts. Finding none, he returned to India to obtain more scriptures; see Douglas and White 1976, 15.

64 Evans-Wentz 1935, 256.

65 Skorupski 2001, 146. The Bön tradition continued the transmission of this practice, but according to my informant Geshe Gelek Jinpa, it is not known if it is still practiced. For an account of this practice in the oral traditions of Lubra, see Ramble 1983, 278.

66 TBRC P 1004. For example, Sangs-rgyas gling-pa's (1340–1396) *'Da 'ka 'chi drod 'pho ba;* see Mei 2004.

67 Deities may include Padmasambhava, Avalokiteśvara, Vajrayoginī, Maitreya, Yamāntaka Vajradhara, Samantabhadra, and Vairocana; see Mullin 1997, 175–178; Yeshe 1991, 1; Mei 2004, 49, 58; Skorupski 2001, 146.

68 Lopez explains that the process of death may occur in a series of eight stages of dissolution where consciousness "gradually retreats from the senses toward the heart and the physical elements of earth, water, fire, and wind lose the capacity to serve as the physical basis for consciousness" (1997, 443). Different signs and stages of death are recorded in Tibetan medical literature (Clifford 1984, 108–114); in religious texts (Fremantle and Trungpa 1987; Germano 1997, 461–466); and in tantric cycles such as the *Guhyasamāja* (Lati Rinbochay and Hopkins 1979).

69 Concerning the physical effects of *phowa,* Guenther states that "after the mantras *hik* and *ka* have been uttered twenty-one times the practice is discontinued for the day and resumed on each following day until lymph or blood appears at the fontanel opening. . . . The oozing of blood or lymph at the fontanel opening is a phenomenon as yet unexplained by the medical sciences, though well attested by all who have performed this practice. Another peculiar phenomenon is that, when a competent Guru imparts this instruction to his disciple, the region of the fontanel opening becomes highly sensitive to touch and remains so for some time. Moreover, when after the instruction he touches the region with Kusagrass, symbolically representing the opening of the passage to the ultimate, the distinct sensation of being pierced from top to bottom is created" (1963, 201). For two scientific studies on the mind-transference technique, see Motoyama 1987; Fujiki 1987.

70 Mei 2009, 144–145.

71 Cornu 1997, 85. Karmay writes that the concepts of *bla* and *bla-bslu* (ransoming the soul) derive from early Tibetan indigenous beliefs. He writes that the *bla* is "conceived of as a support upon which the physiological and intellectual aspects of life rest. It is thus considered the most important of the three

physiological principles, which also include 'respiratory breath' (*dbugs*) and 'vital force' (*srog*). 'Vital force' is as essential as the *bla*, but 'respiratory breath' is perishable and therefore temporary in comparison with the *bla*. As life principle the *bla* pervades all parts of the body, but it depends upon 'respiratory breath' and cannot function without it" (1998, 311).

72 Chagmé 2000, 180. Arguably, the controversial Vajrayana practice of ritual killing (*sgrol-ba*) may constitute an exception to this transgression, since it is done for the purpose of liberating a being into the buddha fields; see Cantwell 1997, 111.

73 Tucci 1949, 365.

74 Mei (2009, 111) suggests that the *'Da' ka 'chi brod* may be chronologically earlier than Nyi-zla sangs-rgyas' *Standing Blade of Grass.*

75 The full title of Nyi-zla sangs-rgyas' work is *Zab lam 'pho ba'i gdams pa 'jag tshugs ma'i lo rgyus gdams dag khrid yig dang bcas pa; see Rin chen gter mdzod* (vol. 32, pp. 547–599). "Standing grass" refers to the *kuśa* grass traditionally used to test the opening induced at the fontanel after a successful practice. Mei (2009, 1) reports an eyewitness account of this ritual in Taipei in 1997 during a *phowa* ceremony performed by a lama of the Karma bKa'-brgyud tradition. .

76 According to Kapstein (1998, 95–97), the ninth 'Bri-gung abbot, rDo-rje rgyal-po (1283 or 1284–1350 or 1351), is said to have opened the pilgrimage sites of gTer-sgrom in 1308. The region of gTer-sgrom is located in a side valley northeast of Lhasa, near the monastery and sky-burial grounds of 'Bri-gung-mthil, and it is famous for its mineral hot springs, caves, hermitages, and other distinguishing landmarks. It is said that Padmasamhava and his tantric consort Ye-shes mtsho-rgyal meditated in gTer-sgrom and concealed several Treasure texts there. Some of these were rediscovered in later centuries by the Treasure discoverers rDo-rje gling-pa (1346–1405) and 'Bri-gung Rin-chen phuntshogs (1509–1557), among others.

77 Smith 2001, 238; 114; 328, n. 803. 'Jig-rten-mgon-po's skepticism toward some rNying-ma doctrines contributed to a short-lived tension between the two schools. The 'Bri-gung abbot rDo-rje rgyal-po endorsed the performance of ritual dances of the Vajrakīla cycle, while a century later a devoted adherent of Padmasambhava, the famous 'Bri-gung Treasure finder Rin-chen phuntshogs, integrated elements of the bKa'-brgyud teachings with the rituals and meditational practices of the rNying-ma school; see Kapstein 1998, 97–98.

78 *Myur lam 'pho ba'i gdams pa 'jag tshugs ma'i khrid yig padma can bgrod pa'i pho nya;* Rig-pa 'dzin-pa chen-po chos-kyi-grags-pa's *gSung-'bum* (vol. XIII, 647–670). See also Gu-ru bkra-shis' *Chos 'byung* (1990).

79 *mTsho maṇḍala nag-po* is located in Dwags-po.

80 The three commentaries of the *Zab lam 'pho ba'i gdams pa 'jag tshugs ma'i lo rgyus gdams dag khrid yig dang bcas pa* are as follows: *Myur lam 'pho ba'i rnal 'byor*

dpal 'brug pa'i nyams bzhes 'jag tshugs ma by the bKa'-brgyud Master Yar-'phel dbang-po (1632–1704); Chos-kyi-grags-pa's *Myur lam 'pho ba'i gdams pa 'jag tshugs ma'i khrid yig padma can bgrod pa'i pho nya,* and *Ma bsgom par 'tshang rgya ba'i 'pho ba'i gdams pa mdor bsdus pa 'jag tshugs ma;* see Rig-pa 'dzin-pa chen-po chos-kyi-grags-pa's *gSung-'bum* (vol. XIII, 671–679).

81 See ff 558–559; 572–573; 595–596. The *phowa* lineage prayer is also found in Chos-kyi-grags-pa's *Myur lam 'pho ba'i gdams pa 'jag tshugs ma'i khrid yig padma can bgrod pa'i pho nya* (ff 654–657) and *Ma bsgom par 'tshang rgya ba'i 'pho ba'i gdams pa mdor bsdus pa 'jag tshugs ma* (ff 674–675).

Chapter Six: The Celestial Treasures of Buddha Amitābha

1 Doctor 2005, 17. Often the division between "old" and "revealed" lineages is blurred. Gyatso (1993, 101, n. 9) notes that the scriptural collection of the "transmitted precepts" contains ritual and liturgical sources associated with several canonical texts, which are primarily but not exclusively tantric, while segments of it "involve Treasure-like moments of concealment and disclosure." There are several important studies on this rather complex body of revealed texts in the Treasure traditions. For pertinent discussions and references to secondary literature, see Martin 2001; Thondup 1986; Mayer 1994, 1996; Gyatso 1998.

2 Smith 2001, 15. For Prats the *gter-ma* tradition was not a Buddhist novelty: was not a Buddhist novelty. According to a Bön-po work, the *bStan rtsis* of Nyi-ma-bstan-'dzin, "the first treasures to be rediscovered were some Bon-po texts brought to light by three Nepalese ācārya in 913 which were said to have been hidden during the reign of Gri-gum-btsan-po" (1980, 256, n. 5).

3 Kapstein 2000, 122. Martin (2001, 156–157) examines Sa-skya Paṇḍi-ta's critique of the Treasure tradition. For an eighteenth-century debate over apocryphal traditions in Tibet, see Davidson 2005, 210–243. An informative summary on the status of Treasure literature by modern and traditional Tibetanists is found in Gyatso 1993, 103, n. 14.

4 For a discussion, see Mayer 1996.

5 Davidson 2005, 210–224.

6 Doctor 2005, 20–21. According to the rNying-ma school, Nyang-ral nyi-ma 'od-zer was one of the Five Treasure Kings, who is said to have died going to Sukāvatī with Amitābha's seed syllable *Hrī;* see Dudjom Rinpoche 1991, 754–755.

7 The *gter-tsheg* orthographical markers are used for designating Treasure texts within a cycle of teachings, see Gyatso 1993, 110.

8 Gyatso 1993, 99–100.

9 Doctor 2005, 35.

10 Pure Vision scriptures are commonly included in Treasure literature despite some major conceptual differences between the two. All Buddhist schools in

Tibet admit (to an extent) sacred literature derived from non-human/visionary sources, although this is most conspicuous in the rNying-ma and Bön schools.

11 Gyatso 1997, 97. Thondup (1986, 90), quoting mKhyen-brtse'i-dbang-po (1820–1892), lists three kinds of Pure Vision treasures: those originating from buddhas, sages, and deities; those derived from one's meditative experiences; and those that come from dreams.

12 Meditative techniques utilizing vision abound in rNying-ma scriptures and early Bön sources. They form an essential part in the sNying-thig movement of the rDzogs-chen tradition, and for Davidson (2005, 501, n. 34) they draw their hermeneutic impetus from the context of the Prajñāpāramitā literature. Gyatso explains that "these highly esoteric experiences are believed to dawn in a series of visions by virtue of which ground awareness makes itself apparent to the advanced practitioner as a directly perceived reality.... Finally all deluded manifestations subside forever, replaced by a self-conscious manifestation of a buddha-body. This manifestation, closely reminiscent of the buddhology of a Mahāyāna work like *Ratnagotravibhāga*, produces countless apparitions and displays, like a moon reflected in the water, that work to teach others" (1999, 130–131).

13 Schwieger 1998, 4.

14 Schwieger 1988, 3–5.

15 Mayer 1996, 70–90. The visionary adaptation of Buddhism in Tibet and the Himalayas inspired scholars such as Aris (1988, 59) to explore the relationship between Tibetan Buddhism and shamanism, describing the Treasure discover Padma gling-pa (1450–1521) as a wonder-working "Buddhist-shaman."

16 'Jam-mgon kong-sprul lists Karma chags-med as a discoverer of pure-vision; Treasures; Thondup 1986, 198. There is a wide range of scriptures in the Celestial Treasures: 1) mortuary rites (*byang-chog*); 2) various ritual offerings (*bsang, chab-gtor, bum-gter*); 3) tantric empowerments for long life (*tshe-dbang*), health (*sman-lha-dbang*), and wealth (*nor-dbang*); 4) thread-cross rituals and amulets (*mdos, srung-ba*); 5) propitiations and supplications of protectors and guardians (*chos-skyong, zhing-skyong, gter-srung*), demons (*btsan, gnod-sbyin, bdud*), high heaven spirits (*lha*), mountain deities (*spom-ri, thang-lha*), *nāgas* (*klu*), and earth spirits (*sa-bdag*); 6) divination and astrology (*rde'u dkar-mo, spar-kha, rtsis*); 7) Vajrayana preliminary practices (*sngon-'gro*); 8) large liturgical cycles and specific tantric meditation techniques (*rmi-lam, 'pho-ba, gtum-mo, phur-pa, gcod*) and tantric commentaries (*rgyud-'grel*); among others.

17 Thondup 1986, 88–90. Schwieger (1998, 3–4) notes that a Treasure text by Chos-rgya rdo-rje (1789–1859) questions the rigidity of these distinctions in that it claims to be simultaneously an "earth-treasure," a "mind-treasure," and a "space-treasure."

18 Stories concerning texts falling from the sky (*gnam-mkha' nas glegs-bam bab*)

go back to early Tibet and King lHa-tho-tho-ri snyan-btsan. According to legends, he received Buddhist texts and sacred objects that had fallen from the sky. Richardson (1998, 74–81) introduces an incomplete eighth-century Dunhuang text (no. 370) said to have fallen from the sky (*gnam babs kyi dar ma bam po gcig go*).

19 Mi-'gyur rdo-rje was recognized as a joint emanation of the great translator Pa-gor Vairocana and Shud-bu dpal, both disciples of Padmasambhava. For biographical details about gNam-chos mi-'gyur rdo-rje, see TBRC (P 654); Guru bkra-shis' *Chos 'byung* (pp. 624–647); *gTer ston brgya rtsa'i rnam thar* (pp. 509–512); *Kaḥ thog pa'i lo rgyus mdor bsdus* (p. 97); outer biography (*Tiṣṭuha-vajraśāstra,* NC vol. 10, 1–538), inner biography (NC vol. 11, 1–139), and secret biography (NC vol. 11, 141–457); and in Karma chags-med's biographies (*gSung-'bum,* vols. ka and ga). For references in Western scholarship, see Martin 2001, 26; Gyatso 1997, 145–153; Chagmé 1998, 7–11; 2008; Schwieger 1998, 1978; Tsering Lama 1988, 45–52; Meisezahl 1981, 195–199; Stein 1959.

20 Ten volumes of the *gnam-chos* collection were introduced by Stein in 1959. Meisezahl (1981, 1982) compiled an index to the *gnam-chos* collection by Migot in the Collège de France. Gene Smith updated the NC cycle, adding three additional volumes, 11, 12, and 13, not included in the Migot collection. Mi-'gyur rdo-rje's inner and secret biographies (*rnam-thar*) are in vol. 11; vol. 12 contains rDzogs-chen texts; and vol. 13, written in *dbu-med* script probably from sDe-dge, contains eighteen texts, mostly *sādhanas*.

21 Mi-'gyur rdo-rje died in 1667 at the age of twenty-two. According to some accounts, his rNying-ma predecessor was 'Khrul-zhig dbang-drag rgya-mtsho of the rMog-rtsa *sprul-sku* lineage. Twenty-five emanations were predicted to follow his death. Guru bkra-shis writes that even though sTag-sham nus-ldan rdo-rje (b. 1655) has been claimed as one of these twenty-five emanations, this is a slight error: *rje 'di la sprul pa'i sku nyi shu rtsa lnga 'byung bar gsung pa'i ya gyal gcig ni // ngor klu lding mkhan chen rin chen mi 'gyur rgyal mtshan yin te // mkhan chen de nyid kyi skye brgyud dang rnam thar la dpyad pas shes so // yang mkhan chen de stag sham pa'i skye ba yin zer ba ni cung zad nor ro* (p. 629). In the *gTer ston brgya rtsa'i rnam thar* (p. 512), Kong-sprul claims that a rMog-grub nam-mkha' chos-dbang was one of his succeeding incarnations and lineage holders.

22 Schwieger 1998, 7.

23 Schwieger 1998, 7.

24 *Guru bkra-shis,* pp. 625, 628.

25 That is, holding back his semen (*khams dkar-po*) and forcing the vital energy to enter into the central channel (*dbu-ma*); see Guru bkra-shis, p. 626. Tsering Lama recounts the same event without going into detail (1988, 49). Thondup writes that with a few exceptions pertaining to monks, most Treasure discoverers

must rely on the support of a physical consort (1986, 82–83). Ironically, Mi-'gyur rdo-rje's refusal to marry a *ḍākinī* is said to have been the cause of his premature death; see Meisezahl 1981, 199, n. 12.

26 The *gnam-chos* collection is also preserved in Kaḥ-thog monastery, rediscovered in 1665 by bDud-'dul rdo-rje (1615–1672).

27 In Tibetan: *gNam chos thugs kyi gter kha snyan brgyud zab mo'i skor las bde chen zhing sgrub.* I have translated *thugs-kyi-gter-kha* as "primordial treasury" even though "mind treasury" is a more literal translation, for the reason that "mind treasury" would suggest that *gnam-chos* scriptures belong to a different class of Treasures known as Mind Treasures (*dgongs-gter*).

28 For a brief account of the origins of the Celestial Treasures of Sukhāvatī, see the *gNam chos thugs kyi gter kha las bde chen zhing du 'pho ba'i gdams pa rgyas par bsgrigs pa* (NCG, text 8, 1b–3a); Kapstein 2004, 33. There are precedents in Tibetan literature of the visionary redactions of Buddhist teachings of celestial deities such as Amitābha; see the account of Thang-stong rgyal-po (1461–1485) guided by a red beam of light emanated from Amitāyus to the location of concealment in Gyatso 1997, 103.

29 Kapstein 2004, 51, n. 80. Skorupski's study (2001, 137–181) of the cremation ceremony draws from the *bDe chen zhing gi ro sreg chog ngan song gnas 'dren sdug bsngal mtsho skem gtan bde rab 'bar* (GB vol. Ga, ldeb 21, fol. 83–110; NCG text 7, 21 fol.). His section on the *phowa* liturgy is based on a partial translation of the *gNam chos thugs kyi gter kha las bDe chen zhing du 'pho ba'i gdams pa rgyas par bsgrigs pa* (GB vol. Ga, ldeb 17, fol. 133–164; NCG text 8, 23 fol.); and his translations of effigy rituals draw from the *gNam chos thugs kyi gter kha snyan brgyud zab mo'i skor las bde chen zhing sgrub gi byang chog thar lam dkar po* (GB vol. Ga, ldeb 11, fol. 175–196; NCG text 5, 12 fol.). Also in circulation are independent commentaries on the *gnam-chos* preliminary practices authored by 'Gro-'dul dpa'-po rdo-rje (1842–1924); see the *gNam chos rdzogs chen sangs rgyas lag 'chan sngon 'gro'i khrid yig bde chen lam bzang* (TBRC, W19664); *Rin chen gter mdzod* (vol. 32, 271–283). A systematic study of the scriptures in the various editions and cycles and critical editions of individual texts is beyond the scope of this work.

30 Colophon: *ces gnam chos 'od chog gi brgyud pa'i gsol 'debs nyung bsdus 'di'ang / dge slong karma chos ldan gyis bskul ngor / karma bcu bzhi pas gang shar 'phral du bris pa dge bar gyur cig.*

31 It appears that *"ma mgon lcam dral,"* in the context of the Kar-ma bKa'-brgyud tradition, refers to Protector Ber-nag-can, a form of Mahākāla, and dPal-ldan-lha-mo rang-byung rgyal-mo in union.

32 The title of this work is *rTsa gsum spyi yi sngon 'gro* (see Appendix III: 4.2, 6.2, 7.3, 8.2, 9.2). In the Lhasa edition, this text is located in the *bDe chen zhing gyi sgrub thabs 'don cha* (5.1). The colophon informs us that it was transmitted to Tulku Mi-'gyur rdo-rje by Blo-ldan mchog-sred, one of Padmasambhava's

eight manifestations. Tib. text: *zhes pa sprul sku mi 'gyur rdo rje dgung lo bcu gsum bya lo chu stod zla ba'i tshes gsum la blo ldan mchog sred kyis dngos su gsungs pa'o.* Karma chags-med writes that in 1657, Buddha Amitābha and his attendants bestowed on Mi-'gyur rdo-rje the following Pure Land texts included in *The Means of Attaining the Sukhāvatī Kṣetra* collection: 1) *bDe chen zhing gi sgrub thabs,* 2) *rMi lam dub de chen zhing mjal thabs,* 3) *sNang ba mtha' yas kyi tshe sgrub,* 4) *bDe chen zhing gig sol 'debs,* 5) *bDe chen zhing gi smon lam chen zhing gi dbang,* 6) *rMi lam gzung ba'i gsol 'debs,* 7) *rMi lam gzung ba'i zhal gdams;* see the *Phowa to Sukhāvatī* (*gNam chos thugs kyi gter kha las bde chen zhing du 'pho ba'i gdams pa rgyas par bsgrigs pa,* 1b3–3a4).

33 The text is known as *bKra shis rtags brgyad kyi dbang* (Appendix II: 4.14, 5.10, 6.8, 8.11, 9.11). The eight symbols are the right-coiled white conch shell, the precious umbrella, the victory banner, the golden fish, the Dharma wheel, the endless knot, the lotus flower, and the vase.

34 This text is an abridged version of an extended long-life empowerment that accompanies the *Mahāsukhā Kṣetra Sādhana.* Traditionally, the next highest birth in degree of merit, after buddhas, bodhisattvas, and arhats, is that of a universal monarch (*cakravartin*). According to Skorupski, "this consecration is bestowed in order to gain the state of a *cakravartin,* and to reach the precious sphere of Mahāvairocana as the king of the Dharma. The seven insignia of a monarch (*rgyal-srid sna-bdun*) are: 1) a thousand-spiked golden wheel; 2) a jewel made of lapis lazuli worn on the king's top-knot; 3) a queen; 4) a minister; 5) an elephant; 6) a supreme horse; and 7) a powerful general" (2001, 133).

35 This is not unprecedented. There are symbolic narratives linking the Karmapas with the cult of Amitābha in the hagiography of the Fourth Karmapa Rol-pa'i-rdo-rje (1340–1383); see Mei 2009, 65–66.

36 Kapstein 2004, 24.

37 The mantra reads: *oṃ amidhewa hrīh / padma dhe wa hrī hūṃ / oṃ a ro likā* (DM 1, 162).

38 A more faithful translation of the title of this work would be *Means of Attaining the Sukhāvatī Kṣetra: Empowerment and Oral Instructions,* to accord with previous translations of the phrase "*bde-chen zhing-sgrub.*" However, to avoid confusion with the compilation titled *The Means of Attaining the Sukhāvatī Kṣetra,* I have opted to translate the *sādhana* as *Sukhāvatī Realized: Empowerment and Oral Instructions.*

39 As seen in the first section of this chapter, the *Anthology of Aspirational Prayers* lists three short pure-vision *termas* entitled *gNam chos bde smon,* which, according to the colophons, were orally transmitted to Mi-'gyur rdo-rje by Buddha Amitābha and his retinue (DM 1, 214–216).

40 The Tantric sources of refuge include the lama (guru), the tantric deity (*deva*), and the protectors, which may be "sky-dancers" (*ḍākinīs*).

41 An oral commentary to this practice by the *phowa* master Ayang Rinpoche recommends the visualization of a four-armed Avalokiteśvara.

42 These three places refer to the upper *rtsa-'khor* (Skt. *cakra*), which are simultaneously sensitized by speech modulation and color frequency: white *oṃ*, red *āḥ*, blue *hūṃ*. The *cakras* correspond to internalized sites located roughly at the heart (*chos kyi 'khor-lo*), the throat (*longs-spyod kyi 'khor-lo*), and the fontanel (*bde-chen gi 'khor-lo*). As we have seen in Chapter Five, the *cakra* of great bliss (Skt. *mahāsukha*) serves as a point of entry for the wisdom-beings (*ye-shes-pa*) and as point of exit for one's subtle consciousness during the practice of *phowa*.

43 This section refers to the visualized couple known as the pledge-beings (Tib. *dam-tshig sems-dpa'*; Skt. *samayasattva*) and the wisdom-beings (*ye-shes sems-dpa'*; Skt. *jñānasattva*), their enlightened counterparts in Sukhāvatī. The symmetrical correspondence between the "structured-imaginary" (the pledge-beings in the visualization) and the "expansive-real" (the wisdom-beings in the Pure Land) is enacted through the emanation of the white, red, and blue light rays. The pledge of the tantric practitioner to attain enlightenment is symbolically and conceptually indivisible with the state of enlightenment embodied by the arrival of the *ye-shes-pa*.

44 These mantras are now sealed by the enunciation of secret syllables. The term *rgya* ("seal") may be an abbreviation of *phyag-rgya* (Skt. *mudrā*), where a particular hand gesture (*mudrā*) is expected; it may be derived from *rgya-ba*, "extent" but also meaning "area or region" (JSK, 104–105). More generically, if the term *rgya* is affixed after other words, it indicates something that seals something else to keep the contents hidden, as in a seal on an envelope.

45 The original text renders *bde-chen* instead of *bde-can*. Possible reasons for this conflation are discussed in Chapter Five.

46 Long-life practices commonly involve Amitābha visualized in the *saṃbhogakāya* form of Amitāyus.

47 This passage on the consecration of ritual objects is probably meant as instructions for the propitiating lama. Bentor elaborates on this ritual practice:

> Not only is the consecration performed within the frame of the *sādhana*, it is, in fact, a special application of the *sādhana*. Having completed the generation process (*bskyed rim*), one can apply one's powers to the generation of a receptacle as a deity (*rten bskyed*) through a similar method. The main components at the core of the consecration ritual, common to almost all consecration manuals I have been able to examine, are as follows: (1) Visualizing the receptacle away (*mi dmigs pa*), always performed in conjunction with meditation on emptiness (*stong pa nyid*). (2) Generation of the receptacle as the *dam tshig sems dpa'* (*samayasattva*) of one's *yi-dam* (*rten*

bskyed). (3) Invitation of the *ye shes sems dpa'* (*jñānasattva*) into the receptacle (*spyan 'dren*) and its absorption (*bstim*) into the *dam tshig sems dpa'* (*dam ye gnyis su med pa*). (4) Transformation of the receptacle back into its conventional appearance of an image, stūpa, book, etc. (*rten bsgyur*). (5) Requesting the *ye shes sems dpa'* to remain in the receptacle as long as *saṃsāra* lasts (*brtan bzhugs*) (1996, 291–292).

48 I have not come across any other protecting deities related to Sukhāvatī, except one passing reference in Nebesky-Wojkowitz (1956, 273) of a *ma-mo* type, known as Za-byed spyang rgyal nag-mo, listed among deities that reside in Amitābha's buddha field. On the other hand, there are a many ritual practices dedicated to the Lion-faced Protectors, the Seng-gdong-ma; see GB, vol. tsha.

49 Nebesky-Wojkowitz 1956, vii.

50 Nebesky-Wojkowitz 1956, 5–6.

51 Nebesky-Wojkowitz 1956, 3–4.

52 The four enlightened activities are 1) pacifying (*zhi-ba*), 2) increasing and enriching (*rgyas-pa*), 3) magnetizing and controlling (*dbang*), and 4) subjugating by wrathful means (*drag-po*).

53 Nebesky-Wojkowitz 1956, 65. Tucci (1949, 594) writes that the cult of Seng-ge gdong-ma (Siṃhavaktrā), an aspect of Ye-shes mkha'-'gro-ma, was introduced to Tibet by Ba-ri, who received it from rDo-rje gdan-pa.

54 For a description, see Nebesky-Wojkowitz 1956, 66.

55 It is not altogether clear to what species the *bam-ro* belong, but judging from their description in the *sādhana*, they are daunting hybrids with the heads and feet of monkeys and bird talon-like hands (see bottom of Illustration I).

56 This passage could be translated as: *Hūṃ!* Guardians of the Buddha Infinite Luminosity (*hūṃ snang ba mtha' yas bka' srung ba;* fol. 38).

57 According to Geshe Gelek Jinpa (private correspondence, September 2001), *rkang-gsum* ("three-legged") refers to: 1) swift dexterity (*myur-mgyogs kyi rtsal*), 2) the ability to fly (*rlung gi gshog-pa*), and 3) supernormal powers (*rdza-'phrul gyi rkang-pa*).

58 In the seventeenth chapter of the *Saṃvarodaya-tantra,* the eight cemeteries (Skt. *aṣṭaśmaśāna*) feature as parts of a *maṇḍala:* Caṇḍogra, Gahvara, Vajrajvālā, Karaṅkin, Aṭṭahāsa, Lakṣmīvana, Ghorāndhakāra, and Kilikilārava; see Tsuda 1974, 123. The twenty-four sacred places in tantric lore are generally known as *pīṭhas* but their exact names and numbers are not consistently rendered in the tantras; see Skorupski 2001, 73, n. 16.

59 *Ban-de dam-nyams* likely refers to a monk who violated his vows in a previous life and has returned as a hostile force.

Epilogue

1 Similar instructions are contained in Karma chags-med's works; see Chapter Four.

2 Kapstein asserts, "It is evident that Sukhāvatī is not, for Tibetan Buddhists, the goal of an exclusive allegiance to a particular sectarian strain of the Mahāyāna, but is, rather, an encompassing end that embraces all the possible goals of the Mahāyāna and so accords with all approaches to the path, tantric and non-tantric" (2004, 40).

3 For Blondeau, this theme became popular from the sixteenth century onward and draws its authority from the long *Sukhāvatīvyūha-sūtra,* which states that in Sukhāvatī, as far as birth is concerned, "the name of the four kinds of birth does not exist, except for the miraculous birth under a lotus" (1980, 47). She further notes that in Kama-based Padmasambhava hagiographies (*rnam-thar*), he is described as having had a womb-birth (*mngal-skyes*), while narratives belonging to the Treasure tradition, with the exception of the *Ba-mkhal smug-po,* accord him birth from a lotus (45–46).

4 Rig-'dzin rgod-ldem, author of the *sBas yul mkhan pa lungs gis lam yig sa dpyad dang bcas pa,* is also known for extracting other Pure Land treasures, such as an aspirational prayer to Sukhāvatī attributed to Padmasambhava; see Appendix III. For a discussion on the cult of hidden lands (*sbas-yul*) and especially the terrestrial pure land of mKhan-pa-lung, see Brauen-Dolma 1985; Reinhard 1978, 5–13.

5 Orofino 1993, 256–259. Hidden lands in the Himalayas may resemble pure lands other than Sukhavati. The heart-disciple of the Fifth sGam-po-pa, rDo-rje drag-snang tsal, envisioned the hidden land of Padma-bkod as the paradise of Buddha Maitreya; see Sardar-Afkhami 1996, 10.

6 Compare, for example, the rNying-ma practice of *thod-rgal,* where one trains by "gaz[ing] into the sky . . . to behold points or disks of light within which Buddha figures may appear and give teachings" (Martin 2001, 23).

7 The colophon reads: "The so-called *Praise to the Protector Amitābha: Opening the Door to the Excellent Pure Lands* was composed by the learned vagrant, Blo-bzang grags-pa (Tsong-khapa) among the snow mountains of 'O-de gung-rgyal's Lhasa and Zhol (greater Lhasa)." For references to 'O-de gung-rgyal, see Haarh 1969, 221; Karmay 1998, 387.

8 According to the *Royal Mirror,* in the presence of a thousand buddhas, Avalokiteśvara made the following aspiration: "May these sentient beings (*sems can;* Skt. *sattvas*) who are so difficult to convert and who live in [this] Snow-clad Kingdom (Tibet), a barbarous borderland, a place untrodden by the feet of any Buddha of the Three Times, be brought onto the Path of Enlightenment and Freedom by me! May this barbarous borderland, moreover, become the field (*zhing; kṣetra*) of conversion [done] by me! May I [fur-

ther] be regarded as the parents of all these sentient beings [living there] such as demons etc!" (Sørensen 1994, 97; parenthetical glosses added). Historical details concerning bSod-nams rgyal-mtshan's life have been discussed in Sørensen 1994, 34–35. The mythical story of Tibet's religious conversion to Buddhism is reiterated in many Tibetan historical works and in versions of the oral epic *Gesar of Ling;* see Kornman 1997, 48–49.

9 The Fifth Dalai Lama's secular seat in the Potala palace is said to go back to a former institution erected in the same place at dMar-po-ri by the Tibetan emperor Srong-btsan-sgam-po; see Sangs-rgyas rgya-mtsho 1999. For an informative discussion of the Potala as an historical and symbolic seat of power, see Chayet 2003, 39–52.

10 The term *sprul-sku,* "manifest body of enlightenment" (Skt. *nirmāṇakāya*), refers to a popular Tibetan system for selecting high monastic officials and identifying incarnate bodhisattvas as abbots of Tibet's larger monasteries (*gdan-sprul*). There are hierarchies to these incarnations (*sprul-sku*), which include "supreme incarnations" (*mchog-sprul*), such as the Dalai Lamas and the Karmapas, both of which relate to the celestial bodhisattva Avalokiteśvara.

11 Tambiah (1987) offers an informative discussion on kingship in early Buddhism. A Pāli text, the *Aggaññasutta,* foretells of the gradual degradation of human society. Apparently, at the lowest point in this process, people were forced to elect a "Great Chosen One (Mahāsaṃmata) who will protect the people and their property and administer an equitable justice in return for food." A variety of Buddhist kings, particularly in Burma and Sri Lanka, trace their descent from Mahāsammata; see Harris 1999, 3. The proemium of *rGyal rabs gsal ba'i me long* pays homage to the royal lineage of Mang-pos bkur-ba (Mahāsaṃmata), the first Indian king and mythical progenitor of Śākyamuni; see Sørensen 1994, 43, 49, 50, 52.

12 As I have noted elsewhere, "The persuasive incumbency of the institution of the Dalai Lama reveals an extended overlapping of religious signifiers and their secular interpretation: in the religious sphere through the Mahayana belief in the salvific fortitude of bodhisattvas and their subsequent monastic cults of deification, and in the political sphere, through the reconsignment of pure land cosmology to the project of pan-Tibetan unification and the implementation of Buddhist metaphysical doctrines of rebirth into viable models of political legitimization and succession"; see Halkias 2006a, 5.

Appendix I

1 See Simmler 1992; see Schoening 1995, 179.

2 As reasoned by Harrison:

> [W]hen the editor of a text is faced with an open recension, it is difficult, if not impossible, to establish the wording of a supposed original or archetype

with any degree of certainty. In fact, even if the Bka' 'gyur tradition as we know it were not open, we would still be in trouble in this respect, since all our work appears to take us back to two hyparchetypes, the Tshal pa and Them spangs ma MSS (or later copies of them). Since, then, there are two hyparchetypes, not three, it is impossible in terms of the laws of classical textual criticism to use them to "reconstruct with certainty the text of the archetype at all places." And this would still be the case even if the tradition was closed—which it isn't—and if contamination was not present—which it is (1994, 296).

3 I wish to thank Prof. Paul Harrison for informing me that he found no copies of the DK amongst the Ta-pho manuscripts; however, there is a copy of the Tibetan long *Sukhāvatīvyūha-sūtra* (personal correspondence, February 2006).

4 This is in line with Hinüber's (1980, 28–40) guidelines for text-critical studies. For a discussion of the Og and O Mss, see Chapter Three.

5 The Og reading seems to be a scribal error.

Appendix III

1 See Boord 2011. For the history of the Northern Treasures tradition, see Boord 1993.

2 *'Jigs gling bde smon by Jigs-med gling-pa mkhyen-brtse 'od-zer* (DM 1, 248–252); *bDe ba can gyi smon lam mtha' yas sgo 'byed ma* by Ratna gling-pa (DM 1, 198–203); *gTer ston bdud 'dul rdo rje'i bde smon* by bDud-'dul rdo-rje (DM 1, 240–241); *rDzogs pa'i sangs rgyas 'od dpag tu med pas rgyal ba ka thog pa dam pa bde gshegs la gnang ba'i sgrub thabs las khol du byung ba'i bde smon by Kaḥthog-pa Dam-pa bde-gshegs* (DM 1, 159–163).

3 DM 1, 214–216. I have not been able to locate these works with the same title in the NC or GB collections.

4 *rNam dag bde ba can du skye pa'i smon lam mi tra dzo kas mdzad pa* (DM 1, 163–166).

5 The *bDe chen zhing gi smon lam thar pa'i sgo 'byed* located in the *Sangs rgyas dgongs 'dus 'gro ba kun bsgrol* cycle (DM 1, 166–171).

References

Tibetan Sources

Names of Authors

Bdud-'joms 'jigs-brel ye-shes rdo-rje. 1996. *bDud 'joms chos 'byung.* Si-khron: mi rigs dpe skrun khang.

Bstan-'dzin nor-bu. 1979. *bDe smon gyi spyi bshad byang chub sems dpa'i myur lam.* Paro: Ngodrup and Sherab Drimay.

Bu-ston. 1988. *Bu ston chos 'byung.* Krung-go: shes rig dpe skrun khang.

Chang I-sun. 1985. *Bod rgya tshig mdzod chen mo.* China: mi rigs dpe skrun khan.

Dpa'-bo gtsug-lag phreng-ba. 1986. *mKhas pa'i dga' ston.* Beijing: mi rigs dpe skrun khang.

Dung-dkar blo-bzang 'phrin-las. 1997. *Dung dkar blo bzang 'phrin las kyi gsung rtsom phyogs bsgrigs.* China: shes rig skrun khang.

Gla-bla bsod-nams chos-'grub. 1997. *gSung 'bum.* 1991 dkar-mdzad edition, introduction by Matthew Kapstein. Delhi: dkon mchog lha bris dpar las sri 'zu khan.

Gnam-chos mi-'gyur rdo-rje. 1983. *gNam chos thugs kyi gter kha sngan brgyud zab mo'i skor.* Bhutan: Dilgo khyentse rinpoche. Reproduit d'apres un jeu d'imprimes de l'edition xylographique de rmug-sans preserves dans le fond Migot.

Gu-ru bkra-shis. 1990. *Gu bkra'i chos 'byung.* Beijing: krung go'i bod kyi shes rig dpe skrun khang.

'Jam-mgon kong-sprul blo-gros mtha'-yas. 1997. *Shes bya kun khyab mdzod.* Delhi: Shechen publications.

'Jigs-med chos-kyi-dbang-po. 1970. *gSung 'bum.* Reproduced from Dudjom Rinpoche's collection. Gangtok: Sonam T. Kazi.

'Jigs-med-chos 'phags-kyis-bsgrigs. 1994. *mKhas dbang tshe brtan zhabs drung gi dpyad rtsom mkho bsdus.* Kan-su: mi rigs dpe skrun khang.

Karma chags-med rin-po-che. 1999? *gSung 'bum gyi dkar chag.* Si-khron: zhing chen mi rigs zhib 'jug su'i bod kyi rig gnas zhib 'jug khang.

'Khrul-zhig padma chos-rgyal. 1978–1985. *rTsib ri spar ma dkar chag (Collected Instructional Material on the Practice of the Teachings of the dKar-brgyud-pa and rDzogs-chen Traditions).* Darjeeling: kargyu sungrab nyamso khang.

Kun-dga' rgyal-mtshan. 1992. *Sa paṇ kun dga' rgyal mtshan gyi gsung 'bum.* Gangs-can rig-mdzod Series, no. 25. Lhasa: boḍ ljong bod yig dpe rnying dpe skrun khang.

Mi-pham rgya-mtsho. 1976. *gSung 'bum.* Gangtok: Sonam T. Kazi.

Mkhas-btsun bzang-po. 1973. *Biographical Dictionary of Tibet and Tibetan Buddhism,* 12 vols. Dharamsala: Library of Tibetan Works and Archives.

Rdo grub-chen 'jigs-med bstan-pa'i-nyi-ma. 1974–1975. *gSung 'bum.* Gangtok: Dodrupchen Rinpoche.

Rig-pa 'dzin-pa chen-po chos-kyi-grags-pa. 1999. *Kun mkhyen rig pa 'dzin pa chen po chos kyi grags pa'i gsung 'bum.* Dehra Dun: Drikung Kagyu Institute.

Sa-skya bsod-nams rgyal-mtshan. 1981. *rGyal rabs gsal ba'i me long.* Beijing: mi rigs dpe skrun khang.

Sa-skya rin-chen. 1988. *Yar lung jo ba'i chos 'byung.* Shin-hwa: bod ljongs mi dmangs dpe skrun khang.

Tshul-khrims skal-bzang khang-dkar. 1985. *Bstan pa snga dar gyi chos 'byung 'brel yod dang bcas pa'i dus rabs kyi mtha' dpyod 'phrul gyi me long zhes bya ba bzhugs.* Delhi: Western Tibetan Cultural Association.

——. 2003. *Yul gangs can gyi bka' bstan dkar chag dang bcas pa'i lo rgyus rags tsam brjod pa snar thang dran dbyangs (History of bKa'-'gyur and bsTan-'gyur).* Kyoto: Annual Memoirs of the Otani Shin Buddhist Research Institute, vol. 20.

Tsong-kha-pa. 1997. *gSung 'bum.* bKra-shis lhun-po Edition. Dharamsala: shes rig dpar khang.

Yar-'phel dbang-po. 1978-1985. *Myur lam 'pho ba'i rnal 'byor dpal 'brug pa'i nyams bzhes 'jag tshugs ma.* Darjeeling: kargyu sungrab nyamso khang.

Titles of Texts

Bde smon phyogs bsgrigs. 1994. 2 vols. Si-khron: mi rigs dpe skrun khang.

Bka' chems ka khol ma. 1989. Lanzhou: kan su'u mi rigs dpe skrun khang.

'Bri gung 'pho ba chen mo 'jag tshugs ma. 1982. Third edition. Washington, DC: Drikung Kagyu Tibetan Meditation Center.

Byed brag rtogs byed 'bring ba 'am/sGra sbyor bam po gnyis pa. 2000. Delhi: shes rig dpar khang.

Dba' bzhed. The Royal Narrative Concerning the Bringing of the Buddha's Doctrine to Tibet. 2000. Pasang Wangdu and Hildegard Diemberger, trans. Wien: Verlag der Österreichischen Akademie der Wissenschaften.

Dkar chag 'phang thang ma and sGra sbyor bam po gnyis pa. 2003. Beijing: mi rigs dpe skrun khang.

Dus rabs bdun pa nas dus rabs bcu bdun pa'i bar rgya gar gyi paṇḍiṭa bod rim byon dang bod kyi mkhas pa rgya gar du rim par byon pa'i mtshan tho dang lo dus mdzod rag bsdus bcas phyogs bsdebs rin chen nor bu'i do shal bzhugs. 1978. Dharamsala: Library of Tibetan Works and Archives.

Gangs can mkhas dbang rim byon gyi rnam thar mdor bdus. 1996. Beijing: krung go'i bod kyi shes rig dpe skrun khang.

Gangs can mkhas grub rim byon ming mdzod. 1992. Kan-su: mi rigs dpe skrun khang.

Gsung 'bum dkar chag (Potala Collection). 1990. Bod ljongs: mi dmangs dpe skrun khang.

Gter ston brgya rtsa'i rnam thar. 1976–1980. Paro: Ngodrup and Sherab Drimay.

Khams khul mkhas dbang rnams kyi snyan ngag dper brjod phyogs sgrig. 1987. Si-khron: mi rigs dpe skrun khang gis bskun.

'Phags pa bzang po spyod pa'i smon lam gyi rgyal po. 2000. *Bhadracaryā-praṅidhāna-rāja.* New Zealand: Dhargye Buddhist Centre.

Rdo grub chen 'jigs med phrin las 'od zer gyi rabs rnam thar. 1985. *The Brief Biography of the First rDo grub-chen 'Jigs-med phrin-las 'od-zer (1742–1821) and His Successors in the rDo grub-chen Lineages of Incarnations.* Gangtok: Pema Thinley.

Rin chen gter mdzod chen mo. 1976–1980. Paro: Ngodrup and Sherab Drimay.

Sa skya pa'i bka' 'bum. 1968. *The Complete Works of the Great Masters of the Sa-skya Sect of Tibetan Buddhism.* Tokyo: Toyo Bunko.

Sbrang char. 1982. mTsho-sngon: mi rigs par khang gis dpar.

Secondary References

Agrawala, Ratna Chandra. 1954. "Life of Buddhist Monks in Chinese Turkestan," in J. Agrawal and B. Dev Shastri, eds., *Sarūpa-bhāratī: Or the Homage of Indology: Being the Dr. Lakshman Sarup Memorial Volume,* pp. 173–181. Hoshiarpur: Vishveshvaranand Institute Publications.

Ahmad, Zahiruddin, trans. 1999. *Life of the Fifth Dalai Lama,* vol. IV, part I. Delhi: International Academy of Indian Culture.

——. 2008. *The Song of the Queen of Spring or A History of Tibet by Nag dBaN Blo-bzaN rGya-mTSHo Fifth Dalai Lama of Tibet.* Delhi: International Academy of Indian Culture.

Almond, Philip. 1988. *The British Discovery of Buddhism.* Cambridge, UK: Cambridge University Press.

Amstutz, Galen. 1997. *Interpreting Amida: History and Orientalism in the Study of Pure Land Buddhism.* Albany: State University of New York (SUNY).

——. 1998. "The Politics of Pure Land Buddhism," *Numen* 45 (1): 69–96.

——. 2004. "Steadied Ambiguity: The Afterlife in 'Popular' Shin Buddhism," in Susanne Formanek and William LaFleur, eds., *Practicing the Afterlife: Perspectives from Japan,* pp. 157–179. Wien: Österreichischen Akademie der Wissenschaften.

Apte S. Vaman. 1965. *The Practical Sanskrit-English Dictionary,* Third Edition. Delhi: Motilal Banarsidass.

Aris, Michael. 1988. *Hidden Treasures and Secret Lives: A Study of Pemalingpa (1450–1521) and the Sixth Dalai Lama (1683–1706).* Shimla: Indian Institute of Advanced Study.

Ashikaga, Atsuuji. 1952. "The Sanskrit Text of the Gāthās in the Larger Sukhāvatīvyūha," *Tōyō gaku Ronsō:* 55–68.

——. 1953. "The Sanskrit Text of the Buddhastotra in the Sukhāvatīvyūha," *Bukkyō gaku Kenkyū* 8–9: 1–8.

Bailey, Harold W. 1961. *Indo-Scythian Studies: Being Khotanese Texts,* vol. IV. Cambridge, UK: Cambridge University Press.

——. 1992–1993. *The Larger Sukhāvatīvyūha, Romanized Text of the Sanskrit Manuscript from Nepal,* Parts I and II. Tokyo: Sanki-bō.

Barber, A. W. 1999. "The Anti Sukhāvatīvyūha Stance of the Tathāgatagarbha Sūtra," *The Pure Land* 16: 190–202.

——. 2002. "Darshanic Buddhism: The Origins of Pure Land Practice," *The Pure Land* n.s. 18–19: 29–47.

Basham, Arthur L. 1954. *The Wonder That Was India: A Survey of the Culture of the Indian Subcontinent before the Coming of the Muslims.* Calcutta: Rupa Publications. Reprint, 1993.

Beal, Samuel. 1906. *Buddhist Records of the Western Kingdoms.* London: Trübner and Ludgate Hill.

Bechert, Heinz. 1992. "Buddha-field and Transfer of Merit in a Theravāda Source," *Indo-Iranian Journal* 35 (2–3): 95–108.

Beckwith, Christopher. 1987. *The Tibetan Empire in Central Asia: A History of the Struggle for Great Power among Tibetans, Turks, Arabs and Chinese during the Early Middle Ages.* Princeton, NJ: Princeton University Press.

——. 1991. "The Impact of Horse and Silk Trade on the Economies of T'ang China and Uighur Empire: On the Importance of International Commerce in the Early Middle Ages," *Journal of the Economic and Social History of the Orient* 34 (3): 183–198.

——. 2009. *The Empires of the Silk Road: A History of Central Eurasia from the Bronze Age to the Present.* Princeton, NJ: Princeton University Press.

Benn, Charles. 2004. *China's Golden Age: Everyday Life in the Tang Dynasty.* Oxford, UK: Oxford University Press.

Bentor, Yael. 1995. "Interiorized Fire Offerings of Breathing, Inner Heat and the Subtle Body," in Ernst Steinkellner et al., eds. *Proceedings of the 7th Seminar of the International Association for Tibetan Studies,* pp. 51–59. Wien: Verlag der Österreichischen Akademie der Wissenschaften.

——. 1996. "Literature on Consecration (Rab gnas)," in José Ignacio Cabezón and Roger R. Jackson, eds., *Tibetan Literature: Studies in Genre,* pp. 290–312. Ithaca, NY: Snow Lion Publications.

Beer, Robert. 1999. *The Encyclopedia of Tibetan Symbols and Motifs.* London: Serindia Press.

———. 2003. *The Handbook of Tibetan Buddhist Symbols.* Chicago: Serindia Press.

Bethlenfalvy, Géza. 1982. *A Hand-list of the Ulan Bator Manuscript of the Kanjur Rgyal rtse Themsspangs-ma.* Budapest: Akadèmiai Kiado.

Beyer, Stephan. 1978. *The Cult of Tārā: Magic and Ritual in Tibet.* Buddhist Studies Series 1. Berkeley: University of California Press.

Bhattacharyya, Benoytosh. 1985. *The Indian Buddhist Iconography.* New Delhi: Cosmo Publications.

Bhikkhu Pasadika. 1991. "Once Again on the Hypothesis of Two Vasubandhus," in V. N. Jha, ed., *Kalyana-Mitta: Prof. Hajime Nakamura Felicitation Volume,* pp. 15–21. Delhi: Sri Satguru.

Bishop, Peter. 1993. *Dreams of Power: Tibetan Buddhism and the Western Imagination.* London: Althone Press.

Bjerken, Zeff 2005. "On Mandalas, Monarchs, and Mortuary Magic: Siting the *Sarvadurgatipariśoshana Tantra* in Tibet," *Journal of the American Academy of Religion* 73 (3): 813–841.

Blezer, Henk. 1997. *Kar gling Zhi khro: A Tantric Buddhist Concept.* Leiden: Research School CNWS.

Blondeau, Anne Marie. 1980. "Analysis of the Biographies of Padmasambhava according to Tibetan Tradition: Classification of Sources," in Michael Aris and Aung San Suu Kyi, eds., *Tibetan Studies in Honour of Hugh Richardson,* pp. 45–51. Warminster, England: Aris and Phillips.

Blum, Mark. 1985. "The Sūtra of Contemplation on the Buddha of Immeasurable Life as Expounded by Śākyamuni Buddha," *The Eastern Buddhist* 18 (2): 131–137.

———. 2002. *The Origins and Developments of Pure Land Buddhism.* Oxford, England: Oxford University Press.

Boord, Martin. 1993. *The Cult of the Deity Vajrakīla.* Buddhica Britannica Series IV. Tring: Institute of Buddhist Studies.

———. 2011. *Illuminating Sunshine: Buddhist Death Rituals of Avalokiteśvara.* Berlin: Wandel Verlag.

Boucher, Daniel. 1998. "Gāndhārī and the Early Chinese Buddhist Translations Reconsidered: The Case of the Saddharmapuṇḍarīkasūtra," *Journal of the American Oriental Society* 118 (4): 471–506.

Braarvig, Jens. 2002. *Manuscripts in the Schøyen Collection III.* Buddhist Manuscripts, vols. I–II. Oslo: Hermes Publishing.

Brauen-Dolma, Martin. 1982. "Death Customs in Ladakh," *Kailash* 9 (4): 319–332.

———. 1985. "Millenarianism in Tibetan Religion," in Barbara Nimri Aziz and Matthew Kapstein, eds., *Soundings in Tibetan Civilization,* pp. 245–256. Delhi: Manohar Publications.

Bretfeld, Sven. 2004. "The 'Great Debate' of bSam yas: Construction and Deconstruction of a Tibetan Buddhist Myth," *Asiatische Studien Études Asiatiques* LVIII (1): 15–56.

Brough, John. 1982. "Amitābha and Avalokiteśvara in an Inscribed Gandhāran Sculpture," *Indologica Taurinensia* 10: 65–70.

Bushell, S. W. 1880. "The Early History of Tibet from Chinese Sources," *Journal of the Royal Asiatic Society of Great Britain and Ireland* 12 (4): 435–541.

Butters, Albion. 2005. *Point Blank: The Doxographical Genius of Kun mkhyen kLong chen rab 'byams pa.* PhD dissertation, Columbia University.

Cabezón, José Ignacio. 1994. *Buddhism and Language: A Study of Indo-Tibetan Scholasticism.* Albany: State University of New York (SUNY).

Cabezón, José Ignacio, and Roger R. Jackson. 1996. *Tibetan Literature: Studies in Genre.* Ithaca, NY: Snow Lion Publications.

Cantwell, Cathy. 1997. "To Meditate upon Consciousness as Vajra: Ritual 'Killing and Liberation' in the rNying-ma Tradition," in Ernst Steinkellner et al., eds., *Proceedings of the 7th Seminar of the International Association for Tibetan Studies,* pp. 108–118. Wien: Verlag der Österreichischen Akademie der Wissenschaften.

Chagmé, Karma. 2000. *Naked Awareness: Practical Instructions on the Union of Mahāmudrā and Atiyoga.* Ithaca, NY: Snow Lion Publications.

———. 2008. *Terton Migyur Dorje: All Pervading Melodious Sound of Thunder: The Outer Liberation Story of Terton Migyur Dorje.* Parphing, Nepal: Palri Parkhang.

Chandra, Lokesh. 1965. *Collected Works of Bu-ston.* Śata-piṭaka Series. Delhi: International Academy of Indian Culture.

———. 1985. *Tibetan-Sanskrit Dictionary.* New Delhi: Sharada Rani.

———. 1987. *Buddhist Iconography.* Śata-piṭaka Series. Delhi: Aditya Prakashan.

———. 2002. "Tun-Huang as Power and Virtue," *Acta Orientalia Academiae Scientiarum Hung* 55: 89–98.

Chappell, David. 1977. "Chinese Buddhist Interpretations of the Pure Lands," in Michael Saso and David W. Chappell, eds., *Buddhist and Taoist Studies,* pp. 23–55. Honolulu: University of Hawai'i Press.

Chayet, Anne. 2003. "The Potala, Symbol of the Power of the Dalai Lamas," in Francoise Pommaret, ed., *Lhasa in the Seventeenth Century: The Capital of the Dalai Lamas,* pp. 39–52. Leiden: Brill.

Chen, Kenneth. 1964. *Buddhism in China: A Historical Survey.* Princeton, NJ: Princeton University Press.

Chen, Sanping. 2002. "Son of Heaven and Son of God: Interactions among Ancient Asiatic Cultures regarding Sacral Kingship and Theophoric Names," *Journal of the Royal Asiatic Society* 12: 289–325.

Chen, Shu-Chen. 2007. *Cultural Change of Indian Pure Land Buddhist Teaching in Chinese and Tibetan Buddhism.* PhD dissertation, University of Virginia.

Childs, Geoff. 2004. Tibetan Diary: *From Birth to Death and Beyond in a Himalayan Valley of Nepal.* Berkeley: University of California Press.

Chophel, Norbu. 1982. "The Mirror of Tibetan Omens and Superstitions, by Karma Chagmed," selected and translated by Norbu Chophel, *Tibet Journal* VII (4): 86–93.

Clifford, Terry. 1984. *Tibetan Buddhist Medicine and Psychiatry: The Diamond Healing.* Delhi: Motilal Banarsidass. Reprint, 1994.

Comneno, Maria A. 2007. "Nestorianism in Central Asia during the First Millennium," *Journal of the Assyrian Academic Society* XI (1): 20–67.

Conze, Edward. 1957. *Vajracchedikā Prajñāpāramitā.* Rome: Istituto Italiano per il Medio e l'Estremo Oriente (Is.M.E.O.).

———. 1959. *Buddhism: Its Essence and Development.* Kathmandu: Pilgrims Book House. Reprint, 1997.

———. 1979. *The Large Sutra on Perfect Wisdom.* Delhi: Motilal Banarsidass.

Corless, Roger. 1989. "Pure Land and Pure Perspective: A Tantric Hermeneutic of Sukhāvatī," *The Pure Land* 6 (n.s.): 205–217.

———. 1995. "Pure Land Piety," in Takeuchi Yoshinori, ed., *Buddhist Spirituality,* pp. 242–271. Delhi: Motilal Banarsidass.

Cornu, Philippe. 1997. *Tibetan Astrology.* Hamish Gregor, trans. Boston: Shambhala Publications.

Cozort, Daniel. 1986. *Highest Yoga Tantra: An Introduction to the Esoteric Buddhism of Tibet.* Ithaca, NY: Snow Lion Publications.

———. 1996. "Sādhana (*sGrub thabs*): Means of Achievement for Deity Yoga," in José Ignacio Cabezón and Roger R. Jackson, eds., *Tibetan Literature: Studies in Genre,* pp. 331–343. Ithaca, NY: Snow Lion Publications.

Cuevas, Brian. 2003. *The Hidden History of the Tibetan Book of the Dead.* Oxford, UK: Oxford University Press.

———. 2006. "Some Reflections on the Periodization of Tibetan History," *Revue d'Etudes Tibétaines* 10: 44–55.

Dalton, Jacob. 2002. *The Uses of the Dgongs pa 'dus pa'i mdo in the Development of the rNying-ma School of Tibetan Buddhism.* PhD dissertation, University of Michigan.

Dalton, Jacob, Tom Davis, and Sam van Schaik. 2007. "Beyond Anonymity: Paleographic Analyses of the Dunhuang Manuscripts," *Journal of the International Association of Tibetan Studies* 3: 1–23.

Dalton, Jacob, and Sam van Schaik. 2006. *Tibetan Tantric Manuscripts from Dunhuang: A Descriptive Catalogue of the Stein Collection at the British Library.* Leiden: Brill.

Dargyay, Eva. 1988. "Srong-btsan Sgam-po of Tibet: Bodhisattva and King," in Phyliss Granoff and Koichi Shinohara, eds., *Monks and Magicians: Religious Biographies in Asia,* pp. 99–114. Ontario: Mosaic Press.

———. 1991. "Sangha and State in Imperial Tibet," in Ernst Steinkellner, ed., *Tibetan History and Language: Studies Dedicated to Uray Géza on His Seventieth Birthday*, pp. 111–129. Wien: Universität Wien.

Davidson, Ronald. 2002a. "Hidden Realms and Pure Abodes: Central Asian Buddhism as Frontier Religion in the Literature of India, Nepal and Tibet," *Pacific World* 4: 153–181.

———. 2002b. *Indian Esoteric Buddhism: A Social History of the Tantric Movement*. New York: Columbia University Press.

———. 2005. *Tibetan Renaissance: Tantric Buddhism in the Rebirth of Tibetan Culture*. New York: Columbia University Press.

———. 2009a. "Studies in Dhāraṇī Literature I: Revisiting the Meaning of the Term Dhāraṇī," *Journal of Indian Philosophy* 37 (2): 97–147.

———. 2009b. "The Problem of Secrecy in Indian Tantric Buddhism," in Bernhard Scheid and Mark Teeuwen, eds., *The Culture of Secrecy in Japanese Religion*, pp. 60–77. London: Routledge.

Dayal, Har. 1932. *The Bodhisattva Doctrine in Buddhist Literature*. London: Kegan Paul.

Dehejia, Vidya. 1997. *Discourse in Early Buddhist Art: Visual Narratives of India*. Delhi: Munshiram Manoharlal.

de la Vallée Poussin, Jean. 1962. *Catalogue of the Tibetan Manuscripts from Tun-huang in the India Office Library*. Oxford: Oxford University Press.

Demiéville, Paul. 1952. *Le Concile de Lhasa*, vol. III. Paris: Bibliothèque de l'institut des hautes etudes chinoises.

Dietz, Siglinde. 2007. "Buddhism in Gandhāra," in Ann Heirman and Stephan Peter Bumbacher, eds., *The Spread of Buddhism*, pp. 49–74. Leiden: Brill.

Doctor, Andreas. 2005. *Tibetan Treasure Literature: Revelation and Accomplishment in Visionary Buddhism*. Ithaca, NY: Snow Lion Publications.

Dotson, Brandon. 2006. *Administration and Law in the Tibetan Empire: The Section on Law and State and its Old Tibetan Antecedents*. DPhil thesis, University of Oxford.

———. 2007. "Emperor Mu-rug-btsan and the 'Phang thang ma Catalogue," *Journal of the International Association of Tibetan Studies* 3: 1–25.

———. 2008. "Complementarity and Opposition in Early Tibetan Ritual," *Journal of American Oriental Society* 128 (1): 41–67.

———. 2009. *Old Tibetan Annals. An Annotated Translation of Tibet's First History*. Vienna: Verlag der Österreichischen Akademie der Wissenschaften.

Douglas, Nik, and Meryl White. 1976. *Karmapa: The Black Hat Lama of Tibet*. London: Luzac.

Dowman, Keith. 1985. *Masters of Mahāmudrā*. Albany: State University of New York (SUNY) Press.

Ducor, Jérôme. 1988. *Le Sûtra d'Amida prêché par le Buddha*. Schweizer Asiatische Studien Études asiatiques suisses, monograph, vol. 29. Bern: Peter Lang.

Dudjom Rinpoche. 1991. *The Nyingma School of Tibetan Buddhism: Its Fundamentals and History*, vol. 1. Matthew Kapstein, ed., Gyurme Dorje, trans. Boston: Wisdom Publications.

Dutt, Sukumar. 1962. *Buddhist Monks and Monasteries of India: Their History and Their Contribution to Indian Culture.* London: George Allen and Unwin, Ltd.

Edgerton, Franklin. 1953. *Buddhist Hybrid Sanskrit Grammar and Dictionary.* William Dwight Whitney Linguistic Series. New Haven, CT: Yale University Press.

Eimer, Helmut. 1988. "A Note on the History of the Tibetan Kanjur," *Central Asiatic Journal* 32 (1–2): 64–72.

——. 1993. *Location List for the Texts in the Microfiche Edition of the Phug brag Kanjur.* Series Major V. Tokyo: Bibliographia Philologica Buddhica.

——. 1997–1998. "Three Leaves from a Tibetan Dhāraṇī Collection," *Indologica Taurinensia* XXIII–XXIV: 423–437.

——. 2002a. "Kanjur and Tanjur Studies: Present State and Future Tasks," in Helmut Eimer and David Germano, eds., *The Many Canons of Tibetan Buddhism, Proceedings of the 9th Seminar of the International Association for Tibetan Studies*, pp. 1–13. Leiden: Brill.

——. 2002b. "On the Structure of the Tibetan Kanjur," in Helmut Eimer and David Germano, eds., *The Many Canons of Tibetan Buddhism, Proceedings of the 9th Seminar of the International Association for Tibetan Studies*, pp. 57–72. Leiden: Brill.

Eliade, Mircea, ed. 1987. *The Encyclopedia of Religion.* New York: Macmillan Publishing Company.

Eliot, Sir Charles. 1959. *Japanese Buddhism.* New York: Barnes and Noble.

Elisseef, Vadime, ed. 1998. *The Silk Roads: Highways of Culture and Commerce.* Paris: UNESCO.

Emmerick, E. Ronald. 1968. *The Book of Zambasta: A Khotanese Poem on Buddhism.* London: Oxford University Press.

——. 1992. *A Guide to the Literature of Khotan.* Tokyo: International Institute of Buddhist Studies.

——. 1995. "Part II Inscriptions of the Seleucid and Parthian Periods and of Eastern Iran and Central Asia," in *Corpus Inscriptionum Iranicarum*, vol. V. London: School of Oriental and African Studies.

Enoki, K., G. A. Kosholenko, and Z. Haidary. 1994. "The Yüeh-chih and Their Mi-grations," in János Harmatta, B. N. Puri, and G. F. Etemadi, eds., *History of Civilizations of Central Asia*, vol. II, pp. 171–189. Paris: UNESCO Publishing.

Evans-Wentz, Walter Y. 1927. *The Tibetan Book of Great Liberation.* Kazi Dawa-Samdup, trans. Oxford, UK: Oxford University Press. Reprint, 2000.

——. 1935. *Tibetan Yoga and Secret Doctrines.* London: Oxford University Press.

Francke, August Hermann. 1926. "Chronicles of Ladakh and Minor Chronicles," in *Antiquities of Indian Tibet*, Part II. New Delhi: S. Chand & Co. Ltd.

Frauwallner, Erich. 1951. *On the Date of the Buddhist Master of the Law Vasubandhu.* Serie Orientale Roma 3. Rome: Istituto Italiano per il Medio e l'Estremo Oriente (Is.M.E.O.).

Fremantle, Fransesca. 1990. "Chapter Seven of the Guhyasamāja Tantra," in Tadeusz Skorupski, ed., *Indo-Tibetan Studies, Papers in Honour and Appreciation of Professor David L. Snellgrove's Contribution to Indo-Tibetan Studies,* pp. 101–114. Tring: Institute of Buddhist Studies.

Fremantle, Fransesca, and Chogyam Trungpa, trans. 1987. *The Tibetan Book of the Dead: The Great Liberation through Hearing in the Bardo.* Boston and London: Shambhala Publications.

Fujiki, Takeo. 1987. "EEG Monitored During the Phowa Ritual," *Research for Religion and Parapsychology* 17: 38–44.

Fujita, Kōtatsu. 1970. *A Study of Early Pure Land Buddhism.* Tokyo: Iwanami Shoten.

———. 1987. "Pure and Impure Lands," in Mircea Eliade, ed., *The Encyclopedia of Religion,* pp. 90–91. New York: Macmillan Publishing Company.

———. 1990. "The Textual Origins of the *Kuan Wu-liang-shou ching:* A Canonical Scripture of Pure Land Buddhism," in Robert Buswell, ed., *Chinese Buddhist Apocrypha,* pp. 149–173. Honolulu: University of Hawai'i Press.

———. 1996. "Pure Land Buddhism in India," in James Foard, Michael Solomon, and Richard Payne, eds., *The Pure Land Tradition: History and Development,* pp. 2–41. Taitetsu Unno, trans. University of California at Berkeley: Institute of Buddhist Studies.

———. 1998. "The Origin of the Pure Land," *The Eastern Buddhist* 31: 33–51.

Gaulier, Simone, Robert Jera-Bezard, and Monique Maillard. 1976. *Buddhism in Afghanistan and Central Asia,* Part I–II. Institute of Religious Iconography, State University Groningen. Leiden: Brill.

Germano, David. 1997. "Dying, Death, and Other Opportunities," in Donald S. Lopez, Jr., ed., *Religions of Tibet in Practice,* pp. 458–493. Princeton, NJ: Princeton University Press.

———. 1998. "Remembering the Dismembered Body of Tibet: Contemporary Tibetan Visionary Movements in the People's Republic of China," in Melvyn Goldstein and Matthew Kapstein, eds., *Buddhism in Contemporary Tibet,* pp. 53–94. Berkeley: University of California Press.

———. 2002. "Canons at the Boundaries: The Rnying-ma Tantras and Shades of Gray between the Early and Late Translations," in Helmut Eimer and David Germano, eds., *The Many Canons of Tibetan Buddhism,* pp. 199–202. Leiden: Brill.

Gethin, Rupert. 2006. "Mythology as Meditation: From the Mahāsudassana Sutta to the Sukhāvatīvyūha Sūtra," *Journal of the Pāli Text Society* 28: 63–112.

Getty, Alice. 1978. *The Gods of Northern Buddhism.* Delhi: Munshiram Manoharlal.

Giles, Lionel. 1957. *Descriptive Catalogue of the Chinese Manuscripts from Tunhuang in the British Museum.* London: British Museum.

Glass, Andrew. 2004. "Kharoṣṭhī Manuscripts: A Window on Gandhāran Buddhism," *Nagoya Studies in Indian Culture and Buddhism* 24: 129–152.

Gombrich, Richard. 1988. *Theravada Buddhism: A Social History from Ancient Benares to Modern Colombo.* London: Routledge and Kegan Paul.

Gómez, Luis. 1996. *The Land of Bliss: The Paradise of the Buddha of Measureless Light.* Honolulu: University of Hawai'i Press.

Griffiths, Paul J., Noriaki Hakayama, John P. Keenan, and Paul L. Swanson, eds. and trans. 1989. *The Realm of Awakening: A Translation and Study of the Tenth Chapter of Asaṅga's Mahāyānasaṇgraha.* Oxford, UK: Oxford University Press.

Grinstead, Eric. 1967. "The Manuscript Kanjur in the British Museum," *Asia Major* 13 (n.s.): 48–70.

Guenther, Herbert. 1963. *The Life and Teachings of Nāropa.* Oxford, UK: Clarendon Press.

Gulácsi, Zsuzsanna. 1997. "Identifying the Corpus of Manichaean Art among the Turfan Remains," in P. Mirecki et al., eds., *Emerging from Darkness: Studies in the Recovery of Manichaean Sources,* pp. 177–216. Leiden: Brill.

Gyatso, Janet. 1985. "The Development of the Gcod Tradition," in Barbara Nimri Aziz and Matthew Kapstein, eds., *Soundings in Tibetan Civilization,* pp. 320–342. Delhi: Manohar Publications.

——. 1993. "The Logic of Legitimation in the Tibetan Treasure Tradition," *History of Religions* 33 (2): 97–134.

——. 1997. "Genre, Authorship, and Transmission in Visionary Buddhism: The Literary Traditions of Thang-stong rGyal-po," in Steven D. Goodman and Ronald M. Davidson, eds., *Tibetan Buddhism: Reason and Revelation,* pp. 95–106. Albany: State University of New York (SUNY) Press.

——. 1998. *Apparitions of the Self.* Princeton, NJ: Princeton University Press.

——. 1999. "Healing Burns with Fire: The Facilitations of Experience in Tibetan Buddhism," *Journal of the American Academy of Religion* 67 (1): 113–147.

Gyurme Dorje and Matthew Kapstein. 1991. *The Nyingma School of Tibetan Buddhism,* vol. 2. Boston: Wisdom Publications.

Haarh, Erik. 1969. *The Yar-lung Dynasty.* Copenhagen: G.E.C. Gad's Forlag.

Halkias, Georgios T. 2004. "Tibetan Buddhism Registered: An Imperial Catalogue from the Palace Temple of 'Phang-thang," *The Eastern Buddhist* 36 (1–2): 46–105.

——. 2006a. "Pure-Lands and Other Visions in Seventeenth-Century Tibet: A *Gnam-chos sādhana* for the Pure-land Sukhāvatī Revealed in 1658 by Gnam-Chos Mi-'gyur-rdo-rje (1645–1667)," in Bryan J. Cuevas and Kurtis R. Schaeffer, eds., *Power, Politics and the Reinvention of Tradition: Tibet in the Seventeenth and Eighteenth Century,* pp. 121–151. Leiden: Brill.

——. 2006b. *Transferring to the Land of Bliss.* DPhil thesis, University of Oxford.

——. 2009a. "Compassionate Aspirations and Their Fulfilment: Dol-po-pa's A Prayer for Birth in Sukhāvatī," in Edward A. Arnold, ed., *As Long As Space Endures: Essays on the Kālachakra Tantra in Honor of H.H. the Dalai Lama*, pp. 259–275. Ithaca, NY: Snow Lion Publications.

——. 2009b. "Loss of Memory and Continuity of Praxis in Rampur-Bashahr: An Itinerant Study of Seventeenth-Century Tibetan Murals," in Brandon Dotson, Kalsang Norbu Gurung, Georgios Halkias, and Tim Myatt, eds., *Contemporary Visions in Tibetan Studies, Proceedings of the First International Seminar of Young Tibetologists*, pp. 139–155. Chicago: Serindia Publications.

——. Forthcoming. "When the Greeks Converted the Buddha: Asymmetrical Transfers and Knowledge in Indo-Greek Cultures," in Peter Wick and Volker Rabens, eds., *Trading Religions: Religious Formation, Transformation and Cross-Cultural Exchange between East and West*. Leiden: Brill.

Handa, Omacanda. 1994. *Buddhist Art and Antiquities of Himachal Pradesh*. Delhi: Indus Publishing Company.

Hansen, Valerie. 1995. "Why Bury Contracts in Tombs?", *Cahiers d'Extrême-Asie* 8: 59–66.

——. 1998. "The Path of Buddhism into China: The View from Turfan," *Asia Major* XI (2): 37–66.

——. 1999. "A Brief History of the Turfan Oasis," *Orientations* 30 (4): 24–27.

——. 2004. "Religious Life in a Silk Road Community: Niya during the Third and Fourth Centuries," in John Lagerwey, ed., *Chinese Religion and Society: The Transformation of a Field*, vol. 1, pp. 279–315. Hong Kong: Chinese University Press.

Harmatta, János. 1964. "Sino-Indica," *Acta Asiatic* 12 (1–2): 1–21.

Harmatta, János, B. N. Puri, and G. F. Etemadi, eds. 1994. *History of Civilizations of Central Asia*, vol. II. Paris: UNESCO Publishing.

Harmatta, János, B. N. Puri, L. Lelekov, S. Humayan, and D. C. Sircar. 1994. "Religions in the Kushan Empire," in János Harmatta, B. N. Puri, and G. F. Etemadi, eds., *History of Civilizations of Central Asia*, vol. II, pp. 313–329. Paris: UNESCO Publishing.

Harris, Ian. 1999. "Buddhism and Politics in Asia: The Textual and Historical Roots," in Ian Harris, ed., *Buddhism and Politics in Twentieth-Century Asia*, pp. 1–25. London: Pinter.

Harrison, Paul. 1987. "Who Gets to Ride in the Great Vehicle? Self-Image and Identity Among the Followers of the Early Mahāyāna," *Journal of the International Association of Buddhist Studies* 10 (1): 67–89.

——. 1978. "Buddānusmṛti in the *Pratyutpanna-Buddha-Saṃmukhāvasthita-Samādhi-Sūtra*," *Journal of Indian Philosophy* 6: 35–57.

——. 1992. *Druma-kinnara-rāja-paripṛcchā-sūtra. A Critical Edition of the Tibetan Text (Recension A) based on Eight Editions of the Kanjur and the Dunhuang Manuscript*

Fragment. Studia Philologica Buddhica Monograph Series VII. Tokyo: International Institute for Buddhist Studies.

——. 1994. "In Search of the Source of the Tibetan Bka' 'gyur: A Reconnaissance Report," in Per Kvaerne, ed., *Proceedings of the 6th Seminar of the International Association for Tibetan Studies,* pp. 295–317. Oslo: Institute for Comparative Research in Human Culture.

——. 1996. "A Brief History of the bKa' 'gyur," in José Ignacio Cabezón and Roger R. Jackson, eds., *Tibetan Literature: Studies in Genre,* pp. 70–93. Ithaca, NY: Snow Lion Publications.

——. 2003. "Mediums and Messages: Reflections on the Production of Mahāyāna Sūtras," *The Eastern Buddhist* 35 (1–2): 115–151.

Harrison, Paul, and Helmut Eimer. 1997. "Kanjur and Tanjur Sigla: A Proposal for Standardization," in Ernst Steinkellner et al., eds., *Proceedings of the 7th Seminar of the International Association for Tibetan Studies,* pp. 11–14. Wien: Verlag der Österreichischen Akademie der Wissenschaften.

Hartmann, Jens-Uwe. 1999. "Buddhist Sanskrit Texts from Northern Turkestan and their Relation to the Chinese Tripiṭaka," in John R. McRae and Jan Nattier, eds., *Collection of Essays 1993: Buddhism across Boundaries: Chinese Buddhism and the Western Regions,* pp. 107–136. Sanchung, Taipei: Fo Guang Shan Foundation.

Hazra, Kanai Lal. 1983. *Buddhism in India as Described by the Chinese Pilgrims.* Delhi: Munshiram Manoharlal.

——. 2009. *Buddhism in India: A Historical Survey.* Delhi: Buddhist World Press.

Heller, Amy. 1997. "Buddhist Images and Rock Inscriptions from Eastern Tibet, VIIIth to Xth Century, Part IV," In Ernst Steinkellner et al., eds., *Proceedings of the 7th Seminar of International Association for Tibetan Studies,* pp. 385–403. Wien: Verlag der Österreichischen Akademie der Wissenschaften.

——. 1998. "The Caves of gNas mjal che mo," in Deborah Klimburg-Salter and Eva Allinger, eds., *The Inner Asian International Style 12th–14th Centuries,* pp. 133–141. Wien: Verlag der Österreichischen Akademie der Wissenschaften.

——. 2008. "Observations on an 11th Century Tibetan Inscription on a Statue of Avalokiteśvara," Tibetan Studies in Honour of Samten Karmay, *Revue d'Etudes Tibétaines* 14: 107–116.

Herrmann-Pfandt, Adelheid. 2002. "The Lhan kar ma as a Source for the History of Tantric Buddhism," in Helmut Eimer and David Germano, eds., *The Many Canons of Tibetan Buddhism,* pp. 129–149. Leiden: Brill.

——. 2008. *Die lHan kar ma: ein früher Katalog der ins Tibetische übersetzten buddhistischen Texte. Kritische Neuausgabe mit Einleitung und Materialien.* Wien: Verlag der Österreichischen Akademie der Wissenschaften.

Hideo, Kimura. 1943. "The Smaller Sukhāvatīvyūha," in *Collateral Buddhist Texts Series,* Vol. I, Part 1. Kyoto: Ryukoku University.

Hikata, Ryusho. 1985. *Studies in Buddhism and Buddhist Culture.* Narita, Japan: Naritasan Shinshoji.

Hill, John. 1988. "Notes on the Dating of Khotanese History," *Indo-Iranian Journal* 31: 179–190.

Hirakawa, Akira. 1963. "The Rise of Mahāyāna Buddhism and Its Relationship to the Worship of Stupas," in *Memoirs of the Research Department of the Toyo Bunko,* vol. 22, pp. 57–106. Tokyo: Toyo Bunko.

——. 1990. *A History of Indian Buddhism.* Paul Groner, trans. Honolulu: University of Hawai'i Press.

Hoernle, Rudolf. 1916. *Manuscript Remains of Buddhist Literature Found in Eastern Turkestan.* Oxford, UK: Clarendon Press.

Hoffmann, Helmut. 1961. *The Religions of Tibet.* Edward Fitzgerald, trans. London: Allen & Unwin.

Hopkins, Jeffrey, trans. and ed. 1987. *Tantra in Tibet: The Great Exposition of Secret Mantra,* vol. 1. Selections from the *sNangs rim chen mo* by Tsong-kha-pa (Tsong-kha-pa blo-bzang grags-pa). Delhi: Motilal Banarsidass.

Houston, Garry W. 1980. *Sources for a History of the bSam yas Debate.* Sankt Augustin: VGH-Wissenschaftsverlag.

Huntington, John C. 1980. "A Gandhāran Image of Amitāyus' Sukhāvatī," *Annali dell' Instituto Orientale di Napoli* 40: 651–672.

Imaeda, Yoshiro. 1998. "À propos du manuscrit Pelliot tibétain 999," in Paul Harrison and Gregory Schopen, eds. *Sūryacandrāya: Essays in Honour of Akira Yuyama on the Occasion of His 65th Birthday,* pp. 87–94. Swisttal-Odendorf: Indica et Tibetica Verlag.

——. 2007. "The History of the Cycle of Death and Birth: A Tibetan Narrative from Dunhuang," in Matthew Kapstein and Brandon Dotson, eds., *Contributions to the Cultural History of Early Tibet,* pp. 105–181. Leiden: Brill.

Inagaki, Hisao. 1985. *A Tri-lingual Glossary of the Sukhāvatīvyūha Sūtras, Part Two: Glossary of the Smaller Sukhāvatīvyūha Sūtra, Sanskrit-Tibetan-Chinese.* Kyoto: Nagata Bunshōdō.

——. 1995. *The Three Pure Land Sūtras.* Kyoto: Nagata Bunshōdō.

——. 1998. *Nāgarjuna's Discourse on the Ten Stages (Daśambhūmika-vibhāṣā).* A Study and Translation from Chinese. Kyoto: Ryukoku Gakkai.

——. 1999. *Amida Dhāraṇī Sūtra and Jñānagarbha's Commentary. An Annotated Translation from Tibetan of the Anantamukha-nirhāra-dhāraṇī Sūtra and Ṭikā.* Ryukoku Literature Series VII. Kyoto: Ryukoku Gakkai.

Jäschke, Heinrich. 1949. *A Tibetan-English Dictionary, with Special Reference to the Prevailing Dialects.* London: Routledge and Paul.

Jones, John James. 1949. *The Mahāvastu,* vols. I–III. London: Luzac and Company.

Kagawa, Takao, et al. 1999. *Zoyaku muryojukyo ihon kogohyo (Critical Edition of the Amitābhavyūha-nāma-mahāyāna-sūtra)*. Research Team for the Comprehensive Study of Pure Land. Kyoto: Bukkyo Daigaku Sogo Kenkyujo.

Kajihama, Ryoshun. 1991. "A Study of a Prayer Book on Rebirth in the Land of Bliss (Sukhāvatī) Written by Tsong kha pa," *Monograph Published by the Faculty of International Language and Culture, Setsunan University* 23 (3): 293–322.

——. 1994. "3rd rDo Gruchen Rinpoche's Pure Land Thought (I)," *Journal of Indian and Buddhist Studies* 43 (1): 492–498.

——. 1996. "3rd rDo Gruchen Rinpoche's Pure Land Thought (II)," *Journal of Indian and Buddhist Studies* 44 (2): 948–952.

——. 2002a. "3rd rDo Gruchen Rinpoche's Pure Land Thought (III)," *Journal of Indian and Buddhist Studies* 50 (2): 984–987.

——. 2002b. *Tibet no Jyōdo Shisō no Kenkyū (The Study of Pure Land in Tibet)*. Kyoto: Nagata Bunshōdō.

Kajiyama, Yuichi. 1989. *Studies in Buddhist Philosophy*. Kyoto: Rinsen Book.

Kanakura, Yensho, Token Tada, Ryujo Yamada, and Hakuyu Hadano, eds. 1953. *A Catalogue of the Tohoku University Collection of Tibetan Works on Buddhism*. Sendai, Japan: Tohoku University Press.

Kapstein, Matthew. 1989. "Purificatory Gem and Its Cleansing: A Late Tibetan Polemical Discussion of Apocryphal Texts," *History of Religions* 28: 217–244.

——. 1996. "Tibetan Technologies of the Self," in José Ignacio Cabezón and Roger R. Jackson, eds., *Tibetan Literature: Studies in Genre*, pp. 275–289. Ithaca, NY: Snow Lion Publications.

——. 1998. "A Pilgrimage of Rebirth Reborn: The 1992 Celebration of the Drigung Powa Chenmo," in Melvyn Goldstein and Matthew Kapstein, eds., *Buddhism in Contemporary Tibet*, pp. 95–119. Delhi: Motilal Banarsidass.

——. 2000. *The Tibetan Assimilation of Buddhism: Conversion, Contestation, and Memory*. Oxford, UK: Oxford University Press.

——. 2003. "Pure Land Buddhism in Tibet? From Sukhāvatī to the Field of Great Bliss," in Richard Payne and Kenneth Tanaka, eds., *Approaching the Land of Bliss: Religious Praxis in the Cult of Amitābha*, pp. 1–16. Honolulu: University of Hawai'i Press.

——. 2004. "The Treaty Temple of De ga g.Yu tshal: Identification and Iconography," in Huo Wei, ed., *Essays on the International Conference on Tibetan Art and Archaeology and Art*, pp. 98–127. Chengdu: Sichuan renmin chubanshe.

——, ed. 2009. *Buddhism Between Tibet and China*. Somerville, MA: Wisdom Publications.

Kapstein, Matthew, and Brandon Dotson, eds. 2007. *Contributions to the Cultural History of Early Tibet*. Leiden: Brill.

Karashima, Seishi. 2007. "A Project for a Buddhist Chinese Dictionary," *Annual Report of the International Research Institute of Advanced Buddhology* X: 337–358.

Karetzky, Patricia Eichenbaum. 1997. "The Evolution of the Symbolism of the Paradise of the Buddha of Infinite Life and Its Western Origins," *Sino-Platonic Papers* 76: 1–28.

Karmay, Samten. 1988. *The Great Perfection: A Philosophical and Meditative Teaching of Tibetan Buddhism.* Leiden: Brill.

———. 1998. *The Arrow and the Spindle: Studies in the History, Myths, Rituals and Beliefs in Tibet.* Kathmandu: Mandala Book Point.

Khetsun Sangpo, ed. 1973. *Biographical Dictionary of Tibet and Tibetan Buddhism (Bod du sgrub brgyad shing rta mched brgyad las),* 12 vols. Dharamsala: Library of Tibetan Works and Archives.

Kimura, Hideo, trans. 1943. *The Smaller Sukhavati-vyuha, Collating Sanskrit, Tibetan, Chinese, with Commentarial Footnotes,* pt. I. Collateral Buddhist Texts Series I. Kyoto: Ryukoku University.

Kiyota, Minoru. 1978. "A Study of the Sukhāvatīvyuhopadeśa," in Minoru Kiyota, ed., *Mahayana Buddhist Meditation Theory and Practice,* pp. 249–296. Honolulu: University of Hawai'i Press.

Kloetzli, Randolph. 1983. *Buddhist Cosmology: Science and Theology in the Images of Motion and Light.* Delhi: Motilal Banarsidass.

Kornman, Robin. 1997. "Gesar of Ling," in Donald S. Lopez, Jr., ed., *Religions of Tibet in Practice,* pp. 39–69. Princeton, NJ: Princeton University Press.

Kudara, Kōgi. 2002. "A Rough Sketch of Central Asian Buddhism," *Pacific World* 3-4: 93–107.

Kumamoto, Hiroshi. 1999. "Textual Sources for Buddhism in Khotan," in John R. McRae and Jan Nattier, eds., *Collection of Essays 1993: Buddhism across Boundaries: Chinese Buddhism and the Western Regions,* pp. 345–360. Sanchung, Taipei: Fo Guang Shan Foundation.

Kvaerne, Per. 1971. "The Canon of the Tibetan Bonpos," *Indo-Iranian Journal* 16: 18–56, 96–144.

Lalou, Marcelle. 1939. *Inventaire des Manuscrits tibétains de Touen-huang.* Paris: Librairie d'Amérique et d'Orient.

———. 1952. "Rituel Bon-po des funérailles royals," *Journal Asiatique* 240: 339–361.

———. 1953. "Les textes bouddhiques au temps du roi Khri-sroṅ-lde-bcan. Contribution à la bibliographie du Kanjur et du Tanjur," *Journal Asiatique* 241: 313–353.

Lamotte, Étienne. 1988. *History of Indian Buddhism: From the Origins to the Śaka Era.* Sara Webb-Boin, trans. Louvain: Université Catholique de Louvain.

———. 1994. *The Teachings of Vimalakīrti.* Sara Webb-Boin, trans. Oxford, UK: Pāli Text Society.

———. 1998. *Śūraṃgamasamādhisūtra.* Sara Webb-Boin, trans. London: Curzon Press.

Lancaster, Lewis R., comp. 1979. *The Korean Buddhist Canon: A Descriptive Catalogue.* Berkeley: University of California Press.

Lati Rinbochay and Jeffrey Hopkins. 1979. *Death, Intermediate State and Rebirth in Tibetan Buddhism.* Ithaca, NY: Snow Lion Publications. Reprint, 1980.

Lauf, D. Ingo. 1975. *Secret Doctrines of the Tibetan Books of the Dead.* Boulder, CO: Shambhala Publications.

Laufer, Berthold. 1918. "Origins of Tibetan Writing," *Journal of the American Oriental Society* 38: 34–46.

Lewis, Todd T. 1996. "Sukhavati Traditions in Newar Buddhism," *South Asia Research* 16 (1): 1–31.

——. 2004. "From Generalized Goal to Tantric Subordination: Sukhāvatī in the Indic Buddhist Traditions of Nepal," in Richard Payne and Kenneth Tanaka, eds., *Approaching the Land of Bliss: Religious Praxis in the Cult of Amitābha,* pp. 236–263. Honolulu: University of Hawai'i Press.

Lien, Y. Edmund. 2009. "Dunhuang Gazetteers of the Tang Period," *T'ang Studies* 27: 19–39.

Lindtner, Christian. 1982. *Nagarjuniana: Studies in the Writings and Philosophy of Nāgārjuna.* Copenhagen: Akademisk Forlag.

Litvinsky, B. A., and M. I. Vorobyova-Desyatovskaya. 1996. "Religions and Religious Movements II," in B. A. Litvinsky, Zhang Guang-da, and Shabani Samghabadi, eds., *History of Civilizations of Central Asia,* vol. III, pp. 421–448. Paris: UNESCO Publishing.

Litvinsky, B. A., Zhang Guang-da, and Shabani Samghabadi, eds. 1996. *History of Civilizations of Central Asia,* vol. III. Paris: UNESCO Publishing.

Liu Xinru. 1988. *Ancient India and Ancient China: Trade and Religious Exchanges AD 1–600.* Oxford, UK: Oxford University Press.

——. 1995. "Silk and Religions in Eurasia, c. A.D. 600–1200," *Journal of World History* 6 (1): 25–48.

Lo Bue, Erberto. 1997. "The Role of Newar Scholars in Transmitting the Indian Buddhist Heritage to Tibet," in S. Karmay et al., eds., *Les habitants du Toit du monde. Hommage á Alexander W. Macdonald,* pp. 629–658. Nanterre: Société d' ethnologie.

Lopez, Donald S. 1996. *Elaborations on Emptiness: Uses of the Heart Sūtra.* Princeton, NJ: Princeton University Press.

——. 1997. "A Prayer for Deliverance from Rebirth," in Donald S. Lopez, Jr., ed., *Religions of Tibet in Practice,* pp. 442–457. Princeton, NJ: Princeton University Press.

——. 1998. *Prisoners of Shangri-la: Tibetan Buddhism and the West.* Chicago and London: University of Chicago Press.

Lusthaus, Dan. 2002. *Buddhist Phenomenology: A Philosophical Investigation of Yogācāra Buddhism and the Ch'eng Wei-shih lun.* London: RoutledgeCurzon.

Mabbett, Ian. 1998. "The Problem of the Historical Nagarjuna Revisited," *The Journal of the American Oriental Society* 118 (3): 332–346.

Machida, Soho. 1988. "Life and Light, the Infinite: A Historical and Philological Analysis of the Amida Cult," *Sino-Platonic Papers* 9: 1–46.

Marshak, B. I., and N. N. Negmatov. 1996. "Sogdiana," in B. A. Litvinsky, Zhang Guang-Da, and Shabani Samghabadi, eds., *History of Civilizations of Central Asia*, vol. III, pp. 233–280. Paris: UNESCO Publishing.

Martin, Dan. 1997. *Tibetan Histories: A Bibliography of Tibetan-Language Sources.* London: Serindia Publications.

——. 2001. *Unearthing Bon Treasures: Life and Contested Legacy of a Tibetan Scripture Revealer, with a General Bibliography of Bon.* Leiden: Brill.

Mayer, Robert. 1994. "Indian Precursors of the gTer-ma Tradition," in Per Kvaerne, ed., *Proceedings of the 6th Seminar of the International Association for Tibetan Studies*, pp. 553–544. Oslo: Institute for Comparative Research in Human Culture.

——. 1996. *A Scripture of the Ancient Tantra Collection: The Phur-pa bcu-gnyis.* Oxford: Kiscadale Publications.

Mayer, Robert, and Cathy Cantwell. 2008. "Enduring Myths: smrang, rabs and Ritual in the Dunhuang Texts on Padmasambhava," *Revue d'Etudes Tibétaines* 15: 289-312.

McIntire, Jennifer. 2000. "Visions of Paradise: Sui and Tang Buddhist Pure Land Representation at Dunhuang," PhD dissertation, Princeton University, Princeton, NJ.

Mei, Ching Hsuan. 2004. "'Pho ba Liturgy in 14th Century Tibet," *Tibet Journal* 29 (2): 47–70.

——. 2009. "The Development of 'Pho ba Liturgy in Medieval Tibet," PhD dissertation, Rheinischen Friedrich-Wilhelms-Universität, Bonn.

Michaelson, Carol. 2004. "Jade and the Silk Road: Trade and Tribute in the First Millennium," in Susan Whitfield, ed., *The Silk Road: Trade, Travel, War and Faith*, pp. 43–49. London: The British Library.

Minamoto, Hiroyuki. 1991. "Characteristics of Pure Land Buddhism of Silla," in Lewis R. Lancaster and C. S. Yu, eds., *Assimilation of Buddhism in Korea: Religious Maturity and Innovation in the Silla Dynasty*, pp. 131–168. Berkeley: Asian Humanities Press.

Monier-Williams, Monier. 1964. *A Dictionary of English and Sanskrit.* Delhi: Motilal Banarsidass.

Moriyama, Shin'ya. 2005. "The Gate of Praise in Vasubandhu's Sukhāvati-vyūhopadeśa," *The Eastern Buddhist* 37 (1–2): 235–253.

Motoyama, Hiroshi. 1987. "Psychophysiological Changes due to the Performance of the Phowa Ritual," *Research for Religion and Parapsychology* 17: 1–37.

Mukherjee, B. N. 1979. "A Mathura Inscription of the Year 26 and of the Period of Huvishka," *Journal of Ancient Indian History* 11: 82–84.

Müller, F. Max, and Nanjō Bunyū, eds. 1880. *The Smaller Sukhāvatīvyuha.* Tokyo: Bonzōwaei gappeki jōdo sambukyō. Reprint, 1931.

———. 1883. *Sukhāvatī-vyūha, Description of Sukhāvatī the Land of Bliss.* Anectoda Oxoniensia Aryan Series. Oxford, UK: Clarendon Press.

Müller, Max. 1880. "The Smaller Sukhāvatīvyūha," *The Journal of Royal Asiatic Society of Great Britain and Ireland* 12: 153–188.

———. 1883. *Sukhāvatī-vyūha, Description of Sukhāvatī the Land of Bliss.* Anectoda Oxeniensia Aryan Series, vol. I, part II. Oxford: Clarendon Press.

Mullin, Glen. 1986. *Death and Dying in the Tibetan Tradition.* Boston: Arkana.

Mumford, Stanley. 1990. *Himalayan Dialogue: Tibetan Lamas and Gurung Shamans in Nepal.* Madison: University of Wisconsin Press.

Murakami, Shinkan. 2008. "Early Buddhist Openness and Mahāyāna Buddhism," *Nagoya Studies in Indian Culture and Buddhism* 27: 109–148.

Mus, Paul. 1998. *Barabadur: Sketch of a History of Buddhism based on Archaeological Criticism of the Texts.* A. W. Macdonald, trans. New Delhi: Indira Gandhi National Centre for the Arts, Sterling Publishers.

Nagashima, Shōdō. 1975. "Taishō Daigaku Shozō Chibetto Daizōkyō Naruta-ban Kanjūr Mokuroku," *Taishō Daigaku Kenkyū Kiyō (Memoirs of Taishō University)* 61: 760–766.

Nakamura, Hajime. 1987. *Indian Buddhism: A Survey with Bibliographical Notes.* Delhi: Motilal Banarsidass.

Nanda, Neeru. 1982. *Tawang, the Land of Mon.* Delhi: Vikas Publishing House.

Nattier, Jan. 1990. "Church Language and Vernacular Language in Central Asian Buddhism," *Numen* 37 (2): 195–219.

———. 2000. "The Realm of Akṣobhya: A Missing Piece in the History of Pure Land Buddhism," *Journal of the International Association of Buddhist Studies* 23 (1): 71–103.

———. 2003. "The Indian Roots of Pure Land Buddhism: Insights from the Oldest Chinese Versions of the Larger *Sukhāvatīvyūha*," *Pacific World* 3 (5): 179–201.

———. 2006. "The Names of Amitābha/Amitāyus in Early Chinese Buddhist Translations (1)," *Report of the International Research Institute of Advanced Buddhology* IX: 183–199.

———. 2007. "The Names of Amitābha/Amitāyus in Early Chinese Buddhist Translations (2)," *Report of the International Research Institute of Advanced Buddhology* X: 359–394.

Nebesky-Wojkowitz, Rene. 1956. *Oracles and Demons of Tibet: The Cult and Iconography of the Tibetan Protective Deities.* Delhi: Paljor Publications. Reprint, 1998.

Neelis, Jason. 1992. "A Survey of Recently Discovered Kharoṣṭī Inscriptions," MA thesis, University of Texas, Austin.

Neumaier, Eva. 2007. "The Cult of Amitābha and the Apotheosis of the Tibetan Ruler," *Pacific World* 9: 231–244.

Niang, Quin. 2004. *Art, Religion, and Politics in Medieval China: The Dunhuang Cave of the Zhai Family.* Honolulu: University of Hawai'i Press.

Niyogi, Puspa. 2001. *Buddhist Divinities.* Delhi: Munshiram Manoharlal.

Okazaki, Joji. 1977. *Pure Land Buddhist Paintings.* Elizabeth ten Grotenhuis, trans. Tokyo: Kodansha International and Shibundo.

Onoda, Shunzō. 2001. "Some Variants in the Texts of the Tibetan Smaller Sukhāvatīvyūha-sūtra," *Kagawa Takao Hakushi Koki Kinen Ronsyu Bukkyogaku Jodogaku Kenkyu.* Kyoto: Nagata Bunsyodo.

Orofino, Giacomela. 1993. "The Tibetan Myth of the Visionary Geography of Nepal," *East and West* 41: 239–270.

Pagel, Ulrich. 1995. *The Bodhisattvapiṭaka.* Buddhica Britannica, Series Continua V. Tring: Institute of Buddhist Studies.

Pagel, Ulrich, and Séan Gaffney. 1996. *Location List to the Texts in the Microfiche Edition of the Śel dkar (London) Manuscript bKa' 'gyur (Or. 6724).* London: The British Library.

Pan, Yihong. 1992. "The Sino-Tibetan Treaties in the Tang Dynasty," *T'oung Pao* 78 (3): 116–161.

Pandey, Lalta Prasad. 1971. *Sun Worship in Ancient India.* Delhi: Motilal Banarsidass.

Panglung, Jampa. L. 1994. "New Fragments of the sGra-sbyor bam-po gnyis-pa," *East and West* 44 (1): 161–172.

Pas, Julian F. 1977. 'The Kuan-wu-liang-shu Fo-ching: Its Origins and Literary Criticism," in Leslie S. Kawamura and Keith Scott, eds., *Buddhist Thought and Asian Civilization,* pp. 182–194. Berkeley: Dharma Publishing.

——. 1995. *Visions of Sukhāvatī: Shan-Ṭao's Commentary on the Kuan Wu-Liang-Shou-Fo Ching.* Albany: State University of New York (SUNY) Press.

Pasadika, Bhikkhu. 1991. "Once Again on the Hypothesis of Two Vasubandhus," in V. N. Jha, ed., *Kalyāṇa-mitta: Professor Hajime Nakamura Felicitation Volume,* pp. 15–22. Delhi: Sri Satguru Publications.

Pathak, Suniti Kumar. 1974. *The Indian Nītiśāstras in Tibet.* Delhi: Motilal Banarsidass.

Patrul Rinpoche. 1994. *The Words of My Perfect Teacher.* Translation of Kun bzang bla ma'i shal lung. Sacred Literature Series. Padmakara Translation Group, trans. San Francisco: HarperCollins Publishers.

Paul, Y. Diana. 1985. *Women in Buddhism: Images of the Feminine in Mahāyāna Tradition.* Berkeley: University of California Press.

Payne, Richard. 1997. "The Cult of Aparimitāyus: Proto-Pure Land Buddhism in the Context of Indian Mahāyāna," *Pure Land* 13–14: 19–36.

——. 2003. "Seeing Sukhāvatī: Yogācāra and the Origins of Pure Land Visualization," *Pure Land* 20: 265–283.

——. 2007. "Aparimitāyus: 'Tantra' and 'Pure Land' in Late Medieval Indian Buddhism?" *Pacific World* 3 (9): 273–308.

Payne, Richard K., and Kenneth Tanaka. 2003. *Approaching the Land of Bliss: Religious Praxis in the Cult of Amitabha.* Honolulu: University of Hawai'i Press.

Prats, Ramon. 1980. "Some Preliminary Considerations Arising from a Bibliographical Study of the Early Gter-ston," in Michael Aris and Aung San Suu Kyi, eds., *Tibetan Studies in Honour of Hugh Richardson,* pp. 256–260. Warminster, England: Aris and Phillips.

Przyluski, Jean. 1927. "La ville de Cakravartin. Influences Babylonian sur la civilisation de l'Inde," *Rocznik Orjentalistyczny* 5: 165–185.

Pugachenkova, G. A., S. R. Dar, R. C. Sharma, and M. A. Joyenda. 1994. "Kushan Art," in János Harmatta, B. N. Puri, and G. F. Etemadi, ed., *History of Civilizations of Central Asia,* vol. II, pp. 331–395. Paris: UNESCO Publishing.

Puri, Baij Nath. 1987. *Buddhism in Central Asia.* Delhi: Motilal Banarsidass.

Rabsal, ed. 1996. *Catalogue of the Phodrang Lhankarma.* Sarnath: Central Institute of Higher Tibetan Studies.

Ramble, Charles. 1983. "The Founding of a Tibetan Village: The Popular Transformation of History," *Kailash* 10 (3–4): 267–290.

Rawski, Evelyn S. 1998. *The Last Emperors: A Social History of Qing Imperial Institutions.* Berkeley: University of California Press.

Reinhard, Johan. 1978. "Khembalung: The Hidden Valley," *Kailash* 6 (1): 5–13.

Rhi, Juhyung. 2003. "Early Mahāyāna and Gandhāran Buddhism: An Assessment of the Visual Evidence," *The Eastern Buddhist* 35 (1–2): 152–202.

Rhys Davids, Caroline A. F., ed. 1975. *The Visuddhi-magga of Buddhaghosa.* Pāli Text Society. London: Routledge and K. Paul.

Rhys Davids, T. W. 1894. *The Questions of King Milinda.* Delhi: Motilal Banarsidass. Reprint, 1999.

——. 1899. *Dialogues of the Buddha,* vol. I. London: Oxford University Press.

Richardson, Hugh. 1985. *A Corpus of Early Tibetan Inscriptions.* James G. Forlong Series, no. XXIX. London: Royal Asiatic Society.

——. 1992. "Mention of Tibetan Kings in some Documents from Dunhuang," *Bulletin of Tibetology* 2: 5–10.

——. 1993. *Ceremonies of the Lhasa Year.* London: Serindia Publications.

——. 1998. *High Peaks, Pure Earth: Collected Writings on Tibetan History and Culture.* London: Serindia Publications.

Rockhill, Woodville. 1891. "Tibet: A Geographical, Ethnographical, and Historical Sketch, Derived from Chinese Sources," *Journal of the Royal Asiatic Society of Great Britain and Ireland* (April): 186–291.

Roerich, George. 1946. *The Blue Annals.* Delhi: Motilal Banarsidass. Reprint, 1976.

Roesler, Ulrike. 2002. "The Great Indian Epics in the Version of Dmar ston Chos kyi rgyal po," in Henk Blezer, ed., *Religion and Secular Culture in Tibet*, pp. 431–451. Leiden: Brill.

Roesler, Ulrike, and Hans-Ulrich Roesler. 2004. *Kadampa Sites of Phempo: A Guide to Some Early Buddhist Monasteries in Central Tibet*. Kathmandu: Vajra Publications.

Rowell, Teresina. 1935. "The Background and Early Use of the Buddha-Kṣetra Concept, Chapters 2–3," *The Eastern Buddhist* 6 (4): 379–431.

———. 1937. "The Background and Early Use of the Buddha-Kṣetra Concept, Chapter 4," *The Eastern Buddhist* 7 (2): 132–176.

Ruegg, David S. 1981. *The Literature of the Madhyamaka School of Philosophy in India*. Wiesbaden: Otto Harrasowitz.

———. 1989. *Buddha-nature, Mind and the Problem of Gradualism in a Comparative Perspective: On the Transmission and Reception of Buddhism in India and Tibet*. London: School of Oriental And African Studies.

———. 1995. *Ordre Spirituel et Ordre Temporel Dans la Pensée Bouddhique de l'Inde et du Tibet*. Paris: Collège de France.

———. 2004. "Aspects of the Study of the (Earlier) Indian Mahāyāna," *Journal of the International Association of Buddhist Studies* 27 (1): 3–62.

Sakaki, Ryosaburo. 1916–1925. *Mahāvyutpatti*, vols. 1 and 2. Tokyo: Suzuki Research Foundation. Reprint, 1962.

Salomon, Richard. 1999. *Ancient Buddhist Scrolls from Gandhāra*. London: The British Library.

Samten Jampa. 1987. "Notes on the Lithang Edition of the Tibetan bKa'-gyur," J. Russel, trans., *Tibet Journal* 3: 17–40.

———. 1992. *A Catalogue of the Phug-brag Manuscript Kanjur*. Dharamsala: Library of Tibetan Works and Archives.

———. 1994. "Notes on the Bka'-'gyur of O-rgyan-gling, The Family Temple of the Sixth Dalai Lama (1683–1706)," in Per Kvaerne, ed., *Proceedings of the 6th Seminar of the International Association for Tibetan Studies*, pp. 393–402. Oslo: Institute for Comparative Research in Human Culture.

Samuel, Geoffrey. 1982. "Buddhism and the State in the Eight Century," in Henk Blezer, ed., *Religion and Secular Culture in Tibet*, pp. 1–19. Leiden: Brill.

———. 1986. "Music of the Lhasa Ministrels," in Jamyang Norbu, ed., Zlos-gar: Performing Traditions of Tibet, pp. 13–19. Dharamsala: Library of Tibetan Works and Archives.

Sardar-Afkhami, Hardar. 1996. "An Account of Padma-Bkod: A Hidden Land in Southeastern Tibet," *Kailash* 18 (3): 1–21.

Schaeffer, Kurtis, and Leonard Van der Kujip. 2009. *An Early Tibetan Survey of Buddhist Literature: The Bstan Pa Rgyas Pa Rgyan Gyi Nyi 'Od of Bcom Ldan Ral Gri*. Cambridge, MA: Harvard University Press.

Scherrer-Schaub, Christina. 1991. "Réciprocité du don: une relecture de PT999," in Ernst Steinkellner, ed., *Tibetan History and Language: Studies Dedicated to Uray Géza on His Seventieth Birthday*, pp. 429–434. Arbeitskres für tibetische und buddhistische Studien. Wien: Universität Wien.

———. 1992. "Śa cu: Qu'y a-t-il au programme de la classe de philologie bouddhique?" in Shoren Ihara and Zuiho Yamaguchi, eds., *Proceedings of the 5th Seminar of the International Association for Tibetan Studies*, vol. 1, pp. 209–220. Narita: Naritasan Shinshoji.

———. 1999. "Translation, Transmission, Tradition: Suggestions from Ninth-Century Tibet," *Journal of Indian Philosophy* 27: 67–77.

———. 2002. "Enacting Words: A Diplomatic Analysis of the Imperial Decrees and Their Application in the Sgra sbyor bam po gñis pa Tradition," *Journal of the International Association of Buddhist Studies* 25 (1–2): 263–340.

Schoening, Jeffrey, trans. with annotation. 1995. *The Śālistamba Sūtra and Its Indian Commentaries*, vol. I. Wien: Universität Wien.

Schopen, Gregory. 1975. "The Phrase *'sa pṛthivīpradeśaś caitya bhūto bhavet'* in the Vajracchedikā: Notes on the Cult of the Book in Mahāyāna," *Indo-Iranian Journal* 17: 4–4, 147–181.

———. 1977. "Sukhāvatī as a Generalized Religious Goal in Sanskrit Mahāyāna Sūtra Literature," *Indo-Iranian Journal* 19: 177–210.

———. 1985. "Two Problems in the History of Indian Buddhism: The Layman/Monk Distinction and the Doctrines of the Transference of Merit," in Georg Buddruss, ed., *Studien Zur Indologie and Iranistik*, pp. 9–47. Reinbek: Verlag für Orientalistische Fachpublikationen.

———. 1987. "The Inscription on the Kuṣān Image of Amitābha and the Character of the Early Mahāyāna in India," *Journal of the International Association of Buddhist Studies* 10 (2): 99–135.

Schopen, Gregory, and Richard Salomon. 2002. "On an Alleged Reference to Amitābha in a Kharoṣṭhī Inscription on a Gandhāran Relief," *Journal of the International Association of Buddhist Studies* 25 (1–2): 3–31.

Schwieger, Peter. 1978. *Ein Tibetisches Wunschgebet um Wiedergeburt in der Sukhāvatī.* St. Augustin: VGH Wissenschaftsverlag.

———. 1998. "A Few Remarks on the Function of Vision for Tibetan Literature," *Proceedings of the 8th Seminar of the International Association for Tibetan Studies*, Bloomington, IN (unpublished).

———. 2000. "Geschichte als Mythos–Zur Aneignung von Vergangenheit in der tibetischen Kultur. Ein kulturwissenschaftlicher Essay," *Asiatische Studien Études Asiatiques* LVI (4): 945–973.

Seldeslachts, Erik. 2007. "Greece, the Final Frontier? The Westward spread of Buddhism," in Ann Heirman and Stephan Peter Bumbacher, eds., *The Spread of Buddhism*, pp. 131–166. Leiden: Brill.

Shakabpa, Tsepon. 1967. *Tibet: A Political History*. New Haven, CT: Yale University Press.

Shakya, Min Bahadur. 1994. *The Iconography of Nepalese Buddhism*. Kathmandu, Nepal: Handicraft Association of Nepal in cooperation with ZDH.

Shimin, Geng 2004. "Study of Two Folios of the Uighur Text 'Abitaki,'" *Acta Orientalia Academiae Scientiarum Hung* 57: 105–113.

Silk, Jonathan. 1993. "The Virtues of Amitābha: A Tibetan Poem from Dunhuang," *Būkkyo Bunka Kenkyūjo Kiyō* 32: 1–109.

——. 1994. *The Heart Sūtra in Tibetan. A Critical Edition of the Two Recensions Contained in the Kanjur*. Wien: Arbeitskreis Für Tibetische und Buddhistische Studien Universität Wien.

——. 1997. "The Composition of the *Guan Wuliangshoufo-jing:* Some Buddhist and Jaina Parallels to Its Narrative Frame," *Journal of Indian Philosophy* 25: 181–256.

Simmler, Franz. 1992. "Prinzipien der Edition von Texten der Frühen Neuzeit aus sprachwissenschaftlicher Sicht," in Lothar von Mundt, Hans-Gert Roloff, and Ulreet Seelbach, eds., *Probleme der Edition von Texten der Frühen Neuzeit: Beiträge zur Arbeitstagung der Kommission für die Edition von Texten der Frühen Neuzeit, pp. 36–127. Tubingen: Max Niemeyer Verlag.*

Skilling, Peter. 1992. "The Rakṣā Literature of the Śrāvakayāna," *Journal of the Pāli Text Society* 16: 109–182.

——. 1993. "Theravādin Literature in Tibetan Translation," *Journal of the Pāli Text Society* 19: 69–201.

——. 1994a. "Kanjur Titles and Colophons," in Per Kvaerne, ed., *Proceedings of the 6th Seminar of the International Association for Tibetan Studies*, pp. 768–769. Oslo: Institute for Comparative Research in Human Culture.

——. 1994b. *Mahāsūtras: Great Discourse of the Buddha, Volume I: Texts*. Oxford: Pāli Text Society.

——. 1997a. "From bKa' bstan bcos to bKa' 'gyur and bsTan 'gyur," in Helmut Eimer, ed., *Transmission of the Tibetan Canon*, pp. 87–111. Wien: Österreichische Akademie Der Wissenschaften.

——. 1997b. *Mahāsūtras: Great Discourse of the Buddha, Volume II: Parts I & II*. Oxford: Pāli Text Society.

——. 2001. "The Batang Manuscript Kanjur in the Newark Museum: A Preliminary Report," *Annual Report of the International Research Institute for Advanced Buddhology at Soka University for the Academic Year 2000* 4: 71–92.

Skjaervø, Prods Oktor. 1999. "Khotan, An Early Center of Buddhism in Chinese Turkestan," in John R. McRae and Jan Nattier, eds., *Collection of Essays 1993: Buddhism across Boundaries: Chinese Buddhism and the Western Regions*, pp. 265–344. Sanchung, Taipei: Fo Guang Shan Foundation.

——. 2002. *Khotanese Manuscripts from Chinese Turkestan in the British Library: A Complete Catalogue of Texts and Translations*. Corpus Inscriptionum Iranicarium,

Part II: Inscriptions of the Eleucid and Parthian Periods and Eastern Iran and Central Asia, Volume V: Saka, Texts VI. London: The British Library.

———. 2004. "Iranians, Indians, Chinese and Tibetans: The Rulers and the Ruled of Khotan in the First Millenium," in Susan Whitfield, ed., *The Silk Road: Trade, Travel, War and Faith*, pp. 34–42. London: The British Library.

Skorupski, Tadeusz, ed. 1990. *Indo-Tibetan Studies, Papers in Honour and Appreciation of Professor David L. Snellgrove's Contribution to Indo-Tibetan Studies.* Tring: Institute of Buddhist Studies.

———. 1995. "A Tibetan Prayer for Rebirth in the Sukhāvatī," *The Pure Land* 12 (n.s.): 205–253.

———. 2001. "Funeral Rites for Rebirth in the Sukhāvatī Abode," in Tadeusz Skorupski, ed., *The Buddhist Forum*, vol. VI, pp. 137–172. Tring: Institute of Buddhist Studies.

Smith, Gene. 2001. *Among Tibetan Texts: History and Literature of the Himalayan Plateau.* Boston: Wisdom Publications.

Snellgrove, David. 1978. *The Image of the Buddha.* Paris: Serindia.

———. 1987. *Indo-Tibetan Buddhism.* London: Serindia.

Snellgrove, David, and Hugh Richardson. 1968. *A Cultural History of Tibet.* Bangkok, Thailand: Orchid Press. Reprint, 2003.

Sørensen, Henrik H. 1998. "Perspectives on Buddhism in Dunhuang during the Tang and Five Dynasties Period," in Vadime Elisseef, ed., *The Silk Roads: Highways of Culture and Commerce*, pp. 27–48. Paris: UNESCO.

Sørensen, Per K. 1994. *Tibetan Buddhist Historiography: The Mirror Illuminating the Royal Genealogies. An Annotated Translation of the XIVth Century Tibetan Chronicle: rGyal-rabs gsalba'i me-long.* Wiesbaden: Harrassowitz Verlag.

Sperling, Elliot. 2008. "The Politics of History and the Indo-Tibetan Border (1987–88)," *India Review* 7 (3): 223–239.

Stearns, Cyrus. 1997. "A Quest for 'The Path and Result,'" in Donald S. Lopez, Jr., ed., *Religions of Tibet in Practice*, pp. 188–199. Princeton, NJ: Princeton University Press.

———. 1999. *The Buddha from Dolpo: A Study of the Life and Thought of the Tibetan Master Dolpopa Sherab Gyaltsen.* Delhi: Motilal Banarsidass. Reprint, 2002.

Stein, Marc Aurel. 1907. *Ancient Khotan: Detailed Report of Archeological Explorations in Chinese Turkestan.* Oxford: Clarendon Press.

———. 1912. *Ruins of Desert Cathay.* London: Macmillan.

———. 1921. *Serindia: Detailed Report of Explorations in Central Asia and Westernmost China*, vol. 1. Oxford: Oxford University Press. Reprint, 1981.

———. 1933. *On Central Asian Tracks.* New York: Pantheon Books. Reprint, 1964.

Stein, Rolf A. 1959. *Recherches sur l'Épopée et le Barde du Tibet.* Paris: Presses Universitaires de France.

——. 1970. "Un Document Ancien Relatif Aux Rites Funéraires Des Bon-Po Tibétains," *Journal Asiatique* 258: 155–185.

——. 2010. "The Indigenous Religion and the Bon-po in the Dunhuang Manuscripts," in Arthur P. McKeown, trans. and ed., *Rolf Stein's Tibetica Antiqua, with Additional Materials*, pp. 231–269. Leiden: Brill.

Stoddard, Heather. 1999. "Dynamic Structures in Buddhist Mandalas: Apradaksina and Mystic Heat in the Mother Tantra Section of the Anuttarayoga Tantras," *Artibus Asiae* 58 (34): 169–213.

Strauch, Ingo. 2008. "The Bajaur Collection of Kharoṣṭhī Manuscripts—A Preliminary Survey," *Studien zur Indologie und Iranistic* 25: 103–136.

Suzuki, Daisetz Teitaro. 1930. *Studies in the Lankavatara Sutra*. London: Kegan Paul. Reprint, 2000.

——, ed. 1955–1961. *The Tibetan Tripitaka*. Peking Edition. Reprinted under the supervision of Otani University, Kyoto. Tokyo-Kyoto: Suzuki Research Foundation.

Takakusu, Junjirō, and Kaigyoku Watanabe, eds. 1924–1932. *Taishō shinshū daizōkyō*, 100 vols. Tokyo: Taishō issaikyō kankōkai.

Takasaki, Jikidō. 1965. *Tōkyō Daigaku Shozō Rasa-ban Chibetto Daizōkyō Mokuroku (A Catalogue of the Lhasa Edition of the Tibetan Tripiṭaka in Comparison with Other Editions)*. Tokyo: photocopy.

Takeuchi, Tsuguhito. 1994. "Three Old Tibetan Contracts in the Sven Hedin Collection," *Bulletin of the School of Oriental and African Studies, University of London* 57 (3): 576–587.

——. 1998. *Old Tibetan Manuscripts from Eastern Turkestan in the Stein Collection of the British Library*, vol. II. Descriptive Catalogue. London: The British Library.

——. 2004. "The Tibetan Military System and its Activities from Khotan to Lop-Nor," in Susan Whitfield, ed., *The Silk Road: Trade, Travel, War and Faith*, pp. 50–56. London: The British Library.

Tambiah, Stanley J. 1987. "The Buddhist Conception of Universal King and Its Manifestations in South and Southeast Asia." Lecture delivered at the University of Malaya, Kuala Lampur.

Tanaka, Kenneth K. 1990. *The Dawn of Chinese Pure Land Buddhist Doctrine: Ching-ying Hui-yüan's Commentary on the Visualization Sutra*. Albany: State University of New York (SUNY) Press.

Tanaka, Kimiaki. 1992. "A Comparative Study of Esoteric Buddhist Manuscripts and Icons Discovered at Dun-huang," in Shoren Ihara and Zuiho Yamaguchi, eds., *Proceedings of the 5th Seminar of the International Association for Tibetan Studies*, vol. 1., pp. 275–279. Narita: Naritasan Shinshoji.

Tarthang Tulku. 1980. *rNying ma sde dge bka'gyur and bstan 'gyur (Tibetan Tripiṭaka)*. Berkeley: Dharma Publishing.

Thomas, Edward. 1933. *The History of Buddhist Thought*. London: Kegan Paul.

Thomas, William F. 1935. *Tibetan Literary Texts and Documents concerning Chinese Turkestan.* Vol. I: Literary Texts. London: The Royal Asiatic Society.

——. 1951. *Tibetan Literary Texts and Documents concerning Chinese Turkestan.* Vol. II: Documents. London: The Royal Asiatic Society.

Thomas, William F., and Gérard Clauson. 1927. "A Second Chinese Buddhist Text in Tibetan Characters," *The Journal of the Royal Asiatic Society of Great Britain and Ireland* 59: 281–306.

Thondup, Tulku. 1986. *Hidden Teachings of Tibet.* London: Wisdom Publications.

Thurman, Robert. 1982. *Life and Teachings of Tsong Khapa.* Dharamsala: Library of Tibetan Works and Archives.

——. 1985. "Tsoṅ-kha-pa's Integration of Sūtra and Tantra," in Barbara Nimri Aziz and Matthew Kapstein, eds., *Soundings in Tibetan Civilization*, pp. 372–383. Delhi: Manohar Publications.

Tremblay, Xavier. 2007. "The Spread of Buddhism in Serindia: Buddhism among Iranians, Tocharians and Turks before the 13th Century," in Ann Heirman and Stephan Peter Bumbacher, eds., *The Spread of Buddhism*, pp. 75–130. Leiden: Brill.

Trenckner, Vilhelm. 1889. *Majjhima Nikāya*, vol. I. London: Pāli Text Society.

Tsering Lama Jampal Zangpo. 1988. *A Garland of Immortal Wish-fulfilling Trees: The Palyul Tradition of Nyingmapa.* Ithaca, NY: Snow Lion Publications.

Tsuda, Shinichi. 1974. *Saṃvarodaya-tantra: Selected Chapters.* Tokyo: Hokuseido Press.

Tsukamoto, Zenryu. 1933. *Chinese Buddhism in the Middle Period of the T'ang Dynasty.* Memoir of Tōhō Bunka Gakuin, Kyōto Kenkyūsho, vol. IV, 1–12. Kyoto: The Academy of Oriental Culture.

Tucci, Giuseppe. 1949. *Tibetan Painted Scrolls.* Bangkok: SDI Publications. Reprint, 1999.

——. 1955. "The Secret Characters of the Kings of Ancient Tibet," *East and West* VI (3): 197–205.

——. 1958. *Minor Buddhist Texts.* Delhi: Motilal Banarsidass. Reprint, 1986.

——. 1973. *Transhimalaya.* London: Vikas Publishing.

——. 1988. *The Temples of Western Tibet and Their Artistic Symbolism.* Indo-Tibetica III, Lokesh Chandra, ed. Delhi: Aditya Prakashan.

Uebach, Helga. 2008. "From Red Tally to Yellow Paper: The Official Introduction of Paper in Tibetan Administration in 744–745," Tibetan Studies in Honour of Samten Karmay, *Revue d'Etudes Tibétaines* 14: 57–70.

Ueyama, Daishun. 1983. "The Study of Tibetan Ch'an Manuscripts Recovered from Tunhuang: A Review of the Field and Its Prospects," in Lewis R. Lancaster and Whalen Lai, eds., *Early Ch'an in China and Tibet*, pp. 327–349. Berkeley Buddhist Studies Series 5. Berkeley: University of California Press.

Ui, Hakuju, Munetada Suzuki, Yenshō Kanakura, and Tōkan Tada, eds. 1934. *A Complete Catalogue of the Tibetan Buddhist Canons.* Tohoku University Catalogue of the sDe-dge Edition of the Canon. Sendai: Tohoku University.

Upasak, C. S. 1990. *History of Buddhism in Afghanistan.* Sarnath: Central Institute of Higher Tibetan Studies.

Uray, Géza. 1989. "Contributions to the Date of the Vyutpatti-treatises," *Acta Orientalia* 43: 3–23.

Vaissière, Étienne. 2004. "The Rise of Sogdian Merchants and the Role of Huns: The Historical Importance of the Sogdian Ancient Letters," in Susan Whifield, ed., *The Silk Road: Trade, Travel, War and Faith,* pp. 19–23. London: The British Library.

van Der Kuijp, Leonard. 1993. "Jambhala: An Imperial Envoy to Tibet during the Late Yuan," *Journal of the American Oriental Society* 113 (4): 529–538.

——. 1996. "The Tibetan Script and Derivatives," in Peter T. Daniels and William Bright, eds., *The World's Writing Systems,* pp. 431–442. Oxford: Oxford University Press.

van Schaik, Sam. 2002. "The Tibetan Dunhuang Manuscripts in China," *Bulletin of School of Oriental and African Studies* 65 (1): 129–139.

——. 2006. "The Tibetan Avalokitesvara Cult in the Tenth Century: Evidence from the Dunhuang Manuscripts," in Ronald M. Davidson and Christian K. Wedemeyer, eds., *Tibetan Buddhist Literature and Praxis,* vol. 4, pp. 55–72. Leiden: E. J. Brill.

van Schaik, Sam, and Kazushi Iwao. 2008. "Fragments of the Testament of Ba from Dunhuang," *Journal of the American Oriental Society* 128 (3): 477–488.

Vassiliades, Dimitrios. 2000. *The Greeks in India: A Survey in Philosophical Understanding.* Delhi: Munshiram Manoharlal.

——. 2004. "Greeks and Buddhism: Historical Contacts in the Development of a Universal Religion," *The Eastern Buddhist* 36 (1–2): 134–183.

Verhagen, Pieter C. 1994. *A History of Sanskrit Grammatical Literature in Tibet,* vol. I. Leiden: Brill.

von Hinüber, Oskar. 1980. "Remarks in the Problems of Textual Criticism for Editing Anonymous Sanskrit Literature," in *Proceedings of the First Symposium of Nepali and German Sanskritists,* pp. 28–40. Kathmandu: Tribhuvan University, Institute of Sanskrit Studies.

Vostrikov, Ivanovich A. 1970. *Tibetan Historical Literature.* Chandra Gupta, trans. Calcutta: Soviet Indology Series.

Walleser, Max. 1916. *Aparimitāyur-jñāna-nāma-mahāyāna-sūtram Nach einer nepalesischen Sanskrit-Handscrift mit der tibetischen und chinesichen Version.* Heidelberg: Heidelberg Academie der Wissenschaften.

Walter, Mariko N. 2006. "Sogdians and Buddhism," *Sino-Platonic Papers* 174: 1–66.

Walter, Michael. 1980. "Preliminary Results from a Study of Two Rasāyana Systems in Indo-Tibetan Esoterism," in Michael Aris and Aung San Suu Kyi, eds., *Tibetan Studies in Honour of Hugh Richardson*, pp. 319–321. Warminster, England: Aris and Phillips.

———. 2003. "Jabir, the Buddhist Yogī, Part III: Considerations on the International Yoga of Transformation," *Lungta* 16: 21–36.

———. 2009. *Buddhism and Empire: The Political and Religious Culture of Early Tibet.* Leiden: Brill.

Walter, Michael, and Christopher Beckwith. 2010. "The Dating and Interpretation of the Old Tibetan Inscriptions," *Central Asiatic Journal* 54 (2): 291–319.

Wang, Helen. 2004. "How Much for a Camel? A New Understanding of Money on the Silk Road before AD 800," in Susan Whitfield, ed., *The Silk Road: Trade, Travel, War and Faith*, pp. 24–33. Chicago: Serindia Press.

———. 2007. "Money in Eastern Central Asia before AD 800," in Joe Cribb and Georgina Herrmann, eds., *After Alexander: Central Asia before Islam*, pp. 399–409. Proceedings of the British Academy 133. Oxford: Oxford University Press.

Wangdu, Pasang, and Hildegard Diemberger. 2000. *The Testimony of Minister Ba.* Vienna: Verlag der Österreichischen Akademie der Wissenschaften.

Ward, William E. 1952. "The Lotus Symbol: Its Meaning in Buddhist Art and Philosophy," Special Issue on Oriental Art and Aesthetics, *The Journal of Aesthetics and Art Criticism* 11 (2): 135–146.

Watanabe, Chikafumi. 2004. "A Translation of Mahāyānasaṃgraha III.5–7," *Nagoya Studies in Indian Culture and Buddhism* 24: 99–114.

Whitfield, Susan. 1990. *Caves of the Thousand Buddhas: Chinese Art from the Silk Route.* London: British Museum Publications.

———, ed. 2004. *The Silk Road: Trade, Travel, War and Faith.* London: The British Library.

Whitfield, Susan, Roderick Whitfield, and Neville Agnew. 2000. *Cave Temples of Dunhuang: Art and History on the Silk Road.* London: The British Library.

Williams, Paul. 1989. *Mahāyāna Buddhism: The Doctrinal Foundations.* London and New York: Routledge.

Williams, Paul, and Anthony Tribe. 2000. *Buddhist Thought: A Complete Introduction to the Indian Tradition.* London and New York: Routledge.

Wilson, Jeff. 2006. "Pure Land Iconography and Ritual Intent: A Comparative Study of the Visualization Texts *Kuan wu-liang-shou-fo ching* and Amitābha *sādhana*," *Pure Land* 22: 167–186.

Wilson, Martin. 1986. *In Praise of Tārā: Songs to the Saviouress.* London: Wisdom Publications.

Woodcock, George. 1966. *The Greeks in India.* London: Faber and Faber.

Wong, Dorothy. 1998–1999. "Four Sichuan Buddhist Steles and the Beginnings of Pure Land Imagery in China," *Archives of Asian Art* 56–80.

Xinjiang Rong. 2004. "Official Life at Dunhuang in the Tenth Century: The Case of Cao Yuanzhong," in Susan Whitfield, ed., *The Silk Road: Trade, Travel, War and Faith*, pp. 57-62. London: The British Library.

Yamabe, Nobuyoshi. 1999. "An Examination of the Mural Paintings of Toyok Cave 20 in Conjunction with the Origin of the Amitayus Visualization Sutra," *Orientations* 30 (4): 38–44.

Yamada, Isshi. 1968. *Karuṇāpuṇḍarīka*. London: School of Oriental and African Studies.

Yamaguchi, Zuihō. 1996. "The Fiction of King Dar-ma's Persecution of Buddhism," in Jean-Pierre Drège, comp., *Études Chinoises et bouddhiques offertes à Michel Soymié*, pp. 231–258. Geneva: Droz.

Yeshe Thubten. 1991. *Transference of Consciousness at the Time of Death*. Boston: Wisdom Publications.

Yoritomi, Motohiro. 1990. "An Iconographic Study on the Eight Bodhisattvas in Tibet," in Tadeusz Skorupski, ed., *Indo-Tibetan Studies, Papers in Honour and Appreciation of Professor David L. Snellgrove's Contribution to Indo-Tibetan Studies*, pp. 323–332. Tring: Institute of Buddhist Studies.

Yoshimizu, Chizuko, ed. 1989. *Descriptive Catalogue of the Naritasan Institute Collection of Tibetan Works*. Tokyo: Naritasan Shinshoji.

Yoshimura, Shyuki. 1950. *The Denkar-ma: An Oldest Catalogue of the Tibetan Buddhist Canons*. Kyoto: Ryukoku University.

Young, Serenity. 2004. *Courtesans and Tantric Consorts: Sexualities in Buddhist Narrative, Iconography, and Ritual*. New York: Routledge.

Zabs dkar Tshogs drug rang drol. 1994. *The Life of Shabkar: The Autobiography of a Tibetan Yogin*. Delhi: Sechen Publications. Reprint, 1997.

Zhang Guang-da. 1996a. "The City States of the Tarim Basin," in B. A. Litvinsky, Zhang Guang-da, and Shabani Samghabadi, eds., *History of Civilizations of Central Asia*, vol. III, pp. 281–302. Paris: UNESCO Publishing.

——. 1996b. "Kocho (Kao-Ch'ang)," in B. A. Litvinsky, Zhang Guang-da, and Shabani Samghabadi, eds., *History of Civilizations of Central Asia*, vol. III, pp. 303–314. Paris: UNESCO Publishing.

Zürcher, Erick. 1995. "Buddhist Art in Medieval China: The Ecclesiastical View," in K. R. van Kooij and Henny van der Veere, eds., *Function and Meaning in Buddhist Art*, pp. 1–20. Groningen: Forsten.

——. 1999. "Buddhism across Boundaries: The Foreign Input," in John R. McRae and Jan Nattier, eds., *Collection of Essays 1993: Buddhism across Boundaries: Chinese Buddhism and the Western Regions*, pp. 1–60. Sanchung, Taipei: Fo Guang Shan Foundation.

Index

Page numbers in bold indicate illustrations. Note that Tibetan terms are listed according to their head letters. Thus bSam-yas is indexed under S; for example, the following terms would appear under D and P with the page numbers. Such terms are also cross-referenced under B and D respectively, as noted:

bDe-smon. See under D

dPal-sprul. *See under* P

E